LIBRARY OF NEW TESTAMENT STUDIES

448

Formerly the Journal for the Study of the New Testament Supplement series

Editor
Mark Goodacre

Editorial Board
John M. G. Barclay, Craig Blomberg,
R. Alan Culpepper, James D. G. Dunn, Craig A. Evans, Stephen Fowl,
Robert Fowler, Simon J. Gathercole, John S. Kloppenborg, Michael Labahn,
Robert Wall, Steve Walton, Robert L. Webb, Catrin H. Williams

HEARING
AT THE BOUNDARIES OF VISION

EDUCATION INFORMING COSMOLOGY
IN REVELATION 9

SEAN MICHAEL RYAN

t & t clark

Published by T&T Clark International
A Continuum imprint
The Tower Building, 11 York Road, London SE1 7NX
80 Maiden Lane, Suite 704, New York, NY 10038

www.continuumbooks.com

Sean Michael Ryan has asserted his right under the Copyright, Designs and Patents Act,
1988, to be identified as the Author of this work.

British Library Cataloguing-in-Publication Data
A catalogue record for this book is available from the British Library.

ISBN: HB: 978-0-567-60489-7

Library Of Congress Cataloging-in-Publication Data
A catalog record for this book is available from the Library of Congress.

Typeset by Free Range Book Design & Production
Printed and bound in Great Britain

To Bridget & Ann, with love and gratitude

CONTENTS

Contents

LIST OF FIGURES

Abbreviations

I. Primary Texts

Aratus

Phaen.	Phaenomena

Cicero

De Inv.	De inventione
De Or.	De oratore
Rep.	De Republica

Euripides

El.	Electra
Ion.	Ion
Phoen.	Phoenissae
Tro.	Troades

Eusebius

H.E.	Historia ecclesiastica

Hesiod

Th.	Theogony
W & D	Works & Days

'Hippolytus'

ἔλεγχός	ἔλεγχός κατὰ πασῶν αἱρέσεων (Refutation of all Heresies)
Antichrist	On Christ and Antichrist
Apoc.	Commentary on the Apocalypse
Gaius	Heads Against Gaius

Homer

Il.	Iliad
Od.	Odyssey

Irenaeus

Dem.	Demonstration of the Apostolic Preaching
Haer.	Adversus haereses

Josephus

Ant.	*Antiquities*
Apion	*Against Apion*
Life	*Life*
War	*Jewish War*

Menander

Dysk.	*Dyskolos*
Mis.	*Misoumenos*

Oecumenius

Apoc.	*Commentary on the Apocalypse*

Philo

Abr.	*De Abrahamo*
Aeter.	*De aeternitate mundi*
Agr.	*De agricultura*
Cher.	*De cherubim*
Conf.	*De confusione linguarum*
Congr.	*De congressu quaerendae eruditionis gratia*
Cont.	*De vita contemplativa*
Dec.	*De decalogo*
Fug.	*De fuga et inventione*
Heres.	*Quis rerum divinarum heres sit*
Leg. All	*Legum allegoriarum*
Legat.	*De legatione ad Gaium*
Migr.	*De migratione Abrahami*
Mos.	*De vita Mosis*
Omn.	*Quod omnis probus liber sit*
Opif.	*De opificio mundi*
Plant.	*De plantatione*
Prov.	*De providentia*
QE	*Quaestiones et solutiones in Exodum*
QG	*Quaestiones et solutiones in Genesin*
Somn.	*De somniis*
Spec.	*De specialibus legibus*

Plato

Phaedo	*Phaedo*
Rep.	*Republic*
Tim.	*Timaeus*

Ptolemy

Alm.	*Almagest*
Tetr.	*Tetrabiblos*

Quintilian

Inst. Or.   *Institutio oratoria*

Tyconius

Apoc.   *Expositio Apocalypseos*
LR   *Libellus Regularis*

Victorinus

Fabr.   *De Fabrica Mundi*
In Apoc.   *In Apocalypsin Joannis*

II. Dictionaries/Reference Works

ABD   *The Anchor Bible Dictionary* (6 vols),
                 (ed.) David Noel Freedman,
                 (New York, Doubleday, 1992)
ANF   *Ante-Nicene Fathers, translations of the writings*
                 of the fathers down to 325 AD (10 vols),
                 Alexander Roberts and James Donaldson (eds)
                 (1868–73)(Repr. Grand Rapids, MI, Eerdmans);
                 http://www.ccel.org/fathers.html
BDAG   *A Greek-English Lexicon of the New Testament and*
                 other Early Christian Literature, W. Bauer, F. Danker,
                 W. F. Arndt, and F. W. Gingrich (Chicago, University
                 of Chicago Press, 2000)
BP   *Biblia Patristica* (7 vols), Centre d'Analyse
                 et de Documents Patristiques, (Paris, Éditions
                 du Centre National de la Recherche Scientifique,
                 1975–2000)
DDD   *Dictionary of Deities and Demons in the Bible*
                 [2nd rev. edn], Karel van der Toorn, Bob Becking
                 and Pieter W. van der Horst (eds), (Leiden, Brill, 1999)
LS   *A Latin Dictionary*, C. T. Lewis and C. Short
                 (Oxford, Clarendon, 1966)
LSJ   *A Greek-English Lexicon*, H. G. Liddell, R. Scott, and
                 H. S. Jones [9th edn] (Oxford, Clarendon, 1996)
NT Apoc.   *New Testament Apocrypha* (2 vols), (ed.) Wilhelm
                 Schneemelcher, trans. R. Mc L. Wilson (Cambridge,
                 James Clarke, 1991–2)
OTP I   *The Old Testament Pseudepigrapha, Volume I,*
                 Apocalyptic Literature and Testaments, (ed.) James H.
                 Charlesworth (London, DLT, 1983)

OTP II	*The Old Testament Pseudepigrapha Volume II: Expansions of the 'Old Testament' and legends, wisdom and philosophical literature, prayers, psalms and odes, fragments of lost Judeo-Hellenistic works,* (ed.) James H. Charlesworth, (London, DLT, 1985)
TDNT	*Theological Dictionary of the New Testament* (10 vols), (ed.) Gerhard Kittel, trans. G. W. Bromiley (Grand Rapids MI, Eerdmans, 1964–)

III. *Journals and Series*

AB	*Anchor Bible*
ABRL	*Anchor Bible Reference Library*
ANRW	*Aufstieg und Niedergang der römischen Welt*
APB	*Acta Patristica et Byzantina*
ARW	*Archiv für Religionswissenschaft*
Bib	*Biblica*
BJRL	*Bulletin of the John Rylands Library*
BMCR	*Bryn Mawr Classical Review*
BR	*Biblical Research*
BZ	*Biblische Zeitschrift*
BZNW	*Beihefte zur Zeitschrift für die neutestamentliche Wissenschaft*
CBQ	*Catholic Biblical Quarterly*
CBR	*Currents in Biblical Research*
CH	*Church History*
CJ	*The Classical Journal*
CP	*Classical Philology*
EvQ	*Evangelical Quarterly*
ExpT	*The Expository Times*
Fides et Hist.	*Fides et Historia*
FOTC	*Fathers of the Church*
GCS	*Die griechischen christlichen Schriftsteller*
HeyJ	*The Heythrop Journal*
HSPh	*Harvard Studies in Classical Philology*
HTR	*Harvard Theological Review*

ICC	*International Critical Commentary*
IDB	*Interpreter's Dictionary of the Bible*
IEJ	*Israel Exploration Journal*
Int	*Interpretation*
JBAA	*Journal of the British Astronomical Association*
JBL	*Journal of Biblical Literature*
JECS	*Journal of Early Christian Studies*
JETS	*Journal of the Evangelical Theological Society*
JGrChJ	*Journal of Greco-Roman Christianity and Judaism*
JHA	*Journal for the History of Astronomy*
JJS	*Journal of Jewish Studies*
JP	*Journal of Philology*
JQR	*Jewish Quarterly Review*
JSJ	*Journal for the Study of Judaism*
JSNT	*Journal for the Study of the New Testament*
JSOT	*Journal for the Study of the Old Testament*
JSP	*Journal for the Study of the Pseudepigrapha*
JTS	*Journal of Theological Studies*
K:JNWTS	*Kerux: The Journal of Northwest Theological Seminary*
LCL	*Loeb Classical Library*
LNTS	*Library of New Testament Studies*
LSTS	*Library of Second Temple Studies*
NICOT	*New International Critical Old Testament*
NIGTC	*New International Greek Testament Commentary*
NLH	*New Literary History*
NovT	*Novum Testamentum*
NTS	*New Testament Studies*
OrChr	*Oriens Christianus*
OTL	*Old Testament Library*
OTS	*Oudtestamentische Studiën*
PAAJR	*Proceedings of the American Academy for Jewish Research*
PBR	*Patristic and Byzantine Review*
PG	*Patrologia Graeca (J.-P. Migne)*
PL	*Patrologia Latina (J.-P. Migne)*
PRSt	*Perspectives in Religious Studies*
RB	*Revue Biblique*
RBén	*Revue Bénédictine*

REAug	*Revue des études augustiniennes*
RevQ	*Revue de Qumran*
RSR	*Recherches de Science Religieuse*
SBLDS	*Society of Biblical Literature Dissertation Series*
SC	*Sources chrétiennes*
SE	*Sacris Erudiri*
SHE	*Studia Historiae Ecclesiasticae*
SJT	*Scottish Journal of Theology*
SNTSMS	*Society of New Testament Studies Monograph Series*
SP	*Studia Patristica*
TU	*Texte und Untersuchungen*
TynBul	*Tyndale Bulletin*
TZ	*Theologische Zeitschrift*
VC	*Vigiliae Christianae*
VT	*Vetus Testamentum*
WBC	*Word Biblical Commentary*
WTJ	*Westminster Theological Journal*
WUNT	*Wissenschaftliche Untersuchungen zum Alten und Neuen Testament*
ZAC	*Zeitschrift für Antikes Christentum*
ZNW	*Zeitschrift für die Neutestamentliche Wissenschaft*
ZPE	*Zeitschrift für Papyrologie und Epigraphik*

ACKNOWLEDGEMENTS

I am extremely thankful for the advice, support, and encouragement that I have received from a wonderful group of colleagues, students, and friends during the process of writing and preparing this book for publication.

Hearing at the Boundaries of Vision is a revised version of my PhD thesis, written under the expert guidance of my supervisors, Dr Bridget Gilfillan Upton and Dr Ann Jeffers. It has been an absolute pleasure to undertake research under the tutelage of Bridget and Ann, my colleagues and friends for many years at Heythrop College, University of London. Whatever is deemed to be of merit in this book originates from the creative freedom and critical insights nurtured by my wise guides. I dedicate this book jointly to Bridget and Ann in warm appreciation of their scholarship and friendship.

I am grateful for the advice of my examiners, Prof. Christopher Rowland and Dr Edward Adams, who encouraged me to include a more detailed treatment of the reception-history of Rev 9 in this publication. It is hoped that the exegetical study of the patristic commentaries of Victorinus, Tyconius, and Oecumenius (ch 6) will serve to complement the creative hearer-construct models (chs 4-5). I am also grateful to the staff at Continuum for their professionalism - from the insightful comments of the anonymous referee, to the patience of Dominic Mattos and his team. Particular thanks go to Andrew Mikolajski (Editor) and Alan Rutherford (Typesetter) for their expertise and diligence, not least in their careful handling of the images and fonts.

This study is indebted to a wide range of dialogue-partners, many of whom are named in the General Index, experts in the fields of ancient education, cosmology, and the reception-history of the Apocalypse. It has been a privilege to engage with such a rich and creative treasury of scholarship. I am grateful to Dr Michael Kirwan, Prof. Richard Burridge, Dr Ian Paul and Dr Simon Woodman for the opportunity to present aspects of my research to the Postgraduate Theology Seminars at Heythrop College and King's College London, and the 'Revelation Seminar' at the British New Testament Conference. Particular thanks go to Daria Pezzoli-Olgiati and the outstanding members of the *International Exchange on Media and Religion* project (Zurich/Trento/Oxford/Cambridge/London) for their inspirational creativity and affection.

I am humbled by the support of my colleagues and close friends at Heythrop College, all of whom have been unfailingly encouraging throughout this process. Above all, I express my love and gratitude to the incomparable Dr Anna Abram, for her loving support and confidence in my abilities throughout my academic studies and early teaching career (even when I have lacked such confidence in myself). I have also benefited inestimably from the wise advice of my gifted colleague Dr Jonathan Norton, whose keen eyes proofread the manuscript and who has kindly offered thoughtful and well-considered comments on this study at various stages of its maturation. Jonathan's own erudite study in this LNTS series, *Contours in the Text: Textual Variation in the Writings of Paul, Josephus and the Yaḥad*, (2011), will undoubtedly become a seminal study of textual plurality in antiquity. I would like to offer particular thanks to Prof. Richard Price for his invaluable assistance in my study of the Latin patristic commentaries on the Apocalypse, notably his comments on my translation of Tyconius (although remaining errors are my own), and also to Dr Tony Carroll for his patient encouragement of my German language studies. I thank my biblical studies colleagues at Heythrop, Michael Cox, Charlotte Naylor-Davis, and Dr Dominik Markl, who have encouraged me to continue to probe the intricacies of the Apocalypse, sustained by their friendship and curiosity. I am grateful to the magnificent staff of the Heythrop Theology library, Christopher Pedley, Larry Markey and Vicky Rowley who have tirelessly assisted my requests for elusive titles, and my former PhD colleagues for their collective encouragement throughout the process (Dr Kevin Lu, Dr Simin Rahimi, Dr Deborah Ross, and the late (Dr) Roy Dorey).

I am ever thankful for the care and support afforded by Dr Richard Parsons and Elaine Parsons, for their wise counsel and true friendship throughout this whole process. I thank Dominic West for his spiritual guidance and Gerard Greene for his good sense, and to both for remaining loyal friends despite all the time I spent writing this book. I also thank Anna Lancaricova, Liam Dawson, Paul Simkins, Aidan Mullally, Nathalie Simon, and Ewa Fryst for their sustaining friendship and good humour during the lonely months of study.

Most of all, I thank my devoted family for their love and support during my lengthy academic studies. To my long-suffering parents, Michael Ryan and Anne Ryan, for their untiring love and care, to my sister, Caroline Ryan, for helping me to remain (relatively) normal, and to my supremely gifted brother, Declan Ryan, for his mature example, blessed with poetic gifts that far outstrip my rudimentary scribblings. Thank you all with all my heart.

London, Christmas 2011

Chapter 1

INTRODUCTION

1.1 Aim

The aim of this study is to consider how a significant variable, namely educational-level, may affect an ancient hearer's interpretation of the cosmology of the Apocalypse. The three-tier model of the cosmos depicted in the Apocalypse (heaven-earth-underworld),[1] represents one design-option among a diverse array of competing cosmological models expressed in the extant literature of the Graeco-Roman era.[2] An ancient individual's exposure to the diversity of models available, notably her awareness of the sophisticated multiple-planetary spheres design of Plato's *Timaeus*, would have been influenced by the range of literary authors that she had studied at school. Accordingly, it is plausible to propose that the extent of an ancient student's Greek literary education (ἐγκύκλιος παιδεία) would have had a direct impact – although not a determinative one – on her choice of preferred cosmological template, and accordingly her reception of the cosmology of the Apocalypse.

This study aims to scrutinize this proposition more closely, by considering the responses of two sets of ancient hearers to the cosmology of the Apocalypse:

i. *'hearer-construct' models* – in the absence of extant data of the reception of the Apocalypse's cosmology by its earliest audiences (late 1st–early 2nd century CE), this study will construct two models of plausible ancient hearers of the Apocalypse, with differing levels of educational attainment, to assess the impact of education as a variable.

ii. *reception history* – the responses of the two hypothetical 'hearer-construct' models will be compared with extant evidence of the earliest layers of reception of the Apocalypse, namely, the three earliest recoverable *Commentaries* on the text, in Latin and Greek, by Victorinus (3rd century CE), Tyconius (4th century CE), and Oecumenius (6th century CE).[3]

---

1   McDonough 2008.
2   Cf. Wright 2000: 98–202.
3   An alternative source of information is provided by disturbances in the manuscript tradition, often indicative of reception issues; cf. Hernández 2006 with reference to

1.2 Text-Focus (Rev 9)

The chosen test-case for this study is chapter 9 of the Apocalypse, comprising portions of the fifth (Rev 9:1-12) and sixth (Rev 9:13-21) trumpets in a broader septet (Rev 8:2-11:19). Rev 9 has been selected as a test-case principally on the basis of the rich cosmological imagery contained in this section. All three tiers of the Apocalypse's tripartite cosmos are present: οὐρανός (Rev 9:1, 13), γῆ (Rev 9:1, 3-6, 14-16), and ἄβυσσος (Rev 9:1-2, 11). Access between these three tiers is recounted, and the passage refers to a unique cosmological feature: τὸ φρέαρ τῆς ἀβύσσου (Rev 9:1-2). In addition, Rev 9:14 contains an intriguing reference to the Euphrates as a boundary marker (ὁ ποταμὸς ὁ μέγας Εὐφράτης), with evocative verbal parallels with Rev 7:1, and its depiction of a four-cornered earth.

Previous research on Rev 9 has tended to focus upon two closely intertwined structural and compositional issues:

    i. the place and function of the septet of trumpets (Rev 8:2–11:19) in the broader literary structure of the Apocalypse, especially in relation to the septets of seals (Rev 6:1–8:1) and bowls (Rev 16:1–16:21), as well as the internal structural organization of each septet, including the presence of 'digressions' (cf. Rev 10:1–11:13).[4]

    ii. the underlying sources and literary influences which may have shaped the form and content of the trumpet septet, notably the Egyptian plague cycle (Exodus 10, Pss 78, 105),[5] Joel's locust vision (Joel 1–2),[6] and trumpet imagery in scriptural, and broader Second Temple Jewish literature (e.g. 1QM, War Scroll).[7]

The presence of patterned repetition connecting the Apocalypse's septets of trumpets and bowls was given prominence in the influential early readings of Victorinus (3rd century CE) and Tyconius (4th century CE),[8] and remains a dominant reading-strategy, adopted in a variety of subtle forms, by a range of contemporary commentators.[9] The underlying structural principle of

---

singular readings of the Apocalypse in Codices Sinaiticus, Alexandrinus, and Ephraemi (4th–5th century CE).

    4   Cf. Bauckham 1993: 1–37; Campbell 2004; Giblin 1994; Jauhiainen 2003; Lambrecht 1980; Perry 2009; Schüssler-Fiorenza 1985: 159–80; Steinmann 1992; Tavo 2005; Ulfgard 1989; Yarbro Collins 1976: 13–55.

    5   Cf. Aune 1998a: 499–506; Beale 1999: 465–7; Müller 1960.

    6   Cf. Strazicich 2007: 59–204.

    7   Cf. Bauckham 1993: 210–37; Paulien 1988: 203–34.

    8   Cf. Dulaey 1997; Gryson 2011a.

    9   For a representative list of contemporary commentators who hold some form of recapitulation theory, see Jauhiainen 2003: 543–4, n.2.

In addition to proponents of a 'futurist' approach to the Apocalypse, who favour more strictly linear readings of the narrative (again with a range of different nuances, e.g. with

repetition, with variation, is a characteristic design of orally communicated narrative, structured for the ear of a listening audience, rather than the eye.[10] That the septets of seals, trumpets and bowls are interconnected in the oral-structural design of the Apocalypse, through intercalation, structural correspondence (e.g. seals 4 + 3, trumpets 4 + 3), and verbal reminiscence (e.g. ὁ ποταμὸς ὁ μέγας Εὐφράτης, Rev 9:14; 16:12) can scarcely be doubted. Yet even where an ancient hearer detects such interconnections, he has still to decide how to interpret such a pattern. Is the emphasis to be placed on the parallelism, such that the events of the fifth and sixth trumpets, for example, are understood to describe the same events as the fifth and sixth bowls? If so, the visionary narrative may be divided into a diptych, or perhaps a triptych, of repetitive images.[11] Alternatively, is greater emphasis to be placed on the variation, such that the bowl cycle, for example, represents a more intense progression on the series of trumpets (e.g. trumpet five affects one third of humanity; bowl five all of humanity) with the visionary narrative moving forward in a 'conical spiral' rather than a straight line?[12]

The first ancient hearer-construct model (Chapter 4) will be required to grapple with this complex structural issue in relation to trumpet six (Rev 9:13ff) and bowl six (Rev 16:12ff), closely associated by a cluster of verbal parallels. In that context, I will discuss how the contents of the hearer construct's mental library inform the exegetical decision that is made. The origins of a 'recapitulative' reading of the Apocalypse, and the work's overarching internal design, will also be discussed in some detail in Chapter 6, with reference to the hermeneutical principles of both Victorinus and Tyconius.

In addition to internal structural parallels between the three septets, the individual series may each be seen to imitate, in varying degrees, the structure and/or content of other literary narratives, perhaps most notably the Egyptian plague-cycle. The Egyptian plagues are represented in a variety of different forms within the MT/LXX: a ten-plague cycle in Exodus 7–12, a seven-plague cycle in Ps 77 (78):43–51 LXX, and an alternative seven-plague cycle in Ps 104 (105):27–36 LXX. The Egyptian plague cycle, or at least components of it, are also re-interpreted eschatologically in a variety of Second Temple Jewish texts, predating, or broadly contemporary with, the Apocalypse and its own distinctive treatment of the material in the cycles of trumpets and bowls (cf. Apocalypse of Abraham 30:14-16; III Apoc. Baruch 16:3).[13]

---

respect to the relationship between the seventh seal and the seventh trumpet and the series of seven which follows; cf. Beale 1999: 116–21 for an overview), commentators who regard the final form of the Apocalypse as a second (or later) edition, such as Charles 1920a: l–lv tend to attribute the parallelism to editorial changes rather than literary design.

10   Cf. Barr 1986; Dewey 1989; Gilfillan Upton 2006: 20–52; Havelock 1984; Ong 1982.

11   Yarbro Collins 1976: 13–55.

12   Schüssler-Fiorenza 1985: 159–80.

13   Cf Aune 1998a: 499–500.

An ancient hearer's recollection of the Egyptian plagues' tradition, on hearing Rev 9 orally performed, may be triggered by the presence of precise verbal parallels (e.g. ἀκρὶς, recalling the locust cycle (Ex 10:12-20)), as well as deeper structural affinities evoked by the Apocalypse's re-envisioned cycle of destructive plagues of fire, blood, and darkness (Rev 8:2-13). Furthermore, an ancient hearer's awareness of pre-existing interpretative connections, also shapes her pre-understanding of this text. Perhaps most pertinent for the present study are the interpretative links between Ex 10 and Joel 1–2. Joel 1–2 is itself an eschatological reinterpretation of a facet of Exodus plague imagery, depicting a nightmarish image of locusts like cavalry invading the land of Yehud on the Day of the Lord (cf. Joel 2:1-11).[14] Accordingly, an ancient hearer may already be cognizant of eschatological re-descriptions of portions of the plague cycle prior to hearing Rev 8:2ff orally performed. The visual and verbal interconnections between Ex 10, Joel 1–2 and Rev 9:1ff, and the impact that the resultant images may have on an ancient hearer's response to Rev 9, will be discussed in more detail in the first of the exegetical studies (Chapter 4).

1.3 Method

This study is concerned with the formative stages in the Apocalypse's reception-history (c. 1st–6th centuries CE), creatively engaging with the earliest recoverable exegeses of Rev 9 (Victorinus, Tyconius, and Oecumenius) (Chapter 6), as well as (re-)constructing the irrecoverable voices of the earliest audiences of this text (Chapters 4 and 5). The present study forms part of a burgeoning interest in the reception-history of the Apocalypse, as evidenced, for example by the recent *Blackwell Bible Commentaries Series* volume focused on the history of interpretation of the Apocalypse in art, music and literature, as well as the *Ancient Christian Commentaries on Scripture/Ancient Christian Texts* series which are making patristic commentaries on the Apocalypse more accessible in new English versions (Victorinus, Oecumenius, Andrew of Caesarea, Apringius, Caesarius, Bede).[15]

The 'hearer-construct' models that will be used to determine the hypothetical responses of ancient hearers represents a modified form of an 'implied reader/hearer' construct. Influenced by broader trends originating in the philosophy of language and filtered through literary theorists (e.g. Iser, Fish), biblical studies has, in recent decades, attuned its ears to consider the role of the reader/hearer in creating, or determining, meaning.[16] In this

---

14   Cf. Strazicich 2007.

15   Kovacs & Rowland 2004; Weinrich 2005; Weinrich 2011a; Weinrich 2011b; cf. also Dulaey 1997; Gryson 2011b; Kretschmar 1985; O'Hear 2010; Suggit 2006.

16   Cf. Literary theorists: Chatman 1978, 1990; Fish 1980; Iser 1974; Biblical specialists: Bal 1997; Fowler 2008; Moore 1989.

regard, a host of recent narratological studies of the Apocalypse by Aune, Garrow, Knight, Linton and Resseguie have illuminated the response of an 'implied reader/audience' construct to the persuasive rhetoric of the text's literary design, and/or intertextual echoes of scripture resonating in its oral delivery.[17]

> The 'implied reader' is a hypothetical construct of the implied author and is thoroughly familiar with the literary, historical, social, linguistic and cultural repertoire of the implied author...who is able to interpret the text in the way the implied author intends.[18]

One of the drawbacks of an implied-reader/hearer construct, however, is that it re-presents a mirror-image of the implied author of the text, as this hypothetical audience construct knows *everything* that the implied author presumes that they know, including the full range of literary texts alluded to by means of the verbal and visual echoes within the narrative. But what happens when ancient hearers responded to this text who did not conform to the image of an ideal hearer embedded within the narrative? How might ancient hearers' interpretations have diverged from the 'intended' response, as a consequence of deviations in the range of literary texts that they actually knew?

This study will consider the hypothetical responses of two ancient 'hearer-constructs' (HC1 and HC2, Chapters 4 and 5) to the text of Rev 9, with each construct representing a slightly modified form of the 'implied audience' role encoded in the text. Both of these constructs are hearers, rather than readers, of this text, corresponding to the predominant practice of reading texts aloud in antiquity, in conformity with the type of performance for which the text was created – read aloud by a solitary reader to a larger group (Rev 1:3).[19] The interpretative response of each hearer is informed by the particular range of texts with which each is already familiar, and which constitute the contents of his or her respective 'mental-library'. The term 'mental library' is a shorthand way of referring to the texts, or portions of texts, which an ancient hearer retained in his/her memory (however imperfectly) as a consequence of recurrent hearing, and which she may recall on the basis of visual and verbal reminiscences of the present text currently being performed (in this instance, Rev 9).

A second major distinguishing feature of the present study is that the hearer-construct models are created for one specific purpose: to test the impact of *educational variations* on an ancient hearer's reading of Rev 9. Accordingly, the precise contents of each hearer's mental library will closely correspond to a plausible range of literary texts that ancient hearers studied

---

17   Aune 2006; Garrow 1997; Knight 1999; Linton 2006; Resseguie 2009.
18   Resseguie 2009: 54.
19   Cf. Achtemeier 1990, nuanced by Gilliard 1993.

at various stages of Greek *encyclical* education.[20] Hearer construct one will be presumed to have received a minimal Greek literary education, whilst hearer construct two is envisaged to have undertaken a tertiary level of study. The aim is to create plausible models of ancient hearers, each with his/her own specific set of literary texts (consistent with her educational attainment), and with a requisite exegetical method that is appropriate both for the period in which each hearer is situated, and the degree of literary competence that each possesses (e.g. *progymnasmata* exercises). As a result, whilst my study originates from within contemporary literary-critical theories (i.e. 'hearer-response' critical readings), once the hearer-construct models have been created, the exegetical studies themselves (Chapters 4 and 5) strive to remain close to *ancient* exegetical techniques.

Nonetheless, the hearer-constructs remain *artificial models* created for the sole purpose of testing a significant variable, namely, the impact of differing levels of education on an ancient hearer's response to the cosmology of the Apocalypse. Accordingly, they are artificially restricted to two facets: a range of texts supplemented by an appropriate exegetical method. To this end, my simplified models of ancient persons do not aim for the socio-historical sophistication of the models created by Peter Oakes, in his recent insightful studies of social-groups within the communities of Philippi and Rome, informed by models of the stratified populace of each city and archaeological evidence of Graeco-Roman architecture.[21]

1.4 Structure

Following this introduction (Chapter 1), the study commences with a consideration of Greek literary education (ἐγκύκλιος παιδεία) (Chapter 2). Attention is paid to the range of literary texts studied at various points around the circle of learning, with particular concern taken to distinguish items of significance for an ancient student's cosmological knowledge (e.g. Homer, Hesiod, Aratus, Plato). Next, a range of cosmological templates are explored (tripartite cosmos, seven planetary spheres, hybrid cosmos) (Chapter 3). The correlation between educational attainment and cosmological knowledge is scrutinised with

---

20   This differs from MacDonald's approach to the *implied audience* of the Gospel of Mark, presumed to possess an encyclical education (esp. knowledge of Homer) (cf. MacDonald 2000). I do not propose that the *implied audience* construct of the Apocalypse presumes such a level of education. Rather, this study hypothesizes how an *encyclical* education may affect the interpretation of this text by a minority of its hearers who possessed varying levels of literary education. For a critique of MacDonald's implied audience construct, cf. Sandnes 2009: 249–50.

21   Cf. Oakes 1998; Oakes 2001: 55–76; Oakes 2009.

reference to a range of test-cases (tripartite model, I En 1–36; seven planetary spheres, Philo; hybrid, II Cor 12:1ff), before concluding with an analysis of the cosmology of the Apocalypse.

The next two chapters outline the hypothetical responses of two ancient hearer-constructs, with differing levels of educational attainment, to the cosmological imagery of Rev 9. Chapter 4 is concerned with the response of an ancient hearer with a minimal literary education (HC1), who adopts a tripartite cosmological template. Chapter 5, by contrast, (re-)constructs the response of a tertiary-educated hearer (HC2), with a preference for a seven-planetary spheres design, ornamented by the Aratean constellations.

The underlying premise that informs the hearer-construct models, namely that there is a direct correlation between an ancient hearer's educational attainment and his/her choice of preferred cosmological model, is then tested with recourse to the earliest extant *Commentaries* on Rev 9 (Victorinus, Tyconius, and Oecumenius) (Chapter 6). To what extent has the educational attainment of each author influenced his interpretation of the cosmological imagery of this chapter?

The study concludes with a reflection on the results of the investigation, and with suggestions for further research (Chapter 7).

Chapter 2

GREEK ENCYCLICAL EDUCATION

2.1 Introduction and Overview

This chapter carefully considers the close correlation between the range of literary texts known to an ancient hearer and the extent of his/her education. It begins (§2.2) with an overview of the progressive cycles of Greek *encyclical* education in the Graeco-Roman era. Attention is paid to the pedagogical goals of each cycle, and the close correlation between educational attainment and socio-economic status. Once this framework is in place, the contents of Greek *encyclical* education are scrutinized (§2.3): which literary texts did an ancient pupil study at various, significant, points on his/her educational journey? Having assessed the general parameters of Greek *encyclical* education, the next two sections nuance this presentation by assessing two significant variables: gender and ethnicity. How might a female pupil's gender (§2.4) impact on her experience of Greek *encyclical* education? What effect might a student's ethnicity (§2.5) have on his/her access to Greek *encyclical* education?

In the latter section, my principal concern is to consider how a Greek-speaking student's Jewish ethnic origin may impact on his/her experience of literary education. Would an ethnically Jewish student, especially one resident in the *Diaspora*, be taught to read and write in Greek by embarking on a programme of Greek *encyclical* studies (reading Homer, Euripides and Menander)? Or was there an alternative, or perhaps a parallel, 'Jewish' education system, which substituted texts from the Septuagint (perhaps pre-eminently the Torah or Psalms) in Homer's place? Taking Philo and Josephus as test cases, I assess how a (tertiary-educated) Jewish student's experience of Greek *encyclical* studies may compare with his non-Jewish contemporaries. The chapter concludes (§2.6) by assessing the significance of a student's educational attainment on the contents of his/her mental library, in preparation for the creation of plausible ancient hearer-construct models in the subsequent exegetical component of the study (Chapters 4 and 5).

2.2 Ἐγκύκλιος παιδεία *in the Graeco-Roman World*

A significant factor in the low estimate of literacy among the majority of the general populace of the Roman Empire in the 1st century CE (no more than 15 per cent of the total population) was the prohibitive cost of formal education.[1] The financial burden of school fees and books predominantly lay with the parents of prospective students, and as a result the system itself was weighted in favour of children from more privileged families. As a consequence, formal, literary education was highly stratified in both scope and range: virtually all élite males (of the senatorial, equestrian or decurion *ordines*) were highly literate (in the sense of 'cultivated', able to read and write with ease and familiar with a range of literary authors), but this privileged group constituted only a tiny proportion (*c.*1 per cent) of the total population.[2] The bulk of the remaining educated population, at the sub-decurion level, were predominantly semi-literate, able to read and/or write short texts, slowly.[3] As will be detailed below, the gulf between the educational attainment of élite students and semi-literates was almost as sharp, in many respects, as the gap between semi-literate students and the illiterate majority of society.

From the 1st century BCE onwards, the progressive order of study that ancient students followed was typically referred to as ἐγκύκλιος παιδεία (cf. Philo, *Congr.* 11–18; 74–76; 142; 148–50), literally 'circular', or more figuratively, 'rounded' education.[4] The scope of the educational process was visualized as the completion of a full circle of learning, which simultaneously illustrated the emphasis on *recurrence* in this process. The same methodical technique of progressively moving from the smallest units to more complex forms recurs at each stage, whilst a core of literary authors (notably Homer) were considered time and again, but at increasing levels of detail.

The content of ἐγκύκλιος παιδεία, as enumerated by prominent ancient educational theorists, notably Pseudo-Plutarch, Philo, Quintilian, and Seneca, differ slightly around the edges, but cluster around a nucleus of constitutive subjects: 'Reading and writing, grammar, literature, geometry, astronomy and music seem to be basic to it; rhetoric and dialectic usually come in; philosophy more often does not.'[5] Completion of the full 'circle of

1   Harris 1989: 3–24, 175–284; attendant factors include the availability of literate intermediaries, the predominantly oral culture, and the lack of political/economic stimulus towards mass literacy. Harris' research has been upheld, with minor qualifications, in more recent research: Humphrey 1991; Woolf 2000.

2   Alföldy 1984; Theissen 2001: 74.

3   Harris 1989: 5: '... *semi-literates*, persons who can write slowly or not at all, and who can read without being able to read complex or very lengthy texts.'

4   Cribiore 2001: 3; Morgan 1998: 35–9.

5   Morgan 1998: 36. Morgan's analysis is based on the list of subjects included under the heading ἐγκύκλιος παιδεία (or a Latin equivalent) by Philo, *Congr.* 11–18 [Gk: 1st century CE]; Pseudo-Plutarch, *De liberis educandis*, (Moralia 1–14) [Gk: 1st century

education' by Graeco-Roman students involved a progression through three tiered-levels of primary, secondary and tertiary studies.[6] Greater fluidity between these three-tiered layers has been identified in recent decades, notably by Cribiore and Morgan, informed by the discoveries of hundreds of Graeco-Roman school-text papyri from Egypt.[7] The evidence of these extant school-texts has supplemented and modified the systematized descriptions presented by ancient theorists on education which tend to distinguish sharply between three different teachers/schools for each educational level (i.e. γραμματιστής, γραμματικός and ῥήτωρ). The school-text papyri evidence a much wider range of educational labels and functions:

> [In the papyrii] *grammatistes* and *grammatikos* are exchangeable terms, and teachers may teach the same thing under both names. *Grammatistai* do not appear at all in the papyri; instead we find a bewildering and undefined variety of other terms, including *grammatodidaskalos*, *deskalos*, *kathegetes*, and even the feminine *grammatike* and *deskale*.[8]

Whilst acknowledging that the edges of the ascending tiers of Greek literary education may be somewhat more blurred and overlapping than the neat schemas described by ancient educationalists, nonetheless, three broad stages, or 'cycles' can still be distinguished on the basis of discernible shifts in the 'curriculum' and its pedagogical goals.[9]

The goal of the primary circle of education was to teach basic literacy and numeracy.[10] Students began by learning to read and write the alphabet, and their own name, before progressing in incremental stages through syllables, words, and phrases of increasing length and difficulty.[11] Evidence for these first tentative steps in literate education is provided by the numerous extant papyri remains of *abecaderies*, syllabaries and word-lists from Graeco-Roman Egypt, evidencing a variety of school-hand competencies.[12] The

---

CE]; Cicero, *De Oratore* 1.187ff [Latin: *artes* 1st century BCE]; Quintilian, *Institutio Oratoria* 1.10.1 [Latin: *orbis doctrinae* 1st century CE]; and Seneca, *Epistle* 88 [Latin: *liberalibus studiis* 1st century CE].

6   Bonner 1975: 165–249; Marrou 1956: 150–75; Too 2001.

7   Cribiore 1996: 173–284.

8   Morgan 1998: 28; cf. Booth 1979; Cribiore 2001: 51–9; Sandnes 2009: 20–31.

9   Morgan is critical of a tripartite classification of Greek *encyclical* education, preferring instead to divide the process, on the basis of literary authors studied, into a 'core' and 'periphery' model (Morgan 1998: 70–73).Whilst I find Morgan's division of literary authors insightful, and will draw upon her concept of a 'core' of literary authors in the present study, nonetheless, there are also clear boundary-markers that distinguish three distinct stages in the process (e.g. astronomers studied using a grammatical method; prose authors at tertiary level) which support the retention of a three-circle system; cf. Cribiore 1999.

10   My focus, however, is exclusively on literate education, at the expense of numerate education, as I am principally interested in the range of literary authors studied.

11   Bonner 1977: 165–88; Cribiore 2001: 160–84; Marrou 1956: 142–59.

12   For a descriptive catalogue of extant primary school exercises see Cribiore 1996:

pinnacle of the primary cycle of education was the copying, recitation, and memorization of short extracts from Greek literary authors (predominantly Homer and other classical poets) as well as innumerable short *gnomic* sayings.[13] The limited range of literary authors studied will be examined in more detail below (§2.3), but for the present Cribiore's summary offers a succinct overview: 'Some Homer, a bit of Euripides, and some gnomic quotations from Isocrates formed the cultural package of students at the primary level...'.[14] Short extracts from a narrow range of classical poets were used for exercises in writing and reading practice and to develop a student's calligraphic skills.[15] The same small core of classical poets would be studied, once again, only with much sharper tools, by the reduced number of students who progressed to the second cycle of education.

The most striking distinction between the primary and secondary levels of education lay not so much in the range of texts that formed the syllabus, but rather the *method* – γραμματική – that was taught to enable students to study these poetic authors critically.[16] One of the earliest extant grammar textbooks is the influential work by the Alexandrian grammarian Dionysius Thrax (*c*.170–90 BCE), who wrote a short treatise entitled Τέχνη Γραμματική.[17] The authenticity of the *final form* of this treatise is much debated, with many scholars concluding that the central core of the work derives from later hands, dating perhaps from as a late as the 4th century CE, summarizing educational practices of the preceding centuries.[18] The authenticity of the introduction is not questioned, however, and it provides a succinct summary of the range of literary skills which students were introduced to in this cycle:

> *Grammatikē* is an *empeiria* ('acquired expertise') of the general usage of poets and prose writers. It has six parts: first, accurate reading with due regard for

175–203 – Nos. 1–40 (letters of the alphabet); nos. 41–77 (alphabets); nos. 78–97 (syllabaries); and nos. 98–128 (word-lists).

13   Cribiore 2001: 178–80; Hock 2001; Morgan 1998: 90–151.

A γνώμη is, strictly speaking, a one- or two-line quotation from literature, but Morgan includes under this heading related extracts which were used for such exercises in the extant schooltext papyri, notably χρεία pithy sayings with a punch-line often attributed to Diogenes the Cynic or Isocrates the philosopher, and the short prose fable (μῦθος) attributed to Aesop or Babrius; Morgan 1998: 123–4. The latter two literary forms are rewritten and manipulated by tertiary-educated students in prose compositional exercises (*progymnasmata*).

14   Cribiore 2001: 179.

15   Cf. Cribiore 1996: 269–70, Text No. 379 (short extracts from Euripides *Phoen.* and *Ino* in a schoolhand (3rd century BCE); Cribiore 1996: 216, Text No. 182, Euripides, *Tro.* 876–79 divided into syllables (1st century CE).

16   Bonner 1977: 189–249; Cribiore 2001: 185–219; Marrou 1956: 160–75; Morgan 1998: 152–89.

17   For the Greek text of Dionysius Thrax's Τέχνη Γραμματική, see Lallot 1998 (Greek and French); Swiggers and Wouters 1998 (Greek, German and Dutch).

18   Cf. Law and Sluiter 1995.

the prosody; second, explanation of the literary devices contained; third, the provision of notes on phraseology and subject matter; fourth, the discovery of etymology; fifth, the working out of analogical regularities; sixth, the critical study of literature, which is the finest part of the *technē* ('art').

(Τέχνη Γραμματική 1.1)[19]

The goal of the complete circle of education, that is, the third cycle of ἐγκύκλιος παιδεία was principally identified with formal training in rhetoric.[20]

> [Rhetoric's] importance is out of all proportion to the relatively small number of literates (and the minute proportion of the population) who studied it, because it was widely (though not universally) regarded as the culmination of *enkyklios paideia* and because those who studied it, and went on practicing it all their lives, were among the most prominent and influential members of their society.[21]

Before a student was trained in the formal art of persuasive speech, specifically, the formal components of the three species of rhetoric – forensic (law-court), deliberative (political) and epideictic (funeral oration) (cf. Aristotle, *Ars Rhetorica* 1.3) – however, s/he was first given a firm grounding in prose compositional exercises.[22] The earliest extant handbook of prose compositional exercises (προγυμνάσματα) dates from *c.*50–100 CE and is attributed to the Alexandrian author Aelius Theon.[23] The student is taken through an ordered progression of compositional exercises, commencing with shorter and simpler tasks (e.g. writing and rewriting fables (μῦθοι)), which become progressively longer and more complicated with time and practice (e.g. verbal descrip-

---

19   Cribiore 2001: 185.

On the first step in this process see the *Shepherd of Hermas*, Vision 2.1. Hermas: 'I took it [heavenly book] and went away to another part of the field, where I copied the whole thing, letter by letter (μετεγραψάμην πάντα πρὸς γράμμα), for I could not distinguish between [lit. 'find'] the syllables (οὐχ ηὕρισκον γὰρ τὰς συλλαβάς)'; Ehrman 2003: 184–5; cf. Miller 1988; Miller 1994; Osiek 1999.

20   Bonner 1977: 250–327; Cribiore 2001: 220–44; Marrou 1956: 186–216; Morgan 1998: 190–239.

The role of philosophy, in relation to rhetoric, was variously assessed by ancient educational theorists, sometimes held to be preparatory to rhetoric, sometimes considered an integral subject alongside rhetoric, and sometimes regarded as a further stage building on rhetoric (cf. Philo, *Congr.* 11.15–18, 74–77 and Ps-Plutarch, *De liberis educandis*, 7c). A small number of students chose to study medicine in preference to formal training in education or philosophy; cf. Alexander 1992: 1009–10.

21   Morgan 1998: 190.

22   For an overview of the three species of classical rhetoric and rhetoric's development during the classical, Hellenistic and Roman eras see Kennedy 1994; 2007; Worthington 2007.

23   Cf. Kennedy 2003: 1–72; Patillon and Bolognesi 1997.

tion (ἔκφρασις) and speech-in-character (προσωποποεία)) in preparation for the careful structuring of an extended speech.[24] As in the previous stages, tertiary-level rhetorical education built on both the skills and the literary texts that a student was familiar with from the previous cycles. So, for example, the composition of χρεία built on a student's acquaintance with short maxims since the elementary stage of education when they were read aloud and memorized, and later used as examples in writing practice. Similarly, Homeric books were a favourite choice of students when penning a prose paraphrase (ὑπόθεσις).[25] Yet, the third cycle also marked new developments, notably a shift away from the imitation of poetic verse towards prose composition, in preparation for speech writing, and a consequent emphasis on a student developing his/her own creative writing skills. The transitional nature of the *progymnastic* exercises, however, ensured that a student's creativity was grounded on μίμησις: students learnt to creatively re-write and re-imagine literary classics, rather than simply composing *de novo*.[26] The emphasis on 'imitation' (μίμησις) also continued to mark the transition to prose speech writing, as students learnt to write extended speeches (declamations) through close study, and imitation, of the structure, vocabulary and style of prominent prose orators (notably Isocrates and Demosthenes) and historians (notably Herodotus).[27]

Completion of the cycle of ἐνκύκλιος παιδεία prepared an élite minority of students for an oratorical career in law or politics.[28] Most of the students who embarked on a Greek literary education, however, would have little expectation of attaining such a goal.[29] Instead, students terminated their circuit at a vast array of differing points along the circumference and with a corresponding variety of educational achievements: the vast majority attained merely a basic level of literacy (primary cycle); a smaller group gained an acquaintance with literary classics, notably Homer, and some tools of literary analysis (secondary level); a still smaller minority learnt basic compositional skills (*progymnasmata*); whilst a tiny proportion

24   The precise order of these exercises varies between compositional textbooks, but shorter, simpler units, such as fable, narrative and χρεία, tend to be clustered at the beginning. The compositional unit, ἔκφρασις, will be discussed in connection with the verbal description in Rev 9:7-9, in the reception of a tertiary-educated hearer (Chapter 5).

25   Morgan 1998: 215.

26   Cribiore 2001: 230–1 notes that although, in theory, the *progymnastic* exercises were intended to be exercises in *prose* composition, in practice the influence of poetic verse, familiar from the earlier cycles of education, continued to have a marked effect on the extant school exercises, exemplified by the large number of Egyptian ἠθοποιίαι school-exercises written in verse. On the creative importance of μίμησις in Graeco-Roman παιδεία see Whitmarsh 2001: 41–131 who discusses the connection between μίμησις and the student's replication and appropriation of a Greek cultural identity.

27   Cf. Theon, *Progymnasmata*, 134.24–135.1.

28   Morgan 1998: 226–34 with reference to Quintilian.

29   Cribiore 2001: 187.

received a formal rhetorical education.[30] The resulting close correlation between an ancient student's educational attainment, and the extent of his/ her knowledge of literary texts, will now be assessed.

2.3 The Contents of ἐγκύκλιος παιδεία

A primary source of evidence detailing the range of literary authors studied by Greek *encyclical* students is afforded by Egyptian school-text papyri, which contain 113 extracts from known Greek literary authors written in a school-hand (identified on the basis of handwriting proficiency and the presence of teaching aids, e.g. line-ruling).[31] Of these 113 extracts, the vast majority are portions of *three* major authors: Homer (58), Euripides (20) and Menander (7).[32] Only one or two brief extracts of other notable poetic authors survive in school-hands, such as Aeschylus (2), Callimachus (1), Hesiod (2), or Sappho (1).[33]

The predominant position of the epic poetry of Homer in Graeco-Roman literature is amply attested by the sheer volume of extant extracts of his work that survive in the school-text papyri, accounting for approximately half of the total number of fragments of named literary authors.[34] The surviving fragments exemplify a range of school-hand proficiencies (from poor (7) to middling (27) to good (20)), which suggest that Homeric extracts were utilized across a broad spectrum of educational levels.[35] In addition to demonstrating Homer's pre-eminence and widespread use at each stage of the educational circle, the papyri also illuminate the relative popularity of specific sections within the Homeric corpus. Perhaps the most striking statistic is that the *Iliad* was significantly more popular than the *Odyssey* at a ratio of approximately 6:1.[36]

---

30   Morgan 1998: 197–226 on the skills of a *progymnastic* education (225): 'They teach pupils, most of whom are likely to use their literacy as bureaucratic middlemen in a variety of posts, to read and analyse complicated texts, to articulate and pass on information in clear and concise form.'

31   Morgan 1998: 50–119 plus Tables 13–15 (310–13); cf. Cribiore 1996: 35–118.
   It becomes increasingly difficult to distinguish school-text papyri from 'published' texts once students attain sufficient proficiency; accordingly the evidence of the 'school-text' papyri is less accurate as a guide to the contents of tertiary-level study and needs to be supplemented with the recommended reading lists of ancient educational theorists.

32   Morgan 1998: 313 (Table 15). For a detailed catalogue of short and long extracts from literary authors used as school exercises see Cribiore 1996: 214–53.

33   Morgan 1998: 310–11 (Table 13).

34   According to my calculations, 58 of the 113 papyri (51 per cent).

35   See Morgan 1998: 313 (Table 15).

36   Morgan 1998: 308–9 (Tables 11–12). The total number of excerpts from the *Iliad* surviving in school-hands, and dating from the Ptolemaic and Roman eras, is 66, compared with only 11 such extracts from the *Odyssey*. The predominance of the *Iliad* over the *Odyssey* may even be detected in the portions of the latter work that are most popular in extant school-exercises: books IV and XI. '...both [books] brought back key figures

The opening books of each work were by far the most popular, with 6 of the 11 school-hand fragments of the *Odyssey* deriving from Books I–V, and no fewer than 35 of the 66 excerpts of the *Iliad* containing portions of Books I–II. These figures strongly suggest that ancient (primary and secondary) students were more likely to be familiar with books I–II of the *Iliad* than any other ancient text. Some of the most popular extracts from this section of the *Iliad* were the catalogue of ships (*Il.* II.494–760) that surveyed the principal characters in the drama, their place of origin and family relations, as well as the deceptive dream that Zeus sent to Agamemnon (*Il.* II.1–282).[37] Potential orators were expected to continue their life-long engagement with Homer, especially the *Iliad*, familiarizing themselves not simply with books I–II, but with the whole of the work (cf. Quintilian, *Inst. Or.* 10.1.46–51).[38]

The substantial number of extant school-text fragments of the plays of the Athenian tragedian Euripides (*c.*480–406 BCE), approximately 20 in total, place this playwright second only to Homer in popularity, far outweighing the combined totals of Aeschylus (2) and Sophocles (1).[39] The surviving fragments exemplify a range of school-hand proficiencies (from poor (6) to middling (4) to good (10)) that suggest how fragments of Euripides were equally at home at both the primary and secondary level (supported by the fact that five of the extracts are brief *gnomai*).[40] The 20 short extracts that survive are drawn from twelve of Euripides' plays, by far the most numerous of which are extracts from the *Phoenissae* (8 fragments).[41] The pronounced popularity of Euripides' *Phoenissae* is most likely derived, as Cribiore suggests, from a variety of elements that coalesced to make the work indispensable as a source for both primary and secondary exercises.[42] *Phoenissae* revisited the familiar myth of the downfall of the house of Thebes (much like *Odyssey* books IV and XI revisited characters from the *Iliad*); it was rich in quotable *gnomai* that could be used in primary exercises; and it provided a host of rare words and compound metaphors, as well as reminiscences of Homeric battle-scenes, for secondary pupils to study. Over and above the content of Euripides' plays, however, arguably the single most important reason why Euripides was the tragedian of choice among ancient educa-

---

from the *Iliad*, whom Telemachus met during his voyage and Odysseus encountered in the underworld'; Cribiore 2001: 196. Ancient educationalists (and their pupils) were keen to revisit literary characters familiar from the *Iliad*, such that the *Odyssey* was read largely as a 'sequel' to the *Iliad*.

37   Morgan 1998: 105–12.
38   Russell 2002, Vol. IV, Book 10.
39   Morgan 1998: 115–16 (plus Tables 22–3 (321–2)); cf. Cribiore 2001: 198–200.
40   Morgan 1998: 115, 313 (Table 15).
41   The twelve plays excerpted are: *Electra, Hecuba, Aegeus, Ion, Phoenissae, Bacchae, Telephus, Hippolytus, Medea,* and *Troades,* (Morgan 1998: 322 (Table 23); cf. Kovacs 1994–2003; Collard and Cropps 2008.
42   Cribiore 2001a.

tionalists was the high esteem in which the rhetorical skill of the author was held, such that his plays were considered excellent objects of study for potential orators, (Quintilian, *Inst. Or.* 10.1.68).

The third major literary author with whom Graeco-Roman students would be especially familiar was Menander (*c*.342–290 BCE).[43] Seven brief fragments of his comedies are extant, mostly in a middling (4) or good hand (2), with an even more widespread range of quotations (either attributed or unattributed) extant in the abundant collections of *gnomai*. Students, especially at primary and secondary level, would be far more familiar with memorable 'one-liners' from Menander's comedies than they would be with the actual plots or characters of the plays themselves. These 'one-liners' were often gathered together in ancient collections of *gnomai*, usually grouped by topic, to serve as school-exercises at every level, whether as a brief text to copy or recite, or as an apposite line for a rhetorician to quote during a speech.[44] At a more advanced level, students might copy more extensive sections of Menander's comedies, as evidenced by a 2nd-century CE fragment of the opening 16 lines of Menander's *Misoumenos*, used as a writing exercise, or read a copy of a play in full.[45] Menandrean comedy was perceived by ancient commentators to stand in a line of continuity with the tragedies of Euripides, portraying people 'as they are' rather than 'how they ought to be' (cf. Aristotle, *Poetics* XXV.1460b).[46] In this regard, Quintilian encouraged his students to imitate Menander's unsurpassed craft in creating realistic characters, especially the realistic speeches-in-character at which Menander excelled, to improve their own oratorical proficiency in adopting various personas (Quintilian, *Inst. Or.* 10.1.69–71).[47]

The extant Graeco-Roman school-text papyri suggest that for the majority of pupils who terminated their circuit at the primary, or early secondary stage, their literary education consisted of limited knowledge of portions of three genres (epic, tragedy and *gnome*): Homer (notably *Iliad* Books I–II), some extracts from Euripides (notably *Phoenissae*) and some *gnomic* sayings attributed to Menander and Isocrates (cf. fig. 2.1).

43   Morgan 1998: 117, 313 (Table 15); cf. Cribiore 2001: 199–201.
44   Cribiore 2001: 200. Only a solitary complete play (*Dyskolos*) by Menander and short fragmentary extracts are extant; Arnott 1979; 1997; 2000; Balme 2001.
45   Cf. Cribiore 1996: 242–3, referring to No. 290, a 2nd-century CE fragment of *Misoumenos*, prologue, lines 1–16, written in an 'evolving' school-hand.
46   Halliwell 1995: 128–9. Menander also alluded to characters, lines and plot-devices familiar to his audience from Euripidean drama; see Peter's Brown, 'Introduction' in Balme 2001: xiv–xv; Troupi 2006.
47   Menander restyled the mask-types of his characters, influenced by Theophrastus' *Characters*, in which the philosopher had drawn a correlation between a person's ἦθος and their physiological characteristics. Cf. Wiles 1991: 2–6, 68–99; Diggle 2004; Webster 1995: 1–51 with reference to the mask types enumerated by Julius Pollux (*Onomastikon* 4.143–54) and the archaeological evidence from Lipari.

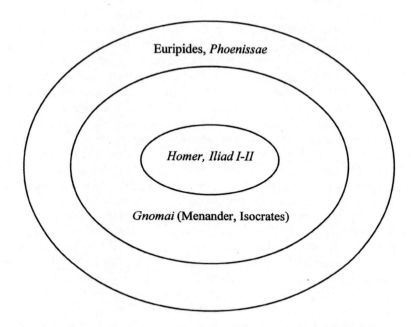

Fig. 2.1 Core of Greek Literary Authors (Homer, Euripides and Menander)

A distinguishing mark of a grammatical-level education was a student's introduction to the elements of astronomy, principally with reference to Aratus' epic poem, φαινομένα.[48] Aratus of Soli, Cilicia (*c*.310–239 BCE) was a Hellenistic philosopher and poet who studied under Zeno, the founder of the Stoic philosophical school, in Athens.[49] The first half of Aratus' φαινομένα (ll.19–757) is essentially a re-casting of Eudoxus' prose φαινομένα, a detailed description of the relative positions of the fixed stars/constellations on the celestial sphere, into the metre of epic poetry (cf. Hipparchus 1.2.1–16).[50] Aratus' epic version of Eudoxus' geometric study

48   Kidd 1997; Mair 1921.
49   Kidd 1997: 3–5; Mair 1921: 359–63. In line with Aratus' Stoic philosophical presuppositions, Zeus is redefined as the rational principle immanent within the cosmos (rather than as a distinct agent outside of it): cf. ll. 2–3 'Filled with Zeus are all highways and all meeting-places of people, filled are the sea and harbours…'. Cf. Kidd 1997: 10–12, 161–74 (commentary on the proem), especially the parallels noted with the contemporary Stoic, 'Hymn to Zeus' by Cleanthes (Thom 2005). On Stoic cosmology see Jones 2003: 328–44.
50   Manitius 1894; the extant extracts of Eudoxus' work are preserved in Hipparchus' commentary.

popularized its contents for an educated Hellenistic audience, and marked the first step in the production of more accessible surveys of astronomy that became a notable feature of the 3rd—1st centuries BCE (cf. especially Geminos' φαινομένα (c.1st century BCE)).[51] These popular surveys and introductions simplified, or omitted, the detailed mathematical proofs of Eudoxus or Euclid, in favour of more general descriptions of the results of such studies. One of the consequences of this more accessible format was the opportunity to include a greater breadth of material within the study (e.g. phases of the moon, eclipses, and astronomical geography).[52] This is precisely what Aratus chose to do, by including an additional section (ll. 758–1141) detailing observable weather signs, comparable to Theophrastus' περὶ σημείων (On [Weather] Signs) (c.371–287 BCE).[53] The net result was an updated version of Hesiod's didactic poem, *Works and Days*, offering practical advice on how to prosper in (agricultural) life through careful scrutiny of calendrical and weather-signs.[54]

Aratus' φαινομένα was phenomenally well-received in the Hellenistic and Roman eras, and was to prove the most popular introduction to astronomy that élite students received in the formal circle of education (ἐγκύκλιος παιδεία), far more so than prose introductions to the subject (e.g. Geminos' φαινομένα).[55] Aratus' poem was principally studied, and taught, as an outstanding example of the epic genre as evidenced by the range of extant *scholia*, written by grammarians, that scrutinize the text using the tools of literary analysis.[56] In addition, the text was also of marked interest to astronomers (μαθηματικόι) such as Hipparchus and Attalus (2nd century BCE) who sought to correct errors of fact so that the text could continue to function as an astronomical textbook.[57] The relative weighting afforded to these respective aspects, influenced the varied perceptions of its genre by ancient teachers and students alike (a mathematical textbook (φαινομένα) more akin to Euclid, and/or an epic poem more akin to Hesiod).

Astronomical study of Aratus' φαινομένα was supplemented by the use of a celestial globe as a visual aid in late Hellenistic and Roman pedagogy (cf. Geminos, φαινομένα xvi. 12, who refers to the use of a 'solid sphere' (σφαῖρα στερεὰ)).[58] Three ancient celestial globes are extant, dating from

51   Evans and Berggren 2006: 8–9.
52   Cf. I Enoch 72–82 (*The Astronomical Book*). On the outdated, and overly schematic, character of much of the astronomical data in I En 72–82, closer to archaic Babylonian lore than Hellenistic astronomical observations, see Otto Neugebauer's Appendix in Black, VanderKam and Neugebauer 1985: 386–414.
53   Hort 1916; Sider and Brunschön 2007.
54   Kidd 1997: 8; Most 2006; West 1978.
55   Marrou 1956: 184–5; Sale 1966. Cf. Cicero, *Rep*. I. xxii, 'Aratus illustrated [the constellations] in his verses...by the ornament of poetic description' (...*sed poetica quadam facultate versibus Aratum extulisse*...)' (Keyes 1928).
56   Cf. Kidd 1997: 43; Martin 1974; (Quintilian, *Inst*. Or. 10.1.46).
57   Kidd 1997: 44–8.
58   Evans and Berggren 2006: 27–43. In addition to the celestial globe (i.e. the solid

the early centuries of the Common Era, namely the Farnese Atlas, the Mainz Globe, and the Kugel Globe.[59] Of these, the Mainz globe (*c.*150–220 CE) is the most representative example of the size (11cm in diameter) and type of (hand-held) celestial globe which could have been used in an ancient educational context, depicting all 48 of the standard Greek constellations as listed by Eudoxus and Aratus (cf. fig. 2.2).[60]

A student who had plotted a complete circle of ἐγκύκλιος παιδεία in preparation for a career as an orator was likely to be familiar with a much more extensive range of literary texts and genres. A maximal sense of the potential gulf between the literary knowledge of a primary educated pupil and a tertiary educated oratorical student is glimpsed by the extensive scope of the recommended reading list of the Roman orator Quintilian (*Inst. Or*) (*c.*95 CE).[61] Quintilian's reading-list is not limited to a selection of the prose speeches of orators, but covers a diverse range of genres, highlighting the authors whose works are recommended as outstanding examples of their type, those whose vocabulary, style or artistry are to be read, and imitated, by budding orators with profit.[62] The comparative list of the principal authors recommended, by genre, are delineated as follows (fig. 2.3):

sphere, σφαῖρα στερεὰ) (xvi. 12), Geminos also refers to an armillary sphere (a 'ringed sphere', σφαῖρα κρικωτή), (xvi. 10, 12) a series of interconnected metal rings representing the most prominent celestial circles (ecliptic, equator, tropics, arctic, antarctic) (32–4). Whilst there are no material remains of a Hellenistic or Roman era armillary sphere, visual representations are extant, e.g. in ancient mosaics (cf. Evans and Berggren 2006: 32, fig. I.5).

59   The Farnese Atlas globe (c. 2nd century CE) is part of a large decorative marble sculpture of the Titan, Atlas, bearing a celestial globe on his back. The celestial globe itself measures 65cm in diameter and displays 40 of the 48 Greek constellations (cf. Künzl 2005: Chapter 6, esp. figs. 6.3, 6.4, 6.7, 6.8). Whilst the Farnese globe itself is dated to the 2nd century CE the date of the celestial globe which its sculptor took as its model may be earlier, perhaps of Hellenistic origin (on the basis of the positioning of the constellations, altered through precession), but evidence is inconclusive; cf. Duke 2006; Schaefer 2005.

The Kugel globe (c. 2nd century CE?) is a high-status decorative object, fashioned from silver and only 6cm in diameter. Cf. Cuvigny 2004: 345–82 who draws a connection with the type of luxury item which the poet/astronomer Leonidas of Alexandria presented to Sabina Poppea (Emperor Nero's wife, c. 62–5 CE) on her birthday, referred to as 'an imitation/copy of heaven' (οὐράνιον μίμημα).

60   Evans and Berggren 2006: 28–31; Künzl 2000. The Mainz globe has a square hole at the top, and a larger, round hole at its base, which suggests that it may have been displayed on a stand or spike (cf. fig. 2.2). Aratus' verbal illustration of the celestial sphere, supplemented by the visual display of the Mainz globe, will inform the tertiary educated hearer's interpretation of Rev 9 (Chapter 5).

61   Cf. Vardi 2003 who also cites a comparable recommended reading list by Dionysius of Halicarnassus (c. 1st century CE).

62   Vardi 2003 draws a connection between the recommended reading lists of orators and earlier selective lists of authors by Alexandrian librarians (notably Aristophanes, 2nd century BCE) representative of specific genres.

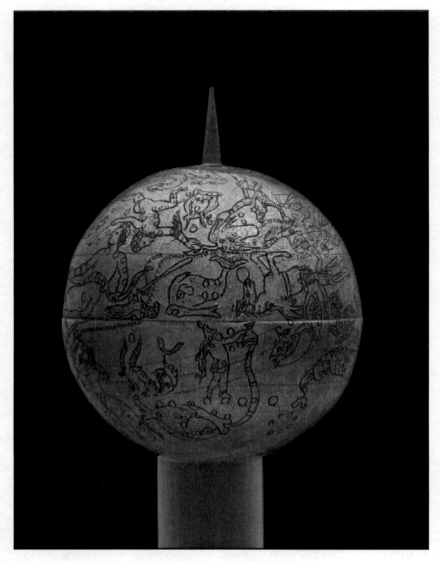

Fig. 2.2 The Mainz Celestial Globe (Replica)[63]

63   Photo/Römisch-Germanisches Museum Mainz, S. Steidl.

Genre	Quintilian (*Institutio Oratoria 10*)	Genre	Quintilian (*Institutio Oratoria 10*)
1. Epic	Homer Hesiod Antimachus Panyassis Apollonius Aratus Theocritus	6. Old Comedy	Aristophanes Eupolis Cratinus
2. Elegy	Callimachus Philetas	7. New Comedy	Menander
3. Iambus	Archilochus	8. History	Thucydides Herodotus Theopompus Philistus
4. Lyric	Pindar Stesichorus Alcaeus Simonides	9. Oratory	Demosthenes Aeschines Hyperides Lysias Isocrates
5. Tragedy	Aeschylus Sophocles Euripides	10. Philosophy	Plato Xenophon Aristotle Theophrastus

Fig 2.3 Quintilian's Recommended Reading List of Greek Literary Authors (Quintilian (Institutio Oratoria 10))

Whilst the vast range of authors and genres listed here represents a maximal list of recommended authors which few ancient students may have actually read in their entirety, nonetheless even the spread of genres itself is significant, covering a wealth of poetic (e.g. epic, tragedy, comedy) and prose forms (history, oratory and philosophy).[64] Students did not progress

---

64 Cf. Hock 2005, who carefully assesses the educational attainment of the implied author (Chariton) of the Greek novel *Callirhoe*. The implied author's extensive range of allusions to Homer's *Iliad* and *Odyssey*, supplemented by one-liners attributed to Menander, and proficiency in epistolography, evidence an education that exceeded the mimimal 'core' of ancient παιδεία. The extent of this excess is hinted at by the range of allusions to prose writers of histories and oratory (notably Herodotus, Thucydides and Demosthenes), combined with an adroit handling of *progymnastic* exercise (διήγημα and ἠθοποιίαι), and an ability to compose persuasively argued rhetorical speeches. The internal evidence of the text strongly suggests that the implied author was the recipient of a tertiary-level education that comprised both compositional exercises and rhetorical speech writing. Yet the extent of Chariton's mental library is also worthy of further scrutiny, in

to the study of prose authors until the tertiary cycle of education, and thus knowledge of the writings of historical, oratorical and philosophical authors in itself constituted an educational boundary-marker that sharply divided élite students from the majority of their peers.[65]

A very limited 'core' of literary texts would have been familiar to almost all students who had embarked on the circle of literary education, principally Homer, but also Euripides and Menander. The recurrent nature of the system was such that students continually returned to the elements, that is, the core authors (Homer) and principles (small units to more complicated forms) that they had met from the very beginning. Yet the continuities were far outweighed by the discontinuities in the breadth of an ancient student's knowledge of these texts: whereas a primary educated student may have some knowledge of *Iliad* Books I–II that s/he has attempted to read, copy and memorize, a tertiary educated student is likely to be familiar with the *Iliad* and *Odyssey* in their entirety, through repeated, critical engagement (Quintilian, *Inst. Or.* 8.5).

2.4 Education Variables I: Gender[66]

The highly stratified nature of Graeco-Roman society, evidenced in the formal literary education of male students, is also replicated in the case of female students, as Cribiore succinctly states: 'the majority of women who attained a degree of literary education belonged to the upper strata of society and came from propertied environments'.[67] Yet the parallelism between male and female students is not exact, and in this respect three significant variations are worthy of note. First, the evidence that we possess, although fragmentary and discontinuous, suggests that a higher ratio of boys received a literary education than girls.[68] Second,

that the range of authors alluded to falls far short of Quintilian's extensive list, barely diverging from the most respected representative of each genre (Homer [Epic], Menander [Comedy], Herodotus and Thucydides [History], and Demosthenes [Oratory]), which he may have studied as school exercises rather than through independent study.

65   A slight caveat to this point is that some brief extracts from the prose fables of Aesop and Babrius may have been familiar to primary educated students as reading and copying exercises.

66   I have drawn on a range of existing surveys of extant Greek evidence pertaining to the extent of female literacy, formal education of women in ἐγκύκλιος παιδεία and literary evidence of female composition in the Graeco-Roman empire, most notably: Bagnall and Cribiore 2006; Cole 1981; Cribiore 2001: 74–101; 2001b; Pomeroy 1981; 1984; 1998.

67   Cribiore 2001: 75, explicitly referring here to the evidence of papyrus letters written by women in Graeco-Roman Egypt.

68   The fragmentary nature of the data (occasional epigraphic evidence, fragmentary papyri (mostly from Egypt), material remains (statues, sarcophagi) and scattered references by male literary authors) creates huge gaps in our knowledge, both temporally and geographically, leading to highly tentative proposals of broader trends in female literacy across the Empire over the course of the Hellenistic and Roman eras.

the extent of a girl's literary education was affected by an additional factor: the age at which she married. Third, although the majority of literate females belonged to the upper strata of society, this was not exclusively the case, as there are pockets of evidence for the existence of female scribes and teachers who appear to be drawn from the sub-decurion strata of society.

The most detailed and extensive body of evidence of female literacy in antiquity is provided by the extant Graeco-Roman papyri from Egypt (1st century BCE–4th century CE).[69] Approximately one-third of the 180 private letters in which a woman is named as sender (*c*.60 letters) are written in a personal, rather than a professional scribal hand, which suggests that either the sender transcribed the letter herself, or dictated it to a family member/ acquaintance.[70] Social etiquette maintained that letters should ordinarily be dictated to a scribe or secretary rather than burdening the author (save for short private correspondence with close friends), so a dictated letter is not a sufficient indication that the sender was illiterate or a 'slow writer', and still affords strong evidence of the composer's educational attainment.[71]

Whilst the papyri are not authored by a homogenous group of women, the economic and social status of these female authors is restricted to a range of women belonging to the élite strata of Graeco-Roman society (i.e. women belonging to families of the senatorial, equestrian or decurion orders).[72] To cite some notable examples Eudaimonis (P. Giss 21–24; P. Brem 63; P. Flor 3.332) and Aline (P. Giss 78) are the mother and wife respectively of Apollonios, who held the office of στρατηγός in upper Egypt – the highest magistracy post in the region – in the early 2nd century CE. The high government office held by Apollonios is reflected in the contents of the letters in this archive, which refer to the purchase of luxury goods (e.g. a child's sleeping rug costing 100 drachmas) and the governance of landed estates (cf. Isidora (BGU 4.1204–7) the partner/sister of the στρατηγός Asklepiades, who refers to a sum of 2,800 drachmas of silver as a payment for land).

These documents provide invaluable data of the educational opportunities for women within the upper strata of élite Graeco-Roman society in the early centuries CE. The financial responsibilities deriving from the management of extensive households and landed estates often required élite women to engage in written correspondence with absent family members and agents.

69   Bagnall and Cribiore 2006; Cribiore 2001b; Pomeroy 1981.

70   For the range of handwriting types in Graeco-Roman papyri, and various criteria for distinguishing between them, see Cribiore 1996: 97–118 (relating to various levels of school hands). For more specific criteria for distinguishing scribal, secretarial and personal hands in private letters consult Bagnall and Cribiore 2006: 42–7.

71   For Graeco-Roman letter conventions see Lieu 2006 and the bibliography cited there.

72   For a nuanced discussion of the range of indicators (property, money, moveable goods, offices) present in these letters that support such conclusions, see Bagnall and Cribiore 2006: 68–74.

As a consequence it was not uncommon for such individuals to compose private/business letters, which they either dictated to a scribe or secretary or penned in their entirety. In preparation for an influential role in household/ estate management, such élite Graeco-Roman women commonly received a sound grammatical education, which included tuition in literacy and letter-composition. The extant papyri provide hints that a number of these women had received private tuition at home, perhaps alongside their brothers, by means of the employment of a καθηγητής who provided them with a grammatical education (cf. Heraidous' education P. Giss 80 and P. Giss 85).

Conversely, these letters also hint at the comparatively limited educational opportunities available to girls from such élite families. Parents of higher social status, encouraged by the valorization of παιδεία among the literary élite and the resultant opportunities for a public career, frequently sought to endow their sons with as extensive an education as their financial means allowed.[73] Élite women, denied access to a comparable public career, had more limited professional opportunities as household managers and businesswomen, for which a grammatical education (the pinnacle of the second cycle) was deemed sufficient.

Hemelrijk's detailed study of the bilingual education of élite Roman women (*c.* 2nd century BCE–3rd century CE) offers a number of insights that are relevant to the present study of Greek literary education.[74] The familiar three-cycles of ἐγκύκλιος παιδεία (primary, secondary and tertiary) often became distorted in Roman womens' experience of this system. Denied access to a public career, the tertiary stage of education was usually viewed as superfluous by their parents, such that few élite women received a tertiary-level formal education. Rare examples of women philosophers, such as the infamous Cynic Hipparchia (partner of Crates, 3rd century BCE), were frequently the objects of ridicule or slander.[75] The second cycle was also frequently truncated by a woman's early marriage (in her early–mid teens), such that Hemelrijk considers that it is more meaningful instead to divide a woman's education into two alternative stages: pre- and post-marital education.[76] Whether or not a woman's literary education terminated at the time of her marriage

---

73   For the ideal of a literary education among educational theorists of the Hellenistic and Roman eras see especially Ps.-Plutarch, *De liberis educandis, Philo, Congr.*, Cicero, *De Oratore*, and Quintilian, *Inst. Or.*

74   Hemelrijk 1999.

75   See Taylor 2003: 173–226 for an insightful study of Philo's depiction of Jewish women philosophers, viewed against a broader context of a range of (mostly negative) reactions to women philosophers by élite male writers (drawing on Hawley 1994).

76   Hemelrijk 1999: 21–2, 28–9: '...upper-class girls usually married in their early or mid-teens, that is, at an age when most boys were only halfway through the second stage of their education (the tuition by a *grammaticus*). Consequently girls lacked the time to complete their education before marriage...' (28–9). Hemelrijk cites the example of Agrippina Maior as an exception (cf. Suetonius, *Augustus*, 86), who did not marry until age 18, and was consequently able to complete a full course of *progymnasmata* exercises.

was usually dependent on the attitude of her husband who assumed pedagogical responsibility for his partner.

Whilst much of the extant evidence from literary sources suggests that literary education was largely restricted to women from élite households, there is some limited evidence that this was not exclusively the case. Although the financial burden of education may have encouraged a higher ratio of male to female literacy, formal elementary education of sub-élite girls is indicated in a selection of sources. An inscription excavated from the gymnasium of Pergamum includes a list of girls who were awarded prizes in contests for epic, elegiac and lyric poetry, reading and calligraphy (καλλιγραφία).[77] This inscription suggests that at least a proportion of Pergamene girls received a formal elementary education at the gymnasium during the Hellenistic era. In addition to isolated examples of private benefactions to fund education in specific cities, material remains of terracotta sculptures of schoolgirls (carrying writing tablets or with a book-roll on her knees) have also been recovered across a broad sweep of the Hellenistic empire (Greece, Asia Minor and Egypt), whose 'mass-production' (using moulds) may indicate a market beyond the upper strata of urban society.[78] The literary evidence is slight, but there are also occasional brief references to women with the status of 'teacher' (ἡ διδάσκαλος, δεσκαλή) in the extant Graeco-Roman papyri from Egypt, which are plausibly interpreted as a reference to an (elementary) teacher, analogous to the reference to male teachers, usually of low social status, referred to elsewhere.[79]

The extant evidence, although fragmentary and discontinuous, suggests that girls from élite families were often educated to at least an elementary level, frequently by means of a private tutor (καθηγητής). Depending on the age at which a woman was married, it was also not uncommon that she should receive a certain level of grammatical tuition, such that she was familiar with a range of Greek literary authors. On rarer occasions, depending on a woman's family status and often also her husband's attitude, she may continue her education after marriage, often

77 Cf. Cole 1981: 231–2; Cribiore 2001: 83–4; Harris 1989: 132, 136 who all refer to a comparable inscription from the city of Teos (2nd century BCE) in which a benefactor, Polythrous, funded the elementary education of all free-born children (explicitly girls and boys) in the city.
Compare Eusebius' reference to Origen's employment of 'girls trained for beautiful writing' (κόραις ἐπὶ τὸ καλλιγράφειν) (H.E. 6.2.3) in his production of commentaries on the scriptures in the 3rd century CE. For a discussion of the evidence for female scribes/copyists/calligraphers in the Hellenistic and Roman eras see Haines-Eitzen 1998 who notes that calligraphic training was particularly important for slaves and freedmen/freedwomen who sought employment as professional scribes, secretaries or copyists.

78 Cole 1981: 231–2; Cribiore 2001: 84–5; Harris 1989: 136–7.

79 Cf. Cribiore 2001: 78–83. It is possible, however, that the term may on occasion refer to a female teacher of apprentices in other trades, notably manual trades such as weaving.

on a less formal basis (through private reading and study). Women from sub-élite families, like their male counterparts, were far less likely than élite children to receive a formal education, although there are traces of evidence that support the existence of female scribes and copyists (καλλιγραφαί) and even (elementary-)teachers (δεσκαλαί).[80]

2.5 Education Variables II: Ethnicity

The highly stratified character of Graeco-Roman παιδεία was mirrored, with its own distinctive variations, in literate education of Judeans/Jews in Palestine and the *Diaspora* during the same era. With respect to the former region, Heszer's exhaustive study of Jewish literacy builds on the method and findings of Harris to focus on the specific test case of Judea.[81] In contrast to previous studies which tended to envisage a higher rate of literacy among the Jewish populace, in view of the centrality of the study of the Torah, Hezser persuasively argues that instead the overall literacy rate was likely to be lower in the predominantly rural region of Palestine than in other more metropolitan regions within the Empire.[82] Applying the same criteria for mass literacy that Harris delineated (e.g. widespread dissemination of texts; extensive, subsidized school network; economic and political support for mass literacy), Hezser concludes that the overall literacy rate among Graeco-Roman Jews was likely to fall short of the 10 per cent figure that Harris identified for the Graeco-Roman empire in general, as almost all the relevant factors were absent:

> Although the exact literacy rate amongst ancient Jews cannot be determined, Meir Bar-Ilan's suggestion that the Jewish literacy rate must have been lower than the literacy rate amongst Romans in the first centuries CE seems very plausible. Whether the average literacy rate amongst Palestinian Jews was only 3 percent, as Bar-Ilan has reckoned, or slightly higher, must ultimately remain open. The question naturally depends on what one understands by 'literacy'. If 'literacy' is determined as the ability to read documents, letters and 'simple' literary texts in at least one language and to write more than one's signature oneself, it is quite reasonable to assume that the Jewish literacy rate was well below the 10–15 percent (of the entire population, including women) which Harris has estimated for Roman society in Imperial times.[83]

80   Cf. Cribiore 2001: 78–83.
81   Hezser 2001; cf. Bar-Ilan 1988; 1992; Crenshaw 1998; Niditch 1996; Young 1998.
82   Former studies which argued for a high rate of literacy in 1st-century CE Judea, stimulated by a widespread network of Jewish elementary (Torah) schools as referred to in the rabbinic literature (b. B. B. 21a, y. Meg 3.1, 73d, y. Ket 13.1, 35c), include Ebner 1956: 38ff; Gerhardsson 1961: 57–9; Safrai and Stern 1974: 149ff.
83   Hezser 2001: 496; Cf. Bar-Ilan 1992: 46–61 whose estimate of a 3 per cent literacy rate for the whole population can be broken down into three sub-categories:

One of the most significant factors behind the recent re-evaluation of literacy rates in first century CE Judea has been a reappraisal of the rabbinic evidence (notably Babylonian Talmud b. B . B. 21a), critically reassessed as a reading back of a later 2nd/3rd-century CE network of Torah schools onto the 1st century CE, rather than providing an accurate snapshot of the Second Temple era.[84]

More helpful, perhaps, than a stark percentage estimate of the populace's overall literacy rate, however, is an awareness of the highly stratified character of literate education in 1st-century CE Judea. At the centre of a concentric circle of Jewish literacy, as in Graeco-Roman society more generally, lay the ruling élite (e.g. Josephus and other aristocratic families, especially in Jerusalem), who, at least since the Maccabean era, had been open to receive a private education, predominantly by personal tutors, in both Greek and Hebrew/Aramaic (cf. Jos. *Ant.* 12.4.6–7).[85] Beyond this élite group were broader circles of professional scribes, who had been instructed to read and/ or copy texts and documents, pre-eminetly the Torah (e.g. scribes, *yaḥad* (cf. 1QSa 1:6–8).[86] The existence of a network of scribal schools, however, is lacking, although it is plausible that the Jerusalem Temple, as a major employer of scribes during the Second Temple period, may have operated a scribal school or a system of apprenticeships.[87] At the outer edges of this literate circle were the broader population, some of whom were perhaps capable of reading aloud short passages or lists, perhaps as a result of informal education by parents (cf. Jos., *Apion* II. 204),[88] whilst the majority were entirely illiterate and dependent on intermediaries for access to literary texts.

---

a negligible literacy rate among the rural population that comprised 70 per cent of the inhabitants, an estimated 1–5 per cent for the majority of the urban population (20 per cent of total) and an anomalously high rate of 2–15 per cent among the ruling urban élite (10 per cent of the population).

84   On the reappraisal of the rabbinic evidence see Heszer 2001: 39–109. The Babylonian Talmud, b. B. B. 21a, refers to a three stage process: the setting up of school-teachers in Jerusalem [C], the setting up of schoolteachers in all districts (for students entering at age 16–17) [D], and the setting up of schoolteachers in all districts (for students entering at age 6–7). The final stage in this process is credited to R. Yehoshua b. Gamla, high priest c.63–5 CE, such that even the Talmud does not date widespread elementary education prior to the second half of the 1st century CE.

85   Hezser 2001: 90–94; Hengel 1974: 76–7.

86   For a survey of the diversity of social roles and professional functions of Judean scribes in this era, see Horsley 2007: 71–150; Schams 1998: 36–273. On the technical training and skill of the Qumran scribes see Tov 2004, and consult Naveh 1986 for the reclassification of 4Q 341 as a scribal writing exercise.

87   But see Schams 1998: 309–27 who is concerned to nuance the extant textual and artifactual data (especially of the Roman period), to avoid a misrepresentative focus on the role of scribes as 'Torah scholars', at the expense of their broader functions as professional writers in a variety of contexts within Judean society.

88   Josephus, *Ap.* II.204 '[The Law] gave instruction to teach reading (literally 'teach letters' (γράμματα παιδεύειν)), in relation to the laws, and that they know about the deeds of their forefathers [= the historical books]...' (cf. Deut 6:7, 11:19) (Barclay 2007: 287).

My principal concern, however, is to probe the content of literate education among *Greek-speaking* Jews (or Jewish-Christians) resident in the *Diaspora*. Would an ethnically Jewish student, living in the *Diaspora*, be taught to read and write in Greek, using the standard set-texts of ἐγκύκλιος παιδεία, pre-eminently Homer, Euripides and Menander? Or, was there an alternative, 'Jewish' education system, which substituted texts from the Septuagint (perhaps pre-eminently the Torah or the Psalms) in Homer's place? What impact did a student's social standing have on the choice of set-texts that were studied?

Tentative evidence of a perceived rivalry between the writings of Homer and the scriptures may be perceptible in the Mishnah (*c*.200 CE), where divergent views are attributed to different social strata (Sadducees and Pharisees) within Judea.[89]

> The Sadducees say, We cry out against you, o ye Pharisees, for ye say, 'The Holy Scripture render the hands unclean', [and] 'The writings of *Hamiram* (המירם) do not render the hands unclean'.
>
> (Mishnah, *Yadaim*, 4.6)[90]

The passage refers to the writings of 'Hamiram', which most plausibly refers to Homer, and if this is the case it is interesting to note that not only are these books explicitly contrasted with the scriptures, but they are (by inference) regarded as 'inspired' (defiling the hands) by the aristocratic Sadducees, who disagree with the Pharisees on this point.[91] Such an opinion is consistent with a reverence for Homer among the ruling élite of Judean society, who considered Homer to be 'the poet' *par excellence* as a consequence of their study of his writings in their Greek literary education (ἐγκύκλιος παιδεία), in marked contrast to the predominant emphasis on scripture study among professional scribal practitioners. In the second passage where the name occurs (y. Sanh 10:1, 28a), a similar rivalry recurs, in that the books of 'Hamiram' are denigrated as suitable only for recitation (reading lessons?), rather than for serious study.[92] The Greek cultural identity that was promoted in ἐγκύκλιος παιδεία by the close study of Homer, was perhaps perceived as a rival which threatened the specifically 'Jewish'

---

89   Hezser 2001: 70–71.
90   Danby 1933: 784.
91   Cf. Jastrow 1926: 355: 'pr. n m. המירם, a person from whom certain secular books are named (Yad. IV. 6, Y. Sah. X. 28a): conjectures: *Homeros* (Homer); ἡμερησια (βιβλια) diaries; symbolical name = 'the Lord remove them"; cf. Gordis 1948.
92   Hezser 2001: 71.

cultural identity that later rabbis sought to promote through close study of the Torah in Hebrew.[93]

More conclusive evidence that élite students from a Jewish ethnic background received a Greek *encyclical* education is provided by the writings of Philo and Josephus.

2.5.1 *Philo of Alexandria (c.20 BCE–50 CE)*

Philo, who was a member of one of the most influential and affluent Jewish families in Alexandria, had received an extensive Greek literary education in his youth, the broad parameters of which he outlines most extensively in his treatise 'On the Preliminary Studies' (*Congr.* 74–77).[94] In various passages Philo refers to up to seven distinct disciplines that he had studied as part of his *encyclical* studies: 1. grammar; 2. rhetoric; 3. dialectic; 4. geometry; 5. arithmetic; 6. music; and 7. astronomy.[95] Grammar is by far the most prominent element that is referred to by Philo, mentioned in six of the eight passages that are concerned with the topic.[96] Philo divided the study of grammar into two distinct parts, the elementary part, which is concerned with writing and reading, and the more advanced stage that is concerned with exegesis of the literary poets and historians (*Somn.* I. 205).[97]

Something of the breadth of Greek literary authors which Philo himself had studied can be glimpsed from the wealth of allusions to epic poets (e.g. Homer and Hesiod) and tragedians (Aeschylus, Sophocles and Euripides) in Philo's treatises.[98] As Niehoff notes, Philo expresses '…open admiration for specific philosophers and playwrights of the classical period.'[99] The pre-eminent status of Homer in ἐγκύκλιος παιδεία is mirrored in Philo's abundant praise of 'the Poet' (*Abr.* 10) as 'the greatest and most glorious of all poets' (*Conf.* 4), and confirmed by a number of allusions to the *Iliad* that are present in his own writings. Of the tragedians Philo is particularly fond

---

93   Cf. Hezser 2001: 71: 'The rabbinic support of Jewish primary teachers who would introduce children to Torah-reading, reflected in the literature at least from the third century onwards, may have been a more or less conscious effort to provide a particularly Jewish alternative to Graeco-Roman education and thereby provide students with a specifically Jewish identity.'

94   On Philo's social background and education see Borgen 1984: 233–82; 1997: 14–16; Colson 1916/17; Mendelson 1982; Sandnes 2009: 68–78.

95   Mendelson 1982: 5–15.

96   *Congr.* 74–7; *Cher.* 105; *Agr.* 18; *Somn.* I.205; *Congr.* 11.15-18; *QG* III.21.

97   Mendelson 1982: 5–6.

98   Explicit references to Homer (*Conf.* 4; *Abr.* 10; *Omn.* 31; *Cont.* 17; *Legat.* 80); quotations/allusions to the *Iliad* (*Cont.* 17; *Agr.* 41; *Mos.* I.61; *Dec.* 69; *Omn.* 31); Hesiod (*Aeter.* 17, 18.); Aeschylus (*Spec.* III. 15, 16; *Omn.* 143); Sophocles (*Spec.* III. 15, 16; *Omn.* 143); and Euripides (*Leg. All.* I.7; III. 202; *Jos.* 78; *Spec.* IV.47; *Omn.* 25, 99, 101, 102, 116, 141, 146, 152). The range of literary authors listed is not exhaustive, but rather representative, and predominantly based on Earp's 'Index of Names' (Colson 1962).

99   Niehoff 2001: 138.

of Euripides, whose lines he extensively quotes in *Quod omnis probus liber sit* in support of his argument that only the virtuous man is truly free (cf. *Omn.* 25, 99, 101, 102, 116, 141, 146 and 152).

Yet despite the evident esteem in which Philo holds Greek poets and tragedians, he nonetheless considered ἐγκύκλιος παιδεία (or rather μέση παιδεία) as inferior to, and preparatory for, the higher virtue of philosophical study.[100] In this regard Philo adapted a familiar analogy (originating with Ariston of Chios (3rd century BCE), cf. Ps-Plutarch, *Moralia* 7D–E (*c.* 1st century CE)), which compared the preparatory (propaideutic) function of ἐγκύκλιος παιδεία with the maidservants whom Penelope's suitors courted in lieu of their ultimate goal of Penelope herself (representing philosophy).[101] Philo transposed this familiar analogy onto the text of Gen 16:1-4, such that Sarah replaced Penelope as the philosophical goal, and Hagar was substituted for the handmaids as the preparatory schooling of ἐγκύκλιος παιδεία. This exegetical move is indicative of Philo's broader objective of depicting the Torah (wisdom) as the supreme goal for a virtuous life, prepared for by both literary studies and Greek philosophy (*Congr.* 79–80).

Accordingly, Philo maintains a critical stance towards Greek philosophical authors, judged from the standpoint of the Mosaic Torah, which he held to be the ultimate standard of philosophical virtue.[102] Philo's literary dependence on Greek philosophers, most notably Plato (cf. *Opif.*), is readily apparent, as is his effusive praise of Plato as 'great' (*Aeter.* 52), a 'true philosopher' (*Cont.* 57) and even 'most holy' (ἱερώτατος) (*Omn.* 13), 'an adjective otherwise attributed only to Moses'.[103] Yet, for Philo, it is Moses who is the originator of the Platonic idea of the created, yet indestructible cosmos (*Opif.* 21), and Greek philosophers in general are utilized as a negative foil in his portrayal of the Therapeutae as ideal philosophers (*Cont.*).

---

100   Colson 1916–17: 154 considers that Philo's description of education by the adjective μέσος may indicate the neutral value of such education (comparable to the Stoic ἀδιάφορος), or perhaps more likely in this context, of an item with a definite value, although not the highest.

101   Mendelson 1982: xxiii–xxiv; Sandnes 2009: 65–6, 68–71.

102   Niehoff 2001: 137–58 offers a perceptive analysis of Philo's ambivalent attitude towards Greek culture: both heavily dependent on Greek literary authors and philosophers as sources, yet simultaneously maintaining a critical distance from them. Niehoff compares Philo's nuanced response to Greek culture with that of Roman authors of the period, such as Cato, Cicero and Seneca, who were similarly concerned to define their identity in critical dialogue with Greek education and culture.

103   Niehoff 2001: 138. Runia has exhaustively demonstrated that Plato's *Timaeus* was an important source for Philo's cosmological thought (with ten direct quotations and eight paraphrases), especially *Tim.* 27d–29d which summarizes Plato's philosophical principles, and *Tim.* 29d–47c which describes the creative actions of the δημιουργός; (cf. Runia 1986: 365–85).

Greek literary education was, for Philo, one part of a dual-track educational system for aristocratic Jewish students, whose ultimate goal was to prepare its pupils for lifelong, philosophical study. Given that Philo identified the Mosaic Torah as the ultimate repository of such philosophical wisdom, it is logical that for him the more significant component of this dual-track system was the avowedly Jewish element, focused on scriptural study (cf. *Legat.* 210). Unfortunately, Philo's references to elementary Jewish education are brief and allusive, although it does appear that he envisaged Torah study, like ἐγκύκλιος παιδεία, to be taught by professional instructors:

> ...we who, born as citizens of a god-loving community, reared under laws which incite to every virtue (ἐντραφέντες νόμοις ἐπὶ πᾶσαν ἀρετὴν ἀλείφουσι), trained from our earliest years under divinely gifted men (παρὰ θεσπεσίοις ἀνδράσι), show contempt for their teaching [the corrupting teaching of other nations].
>
> (*Spec.* I.314)[104]

The precise context of such instruction, whether by private tutor (as was the case with ἐγκύκλιος παιδεία), parental instruction (Deut 6:1-2; cf. *Spec.* II.229–30), or synagogue study (*Legat.* 312; *Spec.* II.62; *Mos.* II.216), or perhaps a combination of these methods, is unclear.[105] What is apparent from Philo's own exegetical treatises, however, is that Philo himself was a skilled interpreter of the Mosaic Torah, which he carefully analysed by means of a nuanced allegorical method that he derived from his encyclical studies. Philo's extant treatises offer sustained exegetical commentaries on the philosophy of the Mosaic Torah, treating many of the major sections of the Pentateuch (e.g. *Opif.* on Gen 1:1ff; *Leg. All.* on Gen 2:1ff; *Cher.* on Gen 3:24ff, etc).[106]

Philo's treatises exemplify one way in which aristocratic Jewish students could negotiate the demands of a dual Greek and Jewish cultural identity. Encyclical studies and Torah study were not pitted against one another, as rival educational alternatives, but rather both pedagogical tracks were to be followed in tandem, as complementary paths to the ultimate goal of philosophical virtue. Like other philosophical educationalists of his era, for Philo ἐγκύκλιος παιδεία was afforded a preparatory role, to prepare a student for philosophical study. Where Philo differed from his non-Jewish contemporaries was in his identification of the Mosaic Torah as the ultimate repository of philosophical wisdom, and accordingly the pre-eminent path within this

---

104 Niehoff 2001: 177.

105 Sandnes 2009: 77 notes how Philo explicitly describes synagogue services as a type of 'school' (*Legat.* 312; *Spec.* II.62; *Mos.* II.216 'for as for their houses of prayer in the different cities, what are they, but schools of wisdom, and courage, and temperance, and justice, and piety, and holiness, and every virtue...').

106 For further discussion of the possible reception of Philo's treatises in a philosophical school/synagogue context consult Sterling 2004: 21–52 (esp. 28–31).

two-track system is the Jewish component, focused on Torah study, by means of which the student would be instructed in the Divine oracles from his earliest years (*Legat.* 210).

2.5.2 Josephus (c. 37–100 CE)

The Judean aristocrat Flavius Josephus adopts a similar critical stance towards ἐγκύκλιος παιδεία: he is simultaneously concerned to emphasize the superiority of Jewish παιδεία over its Greek counterpart, whilst at the same time displaying the fruits of his own Greek literary education. Although no reference is made to even a primary-level Greek education in *Life* 8–12, where Josephus discusses his formative education in Jerusalem, such silence need not constitute evidence of its non-existence.[107] Within the same volume, he describes his entrance into public life, as part of a delegation to Rome (*Life* 13), a role that conceivably required at least 'conversation-level' Greek. More tangibly, by 81 CE Josephus was sufficiently well-versed in the language to write a voluminous history in stylistically accomplished Attic Greek.[108] It is highly likely, therefore, that Josephus received at least a primary-level Greek education in Jerusalem, perhaps by means of private tuition, in accord with his own description of the educational attainments of other members of the Judean aristocracy, notably the Herodians (cf. *Apion* I.51; *Life* 40).[109]

What is incontestable, however, on the basis of Josephus' own explicit testimony, is that regardless of the extent of his Greek education in Judea, he undertook fresh study of Greek literature during his residency in Rome (*Ant.* XX. 262–3).

> Encouraged by the completion of what I had projected [sc. the *Antiquities*], I would now say plainly that no other person who had wished to do so, whether a Judean or a foreigner, would have been able to produce this work so precisely for Greek speakers. For among my compatriots I am admitted to have an education in our country's customs that far surpasses theirs. And *once I had consolidated my knowledge of Greek grammar* (τὴν γραμματικήν), *I worked very hard also to share in the learning of Greek letters and poetry* (καὶ τῶν Ἑλληνικῶν δὲ γραμμάτων καὶ

107 So, persuasively, Rajak: 1983: 46–64. Rajak emphasizes the rhetorical purpose of this section of the *Life*, which is concerned to stress Josephus' Jewish credentials, as further evidenced by the genealogy that precedes. Furthermore, Mason 2003b: 12ff describes how Josephus is concerned in this section of the *Life*, as elsewhere, to present Jewish *paideia* as parallel yet superior to Greek education. As a consequence, Josephus' idealized account of his education (*Life* 8–12) parallels the structure of Greek education – primary studies, plus three years of further study of rhetoric and/or philosophy – whilst emphasizing the superior nature of its content. Silence with respect to Greek *paideia* could thus be explicable as a corollary of such rhetorical aims.

108 Cf. Thackeray 1929: 104 for his evaluation of the high literary merit of the *War*.
109 Cf. Hezser 2001: 90–92.

ποιητικῶν), though my traditional habit has frustrated precision with respect to pronunciation.[110]

Josephus here indicates that he has read compositions by both prose (γραμμάτων), and poetic authors (ποιητικῶν), in order to enable him to imitate the masters of Greek literary style, in preparation for his *magnum opus*, the *Antiquities*. Direct and indirect references to the structure, vocabulary and style of an extensive range of Greek literary authors, including epic poets (Homer, Hesiod), tragedians (notably Sophocles), and a diverse range of Greek-language historians (e.g. Herodotus, Thucydides, Nicolaus of Damascus, and Alexander Polyhistor), in Josephus' extant writings, amply substantiate his testimony on this point.[111]

Despite Josephus' extensive critical study of Greek literary authors, and the evident influence that these works had in shaping the style, vocabulary and structure of his own literary creations, he, like Philo, remained ambivalent towards such literature. An excellent example of Josephus' negative caricaturing of Greek historians is evidenced in the defence of his own work, the *Judean Antiquities*, in *Contra Apionem*. In response to critical reviews of *Antiquities* which disputed his claims for Judean antiquity in view of the silence of Greek historians on this nation (*Apion* I. 1–5), Josephus wishes to reassure his readership of the veracity of his work by dismissing the value of Greek history writing (*Apion* I. 6–27) and emphasizing the superiority of non-Greek historiography, specifically Judean historiography, arguing that the latter is based on more ancient and accurate testimony, namely a body of prophetically authored 'public records' (ἀναγραφαί), comparable to the 'public records' of the Egyptian and Chaldean priesthoods (*Apion* I. 28–36).[112]

---

110 Translation from Mason 2003b: xiv (emphasis mine), with the Greek text taken from Thackeray 1926. It is worth noting that 'καὶ ποιητικῶν μαθηματῶν' is not present in all manuscripts, although its omission may be the result of *homoioteleuton*.

111 Homer (cf. *Apion* I.12-13; II. 14, 155, 256); Hesiod (*Ant.* 108, *Apion* I. 16); Herodotus (*Ant.* VIII. 253, 260-2; *Apion* I. 16, 73); Thucydides (*Ant.* IV. 328ff; *War* I. 373-9 speeches of Moses and Herod possibly modelled on speech of Pericles); Nicolaus of Damascus (*Ant.* I. 94-5, 107, 159-60; VII. 101-3; XIII. 251; XIV 9, 68, 108; XVI. 184ff); and Alexander Polyhistor (*Ant.* I. 240; Polyhistor was also a prominent anthological source for Josephus' references to Berossus and Manetho).

For further details cf. Feldman 1997, 1998, 2006; Howell Chapman 2005; Schwartz 1990: 23–57, 223–32; and Sterling 1992: 226–310. (Many of the alleged parallels, notably by Howell Chapman, are forced and lack verbal parallels; it is plausible that Josephus' imitation of tragic style may have been mediated, at least in part, by acquaintance with other historians, notably Nicolaus of Damascus; cf. Toher 2003; Varneda 1986: 81–8; 230–8).

112 On the structure and rhetorical argument of *Contra Apionem* as a whole, and I. 6–56 in particular see Barclay 2007: xvii–xxii and 8–42 and Mason 2003a: 131–40.

LSL: ἀναγράφω 'to engrave and set up publicly' – of treaties, laws and public acts. Pass. 'To be inscribed or interred in a public register'. ἀναγραφή 'inscription', 'record', 'register', esp. in pl: 'public record'.

Josephus delineates the scope, genre and content of the 22-volume ἀναγραφαί as follows (*Apion* I. 37–42):[113]

37 Accordingly...then, seeing that the writing (of the records) is not the personal prerogative of everyone, nor is there actual disagreement among any of the things written, but the prophets alone learned the highest and oldest matters by the inspiration of the God, and by themselves plainly recorded events as they occurred, 38 so among us there are not myriads of discordant and competing volumes, but only twenty-two volumes containing the record of all time, which are rightly trusted.

39 Now of these, five are those of Moses, which comprise both the laws and the tradition from human origins until his passing; this period falls little short of 3000 years. 40 From Moses' passing until the Artaxerxes who was king of the Persians after Xerxes, the prophets after Moses wrote-up what happened in their times [or, as they saw things] in thirteen volumes. The remaining four (volumes) comprise hymns toward God and advice for living among humanity. 41 From Artaxerxes until our own time all sorts of things have been written, but they have not been considered of the same trustworthiness as those before them, because the exact succession of the prophets failed.

42 Now it is clear in practice how we approach our special texts: for although such an age has already passed [sc. since Artaxerxes], no one has dared either to add anything or to take away from them or to alter them.[114]

Mason insightfully distinguishes between three intertwined categories that Josephus uses to classify the 22 volumes of Judean public records: authorship, chronology and genre.[115] The material is distinguished between the 5 volumes authored by Moses, and the remaining 17 volumes authored by anonymous prophets. The 5 Mosaic volumes cover the period from creation to Moses' death (*c.*0–3,000), whilst the remaining period covered (*c.*3,000–4,450) is recounted in 13 volumes written by anonymous prophets in chronological succession. The additional 4 volumes are not assigned a separate time-period, but rather overlap with

Josephus elides a distinction between the 'scriptures' and priestly genealogical lists, in order to cite the latter as evidence for the antiquity of the former (Barclay 2007: 24–8).

113   The explicit enumeration of 22 volumes of scripture in *Apion* I. 37ff contrasts sharply with Josephus' claim in *Ant* I. 17 to be simply translating the contents of the Judean ἀναγραφαί into Greek, in a volume in which he paraphrases not simply numerous LXX texts (Pentateuch and Historical books in particular), but also the *Letter of Aristeas*, *I Maccabees* and *Nicolaus of Damascus*. On this basis Josephus' reference to the *Antiquities* itself as an ἀναγραφή (*Apion* I. 47) is suggestive of a close connection, to the point of identification, between these writings, consistent, perhaps with Josephus' own claims to prophetic functions (if not the title itself); cf. his prediction of Vespasian's accession (*War* III. 401–2). For further discussion cf. Gray 1992: 35–79.

114   Translation by Mason 2002: 113.

115   Mason 2002: 113–15.

eras already covered by Moses and/or the 13 anonymous prophets. The 22 volumes comprise 4 generic categories: laws, historical tradition, hymns to God and hortatory material. Josephus' primary concern here, however, is with the 'historical tradition' contained within the 5 Mosaic volumes and the 13 succeeding volumes.

Efforts to identify the 22 works to which Josephus alludes only obscurely in *Apion* I. 37–42, has involved modern interpreters in much conjecture.[116] The Pentateuch is the only grouping that can be securely identified (I. 39). The reference to the 13 prophetically authored volumes, covering Judean history from 3,000–4,450 (I. 40), can be variously identified, as Josephus considers that *all* 22 volumes of the public records are prophetically authored (I. 37), so this category does not necessarily describe volumes that would later be assigned to the *nebiim* in rabbinic terminology. Various combinations of texts drawn from Joshua–II Kings plus I Esdras, Nehemiah, I and II Chronicles and Esther, combined with some, or all, of the classical prophets Isaiah, Jeremiah, Ezekiel, Daniel and the Book of the Twelve (either individually or collectively), are plausible candidates for this grouping.[117] Josephus' knowledge of all these texts is assured on the basis of the extensive rewriting of these volumes in *Antiquities* I–XI. The final 4 volumes mentioned are even more allusive, and whilst the book of *Psalms* is a likely candidate, the precise referent of each volume is impossible to pin down, not least because Josephus' descriptions of the Davidic and Solomonic corpuses (*Ant.* VII. 305, VIII. 44) in *Antiquities* suggest a much more extensive collection of volumes than the 4 books referred to in *Apion* I. 40. What is more readily apparent, on the basis of a comparison with *Ant.* I–XII, are the volumes that Josephus here chooses to omit: the Hellenistic era texts, I Maccabees and the Letter of Aristeas (plus Nicolaus of Damascus and his own *Antiquities*). The boundaries of Judean 'public records' are consciously redrawn in a more restrictive fashion in his later *apologia*.

Unlike Greek literary authors, whether philosophers or historians, for whom the 'canonical' reading lists of ἐγκύκλιος παιδεία constituted the pinnacle of cultural knowledge and wisdom, for the two notable Jewish intellectuals discussed, this privileged role is occupied instead by the Judean

116 Cf. Barclay 2007: 28–32; Beckwith 1985: 78–80; 119–22; Leiman 1989; and Mason 2002.

117 The closest parallels to Josephus' 22 volumes of Judean 'public records' are the scriptural lists contained in the later writings of early Christian authors, Origen (Eusebius, *Hist. Eccl.* vi. 25.2) [c. 320–25 CE, Caesarea, Palestine], Cyril of Jerusalem (*Catech.* 4.35) [c. 394 CE, Bethlehem, Palestine] and Jerome (preface to the Vulgate translation of Samuel and Kings). The number 22, possibly influenced by gematria in view of the 22-character Hebrew alphabet, is arrived at in such lists by conflating a number of books together: Judges and Ruth; I and II Sam; I and II Kgs; I and II Chron; I–II Esdras; Jeremiah and Lamentations; Book of the Twelve. Whilst it is plausible that Josephus' 22 volumes are identical to these later enumerations, not least because all these lists have a Palestinian provenance, the precise referents are unverifiable in view of the sparse details provided by *Apion* I. 37–42.

'public records' (ἀναγραφαί) (Josephus) or the Torah of Moses (Philo). The ambivalence of these authors is comparable to that of other indigenous groups, notably Roman intellectuals, who often responded to Greek *encyclical* education in a similar ambivalent way: receptive, yet critical, in an attempt to both appropriate aspects of Greek culture as their own, whilst maintaining (or creating) a distinctive sense of their own cultural identity.[118] Quintilian's recommended reading-list (*Inst. Or.* 10) succinctly illustrates this point, in that it contains two parallel, or mirrored, reading lists: the first listing Greek authors and the second Roman authors. Quintilian runs through the same generic categories again (poetry, comedy, history, oratory, philosophy, etc.), supplementing each genre with examples of recommended Latin authors (cf. fig. 2.4).

Epic	Elegy	Lyric	Tragedy	Comedy	History	Oratory	Philosophy
Homer	Callimachus	Pindar	Euripides	Menander	Herodotus	Demosthenes	Plato
Hesiod	Ovid	Horace	Sophocles		Thucydides	Isocrates	Aristotle
Virgil					Sallust	Cicero	Cicero
					Livy		

Fig. 2.4 Recommended-Reading List (Bilingual Roman Student), representative selection of Greek and Roman authors (cf. Quintilian, Inst. Or. 10)

As a consequence, a bilingual Roman student could appropriate the best of Greek *encyclical* education, whilst maintaining a sense of his/her own cultural identity, and, on occasion, superiority (cf. Quintilian's evaluation of Cicero's literary merits (*Inst. Or.* 10.1.105ff)). Josephus and Philo, like their Roman intellectual counterparts, also had an expanded mental library, which developed and nuanced their sense of cultural identity, in ways that distinguished them from many of their peers.[119] Unlike their bilingual Roman compatriots, however, Josephus and Philo's additional literary knowledge was not restricted to the same generic categories (of epic, tragedy, history, etc.), but included additional, non-literary, generic categories (e.g. laws, hymns) as well as categories which creatively interacted with Greek literary genres (e.g. Josephus' ἀναγραφαί compared with Greek historians, and the divinely inspired poetry of Moses compared to Homeric epic (cf. Mishnah,

---

118　Cf. Niehoff 2001: 142–3; on Philo's cultural assimilation cf. Barclay 1996: 158–80.

119　I do not imply that a student who identified himself as belonging to the dominant culture only read/heard texts by Greek literary authors, as the mental library of such a hearer undoubtedly also included various liturgical texts (hymns, prayers, etc.), works of 'popular' literature (e.g. street theatre) and inscriptions (material culture); cf. Kaizer 2008; Rüpke 2007; Wiseman 2008. The suggestion here is rather that such additional items were less likely to be perceived as competitive rivals to the contents of ἐγκύκλιος παιδεία; they further developed a person's Greek cultural identity by complementing, rather than rivalling, such Greek literary classics.

Yadaim, 4.6)). Although the extent of cultural assimilation and interaction between Judean/Jewish students and Greek *encyclical* education is much less clear below the level of the élite strata of society, Josephus and Philo afford significant insights as to the range of literary texts, and genres, known to tertiary-educated, Greek-speaking, Jewish intellectuals in the first century CE.

2.6 Conclusion

This chapter has provided an overview of Greek *encyclical* education in the Graeco-Roman era, delineating the literary texts which formed the 'core' and 'periphery' of this progressive educational circle (primary, secondary, tertiary). At the core of this system, the texts which (almost) all literate students could be presumed to have read were portions of Homer (notably *Iliad* I–II), Euripides (notably *Phoenissae*) and *gnomic* sayings attributed to Menander and Isocrates. The further a student progressed around this circle, the more extensive were the range of literary authors, and genres, with which s/he was familiar, with two significant 'boundary' markers indicated by knowledge of the 'astronomical' textbook of Aratus' φαινομένα (grammarian), and the prose authors (historians, rhetors, philosophers) studied at tertiary-level and above.

The chapter has nuanced this broad structural framework by considering the significance of two key variables: gender and ethnicity. It was noted how a female student's experience of Greek *encyclical* education was comparable, in many respects, with that of her male contemporaries, at least at the primary and early stages of secondary education (where social status remained the dominant variable on the extent of a student's educational attainment), but that the lack of opportunities for a public career, coupled with the distorting impact of early marriage, frequently terminated a female student's formal education at that level. Finally, the impact of Jewish ethnicity was considered, with particular reference to the tertiary-level education of two notable Jewish intellectuals, Josephus and Philo. It was noted how both authors had received an extensive tertiary-level Greek *encyclical* education, and that like their Roman counterparts, Josephus and Philo evidenced an ambivalent attitude to their Greek cultural heritage, perceived as being in creative competition with their Judean identity. The phenomenon of a Judean intellectual's expanded mental-library was also considered, containing an additional set of literary authors to interact creatively with the normative Greek literary classics. This nuanced overview of 1st-century CE formal education in Greek will inform the construction of the range of literary authors known to both of the two hearer-constructs which are the focus of the exegetical section in Chapters 4 and 5 of this study.

Chapter 3

GRAECO-ROMAN COSMOLOGIES

3.1 Introduction

This chapter has two principal aims: first, to contextualize the cosmology/cosmic geography of the Apocalypse against a backdrop of a diverse range of competing models of the structure and composition of the universe that were advanced in the first century CE. Second, to consider the correlation, if any, between an ancient hearer's level of *encyclical* education and his/her cosmological preferences.

The appraisal begins (§3.2) with a brief schematic overview of three prominent templates of the universe verbally depicted in Graeco-Roman literature: an archaic tripartite model (heaven, disc-earth, underworld); a Platonic/Aristotelian geocentric cosmos with seven planetary spheres; and a modified tripartite cosmos with multiple heavenly tiers. Each template is then scrutinized (§3.3) with reference to a test-case example: the archaic cosmology of I Enoch 1–36 (3rd century BCE); the Platonic cosmology of Philo (1st century CE); and the multi-tiered heaven of a tripartite universe of Paul (II Cor 12:1ff). On the basis of a nuanced assessment of the correspondences and dissonances between these three broad types, the Apocalypse's visualization of the universe is then positioned in its intellectual context (§3.4), and its distinctive, rhetorical function assessed. The chapter concludes (§3.5) by reflecting on the potential significance of educational attainment as a key variable affecting an ancient hearer's perception of the universe, informed by the test case examples considered. What correlation, if any, is there between an ancient hearer's preferred cosmological model and his/her level of educational attainment? Do tertiary-educated hearers invariably opt for a Platonic model and primary educated hearers a Homeric design? This simple dichotomy is refined with reference to the experience of Jewish/Jewish-Christian hearers whose mental libraries include non-literary genres (e.g. dream-vision, I En 14) that contain modified visualizations of the universe, suggesting that educational attainment is a significant, yet not wholly determinative, variable.

3.2 Graeco-Roman Cosmologies: Three Templates

This study adopts Horowitz's broad definition of cosmology as 'the structure of the universe and its constituent parts', in order to avoid creating an artificial boundary between 'cosmology' and 'geography' which was foreign to ANE and Graeco-Roman thought.[1] Accordingly, I utilize a broadly synonymous term, 'cosmic geography', to denote the geography of the totality of the universe (e.g. the geography of the heaven(s), earth and underworld), which was a characteristic feature of geographical study in the Hellenistic and Roman eras (cf. Strabo, *Geography* I.14ff, *c.*64 BCE–25 CE).[2] This definition is intentionally broad enough to include an ancient author's conception of the 'geography of the heavens', whether that region is understood in a material, or non-material sense, and avoids pre-judging the range of constituent parts that an ancient author may choose to include.[3]

The data for this study are drawn from the verbal descriptions of the cosmos, and/or its constituent parts, in a select range of Graeco-Roman literature, rather than focusing exclusively on extant 'drawn maps' of the universe.[4] Accordingly, the interest is in an implied author's 'mental map' of the cosmos, as a legitimate object of study, regardless of how accurately it depicts (or attempts to depict) the physical structure of the terrestrial or celestial realms.[5] Bautch defines a 'mental map' as: '...the projection of order onto a conceptualized space by which spatial data is processed', which neatly captures how an (ancient) author's cognitive map establishes its own internal order and consistency, revealing something of the implied author's own priorities and interests.[6] On this basis, each literary text that describes

---

1   Horowitz 1998: xii. White 2008: 90 is critical of such a narrow focus on the 'anatomy and physiology' of the created universe in post-Enlightenment definitions of 'cosmology', in that ancients considered the question of the cosmos' origin and purpose to be integral to such enquiry. Whilst I concede the point, which is amply demonstrated by the sites of eschatological judgment that Enoch visits on his celestial tour (I En 17–19; cf. §3.3), the particular focus of this thesis concerns the topography of the universe as a 'stage' for Rev 9.

2   Harley and Woodward 1987: 130–76: (131): 'Although from the Hellenistic period onward the original meaning of the term geography was a description of the earth, *ge*, written or drawn...it is equally clear that Greek mapmaking included not only the representation of the earth on a plane or globe, but also delineation of the whole universe' (cf. Homer, *Iliad* xviii.); cf. Bautch 2003: 7–8.

3   It is hazardous to dichotomise a physical realm from a realm of ideas, especially in dream-vision literature, which often locates the sacred space of heaven above the firmament(s), and describes this space in architectural detail (e.g. I En 14), yet narrates the seer's non-physical entry to this realm in a dream.

4   Cf. Scott 2001: 5–22.

5   Cf. Bautch 2003: 160–1 who is consequently critical of attempts to distinguish 'mythic' geography from more accurate topographical studies or travelogues (e.g. Strabo, *Geography*; Pausanias, *Description of Greece*).

6   Bautch 2003: 160; cf. Alexander 1995; Gould and White 1986.

the structure and constituents of the cosmos provides its own, unique, mental map of this space, worthy of study on its own merits. Whilst not retracting this point, it is nevertheless possible to discern broader trends among the diversity of extant cosmologies, with three prominent templates recurring, with almost infinite minor variations, across a broad spectrum of Graeco-Roman literature.[7]

The first template, of a triple-decker cosmos, has a rich pedigree whose roots stretch back at least as far as ancient Sumerian and Akkadian literature of the second millennium BCE.[8] The Babylonian creation epic, *Enuma Elish* (*c.*1100 BCE), describes how the universe was created when Marduk split the body of the defeated chaos monster/waters *Tiamat* in two, such that the lower part formed the earth and the upper part the heavens.[9] This aspect of the cosmogony utilizes a single-heaven model, dividing the universe into two halves: heaven (*an*) and earth (*ki*).[10] When this is combined with the prior action of Ea in creating his subterranean abode in the defeated corpse of *Apsu* (tablet I, 67–78), a familiar three-decker, single-heaven cosmology of heaven-earth-underworld is described. These three realms are envisaged as the homes of the traditional trio of Sumerian deities: Anu in heaven, Enlil on earth, and Enki/Ea in the *Apsu* (cf. *Atrahasis* tablet 1 (*c.*1700 BCE)).[11]

Heaven –	Anu	
Earth –	Enlil	
Apsu –	Ea	

The middle zone of this scheme, the terrestrial realm, is envisaged as a central continent encircled by a vast cosmic Ocean (*marratu*) (cf. Babylonian, *Mappa Mundi* (*c.*8th–7th century BCE)).[12]

The underworld realm, *Apsu*, is comprised of the primordial chaos waters assigned to Ea closely connected with the terrestrial ocean, such that the two are occasionally indistinguishable (cf. *Gilgamesh* xi. 271–6 where Gilgamesh dives into the *Apsu* but then returns to the shore of *marratu*). A triple-decker universe template (single heaven, disc-earth, subterranean waters) constituted

---

7   For more detailed overviews see Adams 2008; Wright 1995: 11–36; Wright 2000: 98–202.

8   On Mesopotamian cosmology see Horowitz 1998; Pongratz-Leisten 2001; Rochberg-Halton 1993; and Wright 2000: 26–51.

9   Cf. Lambert 2008: 17.

10   Horowitz 1998: 111–14; Lambert 2008: 20–23.

11   Cf. Dalley 1989: 3, 9. The final form of *Enuma Elish* conflates the archaic triple-decker universe of *Atrahasis* with a more elaborate three-heaven scheme with the result that Enlil is relocated to the middle heaven and Marduk assumes his residency on earth; cf. Lambert 2008: 15ff.

12   Horowitz 1998: 20–42, 318–62, 403–7 (plates).

the 'default setting' of ANE and Greek cosmological thought from the second millennium BCE until at least the 4th/3rd centuries BCE, with diverse local variations of this cognitive map evidenced in Hebrew writings of the Persian/ Hellenistic eras (e.g. Gen 1, Pss. 115:16–17, 139:8) and Homeric era Greek literature (cf. Homer, *Iliad xviii*; *Odyssey* xi; Hesiod, *Theogony*).[13]

The second template, of multiple planetary spheres, flowered during the 4th century BCE in the theoretical models of Plato (*Timaeus* 33B–40B) and Aristotle (*De Caelo*), but its roots coiled back through Greek astronomical observation and mathematical enquiry of the preceding two centuries.[14] Plato envisaged the cosmos as spherical in shape (*Timaeus* 33B), perfect in its uniformity, rotating in a regular motion around its own axis (36C). The outer sphere of the cosmos is adorned with the fixed stars, which perfectly follow the revolution of the outer firmament, such that their relative positions remain unaltered (40A–B).[15] Nested within this outer firmament are the seven planetary spheres (Moon, Sun, Venus, Mercury [Mars, Jupiter, Saturn]), which only imperfectly follow the rotation of the world-soul which animates the cosmos, as they are each also guided by a contrary, individual rotation (38C–E). At the centre of this geocentric cosmos resides the spherical earth (40B–C), stationary (in equilibrium) and at rest.[16] Plato's elegant expression of this theory became a touchstone of intellectual enquiry on the topic during the Hellenistic and Roman eras, culminating in the definitive study of Ptolemy (*Almagest*) (2nd century CE).[17]

The third template contains elements in common with both of the previous models: like the first, it envisages a triple-decker universe of heaven, earth and underworld; yet, its modified top-tier, containing multiple heavenly layers (often seven, but with many numerical variations), has certain affinities with the seven planetary spheres of the Platonic universe.[18] The notion of multiple heavenly tiers was in no sense a Hellenistic innovation, as comparable designs occur in archaic Akkadian texts of the second millennium BCE (KAR 307 30–38, AO 8196 iv. 20–22 and *Enuma Elish*, c.1,100/1,000 BCE), which explicitly divide the heavens into an upper, middle and lower realm.[19] A selection of Jewish/Jewish Christian accounts of heavenly ascent/

13   Clay 2003: 12–30, 49–72; Keel 1978; Wright 2000: 52–97.
14   Cf. Wright 1995: 18–30; Wright 2000: 98–104; Kirk, Raven and Schofield 1983.
15   Cf. Carone 2005: 71, who argues that in the *Timaeus* Plato emphasizes the ethical benefits of astronomical study (both through observation of the fixed stars (91D–E) and mathematical study (35B)), in order that individuals imitate the harmonious revolutions of the stars, so perfectly conforming to the motion of the world soul; cf. Cornford 1937: 52–138.
16   There is some debate as to whether Plato envisaged the Earth rotating (in alignment with the world soul), an interpretation which Aristotle explicitly rejected (*De caelo* 2.13), and which would appear to contradict Plato's earlier identification of day and night with the revolution of the Same (cf. Cornford 1937: 120–34).
17   Reydams-Schils 2003.
18   Wright 2000: 139–84; Yarbro Collins 1996a.
19   Horowitz 1998: 3–19; Lambert 2008: 15ff.

dream visions of the early centuries of the Common Era recount a seer's ascent through multiple heavenly tiers (most frequently seven) (Cf. Test. Levi 2:1ff; Testament of Abraham [Recension A & B]; Apocalypse of Abraham; II Enoch; III Baruch) before arriving at the upper celestial tier where the Deity resides. It is uncertain whether, or to what extent, these numbered heavenly tiers may reflect the influence of contemporary intellectual developments in Graeco-Roman cosmological thought.[20] I am unconvinced, however, that multiple tiered heavens in visionary texts reflect a direct, and garbled, borrowing of a Platonic system, not least because there is no attempt to imitate the essential design plan of such a model that locates a specific planet in each tier. Instead, the origin of such a template is more profitably sought in Babylonian divinatory literature (cf. KAR 307.30–38 'heaven seven, earth seven' (an. 7 ki. 7)) and related accounts of heavenly ascent/descent through numbered chambers (cf. *Descent of Innana, Nergal and Ereshkigal*).[21] The apparent renewal of interest in multiple heavenly tiers at the turn of the era (contrast I En 14 (single heaven), with II Cor 12:1ff (multiple heaven)) may, however, hint at a secondary role of cultural competition in stimulating impulses to retrieve comparable ancient analogues.[22]

3.3 Three Cosmological Test-Cases

3.3.1 I Enoch 1-36

I Enoch is a composite work, comprising a collection of writings ascribed to the patriarch Enoch, whose mysterious disappearance at the end of his life, as recounted in Gen 5:21-24, came to be interpreted as a heavenly ascent.[23] Enoch's name is pseudonymously associated with the authorship of a variety of traditions detailing heavenly and terrestrial journeys, and the receipt of esoteric heavenly wisdom. The extant Ethiopic corpus of I Enoch is commonly divided into five major sections as follows: 1) The Book of the Watchers (I En 1–36); 2) The Similitudes (or Parables) of Enoch (I En 37–71); 3) The Astronomical Book (I En 72–82); 4) The Dream Visions (I En 83–90); and 5) The Epistle of Enoch (I En 91/92–107).[24] These booklets,

---

20   Compare and contrast Wright 2000: 183 (pro), Yarbro Collins 1996a: 53–4 (anti).

21   Cf. Horowitz 1998: 208–20, 353–4; so Bousset 1901: 136–69; 229–73.

22   Cf. Hadas, 1959: 72–84; Niehoff 2001: 140–42 on competition between cultures in the Graeco-Roman period. For possible traces of multiple-planetary tiers in I En 14, see §3.3.1, below.

23   VanderKam 1984: 28–33. Note that Gen 5:24 implicitly refers to Enoch's heavenly ascent at the end of his life, in contrast to I En 12–36 (cf. I En 81:5-6; I En 83–4 and Jub 4:21-22).

24   See García Martínez 1992: 45–96; Milik 1976: 58, 77–8, 183–4; Nickelsburg 2001: 7–8. Note that in at least one alternative early collection (4QEn^c, c. 35–1 BCE) a *Book of Giants* was included alongside portions of I En 1–36, I En 85–90 and I En

aside perhaps for I Enoch 37–71, were originally composed in Aramaic, as verified by extant fragments at Qumran, the earliest of which (4QEn[a] (c.199–150 BCE) and 4QEn[b] (c.175–125 BCE)), containing portions of I En 1–36, indicate a *terminus ante quem* of c.200 BCE for the Book of the Watchers.[25]

The exegesis that follows will focus on I Enoch 14, describing Enoch's visionary ascent to the celestial sanctuary, and I Enoch 17–19, Enoch's (first) tour of the perimeter of the terrestrial disc-earth. I will princi-pally discuss the Greek text as preserved in Codex Panopolitanus (G[Pan]) (c.5th/6th century CE), which predates the extant Ethiopic manuscripts (c.15th –19th centuries CE) by almost a millennium, although I will refer to significant variants in the Qumran Aramaic fragments, where these are extant and relevant to the discussion.[26]

I En 12–16 presupposes and reiterates the description of the descent of the angelic Watchers and their divine punishment in I En 6–11 (cf. Gen 6:1–4), which affords a significant new role in this process to the patriarch Enoch who was not mentioned in the former section, but who now undertakes the (angelic) function of a heavenly intercessor (cf. I En 15:2).[27] Enoch is initially commissioned by an obedient angelic Watcher (or group of Watchers (G[Pan])) to announce divine judgment against the disgraced Watchers on earth (I En 12:1-3).[28] In response, the fearful Watchers enlist Enoch's professional services, as a scribe, to write (γράφειν) a memorandum of petition (ὑπόμνημα τῆς ἐρωτήσεως) for them and recite it on their behalf in the presence of the Deity (I En 13:4).[29] Enoch selects the noted divinatory site of the river Dan,

92–105. Cf. Milik 1976: 298–339; Nickelsburg 2001: 10–11 and 172–3; García Martínez 1992: 97–115 and especially Reeves 1992, Stuckenbruck 1997.

25   *The Similitudes of Enoch* (1 Enoch 37–71) are unattested at Qumran, with the result that the language, date and provenance of this portion of the work remain a matter of ongoing debate; cf. Boccaccini 2007.

26   An additional reason why I will focus on the extant Greek version of this text is that the first of my hearer constructs (HC1), Chapter 4, will be presumed to know I En 1–36 in Greek translation.

The Akhmim manuscript (Codex Panopolitanus) (G[Pan]), is a 5th/6th-century Greek codex discovered in a Christian grave in a Coptic cemetery in Akhmim (Panopolis), Egypt in 1886/7 alongside a second, mathematical papyrus. In its 66 pages it contains portions of the *Gospel of Peter* (pp.2–10), the *Apocalypse of Peter* (pp.13–19), followed by I Enoch (I En 19:3–21:9 + I En 1:1–32:6a) (pp.21–66). Cf. Milik 1976: 70–71, Nickelsburg 2001: 12, Black 1970: 8 (text G[Pan], pp. 19–44).

27   Most commentators regard I En 6–11 as a 'rewriting' of Gen 6:1-4, analogous to *Jubilees* and the *Genesis Apocryphon* (cf. García Martínez 1992: 62–5; Nickelsburg 2001: 165–73; VanderKam 1984: 112–13), although Milik 1976: 30–32 suggested Gen 6 was dependent on this originally independent 'myth'.

On Enoch's exalted status in I En 12–16, especially the role reversal with the Watchers, see VanderKam 1984: 129–35; Nickelsburg 2001: 229–32; and Gooder 2006: 38–50 (esp. 45).

28   The fragmentary 4QEn[c] 1 5:19 appears to refer to a solitary Watcher; Black 1985: 141; Milik 1976: 190, 192; Nickelsburg 2001: 234–5.

29   On the scribal functions of the character of Enoch and its possible connection

south of Mt Hermon, as the requisite sacred space from which to enter the celestial sanctuary by means of a dream-vision, summoned, or raised, upwards by various heavenly phenomena (clouds, stars, lightning and wind) (I En 14:8-9).[30]

My principal concern is to investigate the architectural structure of the celestial sanctuary, as a verbal description of the interior of the heaven(s).[31] The first structure that Enoch approaches (ἐγγίζω) is a wall built of hailstones, according to the Ethiopic text (*teqm zahenset*), or 'the wall of a building of hailstones' (τείχους οἰκοδομῆς ἐν λίθοις χαλάζης) according to the Greek (G^Pan). Nickelsburg suggests that the Greek noun οἰκοδομή may represent a corruption of an original verbal form that described 'a wall *built* of hailstones' (as preserved in the Ethiopic text), such that the structure depicts the wall that encloses the *temenos* of the heavenly temple (cf. Ezek 40:5).[32] It is entirely plausible that the earliest recoverable form of I En 14:8ff should be understood in this way, commencing its description of the celestial architecture with the exterior walls of the sacred precinct.[33] Verbal parallels with Zechariah's vision support such a reading: YHWH will be a 'wall of fire' (אֵשׁ חוֹמַה / τεῖχος πυρὸς) around the city of Jerusalem, such that it has no need of manufactured defences (Zech 2:8-9 MT/LXX).[34] An alternative structure is recounted in the Greek version, however, as I En 14:9 (G^Pan) understands Enoch to approach an exterior building (οἰκοδομή), akin to the entrance-chamber (cf. I Kgs 6:3; 7:21; Joel 2:17 (אוּלָם)) of the Jerusalem Temple. This outer chamber is comprised of antithetical materials: hailstone-bricks surrounded by tongues of fire, yet Enoch continues his journey within.

The second structure (I En 14:10–14) is explicitly referred to as a 'great house' (οἶκος μέγας), which like the encircling wall (Ethiopic) or entrance-chamber (G^Pan) before it, is constructed of contrasting materials: the walls and floor of this building are constructed of hailstone slabs (ἐν λίθοις χαλάζης) and snow (χιών), but encircled by fire (πῦρ φλεγόμενος). Visual correspondences with the interior ornamentation of the 'holy place' of the

with the professional ideals and capabilities of the authors of the Enochic corpus see Nickelsburg 2001: 65–7 and Orlov 2005: xii.

30   On the sacred geography of I Enoch see Nickelsburg 1981; 2001; Eshel and Eshel 2003.

The Greek text appears to imagine the winds as spreading out like wings in order to raise Enoch heavenward (ἐκπετάννυμι, literally 'to spread out (like wings)', cf. Hos 9:11, Nah 3:16; cf. Apoc. Abr. 15:2-4).

31   On the celestial temple in I Enoch and related heavenly ascent literature see Himmelfarb 1987; 1993; Morray-Jones 2006 (and additional bibliography, p. 145 n.1).

32   Nickelsburg 2001: 258, 262; Halperin 1988: 81. Whilst a singular noun 'wall' is referred to in the Ethiopic text, the reference to encircling fire in the next line suggests an enclosing (four-sided) wall (so Milik 1976: 198: 'τίχους [sic.], though in the genitive singular, should be understood in the collective plural meaning on account of κύκλῳ αὐτῶν').

33   On temple architecture (wilderness tabernacle, Solomon's Temple, Ezekiel's Temple, 11Q Temple) see Chyutin 2006 which includes detailed architectural plans.

34   Petersen 1985: 166–172.

wilderness tabernacle/Jerusalem temple are readily apparent, most clearly in the description of the ceilings (αἱ στέγαι) where 'fiery cherubim' (χερουβὶν πύρινα), shooting stars (διαδρομαὶ ἀστέρων) and water (ὕδωρ) are located. These decorative images correspond to the woven linen curtains (of blue, purple and scarlet thread) used as hangings, draped over the wooden structure of the wilderness tabernacle, whose coloured threads represent the heavens (cf. Josephus, *War* 5.5.4) and contain embroidered images of cherubim (cf. Exod 26:1, 31; 36:8, 35).[35] They similarly correspond to the interior decorations of the Solomonic temple, whose walls and ceilings were decorated with carved figures of cherubim (cf. I Kgs 6:29, II Chr 3:7, & Ezek 41:15-26). The ceiling of the celestial holy place is as paradoxical as the materials out of which this chamber is constructed, depicting the celestial firmament above, undercutting its own implicit spatial location, positioned above the firmament (cf. I En 14:8-9 'ἄνω... εἰς τὸν οὐρανὸν'). The reference to the temple ceiling as the 'heaven' where the cherubim reside (I En 14:11), 'καὶ οὐρανὸς αὐτῶν ὕδωρ' (i.e. the waters above the earth, cf. Ps 104:3 (Ps 103:3 LXX)), further hints at an awkward conflation of two spatial registers in this vision: the seer's ascent into heaven is principally portrayed as a horizontal movement into the interior of the sanctuary; yet the decorative imagery of the celestial sanctuary itself simultaneously depicts 'heaven' on the vertical plane, where it is equated with the ceiling of the sanctuary building.

The third, climactic structure which Enoch sees in his vision (I En 14:15-25) is glimpsed through an open door from within the great house. It is noteworthy that unlike on the previous two occasions (I En 14:9, 10, 13) Enoch neither approaches (ἐγγίζω), enters (εἰσέρχομαι) nor is brought in (εἰσφέρω) to this house which is greater than the former one (ὁ οἶκός μείζων τούτου). Instead, Enoch describes the interior of the celestial Holy of Holies from his vantage point within the Holy Place.[36] The imagery used to describe this chamber is consistent: its floor and walls are constructed exclusively of fire, reflective of the divine glory (δόξα, τιμὴ, and μεγαλοσύνη), whilst the upper part (τὸ ἀνώτερον) of this chamber, like the ceiling in the Holy Place, is equated with the celestial firmament, replete with stars and lightning. The indications are that the 'greater house' is physically higher than the preceding chamber, such that the stars of the firmament are not located in the ceiling, but rather in an upper chamber (or balcony, given that the ceiling can still be seen), below that level. Once again there are suggestions that this celestial temple vision is working on two planes: the horizontal plane recounting a movement towards the Divine presence, combined, somewhat awkwardly, with a depiction of the celestial firmament that rises vertically above the various chambers, and at different gradients. The celestial temple vision culminates with the seer's vision of the Deity enthroned on the cherubim

---

35 Himmelfarb 1987: 211.
36 Nickelsburg 2001: 264, n.18.

throne (cf. Ezek 1).[37] Whilst echoing a number of components present in Ezekiel's vision (notably the crystalline throne (I En 14:18, κρυστάλλινον), evocative of Ezekiel's crystalline firmament (Ezek 1:22 LXX κρύσταλλος); the presence of the cherubim (Ezek 1:5, 15 (cf. Ezek 10:1ff; I En 14:18); and the glorious appearance of the Deity (Ezek 1:27; I En 14:20)), the text stops short of a direct description of the Deity himself (cf. Isa 6:1ff). That Enoch, like the attendant angelic hosts (I En 14:22), does not enter the Holy of Holies itself, but is brought to the very entrance to converse with the Deity, is indicative of his exalted status and angelic functions: '[One of the holy ones] brought me as far as the door' (μέχρι τῆς θύρας) (1En 14:25). Enoch, according to the spheres of graded holiness in the (celestial) temple, is accorded an analogous status to the displaced Watchers: access to the divine presence at the threshold of the Holy of Holies, and entrusted with a divinely commissioned task of petition and proclamation.

The three-tiered chambers of the celestial sanctuary in I Enoch 14 correspond, in broad outlines, to the architectural structure of the wilderness tabernacle/Solomonic temple, such that the vision recounts Enoch's journey from the boundaries of the sacred precinct (Eth.) (or vestibule (G^{Pan})) to the entrance to the Holy of Holies, at the western end of the Holy Place. Two significant factors within I Enoch's verbal description, however, may significantly alter this simple cognitive map. First, there is repeated reference in I En 14 to the *concentric* structure of the heavenly sanctuary, in that the walls are 'encircled' (κύκλος) by flaming fire (I En 14:9, 12, 22). Such a design plan is consonant with the emphasis on the climactic throne room's appearance, as 'greater than this (house)' (μείζων τούτου) (I En 14:15), i.e. the Holy Place in which Enoch stands, as indicative of size in addition to status. Although the references in I En 14:8ff are to the concentric nature of the flaming fire, rather than explicitly to the walls of the structure, the two are closely linked architecturally in the paradoxical design of the building. It is quite conceivable, therefore, that the celestial sanctuary is envisaged not as a set of adjoining chambers, but rather as a nested set of concentric rooms, with the pre-eminent throne-room at its core.[38]

Second, it is arguable that the multiple heavenly tiers of I En 14:8ff are indicative not of chambered divisions within a solitary heaven (so Nickelsburg and Himmelfarb), but rather a *three-tiered heavenly cosmos* (so Morray-Jones).[39] Morray-Jones proposes that variant models of three- and seven-tiered celestial realms reflect alternative configurations of the graded holiness of the celestial temple (depending on the model chosen, e.g. wilderness tabernacle three grades; Solomonic Temple seven grades).

---

37 Halperin 1988: 78–87.

38 Cf. III Enoch 1:1 (5th/6th century CE): 'When I ascended to the height to behold the vision of the chariot, I entered six palaces, one inside the other, and when I reached the door of the seventh palace, I paused in prayer before the Holy One, blessed be he...' (*OTP I*: 255).

39 Morray-Jones 1993a: 203–5; 2006: 148.

Support for such an equation is provided by the close correspondence in metaphorical imagery across a range of Jewish/Jewish-Christian heavenly ascent literature, that correlate heaven with a temple, and multiple tiers, often the highest tier (but cf. § 3.3.3), with the celestial Holy of Holies/Eden/Paradise (cf. Jub 3:9-13 and II Bar 4:2-7).[40] On the basis of such a close identification of chambers and heavenly tiers, Morray-Jones can conclude (with reference to *The Songs of the Sabbath Sacrifice*):

> As in *I Enoch* and the *Testament of Levi*, the courts and chambers of the temple are, in fact, the celestial levels. The temple is not 'in' heaven; its seven 'sanctuaries' are the heavens.[41]

Support for Morray-Jones' reading is provided by I En 14:11, 17, in which the ceiling of the Holy Place and the upper chamber of the Holy of Holies, respectively, are equated with the firmament of fixed-stars, retaining the symbolism of the terrestrial sanctuary. The spatial imagery of I En 14, as noted in the exegesis above, operates on two planes, the horizontal and the vertical, such that the interior movement within this sacred space is simultaneously depicted as a vertical ascent to the highest heaven.[42] I am inclined to agree with Morray-Jones' reading, on the basis of the textual data noted, thus equating each of the three buildings (G^{Pan}) with a successively higher heavenly tier, corresponding to the three tiers of graded holiness of the wilderness tabernacle. The significance of this tentative line of interpretation will be picked-up again with reference to the 'third-heaven' of II Cor 12:2 (§3.3.3).

Following Enoch's visionary ascent to the celestial temple (I En 14:8–16:4), he is taken on a series of guided tours of the periphery of the terrestrial disc, apparently accompanied by archangels (cf. Uriel 19:1; cf. 20:1-8), where significant locations, especially relating to the eschatological punishment of the Watchers and the post-mortem abode of the righteous, are located (I En 17–19, 20–36).[43] In this sub-section I will offer a concise overview of some significant aspects of the mental map of I Enoch 1–36, limited to chapters 17–19 in view of space constraints (and relevance to Chapter 4, below), in dialogue with previous attempts to sketch the topography of these chapters (Grelot (fig. 3.1), Milik (fig. 3.2) and Bautch (fig. 3.3)).[44]

---

40   Himmelfarb 1991.
41   Morray-Jones 2006: 156.
42   The celestial Holy Place is bounded by the firmament of fixed stars (I En 14:11), whilst the celestial Holy of Holies affords a glimpse of a higher heavenly tier above the fixed stars (I En 14:17).
43   Nickelsburg 2001: 276–332.
44   Grelot 1958; Milik 1976: 15–18, 35–41; Bautch 2003: 162–90; cf. Stock-Hesketh 2000 (I En 20–36).

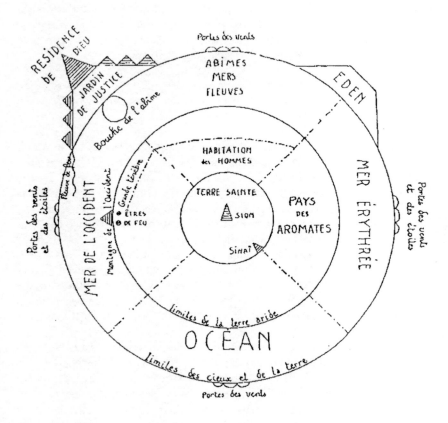

Fig 3.1 The Cosmic Geography of I Enoch and Jubilees (Grelot 1958)[45]

45   Grelot 1958: 46. Grelot's map corresponds to Ionian maps (circular continent, with Jerusalem replacing Delphi at ὀμφαλός (I En 26:1). A flaw is the conflation of data from all the Enochic booklets (I En 1–105) plus *Jubilees*.

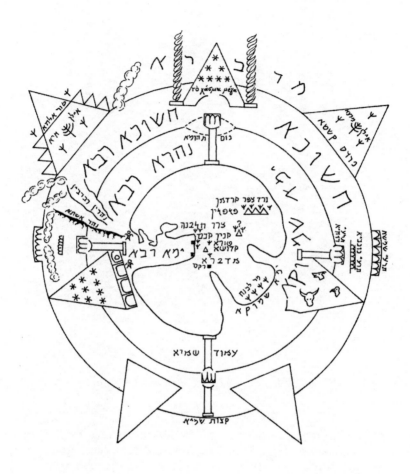

Fig 3.2 The Cosmic Geography of I Enoch (Milik 1976)[46]

46   Milik 1976: 40. By permission of Oxford University Press. Milik's map is distorted by its attempts to conform I En to the template of the Babylonian *Mappa Mundi*, with a resultant misreading of the *nagu* (triangular regions); cf. Horowitz 1998: 30–32.

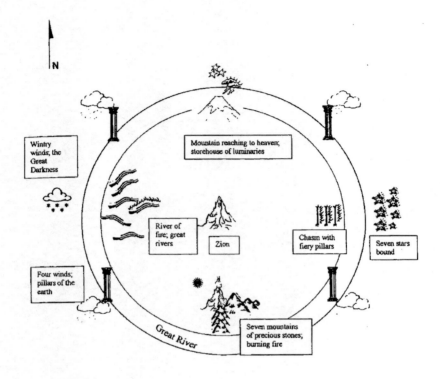

Fig. 3.3 The Cosmic Geography of I Enoch 17–19 (Bautch 2003)[47]

The first significant aspect relates to the overarching template that the implied author presupposes, and onto which the specific spatial features are plotted. Whilst details are hazy the indications that are present in I En 17–19 tend to point in the direction of a central earth, encircled by a terrestrial ocean and topped by a domed firmament. I En 17:5 refers to the 'great river' (ὁ μέγας ποταμός) as a boundary-marker at the perimeter of the west/north-west of the continent of earth, which most likely refers to the terrestrial ocean, especially in the context of other Greek infernal rivers (cf. I En 17:5 and Πυριφλεγέθων).[48] A solitary firmament (τὸ στερέωμα) is referred to in I En 18:2, 12 which rests upon the earth, beyond which Enoch is shown the place of punishment of seven disobedient stars/Watchers (cf. I En 86:1-3),

47   Bautch 2003: 185. Bautch's map corresponds more precisely to the textual data of I En 17–19, but the positioning of some sites is hypothesized on the basis of a proposed circular tour; cf. Stock-Hesketh 2000.
48   So Nickelsburg 2001: 283 contra Bautch 2003: 82–3 for whom θάλασσα μεγάλη = Mediterranean (Num 34:6-7; Josh 15:12; Ezek 48:28) not Oceanus.

constrained from entering within the dome of the firmament. A significant deviation from this model, however, is indicated by the choice of imagery to describe the central earth. Whilst Grelot, Milik and Bautch each depict the earth as a central disc encircled by Oceanus/Bitter River, in line with this unit's predominant Babylonian/Homeric cosmology, the implied author of I En 17–19 does not consistently hold to a single cognitive image. Instead, in I En 18:2-3, the cosmos is depicted not as a domed firmament atop a circular disc, but rather as a square building: the firmament (τὸ στερέωμα) is akin to the roof, the earth to the floor built on a foundation (ὁ θεμέλιος τῆς γῆς) (cf. Ps 82:5 (81:5 LXX), Prov 8:29, Job 38:4, Sir 10:16, 16:19), with the whole structure supported by four pillars of wind (cf. Job 9:6, 26:11).[49] This oscillation in verbal imagery reflects shifts in the text's choice of metaphors, and literary influences (e.g. from Homeric/Hesiodic imagery to Job's lists of revealed things), which defeat attempts to sketch a consistent visual image of the seer's terrestrial journey.[50] The subterranean waters of the abyss are mentioned (I En 17:7), but exclusively with reference to its function as the source (mouth) of the terrestrial waters (including the Ocean). The mouth of the abyss (τὸ στόμα τῆς ἀβύσσου) is situated in close proximity to the realm of the dead ('where no flesh walks') (I En 17:7), but this realm is envisaged as lying to the west of the perimeter of Ocean, on the horizontal plane, rather than as a subterranean realm beneath (cf. *Od.* III.335; IX.26; XIII.241; *Il.* XII. 240).[51]

Just as it is difficult to sketch a drawn map of I En 17–19 in view of a lack of consistent metaphorical imagery throughout (cf. I En 18:1-5), so also it is notoriously difficult precisely to position its spatial features onto a topographical framework. Although particular compass directions are occasionally provided (e.g. I En 17:4 'the fire of the west'), or Enoch's directional movement indicated (e.g. I En 18:10 'beyond these mountains'), more often than not the hearer of the text is given insufficient information to locate precisely the station described. An excellent illustration of this is the difficulty of placing the mountain throne of God (I En 18:6-8; cf. Ezek 28:13-14); the orientation of the mountains is provided, not their compass location. Accordingly Milik and Grelot position this item in the NW, guided by the immediate context (I En 17:1-7), whilst Bautch situates it in the S/ SW guided by the proposed anticlockwise circuit of Enoch's tour.[52] The dreamlike quality of the visual imagery disorientate the hearer and highlight the rhetoric of inaccessibility (I En 19:3).

---

49   Nickelsburg 284–5; Black 1985: 158; Stone 1976.

50   I En 18:1-5 is a summary statement that breaks off the tour (aorist verbs of seeing replace motion).

51   Bautch 2003: 239–40.

52   Cf. Grelot 1958: 40; Milik 1976: 39; Nickelsburg 2001: 285; Black 1985: 158 (all NW); against Bautch 2003: 107–9.

3.3.2 Philo

As discussed earlier (§2.5.1), the aristocratic exegetical philosopher Philo was the recipient of a tertiary-level *encyclical* education, which he retrospectively interpreted as merely a preparatory step towards his ultimate goal of philosophical study (cf. *Congr.* 74–77). Whilst for Philo, true philosophical wisdom was to be sought in the Mosaic Torah (cf. *Cont.*), his extant treatises evidence a sustained critical engagement with the Greek philosophical tradition, notably Plato, whose influence is detectable in both Philo's philosophical treatises (e.g. *Aeter.*) and exegetical commentaries (e.g. *Opif.* on Gen 1–3).[53] Runia has persuasively argued that the apparently low incidence of explicit and implicit references to the *Timaeus* in Philo's writings (ten quotations, eight paraphrases and two direct references without citation) is not to be interpreted as Philo's indirect knowledge of this work (through commentaries and *florilegia*), for two reasons.[54] First, as noted in the previous chapter, Philo's treatment of Plato differs according to the genre of the text he is writing:

> Whereas in the philosophical treatises Philo does not hesitate to mention Plato's name and discuss his views in a direct way, in his exegetical works he tends to avoid mentioning the philosopher's name.[55]

Second, and equally important, is that on closer inspection it appears that Philo's treatment of cosmological topics are saturated with the use of Plato's terminology, reflecting a close engagement with his ideas and imagery.[56] Philo shows a particularly close familiarity with three sections within the *Timaeus* that most closely corresponded to his own theological and cosmological interests: the creation of the cosmos and humanity (*Timaeus* 27d–47e), humanity's psychological make-up (*Timaeus* 69a–72d), and the place of humanity in the hierarchy of the cosmos (*Timaeus* 89d–92c).[57]

Evidence that Philo knew, and appropriated, a form of this Platonic model is proven by Philo's explicit reference to the cosmos as spherical in structure with a spherical earth at its centre surrounded by planetary spheres (cf. *Prov.* II.56).[58]

> ...looking at the things which are really great and deserving of serious attention, namely, the creation of the heaven, and the revolutions of the planets

---

53   Runia 1986: 365–99, 461–7; 2001; cf. Sharples and Sheppard 2003.
54   Runia 1986: 367.
55   Runia 1986: 368, cf. 370–1.
56   Cf. Dillon 1977: 139–81.
57   Runia 1986: 372–5. Philo quotes and paraphrases more passages from the *Timaeus* than all other passages that he cites/alludes to from the rest of the Platonic corpus.
58   Adams 2008: 26; Runia 1986: 461–7.

and fixed stars…and the position of the earth in the most centre spot of the universe…

(*Mos.* I. 212)[59]

Moreover, the dominance of a Platonic cosmological worldview on his thoughts are further evidenced in Philo's allegorical (re)interpretation of passages in the Mosaic Torah (cf. *Heres* 221–4; *Cher.* 21–25) which presuppose such a model of the universe.[60] The influence of the *Timaeus* on the thought-world and terminology of *Cher.* 21–25 is especially apparent, in that he identifies one of the Cherubim (Gen 3:24) as a symbol of the outermost sphere of fixed stars (the movement of the Same), and the other as a symbol of the planetary spheres (the movement of the Different).

For Philo, correctly understood (by means of allegorical exegesis), the Mosaic Torah is a repository of divine wisdom, the goal of philosophical enquiry. Accordingly, the surface-level cosmology of the Torah, describing a tripartite cosmos of heaven, disc-earth and underworld, is effaced in his exegetical commentaries, notably *De Opificio Mundi*, as his exegesis instead privileges a Platonic cosmological worldview that distinguishes the creation of the intelligible cosmos from the creation of the sense-perceptible cosmos, notably with respect to the creation of humanity (Gen 1:26ff; Gen 2:7ff).[61]

A final, crucial piece of evidence is provided by Philo's description of the heavens in the language of visionary ascent. On two occasions, the first drawing on his own experience of inspired interpretation (*Spec.* III.1–6), and the second offering a more general, poetic expression of the heavenly rapture of intellectual study (*Opif.* 69–71), Philo situates visionary ascent against the backdrop of a Platonic, multiple-heaven cosmos (cf. Plato, 'Myth of Er', *Republic*, X.613B–621B; Cicero, 'Dream of Scipio', *De Re Publica*, 6.9–26).[62]

In *Opif.* 69–71, commenting on Gen 1:26-27 with its reference to humanity as the image (εἰκών) of God, Philo unpacks this divine analogy with reference to humanity's intellect (νοῦς), poetically describing the intellect's heavenward journey in search of wisdom. Philo divides the mind's ascent into five stages.[63] It begins by scouring the terrestrial realm (land and sea) for the knowledge that can be discovered therein, before moving on, in stage two, to the ascent proper and the (lower) air (ἀήρ) with its attendant meteorological phenomena. Stage three sees the mind ascend to the upper air, or aither (αἰθήρ), the location of the planets (πλάνητες) in motion, and the fixed stars (ἀστέρες) affixed to the revolving vault of heaven. The fourth stage leaves behind the sensible realm and aims instead at the intelligible realm of

59   Yonge 1993: 479.
60   Wright 2000: 150–2.
61   Runia 2001: 132–5, 321–4.
62   Borgen 1993; Ferrari and Griffith 2000; Bréguet 1980.
63   Borgen 1993: 251–4; Runia 2001: 222–4, the latter privileging Platonic parallels (*Phaedrus*, 246D–249D) over Borgen's suggestion of heavenly ascent literature.

the Forms/Ideas, attainable by philosophical study, yet even this wisdom is insufficient to raise the intellect to the fifth stage, the very presence of God.

The predominant influence on Philo's poetic description is evidently the myth of the ascent of the winged soul to the back of the heavenly vault (cf. Plato, *Phaedrus*, 246D–249D), yet Borgen astutely detects connections with Jewish heavenly ascent literature, where the ascendant's aim is to enter the throne-room of the Deity, here described as 'the Great King' (cf. I En 14:8ff).[64] The most striking impression, however, for the purpose of the present study is that even whilst partially alluding to the motif of heavenly ascent to the divine throne-room, Philo locates his poetic description against the backdrop of a Platonic cosmos of multiple planetary spheres (in contrast to Paul or the seer of the Apocalypse). The same is true for Philo's more succinct account of his own personal ascent in inspired rapture in *Spec.* III.1–6. Compared with *Opif.* 69–71, *Spec.* III.1ff offers a more modest description of divine inspiration, as Philo's mind is borne aloft only as far as the αἰθήρ, the locale of the planets and stars, stopping short of the realm of Ideas or the divine presence.

This brief assessment of Philo's cosmology has demonstrated the significance of Philo's tertiary-level education on his dominant conception of the universe. Philo was cognizant, through first–hand study, of the model of the universe popularized by Plato's *Timaeus*; a spherical cosmos containing a nested series of planetary spheres with a stationary earth at its centre. This conception of the universe proved to be the dominant model of the cosmos among the intellectual élite in the Hellenistic and Roman eras. Although Philo was aware of alternative designs, most notably the tripartite universe of the Mosaic Torah, he perceived instead that when correctly understood (by allegorical exegesis) the Torah itself foreshadowed a model of the universe that Plato later adopted. The pre-eminence of this cosmology in Philo's thought can be seen in passages where he alludes to heavenly ascent (of the mind), fusing Platonic myth (*Phaedrus*) with Jewish heavenly ascent literature. For even here, unlike in I En 14:8ff or II Cor 12:1ff, the cosmological backdrop remains Platonic rather than Homeric.

3.3.3 II Corinthians 12:1-10

In view of space constraints, analysis of the cosmology of the uncontested Pauline epistles will focus exclusively on the description of a heavenly ascent afforded 'a person in Christ' (ἄνθρωπον ἐν Χριστῷ) in II Cor 12:1ff, interpreted within the context of II Cor 10–13.[65]

---

64   Cf. *QG* I.86 where Philo refers to Enoch's translation (μετατίθημι) to heaven (Gen 5:24 LXX); and cf. I En 84:2, 5, 91:3 with respect to God as 'Great King'; Borgen 1993: 253.

65   For broader analyses of Pauline cosmology see Foster 2008: 107–24; van Kooten 2003; and White 2008: 90–106.

II Corinthians 10–13 is a self-contained unit in which Paul appeals (παρακαλῶ, 10:1) to the Corinthian communities in order to defend himself and his apostleship from what he perceives to be hostile jibes by some members of the community. Intimately tied up with the Corinthians' low estimation of his ministry, as Paul perceives it, is their seduction by an alternative group of missionaries, whom he depicts as 'love-rivals' for the community's affection (cf. 11:2, 11), such that he reacts in a jealous and sarcastic tone throughout as he attempts to prove that he is the better man, alone worthy of their affection. Whether or not II Cor 10–13 is perceived to be originally a separate letter-fragment from chapters 1–9 which now precede, there is no doubting the marked shift from the conciliatory tone of the earlier chapters.[66] The immediate context of the passage is the extended 'fool's speech' of II Cor 11:1–12:13, in which irony abounds as Paul attempts to 'boast' of his equality, and more, his superiority, to the rival missionaries on whatever standard of comparison is chosen (cf. 11:21b-23).[67]

In II Cor 12:2 Paul recounts how, fourteen years ago, a 'person in Christ' (ἄνθρωπον ἐν Χριστῷ) known to him was carried off (ἁρπαγέντα) as far as the third heaven. Paul continues in v4 by describing how this same individual was carried off (ἡρπάγη) into paradise, where s/he heard 'unutterable utterances'.[68] My principal concern is to identify the cosmological schema that underlies this passage, specifically, the precise number of heavenly tiers that the implied author describes in these verses. In order to achieve this aim, three interrelated questions require closer investigation: first, who is this unnamed individual, this 'person in Christ', to whom Paul refers? Second, what is the relationship between the two clauses (II Cor 12:2, 4) and their descriptions of 'heavenly abduction'? Did Paul locate paradise in the third heaven, such that vv2 and 3-4 are to be read in parallel, or should these verses rather be read sequentially, describing a two-stage heavenly ascent beyond the third heaven? Finally, what difference does it make for Paul's argument in II Cor 10–13 which heavenly tier this person ascended to?

The majority of interpreters, both ancient and modern, have interpreted ἄνθρωπον ἐν Χριστῷ as an oblique reference to Paul himself, and his own experience of a heavenly ascent. Paul is credited with adopting a third-person style either to distance himself from the charge of 'boasting' in his own abilities, emphasizing his weaknesses instead (cf. II Cor 11:30; 12:1, 6-10), and/or because this reflects the 'ecstatic' nature of the experience, in which the self is viewed as 'other' (cf. vv 2, 4). A good example of a comparable displacement occurs in I En 87:3-4 where the narrator, Enoch, describes his own heavenly ascent as a character within his dream vision. II Cor 12:7,

66   On the integrity of II Corinthians see Martin 1986: xxxix-li; Thrall 1994: 3–48.
67   Welborn 2005.
68   LXX and Gk lit. ἁρπάζω, violent seizure/abduction; transferred sense denoting heavenly abduction of heroes/heroines by gods (cf. Lucian, *De dea Syr* 4; Pausanias 73.18.11; Wis. 4:11; I Thess 4:17); Aune 1998a: 689–90. Passive verbal forms in II Cor 12:2, 4 hint at divine agency in the seizure (cf. Wis 4:11 LXX).

with its explicit reference to an 'abundance of revelations' (τῇ ὑπερβολῇ τῶν ἀποκαλύψεων) which Paul himself received, is widely seen to unmask the identity of the heavenly ascendant of the preceding verses, linking back to the heading of this unit in 12:1 (ὀπτασίας καὶ ἀποκαλύψεις κυρίου).

Notable dissenters include Michael Goulder, who affords greater weight to Paul's explicit distinction between himself (ἐμαυτου) and 'this person' (τοῦ τοιούτου) (II Cor 12:5), arguing that the reference is to a fellow Christian friend of Paul's (ἐν Χριστω), distinguishing Paul's receipt of revelations (II Cor 12:7) from his failure to ascend to the divine throne chariot (ὀπτασία – understood as a technical term for the latter experience), and Morton Smith who identifies Jesus as the ἄνθρωπος.[69] The central pillar of Goulder's argument, namely the sharp distinction between ὀπτασία and ἀποκαλύψις, is too unstable to support the proposal that the implied author is distancing himself from the content of vv1-5. The noun ὀπτασία is not exclusively used as a technical term restricted to visions of the Deity enthroned in the heavenly temple, as it occurs in a variety of other contexts elsewhere in Second Temple literature, for example, to describe the (heavenly) man *by the banks of the Tigris river* (Dan 10:1, 7, 8, 16). It is impossible to verify whether Paul restricted ὀπτασία to references to the *merkabah* throne, as Goulder suggests, because the term at II Cor 12:1 is a *hapax legomenon* in the Pauline literature, and so there is insufficient evidence on which to base a case for a distinctive Pauline meaning. The noun ἀποκαλύψις is used of a variety of forms of visual (e.g. Rom 8:19; II Thess 1:7) and auditory (e.g. I Cor 14:6) disclosures in Pauline literature, such that it is plausible that this term is a broader umbrella-concept that *overlaps* with the more specific visionary term ὀπτασία, rather than being interpreted as an entirely distinct concept.

The striking literary parallelism between vv2 and 3-4 pose a herme-neutical puzzle for exegetes: should the interpretative weight be placed on the repetition (parallel descriptions of the third heaven) or the variation (sequential descriptions of a two-stage ascent)?[70] A closer consideration of the spatial relationships between 'paradise' and the 'third heaven' in heavenly-ascent literature of the Hellenistic and Roman eras may provide helpful clues as to the cosmological worldview that underlies II Cor 12.[71] Three extant heavenly ascent narratives, *Greek Life of Adam and Eve* 37:5, *II Enoch* 8, and *III Baruch* 4, each locate 'paradise' in the third tier of a multiple heaven cosmos. In each of these three texts, moreover, paradise constitutes one of the lower heavenly realms, distinct from the dwelling place of God in the highest heaven.[72]

---

69   Goulder 1994; Smith 1981.
70   Cf. Bietenhard 1951: 162–8.
71   Cf. Gooder 2006: 36–82; Tabor 1986.
72   According to the revised stemma of T. Levi, Levi ascends through seven, not three heavens; cf. De Jonge 1975: 63–86; Hollander and De Jonge 1985: 10–17.

The *Greek Life of Adam and Eve* (*GLAE*) 31–42 (*c.* 2nd–4th century CE) offers a detailed account of the separation of Adam's body and spirit at death.[73] In this recension the divine presence, enthroned on the cherubim throne, is resident in the uppermost heaven of a seven-heaven cosmos, from which the Deity, seraphim and angelic entourage descend to undertake the funerary rites for Adam (*GLAE* 32:4–33:2; 35:2). Adam's spirit is transported to its celestial resting-place in *Paradise*, located in the *third tier* of the heavenly realm (*GLAE* 37:3–6) whilst his body is interred in the verdant garden of the terrestrial paradise (*GLAE* 38–42). A similar cosmological model underlies *II Enoch* [Recension A] (late 1st/early 2nd century CE).[74] The text divides the celestial realm into seven heavenly tiers, with the Deity enthroned in the uppermost, seventh heaven (II Enoch 20). In II En 8–10 the contents of the third heaven are imagined either as a simple split-tier realm, with the place of punishment of the unrighteous (II En 8–9) located above, literally to the north of (10:1), the celestial paradise (II En 10), or, if the additional description of paradise from II En 42 [J] is included, at alternative compass points (east versus north). In the third example, *III Baruch* 4–9 (1st—3rd century CE), the precise number of heavens envisaged remains elusive as Baruch is transported to the gates of the fifth heaven, but does not pass inside.[75] All that can be said with certainty is that the third tier is not the highest heaven. Although the explicit term 'paradise' is not used, one of the many fantastic items that Baruch is shown in the vast plain of the third heaven is 'the tree which caused Adam to stray' (4:8), once again indicating that (aspects of) the celestial paradise are relocated to the third heavenly tier.[76]

If the cosmological frameworks of *GLAE*, *II Enoch* and *III Baruch* are superimposed onto II Cor 12:1ff, then the text envisages a single-stage heavenly ascent to the third tier of heaven where paradise is situated (vv2 and 4 in synonymous parallelism). Significantly, this heavenly realm is *not* the highest heavenly tier where the Deity is enthroned but rather an intermediate level, where the righteous dead are temporarily interred prior to the eschaton.[77] The visionary is afforded a privileged preview of the post-mortem dwelling place of the righteous dead, and it is in this realm that the 'unutterable utterances' are disclosed to him.

Gooder argues that such an interpretative framework offers the most plausible reading of II Cor 12:1ff.[78] Paul here describes a former *failed*

---

73   De Jonge and Tromp 1997; Eldridge 2001; Johnson, *OTP II*: 249–96; Nickelsburg 2005: 327–32.

74   Andersen, *OTP I*: 91–213; Collins 1998: 243–7; Macaskill 2007; Nickelsburg 2005: 221–5.

75   Collins 1998: 248–51; Gaylord *OTP I*: 653–79; Harlow 1996.

76   Wright 2000: 164–74; Yarbro Collins 1996a: 43–6.

77   Bietenhard 1951.

78   Gooder 2006: 165–211; (191–2, n. 5 – but stresses that her thesis is not dependent on the seventh heaven being the highest tier); cf. Betz 1972.

attempt by himself to ascend to the highest heavenly realm, as he was prevented from rising any further by an 'angel of Satan' (which constitutes his 'thorn in the flesh') (II Cor 12:7).[79] Gooder contends that 'chapters 10–13 make more sense if 12.1–10 is understood as another example of failure'.[80] If the heavenly ascent itself is understood as a failure, then II Cor 12:1-7a, and not simply II Cor 12:7bff, provides a further example of Paul's weaknesses and disappointments (cf. II Cor 11:30), corresponding to his ignominious descent from the walls of Damascus (II Cor 11:32-33). Furthermore, both passages are seen to be linked by a common thread of opposition: Paul is prevented from residing in Damascus by Aretas IV, and prevented from ascending to the throne-room of the Deity in the highest heaven by an angel of Satan.

Interpreting II Cor 12:1ff as an ascent within the context of a seven-tiered heaven, however, does not provide the most satisfactory interpretation of the data of the Pauline text. Three points strongly suggest that Paul describes a successful ascent to the highest heavenly tier. The first point concerns the sense of the crucial clause 'ἐλεύσομαι δὲ εἰς ὀπτασίας καὶ ἀποκαλύψεις κυρίου' (II Cor 12:1b). I would contend that both nouns, 'visions and revelations' (ὀπτασίας καὶ ἀποκαλύψεις), govern the genitive of κυρίού, as they are both coordinated by a single preposition (εἰς).[81] Furthermore, whilst a majority of commentators read κυρίού as a genitive of origin, denoting the risen Lord as the source of the revelations, I am inclined to include an objective sense as well. Although II Cor 12:1ff does not explicitly describe a vision of the risen Lord, this may simply stem from the visionary's refusal to disclose the contents of the vision, rather than discounting its occurrence at all. In support of this argument, Rowland has noted that in other instances where Paul qualifies ἀποκαλύψις with a genitive, the noun in the genitive denotes the content of the revelation (cf. Rom 2:5, 8:19, I Cor 1:7, Gal 1:12).[82] On this interpretation, II Cor 12:2ff describes a visionary and revelatory experience of the risen Lord, by means of a heavenly ascent (cf. II Cor 4:6). If this is the case, then the location of this experience must be envisaged as the *highest-heaven*, that is, the divine throne room, where Christ is enthroned at the right of the Deity (cf. I Cor 15:25/ Ps 109:1 LXX). As a consequence, for the implied author of II Cor 12:1ff (and in contrast to *GLAE*, *II Enoch* and *III Baruch*), 'paradise' is identified with the highest heavenly realm, where the Deity and Christ are enthroned, and not considered a distinct and relatively inferior intermediate level.

---

79   Gooder 2006: 190–203 suggests that the double-meaning of the verb ὑπεραίρομαι (II Cor 12:7), meaning both physically 'raise-up' and metaphorically 'exalt', may hint that the thorn in the flesh (= angel of Satan) prevented the visionary from ascending any higher; cf. Morray-Jones 1993a, 1993b; Segal 1990: ch 2.

80   Gooder 2006: 203.

81   Thrall 2000: 774–5.

82   Rowland 1982: 380.

Second, a connection between 'paradise' and the celestial throne room is further strengthened by the nature of the revelation that is disclosed: 'καὶ ἤκουσεν ἄρρητα ῥήματα ἃ οὐκ ἐξὸν ἀνθρώπῳ λαλῆσαι'. The revelatory experience of ἄνθρωπον ἐν Χριστῷ recounted in II Cor 12:4 focuses exclusively on the auditory aspect: the heavenly abductee heard 'unutterable utterances' (ἄρρητα ῥήματα) that are not permissible to disclose. The adjective ἄρρητος connotes both words that are beyond human powers of expression, as well as words that are forbidden to express, with the emphasis explicitly falling on the latter here on the basis of the explanatory clause (οὐκ ἐξὸν).[83] The term was commonly used to describe rites and secrets (e.g. the Eleusinian mysteries) that were not to be disclosed to the uninitiated (cf. Euripides, *Bacchae* 471–2; Plutarch *Mor.* 360F; Philo, *Somn.* I.91). Further speculation as to the content of the revelation can only result in unverifiable conjecture (e.g. angelic song/divine Name), but a consideration of the functional significance of 'paradise' for the nature of the revelation may prove more fruitful.[84] A decision as to whether paradise is imagined as an intermediate level in a multiple heaven cosmos of up to seven tiers, or the uppermost of a seven-heaven cosmos, involves distinguishing the function of paradise for the implied author of II Cor 12:1ff. Is paradise simply the abode of the righteous dead, or is it the abode of the righteous dead located in the presence of the Deity (cf. Rev 6:9)? Given that the revelation is to be kept secret from the uninitiated Corinthian audience (who have not experienced heavenly ascents), it would appear more probable that the latter alternative is intended. The heavenly dwelling places of the righteous (and the corresponding places of punishment for the unrighteous) comprise a large proportion of the content of other heavenly ascent texts (e.g. I Enoch 21–32; II Enoch 8–10), disclosure of whose content to the target audience is a primary purpose of such literature (cf. I En 104:12–105:2). Similarly, Paul has earlier disclosed 'mysteries' relating to the post-mortem status of the righteous, and the events surrounding the eschaton (cf. I Cor 15:15 μυστήριον), and so these appear to be unlikely topics to conceal from the audience here. On this basis I would argue that the ἄρρητα ῥήματα are most plausibly interpreted as a divine disclosure that the heavenly abductee received whilst in the uppermost heavenly realm/paradise/celestial throne-room.

Third, the closest cosmological analogy to Paul's ascent to the heavenly realm may be provided by the heavenly ascent of the patriarch, Enoch, in I Enoch 14:8-23 (*c.* 3rd century BCE) (§3.3.1). As discussed above, in this heavenly ascent vision, the seer, Enoch, ascends to the celestial sanctuary

83   Thrall 2000: 794–8.
84   Angelic song is often proposed, in view of its prominence in heavenly ascent accounts (e.g. II Enoch 17 [J] which similarly describes the content as impossible to recount, presumably owing to its beauty), and overlaps with alternative suggestions as to the content of such song (e.g. divine names) (e.g. Furnish 1984: 545; Morray-Jones 1993b: 281).

where he passes through two outer buildings (G^Pan), corresponding to the vestibule and Holy Place, and peers into a third (Holy of Holies). Although the text is widely interpreted as a single heaven with three inner-chambers (e.g. Nickelsburg, Himmelfarb), there are indications in the passage, notably the interaction of horizontal movement and vertical ascent, which strongly hint that the chambers may closely correspond to a three-tiered heaven. If this is the case, I En 14:8ff constitutes a closer cosmological template in which to position the heavenly abduction in II Cor 12:1ff than the more widely discussed parallels with *GLAE, II Enoch* and *III Baruch*. Connections between Paradise/Eden and the Holy of Holies elsewhere in Second Temple Jewish literature (e.g. Jub 4:21–26; Rev 4–5) strengthen the suggestion that Paul here describes an ascent to the celestial Holy of Holies/ Paradise, the inner sanctum of the celestial Temple (II Cor 12:1ff), where the Deity and risen Christ are enthroned.[85] Such a location is also consistent with the location of an angelic adversary (angel of Satan) (cf. Zech 3:1ff הַשָּׂטָן (= ὁ διάβολος LXX)).

The reading of II Cor 12:1ff proposed is consistent with the broader context of Paul's 'fool's speech' in II Cor 11:1–12:13 in which Paul's boasts oscillate between items in which he prides himself in more than matching the positive credentials of the 'superlative apostles' (cf. 11:21ff), and items in which he prides himself on his own weaknesses (cf. 11:30, 12:5). Unlike II Cor 11:21-29 where an explicit contrast is made with the superlative apostles, there is no explicit suggestion in 11:30ff that Paul's rivals claimed superiority in revelatory experiences.[86] Instead, Paul's heavenly ascent to the celestial throne room, the dwelling place of the Deity and the risen Christ, is a source of unmitigated pride (II Cor 12:5a).

3.4 The Cosmology of the Apocalypse[87]

This section commences with an assessment of the Apocalypse's cosmological template (triple-decker cosmos: single heaven, earth, subterranean abyss), before offering an overview of the topography of each realm. The Apocalypse's distinctive mental map of the cosmos is then assessed in the light of resonances and dissonances with the cosmologies of I En 14, Philo and II Cor 12, and its rhetorical function evaluated.

---

85   So Morray-Jones 2009: 341–419 (esp. 390–6) who interprets II Cor 12:2-4 as a two-stage ascent to the highest heavenly tier, that is, the celestial Holy of Holies/Paradise which constitutes the third heaven. Paul initially ascends as far as the gates (ἕως τρίτου οὐρανοῦ), before subsequently entering inside (εἰς τὸν παράδεισον).

86   Cf. Gooder 2006: 167.

87   Cf. Aune 1997: 317–19; Friesen 2001: 152–66; McDonough 2008: 178–88; Malina 1995; Malina and Pilch 2000; Minear 1962; Wright 2000: 133–5.

One of the most striking aspects of the Apocalypse's mental-map of the cosmos is the retention of an archaic ANE tripartite division of the universe into three realms: heaven, earth and underworld.

καὶ οὐδεὶς ἐδύνατο ἐν τῷ οὐρανῷ οὐδὲ ἐπὶ τῆς γῆς οὐδὲ ὑποκάτω τῆς γῆς[88] ἀνοῖξαι τὸ βιβλίον οὔτε βλέπειν αὐτό

And no one in heaven or on earth or under the earth was able to open the scroll or to look into it.

(Rev 5:3)

A comparable division of the totality of the universe into three tiered zones is also evidenced in the Septuagint (e.g. Exod 20:4, ἐν τῷ οὐρανῷ ἄνω καὶ…ἐν τῇ γῇ κάτω καὶ…ἐν τοῖς ὕδασιν ὑποκάτω τῆς γῆς) and other early Christian literature (cf. Phil 2:10 and Ignatius, *Tralles*, 9:1, ἐπουρανίων καὶ ἐπιγείων καὶ καταχθονίων).[89] Elsewhere in the Apocalypse the central tier of this model is further subdivided into two component parts, 'earth and sea' (γῆ καὶ θάλασσα) (cf. Rev 7:1-3; 10:5, 6; 12:12), although the terrestrial surface water (θάλασσα) has various shades of meaning, such that it is often indistinguishable from the chaos waters under the earth (cf. Rev 13:1; 14:7; 21:21) otherwise referred to as ἡ ἄβυσσος (Rev 9:1, 2, 11; 11:7; 17:8; 20:1, 3).[90]

καὶ πᾶν κτίσμα ὃ ἐν τῷ οὐρανῷ καὶ ἐπὶ τῆς γῆς καὶ ὑποκάτω τῆς γῆς[91] καὶ ἐπὶ τῆς θαλάσσης[92]

And every creature that (is) in heaven and upon the earth and underneath the earth and upon the sea…

(Rev 5:13)

88   It is noteworthy that the clause 'οὐδὲ ὑποκάτω τῆς γῆς' is absent from ℵ, 1854, 2344, possibly as a result of *homoioteleuton*, as a scribe's eye may have skipped from the first to the second γῆς. On possible ideological excision, cf. Rev 5:13 below.

89   Cf. Swete 1906: 75 and Charles 1920a: 139.

90   For the overlap between sea and abyss in the Septuagint see Exod 20:4/Deut 5:8 (ἐν τοῖς ὕδασιν ὑποκάτω τῆς γῆς), especially the synonymous parallelism between θάλασσα and ἄβυσσος in Pss. 32:7, 105:9, Job 41:23 and Sir 24:29.

91   As in Rev 5:3 the clause 'ὑποκάτω τῆς γῆς' is absent from Codex Sinaiticus ℵ and also fam. 1611 (1854, 2050, 2329, 2344), Oecumenius 2053, and certain manuscripts of the Vulgate, strongly suggesting that the clause has been deliberately omitted by some tradents who excluded the inhabitants of the underworld from joining in the praise of the Deity and the Lamb.

92   Cf. Ps 134:6 LXX (ἐν τῷ οὐρανῷ καὶ ἐν τῇ γῇ ἐν ταῖς θαλάσσαις καὶ ἐν πάσαις ταῖς ἀβύσσοις). The preposition ἐπὶ in Rev 5:13 suggests that θάλασσα refers to the terrestrial sea, but its placement in the verse, following ὑποκάτω τῆς γῆς in a list of zones of the universe in descending order, points to an abyssal nuance. Aune 1997: 366 interprets this clause as a three-level cosmos with four sectors (i.e. earth and sea) (cf. Job 11:8-9; Jub 2:16 (Gk fragment) 'ὅσα ἐν τοῖς οὐρανοῖς καὶ ἐν τῇ γῇ, ἐν ταῖς θαλάσσαις καὶ ἐν ταῖς ἀβύσσοις').

In stark contrast to many other Graeco-Roman heavenly ascent texts (e.g. II Cor 12:1ff, II Enoch, III Baruch, Apocalypse of Abraham), which recount a visionary's ascent through multiple heavenly tiers, the Apocalypse appears to envisage a solitary heavenly realm. The text refers to 'heaven' in the singular on fifty occasions, whilst a plural form occurs only once, in Rev 12:12.[93]

διὰ τοῦτο εὐφραίνεσθε, [οἱ] οὐρανοὶ καὶ οἱ ἐν αὐτοῖς σκηνοῦντες. οὐαὶ τὴν γῆν καὶ τὴν θάλασσαν, ὅτι κατέβη ὁ διάβολος πρὸς ὑμᾶς ἔχων θυμὸν μέγαν, εἰδὼς ὅτι ὀλίγον καιρὸν ἔχει.

Therefore rejoice O heavens [plural] and those who dwell in them [plural], woe (is) the earth and the sea, because the devil descended to you (in) great anger, because he knows that he has (only) a little time.

(Rev 12:12)

The plural number (οὐρανοὶ) of Rev 12:12 is unlikely to refer to multiple heavenly tiers, however, for two major reasons. First, on the basis of coherence, a solitary reference to a plural noun is not a strong indicator of an alternative mental map. The second reason is that the plural form is more readily explicable as an echo of the language of the Septuagint, where the dual form of the Hebrew שָׁמַיִם (lit. 'heavens') is occasionally translated by a plural form (οὐρανοί), rather than the more common singular translation (οὐρανός), particularly in poetic passages where the translation aims to retain a sense of a hyperbolic, or hymnic, style, as is the case in Rev 12:12 which calls on the animate heavens to rejoice.[94] As noted by Charles, the solitary reference to a plurality of heavens most likely evidences an allusion to a poetic line from the Septuagint (e.g. Isa 49:13 εὐφραίνεσθε οὐρανοί καὶ ἀγαλλιάσθω, Ps 95:11 εὐφραινέσθωσαν οἱ οὐρανοί καὶ ἀγαλλιάσθω ἡ γῆ), out of keeping with the implied author's more usual reference to heaven in the singular (cf. Rev 18:20 Εὐφραίνου ἐπ' αὐτῇ, οὐρανὲ).[95]

The cosmological framework of the Apocalypse is thus an archaic, three-level cosmos: a single heavenly tier at the top, a central zone divided into earth and sea, and an underworld realm that interacts with the realm above (notably by means of a degree of fluidity between sea and abyss). A brief discussion of each component of this tripartite universe follows, commencing with the predominant image of the heavenly realm as a celestial temple.

---

93   Wright 2000: 133–4.

94   The dual form (שָׁמַיִם) is most commonly translated by the singular noun οὐρανὸς (371 occasions) in the LXX, but much less frequently (51 occasions) by the plural οὐρανοι, the latter almost always in poetic contexts. Cf. Aune 1998a: 655 n. 12d; Yarbro Collins 1996a: 23–4; Wright 2000: 133–4; Houtman 1993; Gerhard von Rad, 'οὐρανὸς', B. Old Testament, *TDNT* 5 (1967), pp.502–8 and Helmut Traub, 'οὐρανὸς', C. Septuagint and Judaism, *TDNT* 5 (1967), pp.509ff.

95   Charles 1920a: 329.

The Apocalypse, like a significant number of other Second Temple Jewish heavenly ascent texts (e.g. I Enoch 14:8ff, Testament of Levi, II Enoch, III Baruch; cf. Songs of the Sabbath Sacrifice) envisions the celestial realm according to the architectural design of the wilderness tabernacle/Jerusalem temple.[96] The Apocalypse is explicit on this point, openly referring to ὁ ναὸς τῆς σκηνῆς τοῦ μαρτυρίου ἐν τῷ οὐρανῷ (the sanctuary, that is, the tent of witness in heaven) (Rev 15:5), indicating that the architectural plan of the wilderness tabernacle (cf. Exod 25:40) informs its vision of the sacred space of heaven (cf. Heb 8:2, 9:11; cf. 4Q 405 22 col. 2 7 (מִשְׁכָּן)).[97] A schematic representation of the areas of 'graded holiness' within the celestial sanctuary (ὁ ναός) in Rev 4–5 and 8–9 can be tentatively plotted, informed by the spatial design of the wilderness tabernacle (cf. Exod 25ff), whilst remaining attentive to the spatial references within the text (fig. 3.4).[98]

At the epicentre of the celestial sanctuary is the central throne (θρόνος) (Rev 4:2) on which the Deity is enthroned, both consisting of, and encircled by, four living creatures (τέσσαρα ζῷα) (4:6).[99] The image is of an animate version of the inanimate cherubim-throne located in the Holy of Holies of the wilderness tabernacle, modified in the light of Ezekiel's vision of the 'living creatures' that propel the Deity's throne-chariot (cf. Exod 25:10-22; and cf. Ezek 1:1-28). The four living creatures constitute part of the animate celestial furniture, one positioned at each corner of the Deity's throne, such that they also encircle the throne to offer their praise (cf. Rev 5:8, 19:4).[100]

96   Barker 1991; Briggs 1999: 45–110; Morray-Jones 2006.

97   By itself ὁ ναός usually renders the Hebrew הֵיכָל, referring to the three-chambered sanctuary building (Holy of Holies, Holy Place, Vestibule), excluding the outer courts of the broader temple (ἱερόν) complex, although it can also be used to denote either the Holy Place or the Vestibule within (but never the Holy of Holies by itself (cf. Aune 1998a: 877)).

98   Cf. Chyutin 2006: 4–36; Jenson 1992: 89–114.

99   The precise spatial positioning of the four living creatures in relation to the throne is obscure, as they are described as being both 'in the midst of' (ἐν μέσῳ) and 'encircling' (κύκλῳ) the throne (Rev 4:6b). The latter preposition corresponds to the location of the seraphim in Isa 6:2 LXX, rather than the 'living creatures' (ζῷα) of Ezek 1:5-25, who are located beneath the throne, set on the likeness of the firmament, which is above their heads (ὑπὲρ κεφαλῆς αὐτοῖς) (Ezek 1:22 LXX) (cf. Pss 80:1, 99:1, etc.). I am inclined to adopt the suggestion of Hall 1990, who considers that the living creatures function as the supporting legs of the throne, both surrounding and supporting it, which corresponds more closely to the image of the cherubim-throne in Exod 25:18ff with a cherubim at either side of the throne; cf. Halperin 1988: 92.

100   It is plausible that a 'living creature' is positioned at each corner of the throne, such that each summons a rider from one of the four compass-points (Rev 6:1-8).

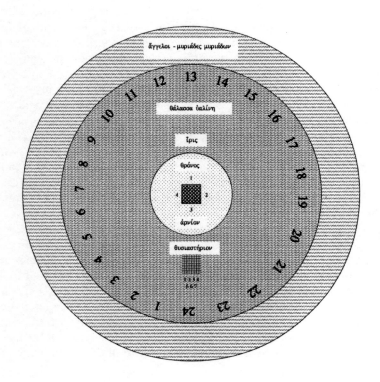

Fig. 3.4: The Celestial Sanctuary of the Apocalypse (Rev 4–5; 8–9)[101]

Corresponding to the four living creatures who form an inner-ring, encircling the throne (κύκλῳ τοῦ θρόνου) (Rev 4:6b), is a second concentric ring formed by the twenty-four enthroned elders who similarly encircle the throne (κυκλόθεν τοῦ θρόνου) (Rev 4:4).[102] These elders are further removed from the centre than the four living creatures, reflected in their subordinate role

101   Cf. Charlesworth and Newsom 1999: 11–12 on the concentric design of the sanctuary in Rev 4–5 & III En 1:1-2 (5th/6th century CE) with reference to the Dura Europus mural.

102   The identity of the twenty-four elders remains a keenly disputed point. For an overview of the major positions (which include heavenly counterparts to the heads of the priestly courses; the twelve sons of Israel; the twelve apostles; astronomical decans) with additional bibliography see Aune 1997: 287–92; Briggs 1999: 47–9; Halperin 1988: 88–9. I interpret these figures as angelic priestly functionaries who correspond to the heads of the twenty-four priestly divisions in the temple (cf. I Chron 23:6, 24:7-18; cf. 4Q *Mishmarot*), primarily because of the evidence of angels as priestly functionaries in other Second Temple Jewish texts (eg. *Jubilees, Songs of the Sabbath Sacrifices*) consistent with the depiction of heaven as a celestial sanctuary in Rev 4–5 (cf. Barker 2000: 123–4).

in relation to them: the four living creatures lead the celestial liturgy and are followed by the elders (Rev 4:9-11), who are generally mentioned second when both groups are referred to (cf. Rev 5:8-10; 14:3).[103] That the circle of enthroned elders demarcates the perimeter of the celestial scene described in Rev 4–5 is hinted at by the implicit location of the seer, in close proximity to this group, staring inward at the central throne, in conversation with one of the adjacent elders (cf. Rev 5:5).[104]

Between the inner-circle of the four living creatures, and the perimeter circle of the twenty-four elders, where the seer is located, are a range of other items that re-imagine aspects of the furnishings of the wilderness tabernacle, most notably the golden altar of incense and the seven-lamped menorah. The seven lamps (ἑπτὰ λαμπάδες) of Rev 4:5 explicitly identified as the seven spirits of God (τὰ ἑπτὰ πνεύματα τοῦ θεοῦ) create a cluster of associative images. These seven lamps located in the celestial sanctuary resonate with the imagery of a solitary seven-lamped menorah positioned in the Holy Place of the wilderness tabernacle (Exod 25:31-40), as well as the visionary re-imagining of this item in both Zech 4:2ff and Rev 1:12-20.[105] Furthermore, the explicit identification of these lamps with the seven spirits of God (Rev 1:4, 3:1, 4:5, 5:6) suggests a further layer of meaning, correlating these celestial lamps with the seven spirits = angels who stand before the throne (cf. 4Q ShirShabb, Similitudes of Enoch).[106] It is highly plausible, therefore, that the seven (trumpet) angels who stand before God (Rev 8:2 τὰ ἑπτὰ ἀγγέλους οἳ ἐνώπιον τοῦ θεοῦ ἑστήκασιν) are to be identified with these same seven spirits (= angels) who stand in the presence of God's throne, denoting the seven archangels familiar from other heavenly ascent literature

103 Halperin 1988: 91. In Rev 7:1 they are listed in reverse order, from the perspective of the angelic throng.

104 The temporary location of the seer, when he ascends to the heavenly throne-room in Rev 4:1ff, appears to be at the edge of the concentric ring of enthroned elders, where he converses with one of their number (cf. Rev 5:5; 7:13-14). The vision is focalized from the perspective of a viewer directly facing the seven spirits, the golden altar of incense and the One on the throne (i.e. approximately where elder no.24 is positioned in fig.3.4). As a consequence the seer's celestial status is on a par with one of the 24 enthroned elders/ heads of the celestial priestly-courses.

The spatial location of the righteous witnesses (martyrs) in Rev 7:9-17; 15:2-4 is difficult to pin-down, but they appear to be in closer proximity to the throne than the seer (cf. Rev 7:9 ἐνώπιον τοῦ θρόνου καὶ ἐνώπιον τοῦ ἀρνίου, (cf. 7:15)) that is, they are standing in the sacred-space between the enthroned elders and the throne, on the sea of glass (cf. Rev 15:2); thus pre-eminent over the living seer.

105 For associative connections between the seven lamps of Rev 4:5 and the seven-lamped menorah (Exod 25; Zech 4) see Briggs 1999: 55–66, and the additional bibliography cited there.

106 For the association of the seven 'spirits' of Rev 1:4 with seven angelic functionaries (rather than the sevenfold spirit of Isa 11), in the light of such an identification at Qumran (e.g. Songs of the Sabbath Sacrifice) and the Similitudes of Enoch, see Aune 1997: 33–5. Cf. also Halperin 1988: 90 for exegetical connections between the torches of Ezek 1:13 and the spirit sent out into all the earth in Zech 6:1-6.

(e.g. I En 20:1; T. Levi 8:2; cf. 'the seven chief princes' of *4Q ShirShabb*).[107]
Finally, the altar (θυσιαστηρίον) (Rev 8:3; cf. Rev 6:9, 8:5, 9:13, 14:18,
16:7), whilst absent from the initial vision of Rev 4–5, is carefully described
in the trumpet-cycle (Rev 8:1ff). The altar described in Rev 8:3-5 functionally
corresponds to the golden-altar of incense (cf. θυμίαμα, 8:3; cf. Rev 9:13)
immediately positioned before the veil in the Holy Place of the wilderness
tabernacle (cf. Exod 30:1-6). Although it is uncertain whether this is the sole
altar referred to in the Apocalypse, as other references (notably Rev 6:9)
may describe the altar of burnt offerings located in the court of priests, it is
apparent that the altar of incense is the intended referent in this context.[108]
Accordingly, it is plausible that the seer, located at the periphery of the circle
of elders, and gazing inward at the central throne, perceives the celestial
equivalent of the menorah (i.e. the seven trumpet (arch)angels) in close
proximity to the celestial golden altar of incense, and that this serves as the
context for his visionary descriptions of the interior of the celestial sanctuary
in Rev 4–5 and 8–9.

Space constraints preclude a more extended discussion of the celestial
temple furnishings and occupants, save for a brief mention of two further
items of spatial significance. A third concentric ring is formed by the myriads
of angels that form an outer circle around the throne (5:11, cf. Dan 7:10),
whilst the crystalline floor of the celestial sanctuary, or sea of glass (θάλασσα
ὑαλίνη) (4:6, cf. Ezek 1:22), most likely corresponds to the dome of the
celestial firmament on which the sanctuary is situated.[109]

Two significant contrasts with the description of the celestial sanctuary
in I Enoch 14:8ff are immediately apparent. First, there is no suggestion of
movement on the part of the seer of the Apocalypse, in marked contrast to
Enoch's inward journey towards the sacred space of the celestial throne room
in I En 14:8-25.[110] Second, and closely related to the previous point, the seer of
the Apocalypse views items that are present in the celestial Holy of Holies (the
throne and living creatures) and the celestial Holy Place (golden incense altar,
menorah) from the outset of his vision. The explanation for both of these
contrasts with I En 14:8ff lies in the vantage point of the seer throughout
Rev 4–5 and 8–9: he is located at the perimeter of the Holy Place within the
wilderness tabernacle in heaven, from where he can gaze on the enthroned
Deity in the celestial Holy of Holies.[111] Rev 4:1ff does not describe the seer's

107   So also Aune 1998a: 508–10; Charles 1920a: 11–13, 224–5; minus seven spirits
Swete 1906: 5–6, 105; Beale 1999: 189–90; for an overview cf. Bucur 2008.

108   Cf. Charles 1920a: 226–30; Briggs 1999: 74–85.

109   Halperin 1988: 93–6.

110   Gooder 2006: 101–2 interprets Rev 4ff as an inversion of I En 14:8ff, a movement
outwards from the central throne; but the text makes no reference to spatial movement –
the seer's gaze moves outwards whilst he remains stationary.

111   Cf. I En 14:25 where Enoch is brought to the threshold (μέχρι τῆς θύρας) of the
celestial Holy Place, without actually entering, in order to communicate with the enthroned
Deity, yet on entering the Holy Place he had already been in a position to see the enthroned
Deity through an open door (I En 14:15ff).

journey through the chambers of the celestial sanctuary, but instead cuts straight to a description of his vision of the One on the throne from within the Holy Place. Rev 4:3ff commences its vision of the celestial sanctuary at the point that Enoch reached in I En 14:13 (entrance into the celestial Holy Place), a point from which no further movement was required to see the enthroned Deity (cf. I En 14:18ff).[112]

Two further questions are raised by this observation: first, why did the author of the Apocalypse not include a description of his visionary ascent to the celestial Holy Place? Second, are there any indications of a boundary between the Holy Place and the Holy of Holies in this vision? In response to question one, it is possible, although highly conjectural in view of the absence of any manuscript support, that an earlier edition included an account of the seer's ascent through three tiered chambers/heavens (comparable to I En 14:8ff), but that this was later removed when the text was redacted, to focus on a singular celestial realm.[113] A tentative response to question two is the suggestion that the rainbow (ἶρις) referred to in Rev 4:3 (cf. Ezek 1:28) may function like the inner 'veil' (פָּרֹכֶת / καταπέτασμα) of the wilderness tabernacle (cf. Exod 26:31, II Chron 3:14).[114] Just as the veil of the wilderness tabernacle was a multi-coloured screen which concealed the Glory of God from the priests in the Holy Place, woven from blue (תְּכֵלֶת / ὑάκινθος) (cf. Rev 9:17), purple (אַרְגָּמָן / πορφύρα) and scarlet (שְׁנִי תּוֹלַעַת / κόκκινος) thread, so also the rainbow in Rev 4:3 is a coloured (σμαργάδινος, 'emerald') screen which conceals the Glory of the enthroned Deity from the seer. Yet, the complete absence of verbal parallels militates against this functional reading for an ancient audience despite the rainbow's apposite spatial location, encircling the cherubim-throne.[115] As a consequence it may be preferable to concede that Rev 4–5, like I En 14:13ff, describes a seer's vision of the enthroned Deity in the Holy of Holies from a privileged vantage point within the celestial Holy Place, as a consequence of the veil having been drawn back (cf. II Cor 3:13-16 (τὸ κάλυμμα)).

Architecturally, the spatial design of the celestial sanctuary has striking verbal parallels with the concentric design of I En 14:8ff, with both texts describing tiers of graded holiness within the shrine as a series of concentric patterns that 'encircle' (κύκλος) the inner sanctum (cf. §3.3.1 above). Whilst these grades are represented by encircling fire around the buildings which divide the temple complex in I En 14:9, 12, in Rev 4ff an analogous function

---

112 Note that the prostrate Enoch does not move again until I En 14:25 – after he has described his vision of the enthroned Deity.

113 Aune 1997: cv–cxxxiv, (First Edition [Rev 1:7-12a + 4:1-22:5], consisting 'almost entirely of a heavenly ascent of the seer' (cxxiv); Charles 1920a: 144–54.

114 For a discussion of the veils of the wilderness tabernacles, especially in relation to the vestments of the High Priest, see Barker 1991: 104–32 and Barker 1998.

115 Each of the three gemstones (ἴασπις, σαρδίον and σμαργάδινος) that are used in Rev 4:3 to describe the multicoloured vision of the One on the throne corresponds rather to gemstones on the High Priest's breastplate (cf. Exod 28:17-18, 36:17-18).

is undertaken by the heavenly occupants themselves (cf. Rev 4:3-4, 6, 8). An interesting contemporary analogue is provided by the architectural design of the utopian Temple in *11Q Temple*, in which the three outer-courts, although not the inner sanctuary itself, are patterned as a series of nested-boxes that emanate outwards from the central sanctuary.[116]

The simplified aerial plan of the boundaries of the οἰκουμένη and the idealized borders of the land of Israel within that are sketched in the Apocalypse's mental map of the earth (cf. Rev 7:1-3; 9:13-15; 20:8) are strongly influenced by comparable sets of four-point border lists (Exod 23:31; Deut 11:24; cf. more elaborate multiple-point descriptions in Ezek 47:15-20 and Num 34:3-12), which envisage these territories as simple four-sided rectangles with four corner-points.[117] These schematic, topographic maps sketch the *political boundaries* of a territory by means of natural landmarks (e.g. river (יָם־סוּף)) and/or civic locations (e.g. Damascus (Ezek 47:17)).

The land mass of the earth (γῆ) is pictured in Rev 7:1 as a square or, more precisely, a three-dimensional cube, with four corners (τέσσαρες γωνία), akin to a four-cornered altar (cf. Ezek 43:20, 45:19 LXX) or four-cornered building (cf. Job 1:19 LXX; cf. I En 18:2-3).[118] This simplified model presents an aerial view of the land mass of earth as it is perceived by a viewer looking down from the celestial sanctuary.[119] Akin to the archaic cosmologies of Homeric era literature, this central land-mass is envisaged to be surrounded by an encircling ocean, referred to as the sea (θάλασσα), which constitutes the corresponding component of the terrestrial sphere (cf. Rev 10:6). The orientation of the four corners of the earth is hinted at in Rev 7:1 by the direct correspondence expressed between the four corners of the earth (αἱ τέσσαρες γωνία τῆς γῆς) and the four winds of the earth (αἱ τέσσαρες ἄνεμοι τῆς γῆς), which emanate from the principal compass points, east, west, north and south (cf. I Chron 9:24 LXX).

Within this broader land-mass (οἰκουμένη) are located the internal borders of the land of Israel (usurped, in the implied author's rhetoric, by the Roman empire) with the river Euphrates functioning as the eastern border (Gen 15:18 LXX; cf. Ex 23:31; Deut 1:7, 11:24; Jos 1:4), forming the eastern side of this interior rectangle.

---

116   Aune 1999; Crawford 2000; Maier 1985; Yadin 1983: 252 (fig. I).

117   Alexander, P. 1992: ABD 2: 985–6; Block 1998: 705–19; Galil and Weinfeld 2000.

118   Aune 1998a: 450–2; Charles 1920a: 203–4; Swete 1906: 94.

119   Cf. also Isa 11:12 and Ezek 7:2 which utilise an analagous cosmic geography but using slightly different terminology, by referring to the 'four wings' (אַרְבַּע כַּנְפוֹת הָאָרֶץ) / (τὰς τέσσαρας πτέρυγας τῆς γῆς) of the earth.

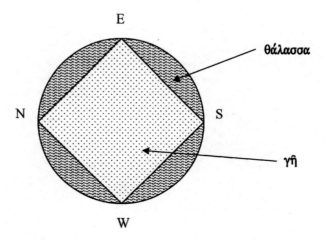

Fig. 3.5 Aerial view of the cuboid earth (γῆ), with four corners (αἱ τέσσαρες γωνία τῆς γῆς) at the principal compass points of the four winds (αἱ τέσσαρες ἄνεμοι τῆς γῆς) (E, S, W, N)[120]

120 On the eastern orientation of Jewish maps see *Jub* 8:22-23 where south is described as lying on the right-hand side. This orientation relates to a common system in the Hebrew Bible that related the compass points to the observer's body: east (front); north (left); west (behind); south (right) (cf. Gen 2:8, 14:15, I Sam 23:24, Job 23:8, 39:26) (cf Alexander, P. 1992: *ABD* 2: 979).

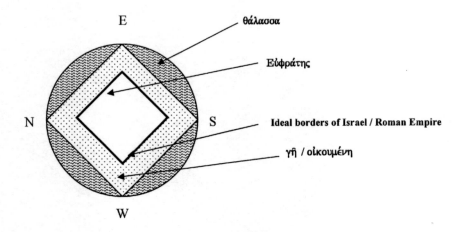

Fig. 3.6 Aerial view of the cuboid earth with interior political boundaries of Israel/Roman empire (Rev 7:1-3; 9:14-15)

The underworld feature that most concerns this study is the 'abyss' (ἄβυσσος) in Rev 9 (Rev 9:1, 2, 11; cf. Rev 11:7; 17:8; 20:1, 3). The term ἄβυσσος (literally, 'without-depth', 'bottomless' (ἄ- βυθός)) is the Septuagint translators' most common translation equivalent for the Hebrew noun תְּהוֹם (primeval, chaos waters) (e.g. Gen 1:2, Amos 7:4, Isa 51:10, Ezek 31:15).[121] The close spatial connection between the subterranean deep and an underworld abode of the shades in Hades creates cosmological associations between these two realms, such that Sheol (Hebrew שְׁאוֹל, Greek ᾅδης) is frequently described as a watery abyss, beneath the terrestrial realm (cf. Jonah 2:1-6; Pss 18:5-6 (17:5-6 LXX); 42:8 (41:8 LXX); 88:3-7 (87:3-7 LXX)).[122] This close correlation between Hades as the realm of the dead located under the earth in close proximity to the surrounding waters of the abyss (or, on occasion, synonymous with the abyss, cf. Jonah 2:3-4; Ps 68:2-3 LXX), creates associative images connecting Hades, the Deep and a Well which will be considered in the exegetical reading of Rev 9:1ff (ch 4).[123] In addition to connections between the subterranean chaos waters of the abyss and Sheol/Hades, Rev 9:2ff also evokes resonances of the subterranean realm as a region of fiery punishment (cf. Isa 66:24; I En 10:6), akin to a

121   Cf. Jeremias, 'ἄβυσσος', TDNT I: 9; Horowitz 1998: 334–47.
122   Aune 1997: 348; Jeremias, 'ᾅδης', TDNT I: 146–9.
123   Bautch 2003: 239–40.

distinctive subterranean mechanism of judgment in the Apocalypse, 'the lake of fire' (ἡ λίμνη τοῦ πυρός) (cf. Rev 19:20; 20:10, 14, 15; 21:8). ἡ λίμνη τοῦ πυρός has perhaps its closest antecedent in the subterranean *river* of fire Πυριφλεγέθων, literally, 'fire-blazing', located in Hades in Greek mythology; cf. Homer, *Odyssey* x. 513; Plato, *Phaedo* 112E–113C; cf. I En 17:5; II En 10:2, which similarly functions as a mode of divine punishment (evocative of theophanic fire).[124]

The cosmic geography of the Apocalypse conforms most closely to an archaic triple-decker template of single heaven, disc-earth, and subterranean abyss. Although there are striking spatial correspondences with the cosmic geography of I En 14:8ff, notably the visualization of heaven as a celestial sanctuary (cf. also II Cor 12:1ff) according to a circular (κύκλος) design-plan, the two texts differ in emphasis with respect to interior divisions. I En 14:8ff foregrounds a sense of movement within three interconnected buildings, which may most plausibly be interpreted as an ascent through three tiered heavens (cf. §3.3.1), whereas the Apocalypse eschews all reference to motion: the seer is positioned already within the celestial Holy Place on entering the heavenly realm (Rev 4:2ff), and there is no evident architectural division between this space and the inner sanctuary. The combination of these two factors supports the Apocalypse's consistent emphasis on a singular heavenly tier (but cf. Rev 12:12; §3.3.1), additionally distinguishing its cosmic-geography from that of II Cor 12:1ff, which explicitly refers to an ascent to (at least) the third heaven.

The Apocalypse's geography of the terrestrial and subterranean realms has most in common with that of I En 17–19 in that both subscribe to a Babylonian/Homeric disc-earth model in which a central continent is surrounded by terrestrial waters, supplied by the underworld abyss (I En 17:7; cf. Rev 9:2ff). Both texts also mix their metaphors, simultaneously depicting the central continent as a four-cornered cube (analogous to a building; cf. I En 18:2-3; Rev 7:1ff), with significant winds at its four compass points. Neither author is particularly interested in detailing the topography of the subterranean realm, although the Apocalypse does equate the abyss with a subterranean Pit/Prison/Sheol (cf. Rev 11:7, 17:8, 20:1, 3), whereas I En 17–19 tends to locate such phenomena at the periphery of the disc-earth (cf. I En 17:7; 18:12, 14).

The Apocalypse's cosmic geography has fewest points of contact with the multiple planetary spheres of Philo's universe, as there is little suggestion within the text that the implied author has been influenced by the ideas, or terminology, expressed in Plato's *Timaeus*.[125] The lack of engagement with a Platonic cosmology may be seen as a further indication of the implied author's limited educational attainment, at least with respect to ἐγκύκλιος

124 Aune 1998b: 1065–7; Charles 1920a: 239–42; Nickelsburg 2001: 282–3.
125 Contra Malina 1992: 2–10 who inaccurately *presupposes* that the Apocalypse ascribes to a multiple planetary spheres model.

παιδεία, demonstrated throughout by the various solecisms and grammatical inelegancies that characterize the language and style of this text.[126] A lack of engagement with Plato's prose *Timaeus* is consistent with a sub-tertiary level *encyclical* education. Yet even if the implied author of the Apocalypse had reached the tertiary cycle it is unlikely that he would have adopted the cosmological worldview associated with the predominant culture as the text offers a counter-voice to the ideological centring of space (Rome) and time (eternity of Roman empire) in imperial ideology: [127]

> [John] tried to disabuse his audience of the notion that Jerusalem, Rome, or any earthly city could function as the geographic center of reality. He instead looked upward, defining God's throne as the meaningful center that infuses all other space with meaning...Rather than settling for the flawed eschatology of the imperial cults in which one prays for the eternal reign of the Roman emperor, John chose a thorough eschatology that held strictly to the integrity of absolute being and demanded the eventual demise of all symbols.[128]

The ordered motion of the heavenly spheres, appealed to as a guide to moral harmony by political philosophers, could never sit comfortably with the Apocalypse's radical re-ordering of spatial categories (cf. Rev 20:11, 21:1).

3.5 Conclusion and Evaluation of Chapters 2–3: Education and Cosmology

The progressive, recapitulative cycles of ἐγκύκλιος παιδεία considered in Chapter 2 indicated a close correlation between the extent of an ancient student's educational attainment and the breadth of literary authors that a student would have studied. One significant transitional point noted was the movement from the predominance of poetic authors and a corresponding shift towards prose writers that characterized the tertiary cycle of education. Accordingly, it is reasonable to hypothesize that the extent of an ancient hearer's educational attainment would influence the cosmological worldview that he adopted and which formed the dominant template of his mental map of the cosmos. Primary/secondary educated students, whose literary knowledge was limited to extracts from epic poets, tragedians and comics, would most plausibly ascribe to a Homeric triple-decker template. Students from more illustrious families, by contrast, who attained to the pinnacle of the educational cycle,

---

126   Aune 1997: clx–ccvi; Charles 1920a: cxvii–clix; Mussies 1971; Porter 1989; but cf. the caveat by Beale 1997 that some solecisms function as signals (to the hearers) of scriptural allusion.

127   Friesen 2001: 122–31,152–66.

128   Friesen 2001: 165–6.

could be expected to perceive the world through Plato's template of planetary spheres, given precedence over alternative models with which he was cognizant.

The validity of such a hypothesis has been given added credence in this chapter by the concise discussion of Philo's mental map of the cosmos (§3.3.2). This tertiary-educated hearer's cosmological perspective has indeed been shaped by his study of Plato's *Timaeus*, such that alternative models (e.g. the triple-decker universe of the Torah) are re-focused through these lenses, allegorically interpreted to conform to, rather than critique, his dominant cognitive map. Yet this simplistic dichotomy requires further nuancing to prevent educational attainment from being innacurately perceived to be the sole determinative variable on an ancient hearer's cosmology. In this regard, Paul's divergent, hybrid cosmology is a pertinent reminder of additional factors. The precise level of education which Paul attained remains a keenly disputed point, with some interpreters (e.g. Hock) arguing for an extensive tertiary level education on the basis of the rhetorical subtlety of Paul's letter composition, while others more cautiously position him at a secondary stage of tuition (e.g. Barclay, Porter and Pitts (*progymnasmata*)).[129] Yet regardless of the precise level attained, Paul confounds expectation by subscribing to a hybrid-cosmos which neither Homer nor Plato could wholly claim authorship. In short, the hybrid cosmology of a triple-decker universe with a multi-tiered heaven evidences influences from literature outside the confines of genres and authors that Paul was likely to have studied as part of a Greek *encyclical* course of studies.

The educational attainment of an ancient student is undoubtedly a significant factor in determining an individual's cosmological worldview, but must not be collapsed into a direct correlation. Unlike Philo, Paul describes his ascent to the heavenly realm using language that is more consistent with the visionary ascent literature of I Enoch than the recommended reading lists of ἐγκύκλιος παιδεία. In view of diverse streams of influence that combine to constitute the contents of an ancient hearer's mental library many hearers are required to decide which mental map is predominant for them, selecting from a range of alternative templates contained in their mental library, specifically tailoring the choice to suit the specific context (or literary genre) which they are writing or hearing.

A comparably nuanced assessment of the correlation between a student's educational attainment and the breadth of literary authors known was outlined in Chapter 2. Whilst a student's mental library progressively expanded as she traverses the circle of ἐγκύκλιος παιδεία, as additional

---

129   Barclay 1996: 383–4; Hock 2003; Porter and Pitts 2008. For recent critiques of interpreting Paul's epistles according to the conventions of Graeco-Roman rhetoric (presuming a tertiary-level education); cf. Andersen 1999; Kern 1995; Tolmie 2005, in sharp contrast to Mitchell 1991 who offers a nuanced interpretation of I Corinthians according to the conventions of deliberative rhetoric.

authors (e.g. Aratus) and genres (e.g. prose histories (Herodotus)) are encountered at significant transitional points, the full breadth of an ancient hearer's mental library is rarely supplied by this solitary stream. The two test case examples of Philo and Josephus (§§2.5.1 and 2.5.2) amply demonstrated how additional, non-literary texts could be added from alternative cultural contexts, to create a unique mental map for each ancient hearer.

The foregoing analysis of Greek *encyclical* education, with its significant, yet not determinative, influence in shaping the distinctive mental library of each ancient student will inform the exegetical studies that follow (Chapters 4 and 5). The contours of each hearer-construct's mental library will be carefully shaped to include a set of literary texts that are consistent with his/her level of educational attainment, supplemented by an additional set of 'extra-curricular' scriptural texts. Accordingly, each hearer-construct's preferred cosmological model will reflect a conscious choice, selected from the range of alternative mental maps of which s/he is cognizant. The overall aim of chapters 4 and 5 is to offer two nuanced, and historically plausible, readings of Rev 9:1ff, that creatively interact with this passage's cosmology and visionary imagery, informed by the pre-existing contents of each hearer-construct's mental library.

Chapter 4

HEARER-CONSTRUCT ONE (HC1):
Interpretation of the Cosmology of Rev 9:1-19

4.1 Introduction

This chapter outlines the first of two hearer-construct readings of Rev 9, focusing upon the hypothetical response of an ancient hearer with a minimal Greek *encyclical* education. The contents of hearer-construct one's (HC1's) mental library is first delineated (§4.2). HC1's mental library is dominated by a carefully prescribed range of scriptural texts, and supplemented by a minimal set of literary authors (Homer, *Iliad* I–II; Menander, *Misoumenos*; Euripides, *Phoenissae*). Next, HC1's interpretative method is sketched (§4.3), informed by ancient theories of memory and recollection, and attentive to the influence of pre-existing interpretative traditions.

HC1's response to the cosmology of this chapter is divided into two parts: trumpet five (Rev 9:1-12) (§4.4) and trumpet six (Rev 9:13-19) (§4.5). In each section a central concern is plausibly to (re-)construct how HC1 may interpret the cosmic-geographical imagery, on the basis of the specific range of texts contained in her mental library, informed by her pre-existing cosmological knowledge, and interpretative method. As a consequence, particular attention is paid to 'the well of the abyss' (τὸ φρέαρ τῆς ἀβύσσου) (Rev 9:1-2), and the great river Euphrates (ὁ ποταμὸς ὁ μέγας Εὐφράτης) (Rev 9:14-15). In addition, HC1's interpretation of the hybrid locusts (Rev 9:7-9), bound angels (Rev 9:14-15), and trimorphic cavalry (Rev 9:17-19) that populate the cosmological template will be assessed.

The chapter concludes (§4.6) by considering the influence exerted on HC1's interpretation by a limited range of visual and verbal images evoked by Joel 1–2, Ezek 38–39, Amos 7:1 LXX, Deut 11:24, and I En 16–17, plus an evaluation of the relative significance of her *encyclical* education.

4.2 HC1: Definition and Mental Library

Hearer-construct one, who is the focus of this first exegetical study (hereafter HC1), is situated in a major urban centre within Asia Minor in the late first or early second century CE. HC1 is credited with a formal Greek literary education, but only to a basic level of competence (completion of the first cycle of education): she is able to read public inscriptions and contracts, and to read, and copy short passages in an 'alphabetic' school-hand.[1]

HC1 is an imaginative construct informed by textual clues as to the approximate compositional date of the Apocalypse, and the provenance of its earliest 'intended audiences', but stops short of a sociological study of this text's earliest recipients.[2] The 'target audience' of the Apocalypse has long been a central component in the interpretation of the work, not least because of the embedded proclamations addressed to seven assemblies in the western Asia Minor cities of Ephesus, Smyrna, Pergamum, Thyatira, Sardis, Philadelphia and Laodicea (Rev 2–3).[3] The advantage of such research has been an acute awareness that, from a socio-historical perspective, the intended audience of the Apocalypse was not an amorphous block but rather a variety of groups each exhibiting a diversity of responses to issues that concerned the author (notably with respect to the degree of assimilation to the surrounding civic culture):

> Revelation had several social settings, not one...The fact that the early chapters of Revelation address assemblies in seven different urban centers... suggests that we are dealing with a complicated interaction of one writer with several social settings. We cannot assume a homogenous audience for

1   Cribiore 1996: 112: Alphabetic hand: 'This is the hand of a learner, or someone who may be relied upon to write the alphabet accurately and without hesitation but who has not yet developed hand-eye coordination...and he always seems to proceed at a slow pace. This kind of hand is not trusted to do a lot of writing, and it obtains poor overall effects.' Characteristic examples of this second grade of handwriting are provided by papyri 192 and 193; Cribiore 1996: 218. The former is a copy of a saying of Diogenes and a short extract from a Euripidean satyr play, and the latter selected lines from *Iliad* II (*Il.* II. 527, 536, 546, 581, 557, 591, 559, 569, 484).

To avoid the infelicitous use of s/he, his/her, etc. throughout the exegetical chapters HC1 will be referred to using the feminine pronoun and HC2 with the masculine pronoun. Whilst these hearer-construct models are self-evidently 'neither male nor female' but rather collections of texts with an ascribed method, nonetheless, the decision to refer to HC1 using the feminine gender is consistent with the greater likelihood that a female would attain a primary/secondary level of encyclical education than a tertiary level education (cf. §2.4).

2   On dating see Aune 1997: lvi–llxx; Beale 1999: 4–27; Friesen 2001: 135–51; Thompson 1990; vanKooten 2007; Yarbro Collins 1984.

On the basis of internal references that most plausibly presuppose the death of Nero (68 CE), coupled with external attestation of the work by Justin (d. c.160 CE), possibly Papias (d. c. 130 CE) and P[98] (c. 2nd century CE), I would situate the final form of the Apocalypse in the period c.68–120 CE. The conflicting and ambiguous nature of much of the internal evidence (esp. Rev 17:9-11), perhaps indicative of redactional stages in the text's composition, caution against a more precise date, such that Irenaeus' testimony of a date late in Domitian's reign (*Adv. Haer.* 5.30.3) remains a plausible, but ultimately unverifiable, option.

3   Cf. Ascough 2005; Duff 2001; Hemer 1986; Ramsay 1904.

John's visions nor can we assume that the visions addressed one uniform situation.[4]

A narratalogical focus on a singular, homogenized response by a mono-lithic 'implied audience' construct fails to come to grips with the mul-tilayered social contexts of the communities addressed in Rev 2-3.[5] Yet this 'flattening out' of the diversity of responses of the target audience appears to be one of the central rhetorical aims of the implied author. Outside of Rev 2-3 all the diverse members of the target audience are characterized as a unified group, the one people of God (cf. Rev 7), com-prising saints, apostles, prophets and martyrs (cf. Rev 6:9-11; 18:20) dualistically opposed to the forces of chaos.[6] The Apocalypse's intended hearers are persuaded, by the textual rhetoric, to reassess their internal disagreements and varying degrees of external assimilation in the light of the total picture of reality that is painted, in starkly monochrome colours, in the mytho-poetic visions of Rev 4–22.[7] The diverse members of the target audience are encouraged to imitate the single-minded faith-fulness of the people of God in the visions, and avoid assimilating with the prevailing culture, which the author caricatures as a demonic Other, the kingdom of the Beast (cf. Rev 13–17).

This chapter focuses on the reception of the Apocalypse by a hypothetical early hearer of this text as it was read aloud in a worship setting in an Asia Minor city. HC1 is envisaged as being familiar with the whole of Rev 1–22 through frequent, and repeated, oral delivery; HC1 is not a 'first-time hearer' whose experience of the text is limited to the preceding chapters of the visionary narrative.[8] The aim is to utilize this model to consider the impact that an ancient hearer's educational background had on his/her inter-pretation of Rev 9. Accordingly, I will begin by delineating the contents of HC1's mental library, indicating the range of literary texts with which this hearer-construct was already familiar.

HC1's mental library will be limited to two streams of influence, for the purposes of the present investigation: 'scriptural' texts heard in the context of an Asia Minor assembly, and portions of literary texts studied as part of her *encyclical* education. The precise range of 'scriptural' texts that HC1 will be presumed to know is not an arbitrary list, but rather closely corre-sponds to the core group of texts that are most frequently alluded to within the Apocalypse, and which are thus most integral to an ancient audience's competent interpretation of this work. On this basis HC1's mental library will partially overlap with the mental library of the implied audience of the Apocalypse, the textual construct of the monolithic 'target audience' of the

4   Friesen 2005: 352.
5   Cf. §1.3.
6   Cf. Pattemore 2004: 68–116.
7   Friesen 2005: 371–2.
8   Cf. Barr 1986.

composition presupposed by the implied author, as indicated, in part, by the range of verbal parallels and allusions to scriptural texts within the work.[9]

In view of the subjective nature of the process, coupled with variations in the range and definition of terminology (quotation, allusion, echo, etc.), the precise contours of the lists of literary texts alluded to in the Apocalypse differ almost from scholar to scholar.[10] Despite the very real divergences between scholars in their detection and adjudication of scriptural parallels on a case-by-case basis in the Apocalypse, a dominant core-group of five subtexts nonetheless remains broadly consistent across a range of studies: Isaiah, Daniel, Ezekiel, Jeremiah and Psalms.[11] This dominant core-group is closely followed by an extensive range of parallels to individual booklets within larger collections, that is, the Twelve (notably Zechariah, Joel, Amos and Hosea) and the Pentateuch (notably Exodus).[12] This core list of ten scriptural texts will be supplemented by one additional prophetic booklet, namely I Enoch 1–36 (especially I En 14 and 17–19 (cf. §3.3.1)). The high regard in which portions of I Enoch were held by a range of early Christian authors is widely documented, with a number of references to Enoch as a 'prophet' (Jude 14–15; cf. II Pet 2:4-5) and his prophecies formally cited or paraphrased, (cf. Irenaeus, *Adv. Haer.* 4.16.2; Tertullian, *De cult fem* 3; Origen, *De principiis* 4.4.8).[13]

In addition to the eleven prophetically authored texts that HC1 is familiar with from oral proclamations in her Asia Minor assembly, her mental library also contains a small core of literary texts derived from her formal Greek *encyclical* education: Homer, *Iliad* (Books I–II), and some short extracts from Euripides (*Phoenissae*) and Menander (*Misoumenos*). The 'core' and 'periphery' of the contents of HC1's mental library are represented in fig. 4.1.

---

9   Cf. Aune 2006: 45–7.

10   Cf. Köstenberger 2006.

11   Cf. Beale 1984; 1998: 60–128; Charles 1920a: lxviii–lxxxiii; Fekkes 1994; 2006; Kowalski 2004; Moyise 1995: 14–18; Swete 1906: cxlviii–cxlix.

12   Cf. Charles 1920a: lxv; Jauhiainen 2005; Moyise 1995: 16; Strazicich 2007: 335–77.

13   Nickelsburg 2001: 82–108; vanBeek 2000; VanderKam 1996.

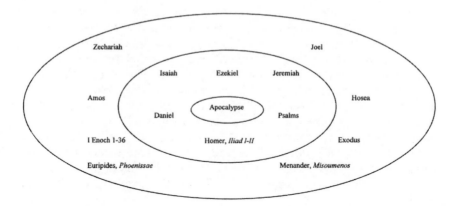

Fig. 4.1 The Contents of HC1's Mental Library

4.3 HC1's Interpretative Method

> This is the interpretation of this vision that you have seen: The eagle that you
> saw coming up from the sea is the fourth kingdom that appeared in a vision
> to your brother Daniel.
> But it was not explained to him as I now explain to you or have explained it.

> haec est interpretatio visionis huius quam vidisti: aquilam quam vidisti ascen-
> dentem de mari, hoc est regnum quartum, quod visum est in visu Danihelo
> fratri tuo, sed non est illi interpretatum, quomodo ego nunc tibi interpretor
> vel interpretavi.

(IV Ezra 12:10-12)[14]

The target audience of the collection of dream-visions attributed to Ezra
(late 1st century CE) is guided to perceive a correlation between the
eagle vision of IV Ezra 11:1–12:3 and the former vision of the prophet
Daniel (Dan 7).[15] The visionary experience of the seer, Ezra, is placed in
continuity with that of his brother (*frater*) Daniel, as he is portrayed as
're-envisioning' Daniel's vision of the four kingdoms.[16] Yet the interpre-

---

14   NRSV/Vulgate.
15   On the date, provenance and genre of IV Ezra see Longenecker 1995: 1–32; Stone
1990 and for its reception-history see Hamilton 1999.
16   Cf. Rev 22:9 'οἱ ἀδελφοὶ σου τῶν προφητῶν' for a similar correlation between
the seer of the Apocalypse and other early Christian prophets and (implicitly) former,
'scriptural' prophets notably Isaiah, Ezekiel and Daniel whose visions are continually re-
imagined throughout the text: cf. Aune 1989.

tative comments, if not also the visual content, are afforded a new and implicitly 'fuller' sense in Ezra's case (cf. IV Ezra 12:35-36). The exegetical (re-)interpretation of Daniel 7 that is evidenced in IV Ezra 11–12 is not presented in the form of a commentary on the former text, but rather the content of Dan 7 is recast in a new visionary form in these chapters, and provided with its own divinely revealed interpretation.

HC1's reception of Rev 9:1ff is closely comparable to that of the target audience of IV Ezra, in that she too interprets the orally received disclosure as a 're-envisioning' of former visions, rather than as a scribal re-interpretation of scripture.[17] By extension, the analysis that follows is not centred on a compositional study of the author of the Apocalypse's 'use' or 'exegetical reinterpretation' of scripture.[18] Instead, it is intended to elucidate how HC1's reception of Rev 9:1ff is guided by her recollection of former visions contained in her mental library, which Rev 9:1ff evokes in a modified or expanded form.

What criteria does HC1 use to single out which vision, or cluster of visions, are 're-envisioned' by the seer in Rev 9:1ff? The first criterion is *visual reminiscence*: which images in HC1's mental library are recalled by the striking verbal images conjured up by the text currently being performed? In ancient Greek theoretical treatises on memory, notably Aristotle's *On Memory and Recollection* (περὶ μνήμη καὶ ἀναμνήσεως), every item of knowledge, received through the five senses, is understood to be absorbed into the memory and stored as a collection of *mental images* (φαντάσματα), indented on the subject's ψυχή, like a series of impressions formed on a wax tablet:[19]

> It is, then, obvious, that memory (ἡ μνήμη) refers to that part of the soul (ψυχή) to which imagination (φαντασία) refers; all things which are mental pictures (φάντασμα), are in themselves subjects of memory...For it is obvious that one must consider such a thing which occurs in the soul by means of the sense perception, and in that part of the body which contains the soul as a kind of painted portrait (ζωγράφημα) – an affection (πάθος), the lasting state of which we describe as memory; for the movement produced implies some impression of sense movement (οἷον τύπον τινὰ τοῦ αἰσθήματος), just as when men seal with signet rings (καθάπερ οἱ σφραγιζόμενοι τοῖς δακτυλίοις).
>
> (Aristotle, *On Memory*, 450a22ff)[20]

17   On the issue of whether genuine visionary experience lies behind the Apocalypse, see Rowland 2006.

18   On various criteria used to define and distinguish citations, allusions and echoes of scripture in the Apocalypse see Beale 1997, 1999; Hays 1989; Moyise 2000; Paul 2000; and Paulien 2000.

19   Cf. Carruthers 2008: 18–37; Small 1997: 81–94; Yates 1966: 42–53.

20   Hett 1935: 286–9; cf. Bloch 2007: 53–79 who proposes that φάντασμα is used to denote a pictorial image which forms a memory impression, that has both physical and non-physical components, and functions as an image of a past sensation.

To recollect (ἀναμιμνῄσκω) items stored in the memory as a mental picture (φάντασμα), involved 'seeing again' the internal pictures, stimulated by the visual senses: '…recollection is the search for a mental picture in a body' (ἡ ἀνάμνησις ζήτησις ἐν τοιούτῳ φαντάσματος) (*On Memory*, 453a13–14).[21] Such recollection involved an affective (πάθος) remembrance of both the image and the emotional impression formed when it was first imprinted on the memory (cf. Aristotle, *On Memory*, 451b1–29).[22] As Vasaly describes, an ancient orator's ability to 'move', and thus to persuade, his listening audience, tapped into the emotive and pictorial aspects of memory and recollection: the orator first recalled evocative mental images stored in his own memory, before verbally describing the same images (using the technique of ἔκφρασις) to create comparable, vivid, mental images in his audience's mind (cf. Quintilian, *Inst. Or.* vi.2.8, 20–36 on πάθος/*adfectus*):[23]

> …the speaker first summons images [φαντάσματα/*visiones*] from his memory where they are stored; if the orator is skilful and imaginative, these stimulate the particular emotional response that he had hoped to create in himself; the orator then, through vivid description [ἔκφρασις], stimulates corresponding *visiones* in the minds of his audience; and these, in turn, produce a seemingly inevitable emotional reaction in his listeners. The process by which the mind of the orator is moved and that by which his audience is moved is, in essence, the same. A particular image (*visio*), summoned to mind, sets in motion a predictable emotional response (*pathos*).[24]

Techniques of *artificial* memory retention and recall, practised to varying degrees by Graeco-Roman orators, required the subject to memorise the components of a case or the parts of a speech (*res*), or even the entire verbal contents of a declamation (*verba*), by representing them as a series of mental images (*imagines*),[25] arranged on a carefully ordered set of imaginary backgrounds (τόποι/*loci*) (usually a mental image of an architectural structure, such as the rooms of a *domus*) (cf. *Rhetorica ad Herennium*, 3.28–40; Cicero, *De Oratore* 2.350–60; Quintilian, *Inst. Or.* 11.2.1–51).[26]

---

21   Hett 1935: 304–5.
22   Carruthers 2008: 19, 62–5. Yates 1966: 48.
23   The compositional technique of ἔκφρασις, as taught in *progymnastic* exercises, will be recalled in the next chapter (§5.3).
24   Vasaly 1993: 88–130 (96–7).
25   *Rhetorica ad Herennium* 3.29: 'An image (*imagines*) is, as it were, a figure (*formae*), mark (*notae*), or portrait (*simulacra*) of the object we wish to remember.' Caplan 1954: 208–9.
26   Caplan 1954; Russell 2001; Sutton and Rackman 1942; cf. Small 1997: 81–116; Small 2007; Yates 1966: 17–41.
Note the striking visual clarity of such mental images: recommended backgrounds are abandoned structures, that are well-lit, with numerous rooms, and with each *locus* no more than thirty feet apart (or the viewer no more than thirty feet from the image, Carruthers 2008: 90); (*Rhetorica ad Herennium* 3.31–2); Caplan 1954: 99–100.

The orator then travels through these memory-rooms, in his mind's eye, when making the speech, recalling the images deposited in each *loci* and accordingly the *res* or *verbum* that each one represents.[27] Particularly noteworthy is the brief description of the vivid set of *imagines* most recommended by the author of *Rhetorica ad Herennium* for creating a lasting, memorable, impression:

> We ought, then, to set up images (*imagines*) of a kind that can adhere longest in the memory. And we shall do so if we establish likenesses (*similitudines*) as striking as possible; if we set up images that are not many or vague, but *doing something* (*agentes imagines*); if we assign to them exceptional beauty (*egregiam pulcritudinem*) or *singular ugliness* (*unicam turpitudinem*); if we *dress some of them with crowns* (*coronis*) or purple cloaks, for example, so that the likenesses may be more distinct to us; or if we somehow disfigure (*deformabimus*) them, as by introducing one stained with blood or soiled with mud or smeared with red paint, so that its form is more striking, or by assigning certain comic effects to our images, for that, too, will ensure our remembering them more readily.
>
> (*Rhetorica ad Herennium*, 3.37)[28]

The grotesque depiction of the active verbal images of the hybrid locusts (Rev 9:7-9), disfigured and crowned, or the vibrant colour-terms associated with the galloping tri-morphic cavalry (Rev 9:17-19) would be regarded as ideally memorable images, strikingly evocative of comparable verbal depictions already impressed upon an ancient hearer's memory (notably the hybrid locust army of Joel 1–2), designed to evoke an affective, emotional response (πάθος) in the listening audience.[29] The principal criterion, therefore, concerns the detection of associative mental images (φαντάσματα) contained in the hearer-construct's mental library, and the resulting 'rebirth of those images' that occurs in their reconfigured form as the hearer listens to the orally performed text.[30]

---

27   Such a technique has suggestive connections with the movements of a seer through the ordered rooms of the celestial temple in a dream-vision (e.g. I En 14), recalling the fantastic *imagines* located therein.

28   Caplan 1954: 220–1 (my italics).

29   Neither the implied author of the Apocalypse, nor HC1, are understood to possess a rhetorical education, by which they might have learned artificial memory techniques. The oratorical examples are used here to highlight the intimate connection perceived between memory, internal memory-pictures, and emotional response to images in the cultural context of the Graeco-Roman era.

30   The incomparable Austin Farrer eloquently evokes the poetic associations of the rich networks of images that are reshaped and reborn in the Apocalypse: 'We can study in this book not only the images, but the process of inspiration by which they are born in the mind...If we appreciate the connexion [between images] rightly, we feel the new image emerging out of the hidden mind under the evocation of the images already in place...'; Farrer 1949: 13–22 (18).

The second, interrelated, criterion concerns the density, or 'volume' to utilize Hays' terminology, of *verbal reminiscences*.[31] Previous oral performances of comparable visions and imagery are recalled by HC1, from the contents of her mental library, where there are a significant cluster of *precise verbal parallels* of the former vision in the context of the orally delivered narrative. This criterion supplements and supports the principal criterion of *visual reminiscences*, by offering a standard by which to identity resonant images in the hearer-construct's mental library.

Yet an ancient hearer's memory recall did not simply function like a concordance, but rather the recollection of a significant former vision carries along with it a cluster of associative parallels, based on pre-existing interpretative traditions. In this regard, HC1's mental library may be metaphorically compared to physical 'memory aids', in the form of notebooks and *testimonia*, in which passages were exegetically interrelated by being juxtaposed on the same leaf or scroll (cf. 4Q 174 *(florilegium)*, 4Q 175 *(testimonia)*).[32] Such an approach conforms to ancient metaphors of memory, already noted, which likened memory to a wax-tablet, or scroll, inscribed with images (cf. Cicero, *De oratore* 2.86–8; *Rhetorica ad Herennium* 3.17).[33] HC1's recollection of Joel's former vision (Joel 1–2), on the basis of visual reminiscences evoked by the Apocalypse's hybrid-cavalry, and supplemented by the high 'volume' of verbal parallels, recalls, alongside it, pre-existing exegetical connections (with Exodus 10, Ezekiel 38–39 and Amos 7:1 LXX) which informed her pre-understanding of eschatological locust-cavalry. The third criterion is therefore the presence of *pre-existing interpretative traditions* that formed clusters of associative meaning.

Finally, HC1's interpretation of the cosmic-geography of Rev 9:1ff will be informed by the range of cosmological templates contained in her mental library, and in particular her predisposition to favour the triple-decker template that is predominant (cf. esp. I En 1–36, Homer, *Iliad* I–II).

4.4 HC1's Interpretation of the Fifth Trumpet (Rev 9:1-12)

4.4.1 The Well of the Abyss (Rev 9:1-2)

¹ Καὶ ὁ πέμπτος ἄγγελος ἐσάλπισεν· καὶ εἶδον ἀστέρα ἐκ τοῦ οὐρανοῦ πεπτωκότα εἰς τὴν γῆν, καὶ ἐδόθη αὐτῷ ἡ κλεὶς τοῦ φρέατος τῆς ἀβύσσου

---

31   Hays 1989: 29–32.
32   4Q 174 juxtaposed a range of texts including Ex 15:17-18, Amos 9:11, Ps 1:1, Isa 8:11, Ps 2:1, Dan 12:10. 4Q 175 juxtaposed Deut 5:28-29, 18:18-19; Num 24:15-17; Deut 33:8-11; Jos 6:26; cf. García Martínez 1994: 136–8.
    Compare Skarsaune 1987 for a discussion of Justin's knowledge and use of collections of 'proof-texts', which similarly extracted and arranged exegetically related passages.
33   Cf. Carruthers 2008: 32–33.

² καὶ ἤνοιξεν τὸ φρέαρ τῆς ἀβύσσου, καὶ ἀνέβη καπνὸς ἐκ τοῦ φρέατος ὡς καπνὸς καμίνου μεγάλης, καὶ ἐσκοτώθη ὁ ἥλιος καὶ ὁ ἀὴρ ἐκ τοῦ καπνοῦ τοῦ φρέατος.

1. And the fifth angel trumpeted: and I saw a star which had fallen out of heaven onto the earth, and the key of the well of the abyss was given to him. 2. And he opened the well of the abyss, and smoke ascended from the well like (the) smoke of a great furnace, and the sun was darkened and the air because of the smoke of the well.

The tripartite cosmological template of the Apocalypse is explicitly enunciated in the opening lines of the fifth trumpet blast: heaven (οὐρανός), earth (γῆ), and abyss (ἄβυσσος) (cf. §3.4). The descending tiers of the cosmos are animated by the movement of a solitary star (ἀστήρ),[34] stationary now on the terrestrial disc, after a prior decent from the firmament above (πεπτωκότα), having unlocked the access-point to the lowest tier (τὸ φρέαρ τῆς ἀβύσσου).

The third trumpet blast (Rev 8:10-11) similarly resulted in a solitary star (ἀστήρ) falling (πίπτω) from heaven to earth, but on the former occasion it had descended upon more broadly defined targets, a third of the rivers of the (disc)-earth, and the adjacent springs. Its designation, ὁ Ἄψινθος, is unique, as no star or constellation is so named in Graeco-Roman antiquity (cf. Aratus, *Phaenomena*),[35] descriptive, rather, of its effects in turning the water courses bitter, due to its herbal properties (absinth).[36] Whilst that star, in line with Neoplatonic thought, is regarded as a living being (cf. Plato, *Laws*, 898D–899D), the emphasis in Rev 8:10-11 is on its vast size (ἀστὴρ μέγας), rather than its living agency, such that its impact covers a third of the (disc)-earth.

The great burning mountain (ὄρος μέγα πυρὶ καιόμενον) (Rev 8:8-9) that plunged into the sea at the blowing of the second trumpet is similarly reminiscent of a star/heavenly being, not least because of a comparable image in HC1's mental library. I Enoch 18:6-16 locates the place of punishment of seven errant stars 'like great burning mountains' (ἑπτὰ ἀστέρας ὡς ὄρη μεγάλα καιόμενα) (I En 18:13), in a great chasm (χάσμα μέγα) beyond the firmament (cf. figs. 3.1–3.3).[37] Seven disobedient stars who failed to come out at their (appointed) times (I En 18:15; cf I En 80:4-6) are punished by being denied all access to their divinely apportioned station, the interior vault

---

34   A singular reading in the original hand of Codex Sinaiticus (א*) significantly alters the meaning: a plurality of stars (ἀστέρας) form a pyrotechnic prelude to the opening of the well of abyss (cf. Rev 6:12–13), whilst the key of the abyss is entrusted to the fifth trumpet angel (the nearest antecedent to αὐτῷ) not the descended angel; cf. Hernández 2006: 204.

35   Kidd 1997.

36   Cf. Aune 1998a: 521–2.

37   Black 1970: 31.

of the celestial hemisphere, sentenced instead to a ten thousand-year impris-onment in a fiery void, located outside the borders of heaven and earth. The precise identity of these seven errant stars is not explicated in the text, but it is plausible that they denote either the wandering (πλανάω) orbits of the seven planets (cf. Rev 1:16), or a seven-starred constellation.[38]

The fallen 'star' of Rev 9:1-2 evokes ambiguously conflicting images in HC1's mental library. There are strong resonances of the recently recited second and third trumpets in the septet (Rev 8:8-11; cf. I En 18:6-16), which serve to relate this celestial functionary to the declination of an errant star or planet, deviating from its regulated orbit, so as to function as both prodigy and agent of cosmic destruction.[39] Yet the divinely designated nature of its task (ἐδόθη, Rev 9:1γ) tempers such wholly negative associations, and hints at affinities with the angelic functionary of Rev 20:1-3 who will similarly descend (καταβαίνω, not πίπτω) from heaven with the key of the abyss (ἡ κλεὶς τῆς ἀβύσσου), but on that occasion to detain the Devil for a millennium, prior to his trial and execution (Rev 20:10), rather than unleash the chaos forces within.[40]

HC1's understanding of the spatial location and function of τὸ φρέαρ τῆς ἀβύσσου is informed by her pre-existing mental map of the cosmos. Whilst the range of texts that constitute HC1's mental library do not depict a uniform model, they do, nonetheless, exclusively subscribe to an archaic triple-decker template (single heaven, disc-earth, subterranean abyss), which is consistent with the cosmological template expressed in the Apocalypse.[41]

Whilst the precise phrase τὸ φρέαρ τῆς ἀβύσσου is unattested in the LXX or the extant Greek fragments of I Enoch 1–36, HC1 is nonetheless already conscious of a close connection between a network of subterranean wells (φρέατα) and the Deep (ἄβυσσος); metaphorical depictions of Hades (ᾅδης) as a well/pit; and a significant, solitary shaft that functions as the source of the terrestrial waters.[42] A consideration of the functional significance of a

38   Cf. Aune 1997: 97–8: οἱ ἑπτὰ ἀστέρες predominantly denote either the seven planets, or certain seven-starred constellations, e.g. the Great Bear (ἡ μεγάλη Ἀρκτος) (cf. Aratus, *Phaenomena* 26–44), in the Hellenistic and Roman eras; cf. Nickelsburg 2001: 289.

39   On 'falling stars' as portents or prodigies of cosmic destruction, cf. Adams 2007: 52–132; Aune 1998a: 416–19.

40   In Roman law imprisonment functioned primarily as a means of detention for those awaiting trial (or the completion of the judicial process) rather than as a judicial sentence of imprisonment following trial; cf. Rapske 1994: 9–35.

41   As noted in §3.3.1 I Enoch 14:8ff may depict three heavenly tiers, rather than a single heaven divided into three chambers, but such a reading is not unambiguous, and HC1 is accordingly more likely to read Rev 9 in line with her predominant cosmological template.

42   HC1's mental library (LXX):

i) φρέαρ – Gen 14:10; 16:14; 21:14, 19, 25, 30, 31, 32; 22:19; 24:11, 20, 62; 25:11; 26:15, 18, 19, 20, 21, 23, 25, 32, 33; 28:10; 29:2, 3, 8, 10; 46:1, 5; Ex 2:15; Num 21:16, 17, 18, 22; Ps 54:24; 68:16; Amos 5:5; Isa 15:8; Jer 14:3; 48:7, 9.

ii) ἄβυσσος – Gen 1:2, 7:11, 8:2; Deut 8:7, 33:13; Ps 32:7; 35:7; 41:8; 70:20, 21; 76:17;

well (φρέαρ) and closely related phenomena (such as a pit or spring) in ANE cosmology as evidenced in poetic texts contained in HC1's mental library, as well as the spatial location of 'the mouth of the abyss' (τὸ στόμα τῆς ἀβύσσου) in the cosmic geography of I En 17, will elucidate the potential significance of τὸ φρέαρ τῆς ἀβύσσου for HC1.

In ANE cosmic geography the water of a 'well' (Hebrew: בְּאֵר, Greek: φρέαρ) or 'spring' (Hebrew: עַיִן or מָקוֹר, Greek: πηγή) is supplied by the subterranean waters (*Apsu*) beneath the surface of the earth.[43] In principle a well-shaft (φρέαρ) is distinguished from a spring (πηγή) on the basis of its formation: a spring is a natural fissure in the disc-earth, whereas a well is an artificial shaft that is cut-down into the bed-rock (cf. Gen 21:25-33; 26:15-33).[44] This sharp distinction cannot be pressed, however, as in a number of passages in the LXX φρέαρ is placed in synonymous parallelism with πηγή (cf. Gen 16:7-14, 24:16-20).[45] The functional correspondence between a well and a spring, as a point of access between the disc-earth and the watery abyss, unites these two types of shaft, regardless of the means of their production. Whilst the principal function of a well or spring is to enable the inhabitants of the disc-earth to gain access to the primeval subterranean waters beneath the earth (Hebrew: תְּהוֹם, Greek: ἄβυσσος) it may also function as a passageway through which the shades of the watery underworld may ascend (cf. I Sam 28 and the νεκυία in *Odyssey* xi.), or inhabitants located on the disc-world may descend to the realm beneath (cf. Aristophanes, *Frogs*; Pausanius, 'The Oracle of Trophonius at Lebadeia (Boetia)', *Description of Greece* IX.39.1–IX.40.2).[46]

The term ἄβυσσος (literally, 'without-depth', 'bottomless' (ἀ- βυθός)) is the Septuagint translators' most common translation-equivalent for the Hebrew noun תְּהוֹם (primeval, chaos waters) (e.g. Gen 1:2, Amos 7:4, Isa 51:10, Ezek 31:15).[47] The close spatial connection between the subterranean deep and an underworld abode of the shades in Hades creates cosmological associations,

---

77:15; 103:6; 105:9; 106:26; 134:6; 148:7; Amos 7:4; Jon 2:6; Hab 3:10; Isa 44:27; 51:10; 63:13; Ezek 26:19; 31:4, 15; Dan 3:55.

iii) φρέαρ + ἄβυσσος – Rev 9:1, 2.

(But cf. πηγή + ἄβυσσος Gen 7:11; 8:2, 7, Deut 33:13; Ps 17:19; and στόμα + ἄβυσσος I En 17:8).

43   Horowitz 1998: 318–62 (esp. 337–41). Gen 7:11, 8:2 LXX describes the opening and closing of all αἱ πηγαὶ τῆς ἀβύσσου (כָּל־מַעְיְנֹת תְּהוֹם) which control the release of the waters of the abyss to flood the surface of the earth.

44   Heintz, 'בְּאֵר' TDOT, I: 463–6.

45   φρέαρ occurs on 49 occasions in the LXX, predominantly as a translation equivalent of בְּאֵר (cf. Gen 14:10; 16:14; 21:14, 19, 25, 30, 31, 32, 33; 22:19; 24:11, 20, 62; 25:11, 15; 26:18, 19, 20, 21, 23, 25, 32, 33; 29:2, 3, 8, 10; 46:1, 5; Ex 2:15; Num 21:16, 17, 18, 22; I Kgdms 19:22 (בור); II Kgdms 3:26 (בור); I Macc 7:19; II Macc 1:19; Ps 54:23; 68:15; Prov 5:15; 23:27; Song 4:15; Amos 5:5; Isa 15:8; Jer 14:3 (גב); 48:7 (בור), 9 (בור).

46   Betz 1983; Dieterich 1893; Edmonds 2004: 111–58; Himmelfarb 1983; Jeffers 2007: 136–8; Jones 1935; Tsagarakis 2000.

47   Jeremias, 'ἄβυσσος', TDNT I: 9.

in various Jewish texts known to HC1, between these two realms, such that Sheol (Hebrew שְׁאוֹל, Greek ᾅδης) is frequently described as a watery abyss, beneath the terrestrial realm (cf. Jon 2:1-6; Pss 18:5-6 (17:5-6 LXX); 42:8 (41:8 LXX); 88:3-7 (87:3-7 LXX)). This close correlation between Hades as the realm of the dead located under the earth in close proximity to the surrounding waters of the abyss (or, on occasion, synonymous with the abyss, cf. Jon 2:3-4; Ps 68:2-3 LXX), creates associative images connecting Hades, the Deep and a Well.[48]

Ps 68:15-16 LXX

Do not let me be drowned by a storm of water
μή με καταποντισάτω καταιγὶς ὕδατος

or let the Deep swallow me down
μηδὲ καταπιέτω με βυθός (MT: מְצוּלָה)

or let the Well close-up its mouth upon me.
μηδὲ συσχέτω ἐπ' ἐμὲ φρέαρ τὸ στόμα αὐτοῦ
(MT: וְאַל־תֶּאְטַר־עָלַי בְּאֵר פִּיהָ)

A range of images coalesce in these poetic lines, describing the under-world as the abyssal waters of the deep that are metaphorically rising over the psalmist in his distress, and as a subterranean cavern, like a gigantic living-being, closing its mouth after swallowing its victim whole.[49] Accordingly, a well (φρέαρ) need not be understood by HC1 as a geographical feature that is *distinct* from Hades, merely a 'shaft' which connects the underworld and terrestrial realms. Instead Sheol itself can be envisaged as a gigantic Well (or Pit) (cf. Ps 69:15-16 (68:15-16 LXX); 88:4-5 (87:4-5 LXX)), akin to a subterranean living-being whose throat (φρέαρ) (cf. Isa 5:14, (נֶפֶשׁ)), or throats (φρέατα) stretch upwards to the terrestrial realm, where its open mouth (στόμα) lies in wait for its victims.[50]

---

48   There is a certain ambivalence, especially among Greek authors, in the pre-cise spatial location of Hades: it is envisaged both as a subterranean realm beneath the disc-earth (cf. Homer, *Il.* xv. 191; *Od.* xi. 57, 155; Hesiod, *Theogony* 729; and (by the same authors) as a realm beyond the (western?) perimeter of the disc earth (cf. Homer, *Il.* xii.240; *Od.* iii. 335; ix. 26) (cf. Bautch 2003: 239–40). A mediating position is also evidenced by descriptions of the terrestrial entrances to the subterranean realm of Hades located at the (western) perimeter of the earth. The juxtaposition of images of Hades as both a subterranean realm (e.g. Ps 68:15 LXX) and as a region at the western perimeter of the disc-earth (I Enoch 17:7–8) within HC1's mental library is therefore not unusual in the Hellenistic/Graeco-Roman era.

49   Dahood 1968: 153-60; Kraus 1989: 61; Tate 1990: 186–202; Weiser 1962: 491–4.

50   See Gen 29:2, 3, 8, 10 LXX for additional references to the terrestrial 'mouth'

For HC1, Hades is poetically imagined in two alternative guises within the Apocalypse. One portrayal is as a multiple-headed living-being whose vast network of throats puncture the terrestrial-disc above (αἰ πηγαὶ τῶν ὑδάτων, Rev 8:10, 16:4; cf. Gen 16:14, 21:19, 24:11; Song 4:15; Jer 14:3 LXX), akin to the polymorphic creatures that reside in its depths (cf. Virgil, *Aeneid* VI. 268–94). An alternate description, which is privileged in Rev 9, is of a vast chthonic living-being with a solitary jaw (τὸ φρέαρ τῆς ἀβύσσου) (Rev 9:1-2; cf Isa 5:14), which the Deity alone can control (cf. Job 40:25-26; 41:6 LXX regarding Leviathan).[51] Emphasizing a *solitary* point of access to the underworld (τὸ φρέαρ τῆς ἀβύσσου), that can be locked or unlocked at the Deity's will (cf. Rev 20:1-3), enables the implied author of the Apocalypse to depict the Deity's complete control over the release or suppression of hostile, abyssal forces, at crucial moments in the visionary narrative.

The terrestrial location of the solitary 'mouth' (στόμα) of this monstrous beast, the point on the surface of the earth which Hades' throat (φρέαρ) stretches up towards, is indicated, for HC1, by the positioning of τὸ στόμα τῆς ἀβύσσου on her pre-existing mental map, informed by I Enoch 1–36. The pertinent passage is I Enoch 17:7-8, which describe Enoch's tour of significant sites at the northern and western perimeter of the disc-earth (cf. figs. 3.1–3.3).

I Enoch 17:7-8[52]

7. And I departed (for) where no flesh walks (ὅπου πᾶσα σὰρξ οὐ περιπάτει). I saw the wintry winds of darkness and the gushing of all the waters of the abyss (τὴν ἔκχυσιν τῆς ἀβύσσου πάντων ὑδάτων).
8. I saw the mouth of all the rivers of the earth and the mouth of the abyss (τὸ στόμα τῆς γῆς πάντων τῶν ποταμῶν καὶ τὸ στόμα τῆς ἀβύσσου).

(στόμα) of a well (φρέαρ) which, as in Rev 9:2ff, can be closed/blocked (in this case by a stone). For additional references to Sheol as a pit see e.g. Ps 16:10 (שַׁחַת); 30:3 (בּוֹר); Prov 1:12 (בּוֹר); Isa 14:15 (בּוֹר); 38:18 (בּוֹר); Ezek 31:16 (בּוֹר). Isaiah 5:14 similarly personifies Sheol, and describes her opening wide her throat (נֶפֶשׁ) to receive the multitudes that go down into her (cf. Wolff 1974: 11–15).

Note also the metaphorical use of φρέαρ to denote female sexuality/sexual organs (Prov 5:15-18; Song 4:15; cf. Lev 12:7, 20:18) which indicates an alternative anthropological model for visualizing Sheol's well and mouth, adapted for use in rhetorical warnings against exogamous sexual relations (cf. Exum 2005: 175-80; Fox 2000: 189–210).

51   Although Job is not included in the restricted mental library of HC1, there are some interesting parallels with the Deity's exclusive claim to be able to 'open (ἀνοίγω) the doors of [the dragon's] face' (πύλας προσώπου αὐτοῦ) (Job 41:6 LXX), much like the Deity delegates the authority to lock or unlock (implicitly 'the door(s)') of the 'well of the abyss' in Rev 9:1-2; 20:1-3, which may be poetically compared with the throat of a subterranean chaos monster (Hades).

52   Translation, Nickelsburg 2001: 276 amended to conform to G^Pan (Black 1970: 31).

The immediate context of I En 17:7-8 is a description of significant topographical features explicitly located at the *western* periphery of the disc-earth (cf. the fire of the west (πυρός δύσεως) v 4; the great sea of the west (θάλασσα μεγάλη δύσεως) v 5).[53] Arriving at the great river that encircles the perimeter of the inhabited world, Enoch moves across it, to depart where no flesh walks, that is the realm of the dead.[54] Whilst the precise compass direction is not stated explicitly (so also *Od.*, xi.), it appears that the seer moves in a west or north-westerly direction, across the river *Oceanus*, to the land of the dead on its far shore.[55] It is in this topographical location, the west/ north-west of the earth, on the far side of the river *Oceanus*, within the realm of Hades, that I En 17:7-8 situates the mouth of the abyss and the source of the terrestrial rivers. I En 17:7-8 closely correlates the spatial locations of the 'mouth' (στόμα) of the subterranean abyss, which gushes forth water, and the mouth (στόμα) of all the terrestrial rivers on the disc earth. The juxtaposition of these descriptions strongly suggests that the subterranean abyss is envisaged as the *source* of the terrestrial waters, encircling *Oceanus* and all the many rivers of the disc-earth.[56] Such an interpretation corresponds both to ANE conceptions of the intimate connections between the terrestrial watercourses and the waters above and below the earth (cf. Gen 2:6; 7:11), as well as Plato's description of the subterranean waters in *Phaedo* 112C–113C, where he describes how the terrestrial rivers issue from the infernal waters of Tartarus.

On the basis of HC1's pre-existing mental map of the cosmos, informed by I En 17 and the poetic descriptions of Hades as an abyssal well (cf. Ps 68:15-16 LXX), τὸ φρέαρ τῆς ἀβύσσου (Rev 9:1-2) is envisaged as the 'throat' of the chthonic living-being, Hades, whose mouth (στόμα) arises to the surface of the earth at the NW perimeter of *Oceanus* – the terrestrial access-point to the realm of the dead (cf. figs. 4.2 and 4.3).

---

53   Cf. §3.3.1.

54   The description of Hades as a realm of darkness (σκότος) is consistent with its characterization across a vast range of ANE and Greek literature (e.g. *Descent of Ishtar*, *Epic of Gilgamesh* 7.4.33; *Od.* xi. 11-32; Job 10:21-22), which is appropriately located in the west, the region of the setting sun.

55   Whilst the primary emphasis in this section is on Enoch's tour of the western perimeter of the earth there are also hints of a slightly northerly movement, once he crosses *Oceanus*. The depiction of Hades as a region of darkness (σκότος) has affinities with the region he has just visited (I En 17:1-2), a 'dark/gloomy'(ζοφώδη) region in the north/ northwest, given the use elsewhere of the cognate noun ζόφος to denote the realm of the dead (cf *Od.* xi. 57, 155; Hesiod, *Theogony*, 729) (so Bautch 2003: 50–51). In addition, the wintry winds of darkness originate from the north-west, west north-west according to I En 76:11-12.

56   Bautch 2003: 94–5; Nickelsburg 2001: 284.

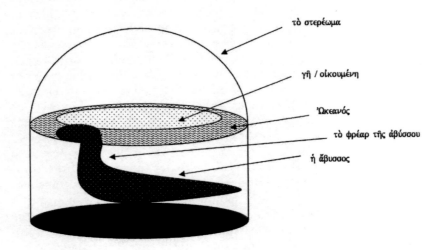

Fig. 4.2. Schematic cross-section of the disc-earth and subterranean realm (Rev 9:1-2)

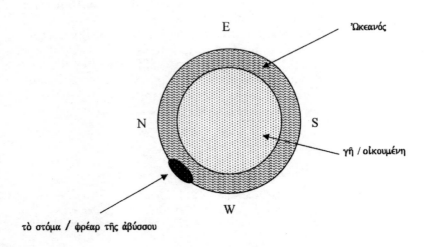

Fig. 4.3 Panoramic view of the disc-earth, encircling Ὠκεανός, and τὸ φρέαρ τῆς ἀβύσσου / τὸ στόμα τῆς ἀβύσσου (Rev 9:1-2; I En 17:7-8) emerging at the NW perimeter of Ὠκεανός/entrance to Hades[57]

57   Cf. Grelot 1958: 46 (fig. 3.1) who similarly locates 'bouche de l'abime' at NW perimeter of Oceanus; contrast Milik 1976: 40 (N) (fig. 3.2); Bautch 2003: 185 (W) (fig. 3.3).

4.4.2 The Abyssal Locusts & The Angel of the Abyss (Rev 9:3-12)

³ καὶ ἐκ τοῦ καπνοῦ ἐξῆλθον ἀκρίδες εἰς τὴν γῆν, καὶ ἐδόθη αὐταῖς ἐξουσία ὡς ἔχουσιν ἐξουσίαν οἱ σκορπίοι τῆς γῆς.
⁴ καὶ ἐρρέθη αὐταῖς ἵνα μὴ ἀδικήσουσιν τὸν χόρτον τῆς γῆς οὐδὲ πᾶν χλωρὸν οὐδὲ πᾶν δένδρον, εἰ μὴ τοὺς ἀνθρώπους οἵτινες οὐκ ἔχουσι τὴν σφραγῖδα τοῦ θεοῦ ἐπὶ τῶν μετώπων.
⁵ καὶ ἐδόθη αὐτοῖς ἵνα μὴ ἀποκτείνωσιν αὐτούς, ἀλλ' ἵνα βασανισθήσονται μῆνας πέντε, καὶ ὁ βασανισμὸς αὐτῶν ὡς βασανισμὸς σκορπίου ὅταν παίσῃ ἄνθρωπον.
⁶ καὶ ἐν ταῖς ἡμέραις ἐκείναις ζητήσουσιν οἱ ἄνθρωποι τὸν θάνατον καὶ οὐ μὴ εὑρήσουσιν αὐτόν, καὶ ἐπιθυμήσουσιν ἀποθανεῖν καὶ φεύγει ὁ θάνατος ἀπ' αὐτῶν.

⁷ Καὶ τὰ ὁμοιώματα τῶν ἀκρίδων ὅμοια ἵπποις ἡτοιμασμένοις εἰς πόλεμον, καὶ ἐπὶ τὰς κεφαλὰς αὐτῶν ὡς στέφανοι ὅμοιοι χρυσῷ, καὶ τὰ πρόσωπα αὐτῶν ὡς πρόσωπα ἀνθρώπων,
⁸ καὶ εἶχον τρίχας ὡς τρίχας γυναικῶν, καὶ οἱ ὀδόντες αὐτῶν ὡς λεόντων ἦσαν,
⁹ καὶ εἶχον θώρακας ὡς θώρακας σιδηροῦς, καὶ ἡ φωνὴ τῶν πτερύγων αὐτῶν ὡς φωνὴ ἁρμάτων ἵππων πολλῶν τρεχόντων εἰς πόλεμον,
¹⁰ καὶ ἔχουσιν οὐρὰς ὁμοίας σκορπίοις καὶ κέντρα, καὶ ἐν ταῖς οὐραῖς αὐτῶν ἡ ἐξουσία αὐτῶν ἀδικῆσαι τοὺς ἀνθρώπους μῆνας πέντε,
¹¹ ἔχουσιν ἐπ' αὐτῶν βασιλέα τὸν ἄγγελον τῆς ἀβύσσου, ὄνομα αὐτῷ Ἑβραϊστὶ Ἀβαδδών, καὶ ἐν τῇ Ἑλληνικῇ ὄνομα ἔχει Ἀπολλύων.
¹² Ἡ οὐαὶ ἡ μία ἀπῆλθεν· ἰδοὺ ἔρχεται ἔτι δύο οὐαὶ μετὰ ταῦτα.

3. And locusts came out of the smoke onto the earth, and authority was given to them like the authority which the scorpions of the earth have.
4. And they were told not to harm the grass of the earth nor any green thing nor any tree but only people who do not have the seal of God upon their foreheads.
5. And it [the authority] was given to them in order that they might not kill them, but in order that they [unsealed people] might be tortured for five months. And their [locusts'] torture (is) like the torture of a scorpion when it strikes a person.
6. And in those days people will seek Death, and they will not find him, and they will long to die and Death flees from them.

7. And the likenesses of the locusts (were) like horses that had been prepared for war, and upon their heads as crowns like gold, and their faces (were) like human faces.

8. And they were having hair like womens' hair, and their teeth were like lions' (teeth).

9. And they were having chests like iron-breastplates, and the sound of their wings (was) like (the) sound of many chariot-horses galloping into war.

10. And they were having tails like scorpions and stings, and their authority to harm people for five months (was) in their tails.

11. They were having over them a king, the angel of the abyss, whose name in Hebrew (was) Abaddon, and in Greek he has (the) name Destroyer.

12. The first woe has passed: behold two woes are still coming after these things.

HC1 perceives the Apocalypse's detailed description of the abyssal locusts, and their leader, primarily as a re-envisioning of a former vision of Joel (Joel 1–2) contained within her mental library. Aspects of this former vision are recalled by HC1, triggered by *visual reminiscences* of the φάντασμα of Joel's locust-cavalry imprinted on her memory, supported by a cluster of close *verbal parallels*, concentrated in Rev 9:7-9. Recollection of this passage (Joel 1–2) carries with it an attendant set of pre-existing interpretative connections with Exodus 10, Ezekiel 38–39 and Amos 7:1 LXX which inform HC1's prior understanding of this passage. The Apocalypse's re-envisioning of Joel 1–2, and its associative images in HC1's mental library, modifies and reorients HC1's preconceived interpretative framework.[58]

The most resonant verbal parallels and associative connections are as follows:

Rev 9:7α

Καὶ τὰ ὁμοιώματα τῶν ἀκρίδων ὅμοια ἵπποις ἡτοιμασμένοις εἰς πόλεμον

(And the likenesses of the locusts (were) like horses that had been prepared for war)

Joel 2:4-5 (LXX)[59]

4α ὡς ὅρασις ἵππων ἡ ὅρασις[60] αὐτῶν

4β καὶ ὡς ἱππεῖς οὕτως καταδιώξονται

5α ὡς φωνὴ ἁρμάτων ἐπὶ τὰς κορυφὰς τῶν ὀρέων ἐξαλοῦνται

5β καὶ ὡς φωνὴ φλογὸς πυρὸς κατεσθιούσης καλάμην

5γ καὶ ὡς λαὸς πολὺς καὶ ἰσχυρὸς παρατασσόμενος εἰς πόλεμον

58   Cf. Strazicich 2007: 354–8.

59   Ziegler 1943.

60   Ziegler accepts א and B (ὅρασις) repetition of מַרְאֵה (MT); contra. Rahlfs following W and Q, ὄψις.

MT מַרְאֶה 29 occurences – LXX: translates: εἶδος (9), ὄψις (7), ὅρασις (1), ὁμοίωμα (0).

(lit. 4α as a vision of horses (is) their vision
    4β and as horsemen thus they will pursue
    5α as the sound of chariots upon the peaks of the mountains,
      they will jump-up
    5β and as the sound of a flame of fire devouring a reed
    5γ and as a great and mighty people being drawn-up for war).

The range of verbal parallels recalling Joel 2:4-5 are neither extensive nor exclusive, as they are limited to three commonly associated words (ἵπποι, εἰς πόλεμον).[61] The significance of this line lies in its role as part of a dense cluster of verbal parallels to Joel 1–2 in the immediate context (Rev 9:7-9), which combine with the resonances of this distinctive simile (locusts compared with cavalry; cf. also Jer 28:27 LXX) to evoke the disturbing vision of Joel and its emotive force (πάθος), from among the range of alternative φαντάσματα contained in HC1's mental library.[62]

The next sustained set of verbal recollections of Joel's former vision occurs at Rev 9:8β, which calls to mind Joel's simile of zoological-dentistry (Joel 1:6).[63]

Rev 9:8β
καὶ <u>οἱ ὀδόντες αὐτῶν ὡς λεόντων</u> ἦσαν
(and their teeth were like lions' (teeth))

Joel 1:6 (LXX)
6a ὅτι ἔθνος ἀνέβη ἐπὶ τὴν γῆν μου ἰσχυρὸν καὶ ἀναρίθμητον
6b <u>οἱ ὀδόντες αὐτοῦ</u> ὀδόντες <u>λέοντος</u> καὶ αἱ μύλαι αὐτοῦ σκύμνου

(lit. 6a because a strong and innumerable nation came up upon my land
    6b its teeth (the) teeth of a lion, and its grinders (those of) a (lion-)cub)

---

61   ἵππος and πόλεμος are closely combined in a diverse range of texts contained in HC1's mental library: Deut 20:1, Hos 1:7; Zech 10:3, 10:5, Jer 6:23; 27:42; cf. also the brief excursus on cavalry horses in Homer, *Il.* II. 763–7; cf. Kirk, 1985: 240–1.

62   ἀκρίς is similarly widely dispersed in HC1's mental library: Ex 10:4, 12, 13, 14, 19; Lev 11:22; Num 13:33; Deut 28:38; Ps 77:46; 104:34; 108:23; Hos 13:3; Amos 7:1; Joel 1:4; 2:25; Nahum 3:15, 17; Isa 33:4; 40:22; Jer 26:23; 28:14.

63   For the combination of ὀδούς and λέων elsewhere in HC1's mental library cf. Ps 57:7 LXX.

HC1 is encouraged to recall the evocative dissonances of Joel's mental image, notably the distinctive combination of a likeness (ὡς) to both cavalry-horses and lions (Joel 2:4α, 2:5γ; 1:6β).[64] The final sustained set of lexical triggers occurs at Rev 9:9β, once again recalling Joel 2:4-5:

Rev 9:9β
καὶ ἡ <u>φωνὴ</u> τῶν πτερύγων αὐτῶν <u>ὡς φωνὴ ἁρμάτων</u> <u>ἵππων πολλῶν</u> τρεχόντων <u>εἰς πόλεμον</u>
(and the sound of their wings (was) like (the) sound of many chariot-horses galloping into war)

Joel 2:4-5 (LXX)
4α ὡς ὅρασις <u>ἵππων</u> ἡ ὅρασις αὐτῶν
4β καὶ ὡς ἱππεῖς οὕτως καταδιώξονται
5α <u>ὡς φωνὴ ἁρμάτων</u> ἐπὶ τὰς κορυφὰς τῶν ὀρέων ἐξαλοῦνται
5β καὶ ὡς <u>φωνὴ</u> φλογὸς πυρὸς κατεσθιούσης καλάμην
5γ καὶ ὡς λαὸς <u>πολὺς</u> καὶ ἰσχυρὸς παρατασσόμενος <u>εἰς πόλεμον</u>

(lit. 4α as a vision of horses (is) their vision
    4β and as horsemen thus they will pursue
    5α as the sound of chariots upon the peaks of the mountains,
        they will jump-up
    5β and as the sound of a flame of fire devouring a reed
    5γ and as a great and mighty people being drawn-up for war).

Rev 9:9β melds the auditory description of the sound of war-chariots (Joel 2:5α), with the visual image of war-horses galloping into battle (Joel 2:4αβ).

The imagery of Joel 1–2 is recollected, by HC1, whilst hearing Rev 9 orally performed, owing to the distinctive, evocative *visual reminiscences* of fearsome locusts envisioned as a vast cavalry-force with leonine attributes, triggered by an associative set of direct *verbal parallels* (ἵπποι, ἀκρίδες, πόλεμος, ὀδόντες, λέοντος, ἅρμα) (Joel 1:6, 2:4-5).

HC1's pre-existing interpretation of the hybrid locusts of Joel 1–2 can be built up in interpretative layers on the basis of verbal parallels and associative imagery which closely connect the depiction of the locust cavalry of Joel 1–2 with related figures in HC1's mental library: the Egyptian plague locusts (Ex 10; Pss 77, 104 LXX); and the enemy from the north/Gog (cf. Joel 2:20; Ezek 38–39; Amos 7:1 LXX).

On the basis of HC1's familiarity with the LXX version of Joel's vision (Joel 1–2), her pre-understanding of the agents described in these chapters

---

64 The conflation of imagery from Joel 1 and 2 to describe the locusts indicates that the implied author of the Apocalypse understood both chapters to describe an eschatological locust invasion. On the relationship between Joel 1 and 2 see Crenshaw 1995; Wolff 1977 (Joel 1 locust invasion; Joel 2 military invasion); Barton 2001; (Joel 1 and 2 locust invasion); Andiñach 1992, (Joel 1 and 2 military invasion).

can be summarized as follows. The agents are an incomparable military force (Joel 2:2) that have been dispatched by the Lord to invade the land (2:1), such that they function as delegated agents of the Lord's eschatological Day of judgment (cf. 2:1-2, 11). These forces are under the direct command of the Lord (cf. 2:11) and as a consequence their invasion is signalled by the theophanic indicators of fire, blazing before and behind (2:3 τὰ ἔμπροσθεν αὐτοῦ πῦρ ἀναλίσκον καὶ τὰ ὀπίσω αὐτοῦ ἀναπτομένη φλόξ (cf. Ps 49:3 LXX, 96:1-3 LXX).[65] Despite the wealth of similes that compare this unsurpassed force with cutting-edge military troops (Joel 2:4-9), this divine army is not envisaged, as might be expected, as the Lord's regular angelic 'host' (αἱ δυνάμεις αὐτοῦ (cf. Ps 148:2 LXX)), but rather is portrayed as a devastating locust-swarm (cf. Joel 1:4, 6) that is likened to (ὡς, 8x Joel 2:4-9) an annihilating army. The decisive textual evidence that supports HC1's equation of this locust-swarm (Joel 1:4, 6) with the Lord's army (Joel 2:11) is provided by Joel 2:25, where the four locust-types of Joel 1:4 are directly identified as 'my [the Lord's] great force' (ἡ δύναμίς μου ἡ μεγάλη), which he dispatched against his people.[66] Supporting evidence is provided by the simile which describes the locusts as 'a powerful and innumerable nation' (ἔθνος... ἰσχυρὸν καὶ ἀναρίθμητον) (Joel 1:6), which overlaps with the description of the military force as 'a large and strong people' (λαὸς πολὺς καὶ ἰσχυρός) (Joel 2:2).[67]

Joel's eschatological locust-army is evocative of the 'plague' of locusts that formerly devastated the Egyptians (cf. Ex 10:1-20; Pss. 78:42-53 (77:42-53 LXX); 105:26-36 (104:26-36 LXX)), with both swarms utterly consuming all vegetation (cf. Joel 1:4; 2:25; Ex 10:12; Ps 104:35 LXX) and closely associated with darkness. The former claims of unparalleled devastation associated with the Egyptian locust swarm (cf. Ex 10:14β) are usurped by the incomparable destruction of Joel's locust-army on the Day of the Lord (cf. Joel 1:2β), such that future generations (Joel 1:2-3) will be taught of the Lord's 'mighty deeds' in response to this event, which exceed the Lord's former mighty deeds (Joel 2:26, τὰ θαυμάσια) at the Exodus (contra Ps 77:3-4 LXX). HC1's pre-existing interpretative connection between Joel 1–2 and the Egyptian locust plague is reinforced by the structural connections between the Egyptian plague cycle and the context of Rev 9:1ff, as an integral component of a series of seven (trumpet) plagues (cf. Rev 9:18, πληγή (cf. Ex 11:1, 12:13)).[68]

In addition to drawing associative connections between Joel's locust-army and the Lord's theophanic host (cf. Ps 49:3 LXX, 96:1-3 LXX), and perceiving that this devastating force surpasses the Egyptian locust-plague in

---

65   Cf. Wolff 1977: 45; Strazicich 2007: 125–8.

66   Cf. Jerome, *In Joel* 163.91ff; cf. Lössl 2004.

67   The verbal parallel closely mirrors the Hebrew parallel (עצום) (mighty) that connects these two verses (Joel 1:6, 2:2).

68   Cf. Aune 1998a: 499–506 for tables displaying synoptic parallels between Rev 8:1–11:19 and Exod 7:8-13:16, Ps 78:43-52; Ps 105:27-36; Amos 4:6-13.

intensity (Ex 10:1-21; Pss 77:42-53; 104:26-36 LXX), HC1 may also have made a connection between Joel's locust-army and the 'Enemy from the north' (Jer 1–6; Ezek 38–39),[69] under the influence of Amos 7:1 LXX. The presence of such an exegetical tradition is debated, so the text of Amos 7:1 LXX requires careful scrutiny before determining whether it is plausible to state that HC1 made such a connection.[70]

The opening vision in Amos' vision-cycle (Amos 7:1-3 MT) has striking verbal and thematic resonance with the Egyptian locust-plague traditions (Ex 10:1-20; Pss. 78:42-53 (77:42-53 LXX); 105:26-36 (104:26-36 LXX) and the re-envisioning of these traditions in Joel 1–2, not least in the Lord's decision to relent (נחם / μετανοεῖν) and avert the threatened destruction (compare Joel 2:13ff with Amos 7:3).[71] The most pertinent line for the purpose of the present study is as follows:

Amos 7:1 (MT)

כֹּה הִרְאַנִי אֲדֹנָי יהוה
וְהִנֵּה יוֹצֵר גֹּבַי בִּתְחִלַּת עֲלוֹת הַלָּקֶשׁ
וְהִנֵּה־לֶקֶשׁ אַחַר גִּזֵּי הַמֶּלֶךְ׃

Thus the Lord YHWH showed me:
and behold one forming a locust-swarm at the beginning of the coming-up of the later growth,
and behold, (the) later growth after the king's mowing.

Amos 7:1 (LXX)

οὕτως ἔδειξέν μοι κύριος
καὶ ἰδοὺ ἐπιγονὴ ἀκρίδων ἐρχομένη ἑωθινή
καὶ ἰδοὺ βροῦχος εἰς Γωγ ὁ βασιλεύς

(Thus the Lord showed me:
and behold an influx[72] of locusts coming at dawn,[73]
and behold one locust, Gog the king)[74]

69　Childs 1959.

70　Cf. Bøe 2001: 61–70; Dines 1992: 213–21; Strazicich 2007: 175–7.

71　ἀκρίδες, Ex 10:4, 12, 13, 14, 19 (x2); Ps 77:46; 104:34; Joel 1:4 (x2) 2:25.

אָכַל / κατεσθιω, Exod 10:5, 10:12, 10:15, Ps 105:35 (104:35 LXX); Joel 2:25; Nogalski 2000: 100–104.

נחם / μετανόησον, Joel 1:14, 2:15-16, Amos 7:3.

72　LXX ἐπιγονή, elsewhere denotes growth or birth of an animal, suggesting the emergence of a vast number of locusts (hence, 'influx'); Cf. Dines 1992: 213; Wolff 1977: 291.

73　LXX ἐρχομένη ἑωθινή (literally, 'coming early') is discordant with MT עֲלוֹת בְּתְחִלַּת ב (literally, 'in the beginning of the coming-up'); plausibly recalling stock phrases linking ἑωθινή with dawn (e.g. Jon 4:7; cf. Joel 2:2), a characteristic time of military attack (cf. Ex 14:24, I Kgms 11:11); Dines 1992: 213–14.

74　LXX reference to Gog in Amos 7:1 is unparalleled in other Greek versions

In Amos 7:1γ (MT) an explanatory clause is provided to unpack the meaning of לֶקֶשׁ (later growth) (Amos 7:1β), such that the crucial term is repeated and then explicated further: 'later growth (that is, after the king's mowing)'.[75] It is widely held that either the LXX translator, or an earlier Hebrew scribe, misread, or perhaps re-read, three of the words in Amos 7:1γ: in place of the noun לקש the locust-term ילק may have been read, which would account for the LXX translation of βροῦχος.[76] The visual similarity of *daleth* and *resh* may account for the misreading, whether deliberate or accidental, of the unpointed Hebrew אחר (after) by אחד (one), resulting in the LXX reading of εἷς. Finally, a comparable visual similarity between *waw* and *zayin* and *gimel* and *yod*, could have resulted in a reading of גוג in place of גֵּזִי, transliterated into Greek as Γωγ.[77]

Each of the individual components in this reconstructive process is plausible in isolation, although the weakest element is undoubtedly the proposal that a scribe/translator misread ילק in place of לקש, not least because this word occurred in the preceding line (Amos 7:1β) where it was rendered by ἐρχομένη.[78] The sustained reinterpretation that is evidenced in Amos 7:1 LXX may reflect not simply accidental scribal errors, but perhaps the conscious influence of an existing interpretative tradition which related the locust-swarm of Joel 1–2 with Gog from Magog. Support for such a suggestion is found within the text of Joel itself, where an explicit reference is made to the 'northerner' in the context of YHWH's reversal of the consequences of the locust-army invasion.

Joel 2:20 (MT)

וְאֶת־הַצְּפוֹנִי אַרְחִיק מֵעֲלֵיכֶם
וְהִדַּחְתִּיו אֶל־אֶרֶץ צִיָּה וּשְׁמָמָה
אֶת־פָּנָיו אֶל־הַיָּם הַקַּדְמֹנִי
וְסֹפוֹ אֶל־הַיָּם הָאַחֲרוֹן
וְעָלָה בָאְשׁוֹ וְתַעַל צַחֲנָתוֹ
כִּי הִגְדִּיל לַעֲשׂוֹת׃

(Aquila, Symmachus or Theodotion); Aquila transliterates גֵּזִי with γαζης; Bøe 2001: 61–2.

75   Wolff 1977: 297.

76   LXX βροῦχος (10): 6x ילק (Ps 104:34; Joel 1:4 (x 2); Joel 2:25; Nahum 3:15 and 3:16); 2x אַרְבֶּה (Lev 11:22, I Kgs 8:27); in synonymous parallelism with אַרְבֶּה (II Chron 6:28, Joel 1:4 (x2), Joel 2:25).

77   Cf. Bøe 2001: 63–5.

78   I am grateful to my colleague, Dr Jonathan Norton, for his insight that the LXX reading could have arisen if a *yod* was read as a variant *mater lectionis* in place of *he* in הנה and the *shin* was interpreted as a contraction of אשר. Divided differently, the Hebrew text could then have been read as follows: והן ילק שאחר גזי המלך 'And behold, a locust which is one גזי the King'.

And I will remove the Northerner from upon you (pl.),
and I will banish him to a land of drought and devastation,
his face to the eastern sea
and his end to the western sea,
and his stench will go up, and his stink will arise
because he has done great things.

Joel 2:20 (LXX)

καὶ τὸν ἀπὸ βορρᾶ ἐκδιώξω ἀφ' ὑμῶν καὶ ἐξώσω αὐτὸν εἰς γῆν
ἄνυδρον καὶ ἀφανιῶ τὸ πρόσωπον αὐτοῦ εἰς τὴν θάλασσαν τὴν
πρώτην καὶ τὰ ὀπίσω αὐτοῦ εἰς τὴν θάλασσαν τὴν ἐσχάτην καὶ
ἀναβήσεται ἡ σαπρία αὐτοῦ καὶ ἀναβήσεται ὁ βρόμος αὐτοῦ ὅτι
ἐμεγάλυνεν τὰ ἔργα αὐτοῦ

And I will drive-out the one from the north from you (pl.), and I will beach
him in a waterless land, and I will destroy his face to the first sea, and his rear
to the last sea, and his rottenness will ascend and his roar will arise because
he extended his actions.

Joel 2:20 (MT/LXX) refers to the mythological northern enemy (הַצְּפוֹנִי /
τὸν ἀπὸ βορρᾶ) (cf. Ezek 38:15) that the Lord pledges to annihilate as
part of a wider programme to reverse the destructive invasion of Joel
1–2 (cf. Joel 2:18-27).[79] Just as the Lord will restore the grain, wine
and oil that the locust-invasion destroyed (Joel 2:18, 25), so also will he
expel and definitively defeat the enemy from the north. The close correlation, to the point of identification, between the locust-swarm and
the innumerable army (cf. Joel 1:4, 2:2, 2:7) that devastates the land
is spelt out most clearly in Joel 2:25, where the four locust-types are
explicitly described as YHWH's 'great army' (חֵילִי הַגָּדוֹל / ἡ δύναμίς μου
ἡ μεγάλη). As a consequence, the context of Joel 2:20 strongly suggests
that the mythological 'northerner' may be readily equated with the devastating military force/locusts that are described in Joel 1–2.
    Is it plausible to regard Amos 7:1 LXX as a further development of implicit
connections between the locust swarm of Joel 1–2 and the enemy from the
north? That is to say, whilst Joel 2 utilizes the 'enemy from the north' traditions in its metaphorical description of locusts as YHWH's innumerable
army (cf. 2:25), Amos 7:1 LXX takes a further step and identifies the leader

---

79   Cf. Ezek 38:15 which refers to Gog, and his forces, originating from 'the extremi-
ties of the North' (מִיַּרְכְּתֵי צָפוֹן)/(ἀπ' ἐσχάτου βορρα); Block 1998: 424–93; Zimmerli 1983:
281–324.

of the locust-swarm as Gog the king? Such an interpretative connection was proposed by Bruce and developed more recently by Strazicich.[80] Strazicich assigns the deviations from the MT *Vorlage* to a deliberate instance of 'midrashic interpretation' on the part of the LXX translator of Amos 7:1:

> The LXX tradent, by means of an *'al tiqre* interpretation (Amos 7:1), makes a midrashic complex, mixing the locust imagery in Joel 2:20 with the enemy topic in Ezek 38–39, which is connected by means of the gentilic noun הַצְּפוֹנִי. This passage is the only text that is able to create a fusion of these two ideas in the OT. Therefore, the LXX tradent of Amos represents the earliest interpretation of Joel 2:20, which identifies Gog as Joel's *Nordfeind*, who is cloaked with the garb of locusts.[81]

Yet a logical gap still remains: whilst it is conceivable that a LXX translator may connect the locust-swarm of Joel 1–2 with the enemy from the north (Ezek 38–39), building on the pre-existing connection in Joel 2:20, what might have prompted an interpreter to *identify one locust with Gog*? Joel 2:20 depicts the collective locust-swarm as a gigantic foe, the 'northerner', echoing the nightmarish enemy forces of Ezek 38–39, yet makes no explicit reference to a leader, Gog. On this point, Bruce may offer a more perceptive hypothesis: a pre-existing exegetical connection between Joel's locusts and the 'enemy from the north' (Ezek 38–39) (cf. Joel 2:20) lay in the background of the scribe's thought, yet the impetus may have come from a difficult or corrupt text, which led to the singling out of *one* (אחד for אחר) of the locusts for a specific identification (גוג instead of גזי).[82] Such an interpretation can account both for a pre-existing connection between Joel's locusts and the 'enemy from the north' that is found in Joel 2:20, and also the lack of evidence of further exegetical development of the unique reading of Amos 7:1 LXX, which explicitly identified one of the locusts as Gog.[83]

On the basis of the contents of HC1's mental library, informed by pre-existing exegetical connections between Joel 1–2 and both the Exodus plagues tradition (Ex 10; Pss 77, 104 LXX) and the 'enemy from the north'/ Gog tradition (Joel 2:20; Amos 7:1 LXX, Ezek 38–39), HC1's perception of the locust-army which Joel envisioned can be stated succinctly as follows. The locust-troops (Joel 1–2) are the Lord's eschatological agents of judgment

---

80   Bruce 1972: 37–52; Strazicich 2007: 175–7.
81   Strazicich 2007: 176–7. There are significant weaknesses in Strazicich's method, not least his presumption that the *Vorlage* of the LXX text closely corresponded to the MT (176); contrast Bøe 2001: 62–3.
82   Bruce 1972: 41.
83   Dines 1992: 215–21; Bøe 2001: 61–2.

(Joel 2:25), who function as his theophanic military 'host' (cf. Ps 49:3 LXX, 96:1-3 LXX), entrusted with a mission to devastate the staple-crops of Israel (cf. Joel 1:4, 2:20; cf. Ex 10:12, 15; Ps 104:35 LXX). This locust-swarm is identified as the devastating 'enemy from the north' (Jer 1–6; Ezek 38–39) that the Lord has co-opted as his agents, under the leadership of their king, Gog (Amos 7:1 LXX; Ezek 39–39).

How is HC1's pre-understanding of Joel's vision modified as a result of the 're-envisioning' of this vision in Rev 9:1ff? Four points are worthy of particular note. First, the pre-eminence of the devastating force of the eschatological locusts is further intensified. Whereas the plague-locusts had been entrusted with the complete devastation of animal fodder in the land of Egypt (Ex 10:12, 15; Ps 104:35 LXX (χόρτος)), indirectly affecting the livestock, this pales into insignificance with the incomparable devastation of Joel's eschatological locusts (Joel 1:2 contra Ex 10:14; Ps 77:1-4 LXX), sent to utterly destroy the staple crops of grain, wine and oil on which the population of Yehud, and the temple service, depended (Joel 1:5, 10; cf. 2:19).[84] The Apocalypse's re-envisioning of Joel's eschatological locusts accentuates still further the severity of the eschatological locusts' commission: they are expressly forbidden from harming the vegetation (Rev 9:4), as instead they are to torture (βασανίζω) unsealed human beings directly, for a five-month duration.[85]

Second, the scope of the northern origins of the hybrid locust-cavalry is extended. The Egyptian plague locusts were carried to the land of Egypt on an east wind (Ex 10:13 MT רוּחַ קָדִים) or a south wind according to the Septuagint (Ex 10:13 LXX ἄνεμον νότον), and removed by a wind from the opposite direction (Ex 10:19 MT west wind (literally 'a wind from the sea', רוּחַ־יָם, Ex 10:19, LXX ἄνεμον ἀπὸ θαλάσσης) which cast the insects into the יַם־סוּף (sea of destruction) (LXX εἰς τὴν ἐρυθρὰν θάλασσαν 'Red Sea').[86] For HC1 the locust-cavalry of Joel's vision, by contrast, is to be correlated with the 'enemy from the north' (cf. Joel 2:20), under the leadership of Gog (cf. Amos 7:1 LXX; Ezek 38–39) originating from the uttermost lands of the north (cf. Ezek 38:15). According to HC1's mental map of the cosmos the abyssal origins of the Apocalypse's locust-cavalry *extends* this 'northern' imagery, as the hybrid creatures are envisioned as rising from the underworld via the 'well of the abyss' (τὸ φρέαρ τῆς ἀβύσσου) (Rev 9:2-3) (= τὸ στόμα τῆς ἀβύσσου, I Enoch 17:8), the terrestrial mouth of Hades (cf. Ps 68:15-16 LXX) that emerges at the NW perimeter of the disc-earth (cf. fig. 4.3). This

84   Ahlström 1971.

85   Although absent from HC1's mental library, it is noteworthy that the *Wisdom of Solomon* reinterprets the Egyptian locust plague, one of a series of seven antitheses, as a direct attack on humans, of even greater ferocity than in Rev 9, as the victims are killed; cf. Wis 16:9: 'For the bites/stings (δήγματα) of the locusts (ἀκρίδων) and flies killed them (οὓς … ἀπέκτεινεν)'; Cheon 1997; Winston 1979.

86   For יַם סוּף as 'the sea of destruction', evocative of the chaos waters (cf. Rev 9:2), see Wyatt 2005: 38.

is consistent with the description of destructive winds that emerge from eight 'wrong-angled' gates in the *Astronomical Book of Enoch* (I En 72-82), through three of which devastating *locust swarms* are propelled:[87]

I En 76:1, 4[88]
1. At the boundaries of the earth I saw twelve gates open for all the winds, from which the winds emerge and blow on the earth.... 4. Through four of them [E, N, S, W] emerge winds of blessing and peace, but, from those (other) eight, winds of punishment emerge; when they are sent they bring devastation on the entire earth and the water on it, all that live on it, and all that are in the water and on the land.

I En 76:10-11 [Winds from the Northern Gates]
10. Following these the winds that are towards the north, whose name is 'sea', and which emerges from the seventh gate that is towards the southeast [NE] – there emerge from it dew, rain, locust, destruction.
11. From the middle gate [N] in a direct way there emerge life, rain, dew; through the third gate that is toward the west [NW], inclining to the north, there emerge mist, hail, snow, rain, dew and locust.

HC1, whose mental map of the cosmic geography of the Apocalypse is heavily influenced by the eschatological cartography of I En 1–36, is thus in a position to draw a close correlation between the emergence of the abyssal locusts from τὸ φρέαρ τῆς ἀβύσσου in Rev 9:2ff (NW perimeter of the earth) and the destructive gates of the winds in I En 34–36/76 (including the NW gate). Accordingly, HC1's pre-existing identification of Joel's locust swarm with the liminal 'northern' foe (Ezek 38–39) is amplified, as the chthonic locusts are imagined to emerge from the north-western perimeter of the disc-earth, the terrestrial entrance to the realm of Hades.

Third, Rev 9:7-10 supplements and extends Joel's metaphorical register to portray this force as a distorted mirror-image of the Deity's angelic host. Their hybrid attributes are extended with new human and animal components: human faces and women's hair (Rev 9:7γ-8α; cf. Apoc Zeph 4:1-7, 6:7-9), with the sting appropriate to scorpions (Rev 9:10α (cf. 9:3β)).[89] Their

---

87   An abbreviated version of I En 76 is contained in HC1's mental library, recounted in I En 34:1–36:4, but with no reference to locusts emerging from the gates.

88   Nickelsburg 2004: 104–5. Cf. Nickelsburg 2001: 331–2 (I En 34:1–36:4 as an abridgement of I En 76); Neugebauer in Black 1985: 403–7 (incl. fig. 2).

Charles 1920a: 191–2, 248–50 equates the underlying source of Rev 9:1ff with I En 76 in which angels at the gates of the earth (cf. Rev 7:1-3) release a plague of natural locusts (NE and NW gates), echoing the enemy from the North tradition; the Apocalypse is understood to modify this source to emphasize the creature's demonic origins. My interpretation adapts Charles' source-critical analysis, reapplying it to the reception of Rev 9 by a hearer (HC1) who presupposes Enochic cosmology.

89   Cf. Apoc. Zeph. 4:1-7, 6:8-9 for polymorphic Hadean figures (Satan and his entourage), with long hair; Wintermute, *OTP I*: 497–515.

military hardware is similarly upgraded by the addition of iron breastplates, appropriate for an armoured cavalry force (θώρακας ὡς θώρακας σιδηροῦς) (Rev 9:9α).[90] Rev 9:7β ascribes a royal status to the abyssal hybrids by endowing each of them with the likeness of a golden crown (ὡς στέφανοι ὅμοιοι χρυσῷ), indicative of their status as client kings of the ruler of the abyss (Rev 9:11, βασιλεύς), and as such, abyssal counterparts to the twenty-four crowned elders (Rev 4:4).[91]

The fourth, and final, way in which HC1's pre-existing perception of Joel's locust-cavalry is distorted by the Apocalypse's 're-envisioning', relates to the identity of their commander. Under the influence of Amos 7:1 LXX (and Joel 2:20), HC1 had previously visualised the eschatological locust cavalry of the northern foe under the command of 'one locust, Gog, the king (βροῦχος εἷς Γωγ ὁ βασιλεύς)' (Amos 7:1 LXX). In the re-envisioned version, command is transferred to a more senior official (Rev 9:11):

Rev 9:11 ἔχουσιν ἐπ' αὐτῶν βασιλέα τὸν ἄγγελον τῆς ἀβύσσου, ὄνομα αὐτῷ Ἑβραϊστὶ Ἀβαδδών, καὶ ἐν τῇ Ἑλληνικῇ ὄνομα ἔχει Ἀπολλύων.

They were having over them a king, the angel of the abyss, whose name in Hebrew (was) Abaddon, and in Greek he has (the) name Destroyer.

The Hebrew form of the king of the locusts' name, that is transliterated by Ἀβαδδών in Rev 9:11, is אֲבַדּוֹן, a poetic expression denoting the realm of the dead as a place of destruction (cf. Prov 15:11, 27:20, Job 26:6, 28:22, 31:12, Ps 88:12; 1QHᵃ xi:32; 4Q 286 7ii:7; 4Q 504 1-2 vii.8).[92] The use of this term to refer to a ruler of the underworld may have been stimulated by the personification of Abaddon, in parallelism with Sheol and Death respectively, in Job 26:2, 28:22.[93] The Greek form of the king

---

90　On first century CE armoured cavalry, characteristically identified with renowned Parthian 'cataphracts', clad in bronze and steel plates (cf. Plutarch, *Crassus* 24–5 and Polybius 30.25.9): see Aune 1998a: 891-4; Sidnell 2006.

91　Cf. Tyconius, *Commentary on the Apocalypse* III.30 who picks up on the verbal parallels to emphasize the imitative nature of the golden crowns of the locusts, 'like gold in imitation of the church (*isti autem similes auro ad imitationem ecclesiae*)'; cf. Gryson 2011: 158.

92　Aune 1998a: 534; Charles 1920a: 245–6; Swete 1906: 117. Note the various poetic terms in apposition to אֲבַדּוֹן in its occurances in the MT and DSS: Sheol (שְׁאוֹל) (Prov 15:11, 27:20, Job 26:6, 1QH 3:16-19); Death (מָוֶת) (Job 28:22), the grave (קֶבֶר) (Ps 88:12), the pit (שַׁחַת) (4Q 286 7ii:7), and the abyss (תְּהוֹם) (4Q 504 1–2 vii.8). The latter example is of particular relevance in view of the explicit reference to the 'abyss' (ἄβυσσος) in Rev 9:11.

4Q 504 (Words of the Luminaries) is a liturgical work whose Sabbath prayers praise God as creator (cf. Rev 4:11, 5:13). 4Q 504 vii. 4-9 recounts the praise of God by all the inhabitants of the cosmos, in descending order from the vault of the firmament to the abyss/Abaddon; Davila 2000: 239–66 (264–5); Garcia Martinez 1994: 416.

93　Compare the personification of the Pit/Well (בְּאֵר / φρέαρ) as an underworld monster that swallows its victims in Ps 69:16 (68:16 LXX), the personification of the god of

of the locusts' name, Ἀπολλύων, is resonant with the most common translation equivalent (ἀπώλεια, 'destruction') for אֲבַדּוֹן in the LXX version (all except Job 31:12), although a more active nuance of 'Destroyer' (Ἀπολλύων, pres. partic. act. nom. sing. masc. vb ἀπόλλυμι 'to ruin, destroy') is here preferred.[94] The identity of this underworld ruler is difficult to tease out precisely from the context, although parallels with the DSS suggest that Belial is perhaps the most plausible candidate:

4Q 286 7ii.7-10
And [again they say, 'Cursed are you, ange]l of the pit and spir[it of destru]ction

([ארור אתה מלא]ך השחה ורו]ח האב[דון)

in all plots of your nature of g[uilt and in all schemes of abomin]ation and [your] counsel of wicked[ness]. And den[ounced are you, in the r[ea]l[m of your iniquity] and in [yo]ur [service of wickedness and guilt], with all the de[filements of Sheo]l and wi[th the taunts of the pi]t [and with the humi]liations of annihilation, with [no survivor and with no acts of for]giveness, with the anger of the rage of [Go]d [for al]l [eternit]ies. Amen. A[men.][95]

4Q286 7ii. is a *yaḥad* composition which recounts a series of curses pronounced by the community (יהד) against Belial (בליעל), the chief of the fallen angels, and his human ('sons of Belial') and heavenly adherents ('spirits of his lot').[96] In the reconstructed line that opens the curse cited above, Belial is identified as 'angel of the pit' ([מלא]ך השחה) and 'spirit of destruction' ((ורו]ח האב[דון)), explicitly identifying this figure as an angel associated with the underworld realm (cf. also 1QM xiii.11–12), and evidencing a word-association with 'destruction' (אֲבַדּוֹן) akin to Rev 9:11.

The king of the locusts (Rev 9:11), poetically described as a personification of the underworld pit which constitutes its domain, is an angelic figure who most closely corresponds to Belial, 'the angel of the pit', in the DSS.[97]

---

the underworld, *Mot* in Ugaritic literature, as well as *Thanatos* as a character in Greek tragedy (cf. Euripides, *Alcestis*; compare *Testament of Abraham*); Ludlow 2002: ch 5; *DDD*: 1999 (Abaddon, Mot).

94   Swete 1906: 117. On possible word-play between Ἀπολλύων (Destroyer) and Apollo (Aeschylus, *Agammemnon*, 1080-2; Euripides, *Phaethon*, frg. 781; Menander *Peric.* 440), perhaps hinting at an allusion to Nero (cf. Suetonius, *Nero*, 53); cf. Aune 1998a: 535.

95   Davila 2000: 59–62 (59).

96   Cf S. D. Sperling, *DDD* 1999: 169–71.

97   In addition to the negative references to Belial as ruler of the abyss, there are also various ascriptions of authority over the abyss/Hades/Tartarus to one of the archangels, notably, Uriel, who is in charge of Tartarus (ὁ ἐπὶ τοῦ ταρτάρου) (I En 20:2); and variations on the name [Je]remiel (cf. I En 20:8), *Apoc. Zeph* 6:15 'the great angel Eremiel who is over the abyss and Hades' (explicitly contrasted with another 'great angel', the Accuser/Satan, who is also located in Hades *Apoc. Zeph.* 6:1-17); IV Ezra 4:36 Jeremiel the archangel in charge of the souls in Hades; and II Baruch 55:3, 63:6, Ramael, in charge of true visions. (Cf. Carol Newsom, 'Uriel', *ABD* 6, p 769; G. W. E. Nickelsburg, 'Jeremiel', *ABD* 3, pp.722–3).

Unlike the proverbial locusts who are free of monarchical rule (Prov 30:27), the polymorphic abyssal-locusts of Rev 9:3-11 fall under the jurisdiction of the 'angel of the abyss', Belial, the ruler of the present age (cf. 1QS i:18).[98] One immediate difficulty is that HC1 is monolingual and has no access to, or knowledge of, the DSS or related Hebrew/Aramaic material, unlike the bilingual implied author of Rev 9. Is HC1 therefore able to draw a connection between ὁ ἄγγελος τῆς ἀβύσσου and Belial/Satan?[99] I think that it may be very difficult for HC1 to make such an interpretative link on the basis of the contents of her mental library alone. Although Rev 11:7, 17:8 will refer to the Beast (τὸ θηρίον) ascending from the abyss, and Rev 20:1-3 to the imprisoning of the Dragon/Satan in this realm, the imagery differs, as the characters are depicted as imprisoned within this realm, rather than ruling over it. As a consequence, HC1 may be more likely to either identify Uriel as ὁ ἄγγελος τῆς ἀβύσσου, given that this archangel is entrusted with authority over Tartarus in I En 20:2, or else interpret the epithet 'Απολλύων as a personification of the underworld itself (= ἀπώλεια, cf. Ps 87:12 LXX).[100]

HC1's pre-understanding of the hybrid locusts visualised by Joel, and supplemented by the descriptions of Moses, Ezekiel and Amos, as the eschatological enemy from the north (Joel 2:20/Ezek 38-39), functioning as the Lord's agents of judgment (Joel 1-2), under the command of Gog, their king (Amos 7:1), is modified as a consequence of the Apocalypse's more expansive vision. The northern origins of this force is reconfigured by their emergence from the *north*-western perimeter of the disc-earth, the entrance to the subterranean abyss (cf. I En 17:7-8; I En 76:10-11), such that this force is re-imagined as a chthonic cavalry force of hybrid angelic beings. Consistent with their abyssal origins is the reassignment of their leader, no longer Gog, but rather the 'angel of abyss', the personified ruler of the underworld pit/ Hades ('Απολλύων, cf. Ps 87:12 LXX).

---

98   Contra. Prov 30:27 LXX: 'The locust is not ruled by a king (ἀβασίλευτόν ἐστιν ἡ ἀκρὶς), yet she marches out, in good order, at a single command.'

99   Neither Abaddon nor Apollyon is referred to again in the Apocalypse, and Belial/ Beliar is never once named in the Apocalypse; instead the preferred designations for the chief anti-God agent are Dragon, Serpent, Satan and Devil (cf. Rev 20:2). Aune 1998a: 534 raises this caveat as a warning against equating 'the angel of the abyss' with Belial/ Satan, yet nonetheless concedes that the presence of the definite article (ὁ ἄγγελος) is more explicable if the intended audience identified this abyssal figure with an existing agent.

100   Possible connections between Nero *rediturus* and Beliar are relevant to the broader discussion but lie outside the narrow parameters of HC1's mental library; cf. Bauckham 1993: 384–452; Collins 1974; Klauck 2001; Kreitzer 1988; Lawrence 1978; Thomas 2008: 91–110; Tuplin 1989; van Henten 2000; van Kooten 2005, 2007; Yarbro Collins 1976: 176–83.

4.5 HC1's Interpretation of the Sixth Trumpet (Rev 9:13-19)

4.5.1 The Cosmic Geography of the Sixth-Trumpet (Rev 9:13-15)

[13] Καὶ ὁ ἕκτος ἄγγελος ἐσάλπισεν· καὶ ἤκουσα φωνὴν μίαν ἐκ τῶν [τεσσάρων] κεράτων[101] τοῦ θυσιαστηρίου τοῦ χρυσοῦ τοῦ ἐνώπιον τοῦ θεοῦ,
[14] λέγοντα τῷ ἕκτῳ ἀγγέλῳ, ὁ ἔχων τὴν σάλπιγγα· λῦσον τοὺς τέσσαρας ἀγγέλους τοὺς δεδεμένους ἐπὶ τῷ ποταμῷ τῷ μεγάλῳ Εὐφράτῃ.
[15] καὶ ἐλύθησαν οἱ τέσσαρες ἄγγελοι οἱ ἡτοιμασμένοι εἰς τὴν ὥραν καὶ ἡμέραν καὶ μῆνα καὶ ἐνιαυτόν, ἵνα ἀποκτείνωσιν τὸ τρίτον τῶν ἀνθρώπων.

13. And the sixth angel trumpeted: and I heard one voice from the [four] horns of the golden altar before God,
14. saying to the sixth angel, the one who has the trumpet: 'Release the four angels who have been bound at the great river Euphrates.'
15. And the four angels were released, who had been prepared for the hour, and day, and month, and year, in order to kill a third of humanity.

HC1's appreciation of the topography of Rev 9:13ff is informed by her pre-existing mental map of two interrelated territories: i) the interior of the celestial temple (cf. I Enoch 14–16, Isaiah 6, Ezekiel 1, 10, 40–48, Daniel 7; cf. *Songs of the Sabbath Sacrifice* (4Q 400–7); ii) the function of the river Euphrates (Rev 9:14) as a boundary marker (cf. Gen 15:18, Deut 1:7, 11:24, etc). I will sketch HC1's pre-existing mental map, deriving from the contents of her mental library, before assessing how this informs her interpretation of the cosmology/cosmic geography of Rev 9:13ff.

HC1 is familiar with depictions of the heavenly realm, the region beyond the firmament, as a celestial sanctuary in which the Deity is enthroned on a cherubim-throne in the heavenly Holy of Holies (cf. I Enoch 14:15-23; Daniel 7:9-10). The contours of the architecture of the celestial sanctuary is equally familiar to HC1 from the architecture of the wilderness tabernacle (cf. Ex 25–30) given that the celestial realm is envisaged as the model (τύπος) of the terrestrial tabernacle (cf. Ex 25:40 LXX).[102] Accordingly, HC1's pre-existing mental map of the interior of the celestial sanctuary is close to the vision recounted in I Enoch 14:8-23, which depicts a tripartite structure:

---

101 For the textual complexities and disturbances in the manuscript tradition in Rev 9:13b, resulting from scribal confusion with regard to the source of the voice: golden altar (ℵ*); (one of the) horns of the altar (A, P⁴⁷, 0207); angel (Tyc.), discussed already by Tyconius, *Commentary* III.38 (cf. Gryson 2011: 160, 286–8), cf. Aune 1998a: 488–9; Hoskier 1929: 248–9; Metzger 1975: 742.

102 Cf. Chyutin 2006.

an outer-court (I En 14:9), inner house (holy place) (I En 14:10-14), and interior holy of holies (I En 14:15-23), perhaps most likely conceived in conformity with Ex 25–30 as an adjoining series of rectangular rooms (§3.3.1). Rev 4–5 re-envisions such a tripartite structure, redesigning the spatial model from a rectangular plan with the Holy of Holies at the far-end of the structure, to a series of concentric circles of graded holiness (§3.4).

The golden altar of incense and the seven spirits/lamps/(arch)angels function as the celestial analogues to the golden altar of incense (cf. Ex 30:1-10) and seven lamps of the menorah (cf. Ex 25:31-40), respectively, in the holy place of the wilderness tabernacle (cf. Rev 15:5). The hierarchical relationship between the golden altar of incense, and the sixth trumpet-angel (Rev 9:13-14) corresponds to the relative spatial location of these heavenly functionaries in the celestial court, measured in terms of their proximity to the central throne (cf. Ex 30:26, 40:24, 26). The pre-eminent spatial location of the golden altar over against the menorah in the holy place of the wilderness tabernacle is consistent with the higher-status of the golden-incense altar in Rev 9:13-14. Accordingly, the animate golden-altar of incense is depicted as hierarchically superior to the sixth trumpet-angel, such that one of its four horns can command the subordinate arch-angel to 'Release! (λῦσον)' the bound angels on the disc-earth (9:14β).

The Apocalypse's description of an animate altar in the celestial sanctuary (Rev 9:13-14; 16:7) has close parallels with the praise of the animate furnishings in the celestial sanctuary/sanctuaries in the fragmentary *Songs of the Sabbath Sacrifice* (4Q 400-407; 11Q 17; Mas 1k).[103] The *Songs of the Sabbath Sacrifice* is a Hebrew liturgical text extant in ten fragmentary copies (nine from Qumran and one from Masada) that date from *c*. 50 BCE–50 CE, and which provides the rubrics for the first 13 sabbaths of the liturgical calendar.[104] Newsom in particular emphasizes the function of such a text in the Sabbath liturgy of the *yaḥad* at Qumran, in which the songs replaced, rather than accompanied, the Sabbath holocaust offerings of the first quarter of the year (cf. Num 28:9-10; Ezek 46:4-5), as one of 'communal mysticism'.[105] The earthly worshippers/priests are called to join in the praise of the angelic priesthood, with its repetitious meditation on the number seven (Songs 6–8), before being led progressively through the courts of the outer-celestial sanctuary (Songs 9–10) to the inner דביר (Song 11), and a vision of

---

103   Cf. Alexander 2006: 13–73; Charlesworth and Newsom 1999; Davila 2000: 83–167; Newsom 1985.

104   The reason why only the first quarter of the liturgical calendar (Sabbaths 1–13) is covered is a puzzle, but recent suggestions of a close connection with the Festival of Weeks (which occurred between Sabbaths 11 and 12), and which marked the Qumran community's covenant renewal ceremony, is plausible, especially as one of the (later) lectionary readings for this festival was the vision of the divine chariot of Ezekiel 1, which underlies much of the imagery of *Sabbath Song* 12; cf. Charlesworth and Newsom 1999: 4; Davila 2000: 88–90.

105   Charlesworth and Newsom 1999: 4–5; Newsom 1990: 113–18.

the divine chariot-throne (מרכבה) (cf. Rev 4–5).[106] The most pertinent extracts concern the descriptions of the animate furnishings of the celestial sanctuary praising the Deity on the throne.

Sabbath Song 7 (4Q 403 frag 1. 2.13-15)[107]

13. And all the decorations of the inner room make haste with wondrous psalms in the inner ro[om ...] (וכול מחשבי הדביר יחושו בתהלי פלא בדביר)
14. wonder, inner room to inner room with the sound of holy tumult. And all their decorations [...] 15. and the chariots of his inner room give praise together (והללו יחד מרכבות דבירו), and their cherubim and their ophannim bless wondrously (וברכו פלא כרוביהם ואופניהם) ...

(4Q 403 frag. 23 1.8-10)[108]

8. ...Whenever the divine beings of knowledge enter by the portals of glory, and whenever the holy angels go out to their dominion, 9. the portals of entrance and the gates of exit make known the glory of the king (פתחי מבואי ושערי מוצא משמיעים כבוד המלך), blessing and praising all the spirits of 10. God at (their) going out and at (their) coming in through the gates of holiness. ...

As in the *Songs of the Sabbath Sacrifice*, so also the celestial furnishings of the Apocalypse are envisaged as animate heavenly beings that join in the praise of the One on the throne (cf. Rev 16:7; cf. 4Q 403 frg. 1 1.41–46; 4Q 405 frgs. 14–15 col. 1; 4Q 405 frg. 19; 4Q 405 frg. 23 1.8–10).[109] More specifically, the golden altar of incense is perceived to be an angelic functionary, which, like the 'living beings' of the cherubim-throne (Rev 4:6b-8), is accorded an exalted position in the angelic hierarchy, on the basis of its proximity to the sacred-space of the Throne.

---

106 Charlesworth and Newsom 1999: 11.
107 Charlesworth and Newsom 1999: 56–7.
108 Charlesworth and Newsom 1999: 94–5.
109 Cf. Allison 1986: 410–11; Elgvin 2009: 268–71; Ulfgard 2009: 260–4.
In Rev 3:12 those who conquer are promised the reward of being transformed into a pillar (στῦλος) in the (celestial) sanctuary (ἐν τῷ ναῷ τοῦ θεοῦ μου), which must similarly constitute a heavenly/angelic status. Cf. II Enoch 20:1 [J] where a range of angelic beings are described: cherubim, seraphim, 'many-eyed thrones' (cf. plural *merkaboth* in the *Songs of the Sabbath Sacrifice*), and '*otanim*' (a likely corruption of the *ofanim* (wheels) of Ezekiel 1), (Andersen, OTP I: 134).

It is uncertain, however, to what extent HC1 would be cognizant of such a celestial hierarchy, on the basis of the contents of her mental-library, which lacks the illuminating background detailed in the *Songs of the Sabbath Sacrifice*. Whilst HC1 could assign the voice to the unspecified angel of 8:3, who stands over (ἐπί) the golden-altar, I will credit the hearer-construct with sufficient wit to perceive that the golden-altar is an animate celestial functionary, simply on the basis of the worldview of the Apocalypse itself, which offers its hearers the opportunity to become a 'pillar' (στῦλος) in the celestial sanctuary (3:12), and describes the four living-beings that comprise the throne (cf. 6:1, 3, 5, 7) and perhaps even the throne itself (6:6, 16:17, 19:5), as animate and vocal functionaries in the celestial hierarchy.[110]

As a result, HC1 may recall Daniel's fractured vision of the animate, vocal horn (κέρας) of the fourth Beast (Dan 7:7-8 LXX), which possesses both human-like eyes (ὀφθαλμοὶ ὥσπερ ὀφθαλμοὶ ἀνθρώπινοι) and a mouth 'speaking great things' (στόμα λαλοῦν μεγάλα). A triangulation of resonances is created by the 're-envisioning' of the vocally-horned creature at Rev 13:1-10, where the composite, ten-horned (κέρατα δέκα) amalgam of the Danielic chaos monsters is afforded a similar vocal proficiency (στόμα λαλοῦν μεγάλα καὶ βλασφημίας) (Rev 13:5).[111] *Visual reminiscences* evoked by Rev 9:13 serve to emphasize the extent to which the speech of the ten-horned Beast from the sea (Rev 13:1-10) constitutes a scandalous mockery of the animate four-horned altar's praise of the Deity (cf. Rev 16:7).

The river Euphrates constitutes a bi-focal boundary marker for HC1 (Rev 9:14). From a political perspective, the river Euphrates formed the natural border of the eastern extent of the Roman Empire, the boundary that separated the Roman empire from the Parthian kingdom (cf. Strabo, *Geography* 11.6.4; 11.9.2–3).[112] Whilst Rome often engaged in military conflict with the Parthians over control of this border territory (especially Armenia), even during the early reign of Nero, the predominant position was of alliances and agreements between the two empires. Nonetheless, the potential threat of the armoured cavalry of Parthia remained a vivid memory, in view of earlier successful military campaigns by the Parthians

---

110   Beale 1999: 505–6 assigns the voice to an unnamed angel (cf. 8:3, so also Swete 1906: 118), or perhaps to Christ (on the basis of Rev 6:6 – a voice which is more plausibly assigned to the animate throne). Beale's perception of the celestial hierarchy brackets-out animate furniture, and so he is forced to revert to an alternative scheme, in which Christ is appealed to as of superior status to the sixth trumpet-angel. Aune 1998a: 536 and Smalley 2005: 235–6 both assign the voice to the celestial altar.

111   Cf. Aune 1998a: 742–3; Beale 1999: 694–6; Smalley 2005: 240.

112   Strabo occasionally extols Roman imperial ideology to the extent that he proclaims Roman dominion over the whole οἰκουμένη (Strabo, *Geogr.* 6.4.2; cf. Philo, *Legat.* 10), but on other occasions he more accurately notes the autonomous kingdom of the Parthians at Rome's eastern border (Strabo, *Geogr.* 11.9.2-3); cf. Clarke 1999; Dueck, Lindsay and Pothecary 2005.

at Carrhae (in 53 BCE) and most notably an incursion into Roman territory in 40 BCE (cf. Appian, *Bell. Civ.* 5.9).[113]

For a scripturally literate hearer, an additional layer of meaning is detected, which vies for attention with the acknowledged Roman imperial significance. The precise phrase present in Rev 9:14 ὁ ποταμὸς τῷ μεγάλῳ Εὐφράτῃ (the great river Euphrates) evokes an alternative configuration of territorial boundaries, namely the 'ideal limit' of the land of God's promise to Abraham and his descendants, extending from 'the river of Egypt, to the great river, the river Euphrates' (ἀπὸ τοῦ ποταμοῦ Αἰγύπτου ἕως τοῦ ποταμοῦ τοῦ μεγάλου ποταμοῦ Εὐφράτου) (Gen 15:18 LXX; cf. Ex 23:31; Deut 1:7, 11:24; Josh 1:4).[114] HC1 is consequently aware of *two rival territorial* boundaries, signalled by the 'great river Euphrates': the ideal limit of the eastern border of the land of Israel, and the usurpation of this same territory by the eastern extent of the Roman empire during the first century CE. For HC1, agents located at the 'great river Euphrates' are evocative both of the threat of a Parthian cavalry invasion of the Roman empire from beyond its eastern border (cf. Rev 9:15-19; 16:12) and of a military campaign to *restore* the rightful territorial boundaries of the 'kingdom of our Lord and his Messiah (ἡ βασιλεία...τοῦ κυρίου ἡμῶν καὶ τοῦ χριστοῦ αὐτοῦ)' (Rev 11:15).

The simplified aerial plan of the boundaries of the οἰκουμένη and the idealized borders of the land of Israel within, that are sketched in the Apocalypse's mental map of the earth (cf. Rev 7:1-3; 9:13-15; 20:8), are strongly influenced by comparable sets of four-point border lists that both the implied author and HC1 are familiar with (Ex 23:31; Deut 11:24; cf. more elaborate multiple point descriptions in Ezek 47:15-20 and Num 34:3-12), which envisage these territories as a simple four-sided rectangle with four corner-points (cf. §3.4). Accordingly, on HC1's mental map of Rev 9:1ff the abyssal locusts are positioned as emerging from the 'well/mouth of the abyss' (Rev 9:2-3; cf. I En 17:7-8), beyond the NW perimeter of the οἰκουμένη, whilst the four bound angels (Rev 9:14-15) and the tri-morphic cavalry (Rev 9:16-19) are stationed within the οἰκουμένη, at the eastern border of the Roman Empire/Israel (cf. Gen 15:18), at the river Euphrates (cf. fig. 4.4).

---

113 Bivar 1983; Edwell 2008; Fowler 2007.

114 Cf. Swete 1906: 119. For a discussion of various texts that describe two-point (N-S) or four-point (N-E-S-W) borders of the land of Israel, the latter envisaging the land as a rectangle (as in Rev 7:1ff), cf. P. Alexander, *ABD* 2: 985–6.

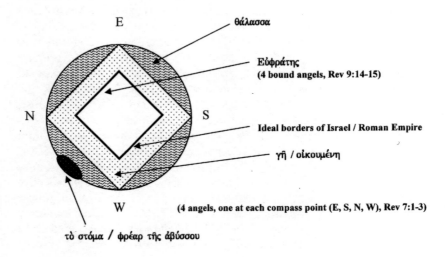

Fig. 4.4 *Aerial view of the cuboid earth with the relative spatial locations of* τὸ φρέαρ τῆς ἀβύσσου *and the two sets of* τέσσαρες ἄγγελοι *(Rev 7:1-3; 9:14-15)*

4.5.2 The Bound Angels (Rev 9:13-15)

On the basis of the contents of HC1's mental library three potential identifications of the four bound angels present themselves: i) the four angels restraining the winds in Rev 7:1-3; ii) the bound Watchers of I Enoch 10; and iii) the deputation of evil angels of Ps 77:49 LXX.[115] The relative strengths of each of these proposals will be considered in turn.

What correlation, if any, might HC1 draw between the four angels of Rev 7:1-3, located at the four corners of the earth, and the four angels bound at the river Euphrates (Rev 9:14)?[116] The four angels (τέσσαρας ἀγγέλους)

---

115   Although not described as 'bound', the angels located at the Parthian border in I En 56:5-7 strongly resonate with Rev 9:13-19, in view of the topographical similarities heightened by comparable metaphorical registers, descriptive of cavalry breaking out 'like lions from their lairs'; cf. Nickelsburg and VanderKam 2004: 70; Arcari 2007. *The Similitudes of Enoch* lie outside the parameters of HC1's mental library, however, and so are not available as a source of resonance.

116   Aune 1998a: 426 notes that the first reference to the four angels in Rev 7:1 is anarthrous, as this group of angels is otherwise unknown to the intended audience, whereas the second reference in 7:2 is articular, representing an anaphoric use of the definite article. Consequently, the presence of the definite article in Rev 9:14 (τοὺς τέσσαρας

(Rev 7:1), entrusted with authority over the four cardinal winds, stand at the four corners of the earth (ἑστῶτας ἐπὶ τὰς τέσσαρας γωνίας τῆς γῆς) (cf. fig. 4.4) in order temporarily to restrain (κρατέω) the (personified) winds originating from these compass points, so as to prevent their gaining access to the interior of the land and sea, and wreaking destruction on the flora and fauna (πᾶν δένδρον) within (Rev 7:1-3, cf. I Enoch 76, §4.4.2 above). Whilst there is a superficial connection between the four angels of Rev 7:1-3 and 9:14-15, with respect to number, the spatial location (gates of the wind at the four compass points (cf. I En 34:1-36:4) versus eastern border of the land of Israel/Roman empire) and role (binding winds rather than being bound themselves) differs too sharply for HC1 to equate these angelic functionaries.[117]

Might the four bound angels of Rev 9:14-15 resonate, instead, with the bound Watchers of I Enoch 10? Azael is 'bound hand and foot' and cast into the darkness of the wilderness, and Shemihazah and his associates are similarly bound and laid in the 'valleys of the earth' (I En 10:4-8; 11-13). The basic connection with Rev 9:14 rests on the description of the 'binding' (δέω) of rebellious angelic Watchers. A major stumbling block relates to the divergent cosmic geography. Azael is bound in fetters like a criminal and cast into a dark opening in the wilderness (I En 10:4) that functions both as a prison-dungeon and as an image of Sheol as a dark (σκότος) chthonic realm.[118] Yet neither the ambiguous topographical reference to Δαδουὴλ (I En 10:4), nor the astronomical reinterpretation of this region (as an abyss beyond the perimeter of the earth in I En 18:6ff), suggests any association with the eastern boundary of the empire.[119] Shemihazah and his associates are detained at a variety of spatial locations dispersed among 'the valleys of the earth' (τὰς νάπας τῆς γῆς) (I En 10:12), again without any suggestion of a connection with the Euphrates.

The third option relates to the 'wonders' (τὰ θαυμάσια) of the Lord that are recounted in the didactic psalm, Ps 78 (Ps 77 LXX), which includes an account of the plague cycle as part of the Lord's deliverance of his people from Egypt (vv 42-53).[120] Seven of the Exodus plagues are recounted: blood, flies, frogs, locusts,[121] hail, pestilence (vv 44-48) concluding with the death of the first-born (v 51). The most striking element, however, relates to the unparalleled reference to the Lord dispatching his wrath among the Egyptians:

ἀγγέλους) suggests that this group of four angels should be familiar to the target audience, either from external sources or as an anaphoric reference back to the angels in Rev 7:1-3.

117 So also Aune 1998a: 536–7 (leaving the narrative role of angels in Rev 7:1-3 unfulfilled); Charles 1920a: 248; Swete 1906: 118–19.

118 Cf. Nickelsburg 2001: 221–2; cf. Prometheus (Aeschylus, *Prometheus Bound*) and the Titans (Hesiod, *Theogony*, 617–735).

119 For the variant readings (e.g. Δουδαηλ) and proposed interpretations, based on reconstructed Hebrew/Aramaic originals, see Milik 1976: 29–30; Nickelsburg 2001: 222.

120 Cf. Dahood 1968: 234–48; Gillingham 1999; Kraus 1989: 118–31; Lee 1990.

121 Ps 77:46 LXX καὶ ἔδωκεν τῇ ἐρυσίβῃ τὸν καρπὸν αὐτῶν καὶ τοὺς πόνους αὐτῶν τῇ ἀκρίδι (He gave the fruit [of their toil] to the rust, and their labours to the locust).

49. He sent among them his anger's wrath (ἐξαπέστειλεν εἰς αὐτοὺς ὀργὴν θυμοῦ αὐτοῦ), anger and wrath and distress (θυμὸν καὶ ὀργὴν καὶ θλῖψιν), a deputation through evil angels (ἀποστολὴν δι' ἀγγέλων πονηρῶν)

50. He made a path for his wrath (ὡδοποίησεν τρίβον τῇ ὀργῇ αὐτοῦ)...

(Ps 77:49-50a LXX)

In the context of Ps 78:49-50 the 'deputation of evil messengers' (מִשְׁלַחַת מַלְאֲכֵי רָעִים) (v.49γ) would seem to refer back to the divine attributes listed in v 49β, depicted as personifications sent out as YHWH's agents (עֶבְרָה וָזַעַם וְצָרָה) (Fury, Rage, and Distress). These agents of divine retribution enable the psalmist to describe the direct action of YHWH against his human adversaries, the Egyptians, whilst retaining the Deity's transcendence. A smooth pathway is metaphorically created for these divine attributes/messengers, to speedily take vengeance against the lives of YHWH's opponents (v 50).[122] In the LXX version, however, the angelic forces are transformed into the mediators of the Lord's divine wrath which is delegated through (διά) their actions, as his celestial military force (cf. Joel 2:25 LXX).

In view of the affective resonances between the plague-cycle of Ps 77 LXX and the trumpet-septet of plagues in Rev 8:1-11:19, might HC1 relate the bound angels of Rev 9:14 with the destructive agents of divine vengeance in Ps 77:49 LXX? Once again, the proposed identification founders on the spatial dissonance between the two verbal images. The 'evil angels' (ἄγγελοι πονηροί) of Ps 77:49 LXX are dispatched wherever a path is laid (ὁδοποιέω) by the Deity (v 50a). By contrast, the 'bound angels' of Rev 9:14 are detained at the eastern boundary of the river Euphrates.

The limited contents of HC1's mental library, deficient in comparison with the 'ideal hearer' of the text,[123] leave her at a loss as to the identity of these four bound angels, as no comparable φάντασμα is recoverable from the multiplicity of mental images impressed on her ψυχή, in which angels are bound at the eastern border of the οἰκουμένη.

---

122 Contrast Kraus 1989: 129 who relates the phrase to 'demonic powers', and Dahood 1968: 244 who modifies the pointing to describe the evil angels as divine escorts, preparing YHWH's path (vv 49–50).

123 Cf. Eagleton 2008: 105 'For the structuralists, the "ideal reader" of a work was someone who would have at his or her disposal all of the codes which would render it exhaustively intelligible.'

4.5.3 The Tri-morphic Cavalry (Rev 9:16-19)

¹⁶ καὶ ὁ ἀριθμὸς τῶν στρατευμάτων τοῦ ἱππικοῦ δισμυριάδες μυριάδων, ἤκουσα τὸν ἀριθμὸν αὐτῶν.

¹⁷ Καὶ οὕτως εἶδον τοὺς ἵππους ἐν τῇ ὁράσει καὶ τοὺς καθημένους ἐπ' αὐτῶν, ἔχοντας θώρακας πυρίνους καὶ ὑακινθίνους καὶ θειώδεις, καὶ αἱ κεφαλαὶ τῶν ἵππων ὡς κεφαλαὶ λεόντων, καὶ ἐκ τῶν στομάτων αὐτῶν ἐκπορεύεται πῦρ καὶ καπνὸς καὶ θεῖον.

¹⁸ ἀπὸ τῶν τριῶν πληγῶν τούτων ἀπεκτάνθησαν τὸ τρίτον τῶν ἀνθρώπων, ἐκ τοῦ πυρὸς καὶ τοῦ καπνοῦ καὶ τοῦ θείου τοῦ ἐκπορευομένου ἐκ τῶν στομάτων αὐτῶν.

¹⁹ ἡ γὰρ ἐξουσία τῶν ἵππων ἐν τῷ στόματι αὐτῶν ἐστιν καὶ ἐν ταῖς οὐραῖς αὐτῶν, αἱ γὰρ οὐραὶ αὐτῶν ὅμοιαι ὄφεσιν, ἔχουσαι κεφαλὰς καὶ ἐν αὐταῖς ἀδικοῦσιν.

16. And the number of the cavalry-soldiers (is) a double myriad of myriads – I heard their number.
17. And thus I saw the horses in the vision and those sitting upon them, having fiery and hyacinthine and sulphurous breast-plates, and the horses' heads (are) like lions' heads, and fire and smoke and sulphur is coming out of their mouths.
18. A third of humanity was killed by these three plagues, from the fire and smoke and sulphur coming out of their mouths,
19. for the authority of the horses is in their mouths and in their tails, for their tails (are) like snakes, (which) have heads, and with them they are doing harm.

The extent of this almost innumerable force, resonant with the angelic hosts engaged in the celestial liturgy (Rev 5:11; Dan 7:10), is beyond the perception of the seer, who is reliant on divine disclosure to comprehend such a vast total (ἤκουσα τὸν ἀριθμὸν αὐτῶν, cf. 7:4). The epic scale of this military invasion bears comparison, for HC1, with the renowned 'Catalogue of Ships' recounted in *Iliad* II. 484–760.[124] The seer, like the poet, is reliant on divine inspiration to recount the scale of such an innumerable force:

Iliad II.484-93[125]
Tell me now, you Muses who have dwellings on Olympus – for you are goddesses and present and know all things, but we hear only a rumour and know nothing – who were the leaders and lords of the Danaans. But the multitude I could not tell or name (πληθὺν δ' οὐκ αν ἐγὼ μυθήσομαι οὐδ' ὀνομήνω), not even if ten tongues were mine and ten mouths and a voice unwearying, and the heart within me were of bronze, unless the Muses of Olympus, daughters of Zeus who bears the aegis, call to my mind all those who came beneath Ilios.

124 Kirk 1985: 166–240; Murray 1999: 96–117.
125 Murray 1999: 96–7.

The conflated verbal echoes of the locust-cavalry of Joel 1–2, refracted through the mythological lens of Gog and the enemy from the north in the immediate context of the fifth trumpet (esp. Rev 9:7-9), continue to exert a considerable influence. As Farrer discerns, these two woes can be perceived, in one sense, as variations on a theme of Joel 1-2:

> There can be no doubt that the description of the cavalry is inspired by the same texts of Joel as the preceding vision. Joel describes the locusts as invading cavalry; St John makes two pictures of it – cavalry like locusts, and locust-like cavalry. He does not even wish to contrast them strongly. The locusts have lions' teeth, yet do all their damage with their scorpion-tails; the cavalry horses have lions' heads, and do their damage with them; but they can hurt with their snake-headed tails as well.[126]

Whereas in the fifth-trumpet the locust-form retained a controlling hold on the description of the monstrous cavalry (Rev 9:7-9), in the sixth trumpet this hold is relaxed, allowing the tri-morphic cavalry to take on new, and ever more fearsome, shape (9:16-19).[127] The original images plucked from Joel 1–2 (specifically Joel 1:6, 2:4-5) that formed the basis of the fifth trumpet's vision are re-imagined and sculpted into new forms in the sixth trumpet that succeeds it. The tri-morphic cavalry share leonine features with the locust-cavalry (Rev 9:8β; 17γ), but in an expanded form, as the whole of their heads are now likened to a lion, and not simply their teeth (καὶ αἱ κεφαλαὶ τῶν ἵππων ὡς κεφαλαὶ λεόντων). The central core of the tri-morphic cavalry remains that of a cavalry horse (ἵππος), now including a mounted soldier (ἱππικον) (cf. Rev 9:16α, 17α, 19α). This added detail develops the reference to cavalry soldiers (ἱππεύς) in Joel 2:4β LXX, an element which was not explicated in the fifth trumpet's re-envisioning of Joel 2:4-5 (cf. Rev 9:7α, 9:9β).

Rev 9:13-19 re-envisions *both* Joel 1–2 and the expansion of this vision in Rev 9:7-9. This dual focus can be seen most clearly in the re-appropriation of innovative additions to Joel 1–2 that were expressed in Rev 9:7-9, most notably the armoured 'breast-plates' (θώρακας σιδηροῦς, 9:9α; θώρακας πυρίνους καὶ ὑακινθίνους καὶ θειώδεις, 9:17β) and the harmful tails (ἐν ταῖς οὐραῖς αὐτῶν ἡ ἐξουσία αὐτῶν ἀδικῆσαι τοὺς ἀνθρώπους, 9:10β; ἡ γὰρ ἐξουσία τῶν ἵππων...ἐν ταῖς οὐραῖς αὐτῶν...καὶ ἐν αὐταῖς ἀδικοῦσιν; 9:19). The tri-morphic cavalry of Rev 9:16-19 are, in no small part, a re-imagined representation of the hybrid locust-cavalry of Joel 1–2, distorted through the lens of the polymorphic abyssal locusts of Rev 9:7-9. In this

---

126 Farrer 1964: 121; cf. Tyconius, *Commentary* III.43; Gryson 2011: 161.

127 An ancient hearer with a more extensive encyclical education than HC1 would doubtless have picked up the visual correspondences with the mythological Chimaera (Χίμαιρα). The Chimaera was a lion-headed, goat-bodied monster with a snake-headed tail, who breathed fire (cf. Homer, *Iliad* VI. 181–2; Hesiod, *Theogony*, 319–24; Euripides, *Ion* 203–4, *Electra* 474–5); cf. Clay 2003: 157–61.

altered vision the locust-form of these monstrous creatures recedes entirely into the background, as the equine attributes of this fearsome cavalry are allowed free-reign.

The fifth trumpet vision had revised HC1's pre-existing interpretation of Joel 1–2 in which she had formerly equated the locust-cavalry with the enemy from the north (Joel 2:20; Ezek 38–39) under the command of Gog (Amos 7:1 LXX). Rev 9:1ff intensified the chthonic imagery to reimagine these creatures as abyssal angelic hybrids, who ascend from the NW entrance to the Pit, under the command of Abaddon (Beliar/the personified ruler of Hades) (Rev 9:2ff). The sixth trumpet creates another image from the same visionary materials, returning once more to Ezek 38–39, but now focusing on the eastern contingent of the northern coalition, rather than Gog's own northern battalions. The spatial location of the tri-morphic cavalry in HC1's mental map, mustered at the eastern border of the Roman Empire/Israel (cf. §4.4 above), evoke the spectre of Parthian cataphracts poised to mount an invasion (cf. Plutarch, *Crassus* 24–25; Polybius 30.25.9; cf. I En 56:5-7; Josephus, *Ant.* 14).[128]

This spatial trigger is supported by verbal parallels with the topography of the sixth bowl (Rev 16:12-16, ὁ ποταμὸς ὁ μέγας Εὐφράτης), encouraging HC1 closely to connect the mustered tri-morphic cavalry of Rev 9:16ff with 'the kings from the east' (οἱ βασιλεῖς τῶν ἀπὸ ἀνατολῆς ἡλίου) (Rev 16:12), crossing the eastern border to invade the territory within.[129] Of even more import for HC1, however, are the additional connections that are forged between the Euphratean cavalry (Rev 9:16ff)/(Parthian) eastern kings (Rev 16:12) and the worldwide coalition of 'the kings of the whole inhabited earth' (οἱ βασιλεῖς τῆς οἰκουμένης ὅλης) (Rev 16:14), which re-ignite her preconceived association of Joel's locust-cavalry with Gog's northern coalition (Ezek 38–39).[130]

The spatial position of the second group of rulers, 'the kings of the whole inhabited earth' (οἱ βασιλεῖς τῆς οἰκουμένης ὅλης) (Rev 16:14, 16), differs, however, from the eastern coalition that precedes (Rev 16:12). Rev 16:13-16 describes the gathering together (συνάγω) of a more extensive coalition force, headed by the kings of the whole οἰκουμένη, strongly echoing Ps 2:2 and Ezek 38–39 (cf. Ezek 39:2). Whereas the mental map of Rev 9:13-19 utilizes four-point border maps of an idealized Israel as its template (cf. Exod 23:31; Deut 11:24), the privileged spatial template that informs Rev 16:13-16 derives rather from ethnographic *Mappa Mundi*, inspired by the cartographic Table of Nations in Gen 10 (cf. Ezek 38–39 and *Jubilees* 8–9) (cf. fig. 4.5).[131] Such ethnographic maps locate Jerusalem at the centre of a

128 Arcari 2007.
129 Note, however, that the coalition force of eastern troops (reminiscent of Parthia and her client kings) contains no explicit connection with Nero *rediturus* in Rev 16:12ff; cf. Aune 1998a: 890–4; Charles 1920b: 46–51; Prigent 2004: 469–70; Swete 1906: 202–5.
130 Cf. Bøe 2001: 76–138.
131 Cf. Alexander 1997; Scott: 1995: 5–56; 2001: 23–42; VanderKam 1994.

circular disc-earth, surrounded by hostile nations, divided into three ethnic groups (the descendants of Shem (east), the descendants of Ham (south) and the descendants of Japheth (north)).[132]

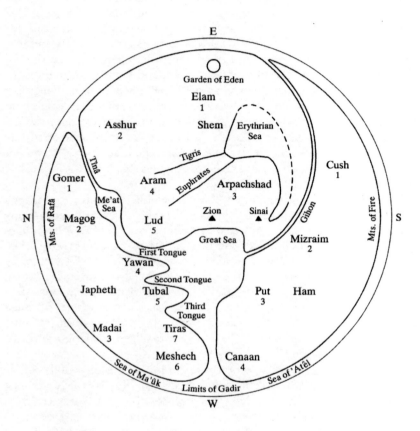

Fig. 4.5. Jubilees 8–9 Mappa Mundi (Schmidt)[133]

132 In Ezek 38:12 and Jubilees 8:19 Jerusalem/Zion is identified as the 'navel' of the earth, taking the place of Delphi in Ionian maps (Strabo, *Geogr.* 9.3.6; Pausanius, 10.6.3) and Rome in Roman maps (Strabo, *Geogr.* 6.4.1); cf. Alexander 1997.
133 Schmidt 1990: 122.

Rev 16:13-16, like Ezekiel 38–39, envisages the convergence of all the surrounding nations of the world onto a central point, explicitly identified as Ἁρμαγεδών (Rev 16:16), perhaps most plausibly a transliteration of the Hebrew הַר מְגִדּוֹ 'mountain of Megiddo', akin to 'τὰ ὄρη τοῦ Ἰσραηλ' of Ezek 39:2 LXX.[134] This shift in mental map at Rev 16:13 creates a disjunction in HC1's reading of the sixth bowl, which initially disassociates the nations which converge from all points on the οἰκουμένη onto Israel, at its centre (Rev 16:13-16; cf. Rev 19:19, 20:7-9), from the singular spatial location of the eastern cavalry/kings at the border of the Euphrates (Rev 9:13-19; 16:12). The convergence of the 'kings of the whole inhabited world' onto the battlefield (Rev 16:13-16) is an intensification of the eastern invasion which preceded, signalling a second stage in the conflict, begun in Rev 9:13-19 and recapitulated, with variation, in Rev 16:12.

Yet the emphasis on Gog, and his forces, emerging from 'the uttermost parts of the north' (מִיַּרְכְּתֵי צָפוֹן) / (ἀπ' ἐσχάτου τοῦ βορρᾶ) (Ezek 38:6, 15, 39:2), and from all the surrounding nations of the οἰκουμένη, need not preclude any connection with the Euphratean locale of Rev 9:13-19. Ezek 38–39 retains a connection with the eastern, Mesopotamian region in its anomalous inclusion of troops from Persia (פָּרַס) / (Πέρσαι) (Ezek 38:5) among the coalition forces of Gog 'from the land of Magog'.[135] The presence of Persia (פָּרַס) / (Πέρσαι) (Ezek 38:5) in this coalition force is anomalous, as it is the only referent that is not drawn from the Table of Nations in Gen 10. The inclusion of Persia, Cush (= Ethiopia) and Put (= Libya) among the allied forces of Gog is often excised as a secondary gloss that distorts a hypothetical original force originating exclusively from the northern tribes of Japheth.[136] Yet for a 1st-century CE hearer (HC1) familiar with Ezek 38:5 LXX, and predisposed to forge a close connection between Joel's locust cavalry and Ezekiel's 'enemy from the north', the inclusion of the tri-morphic cavalry/eastern kings among Gog's coalition forces is entirely appropriate.

Further retrieving HC1's former reading of Joel 1–2, as Gog's northern foe (Joel 2:20) functioning as the Lord's theophanic host (cf. Joel 2:3; cf. Ps 49:3, 96:1-3 LXX), the sixth trumpet vision continues by accentuating the tri-morphic cavalry's role as divine agents of judgment.[137] The cavalry's theophanic agency is evidenced by their troop numbers (δισμυριάδες

134 Cf. Aune 1998a: 898-99; Charles 1920b: 50; Swete 1906: 206.
135 Childs 1959: 196.
136 So Zimmerli 1983: 285, 306, who notes the confusion in the versions on the identity of these nations; yet the LXX simply translates the MT referents using contemporary Greek names: Persia, Ethiopia and Libya (Πέρσαι καὶ Αἰθίοπες καὶ Λίβυες). Block 1998: 439–40 retains the line but interprets פָּרַס not as a reference to 'Persia', but as an otherwise unattested commercial/military ally of Egypt (despite the exclusive use of this noun to denote Persia elsewhere in the Hebrew Bible (cf. Dan 10:1, 13, 20; Ezra 1:1, 2, 8, etc.).
137 So also Steinmann 1992: 73-4, although I do not accept his further interpretative step which (allegorically) identifies these hybrid creatures with 'Christians as witnesses in the world' (74).

μυριάδων, Rev 9:16; cf. Rev 5:11, Dan 7:10; I En 14:22), noted already, reminiscent of the Deity's host, and in addition the three substances which they emit: καὶ ἐκ τῶν στομάτων αὐτῶν ἐκπορεύεται πῦρ καὶ καπνὸς καὶ θεῖον (Rev 9:17γ; repeated Rev 9:18β). The fiery (πυρίνος) and sulphurous (θειώδης) colours of the cavalry's breastplates anticipate the theophanic arsenal of fire (πῦρ) and sulphur (θεῖον) that these monstrous creatures breathe out, as agents of divine judgment (cf. Rev 14:10; 19:20; 20:10; 21:8; Gen 19:24; Ps 10:6; Ezek 38:22; and cf. Rev 11:5 (two witnesses); IV Ezra 13:10 (man from the sea); II Enoch 1:5 (angelic figures)). The correlation between smoke (καπνός) and the colour-term ὑάκινθινος (purple/violet) is less easy to determine, although Swete's suggestion is ingenious, 'the blue smoke of a sulphurous flame'.[138] In any event, Rev 9:17β conflates two sets of familiar pairings: the fire and sulphur of divine judgment (Gen 19:24; Ps 10:6; Ezek 38:22), with the fire and smoke of a theophany (Ex 19:18; Isa 4:5), in order to explicate the divine agency of the tri-morphic cavalry, (cf. Joel 2:3, 2:25).[139]

The tri-morphic cavalry of Rev 9:17-19 brings to realization a nightmare vision of 'newly-created unknown beasts full of rage, or such as breathe out fiery breath, or belch forth a thick pall of smoke' (ἢ νεοκτίστους θυμοῦ πλήρεις θῆρας ἀγνώστους ἤτοι πυρπνόον φυσῶντας ἄσθμα ἢ βρόμον λικμωμένους καπνοῦ ἢ δεινοὺς ἀπ' ὀμμάτων σπινθῆρας ἀστράπτοντας) (Wis 11:18) that the Deity had chosen to avoid dispatching as agents of judgment during the original Exodus plagues. To the extent that HC1's predisposition to equate Joel's locust-cavalry with Gog's coalition forces, implementing divine judgment (Ezek 38–39; Amos 7:1 LXX), is undercut in the fifth trumpet vision, its principal motifs are rehabilitated and restored, but in a more narrowly defined form, in the sixth trumpet vision. In Rev 9:16ff (cf. Rev 16:12ff) hybrid cavalry forces from the east, evocative of Gog's Persian/Parthian allies (Ezek 38:5; cf. I En 56:5-7), undertake the divinely appointed task which Joel had assigned to the full northern force (Joel 2:20; Ezek 38-39). Joel's vision, as HC1 formerly understood it, did not reveal the full picture disclosed to the seer of the Apocalypse: the devastating multitudes described in the sixth trumpet/bowl – whom Joel had formerly glimpsed – (Rev 9:16ff/ 16:12) are merely a *prelude* to the full horror that is to be unleashed when the whole host of Gog's northern forces is unleashed (Rev 16:14ff; 19:17-21; 20:7-10).

---

138 Swete 1906: 120.

139 Another possible resonance is with Leviathan, the fire-breathing chaos monster, which similarly contains fire and smoke within its furnace-like chest (cf. Job 41:12 LXX). The inclusion of θεῖον in Rev 9:17-18, however, indicates that the emphasis is shifted here to depict the tri-morphic cavalry as agents of divine judgement, rather than as negative chaos beasts.

4.6 Conclusion

Concentrated *visual and verbal reminiscences* of Joel's former vision of hybrid locust-cavalry (Joel 1:6, 2:4-5) resonate most vocally among the leaves of HC1's mental library, as the contents of the fifth and sixth trumpet visions (Rev 9:1ff) are orally performed. Pre-existing interpretative associations between Joel's locusts (Joel 2:20), Ezekiel's northerner (Ezek 38–39), and Amos' locust-king, Gog (Amos 7:1 LXX), predispose HC1 to privilege these specific 'scrolls' among the varied contents of her mental library. Joel's locusts are equated with the 'enemy from the north', God's delegated agents of eschatological judgment, under the command of their king, Gog. The seer of the Apocalypse sees it differently (Rev 9:1ff): his 'brothers' Joel, Ezekiel and Amos were not privileged to receive the full disclosure of eschatological events (cf. IV Ezra 12:10-12) which have latterly been revealed to him. The full picture is decidedly more chthonic: the eschatological locust-force are more potent (vv 7-9), arising from the NW entrance to the abyss (cf. vv 2-3; cf. I En 17:7-8), not the northern rim of the οἰκουμένη, and their leader is Belial (v.11) (or personified Hades, for HC1), not the northern commander Gog.

And yet, the former visionaries had attained partial insight (Rev 9:16ff): Joel, Ezekiel and Amos accurately associated these hybrid cavalry troops with Gog's coalition forces, distorted mirror-images of the Deity's celestial troops (cf. Rev 5:11), armed with the characteristic theophanic arsenal of fire and sulphur (vv 17-19; cf. Joel 2:3). The flaw was in equating this extensive cavalry force with the full force of Gog's coalition, when, in truth, they accounted for only one marginal component (Ezek 38:5; Persia/Parthia). The tri-morphic cavalry are delegated a preliminary task (Rev 9:16ff; 16:12) of relaying the Deity's fatal rhetoric: one third of the population are to be annihilated to persuade the rest to reconsider their allegiance (Rev 9:20-21). Joel had been under the misapprehension that the locust-hybrids constituted the full extent of the eschatological woes (cf. Joel 1:2-3); the seer of the Apocalypse discloses that this was merely a prelude to far greater terrors to come (Rev 16:14ff; 19:17-21; 20:7-10).

HC1's apprehension of the visionary images of the fifth and sixth trumpets draws on a limited range of βιβλία deposited in her mental library: Joel, Ezekiel, Amos and I Enoch. Her cognitive map of the topography of Rev 9 is founded on a template primarily derived from Enoch (I En 17), and supplemented by four-point border maps (Ex 23:31; Deut 11:24) familiar from the Pentateuch. The visionary action is limited to liminal, border territories: the NW perimeter of the disc-earth and the eastern border of Israel/Rome, as marginal forces are commissioned by the Deity to invade the centre and terminate Rome's usurpation of an empire over which it has no claim (Rev 11:15-19). The visionary texts recalled are those which have already been rolled-up inside the scroll of Joel 1–2 in HC1's mental library (Ezek

38-39; Amos 7:1 LXX); unfurling with it, they are overwritten together by the imperialist claims of Rev 9:1ff and its expansive vision which re-envisions all that those former visionaries saw. HC1's mental library is more akin to a *florilegium* (cf. 4Q 174, 4Q 175) than a concordance, as texts containing related words, images and themes are already combined, and form a pre-understanding which HC1 brings with her when she listens to each new oral performance in her Asia Minor assembly.

The major contributory factor of HC1's *encyclical* education (Homer, Euripides, Menander) lies in its coherence with her dominant cognitive map – a tripartite 'Homeric' cosmological template – such that she is content to locate the fantastical creatures of Rev 9:1ff at the liminal edges of the disc-earth.

Chapter 5

Hearer-Construct Two (HC2):
Interpretation of the Cosmology of Rev 9:1-12

5.1 Introduction

This chapter outlines the second of two hearer-construct readings of Rev 9, focusing upon the hypothetical response of an ancient hearer with a tertiary level *encyclical* education that included exercises in prose composition (προγυμνάσματα). First to be delineated are the contents of hearer construct two's (HC2's) mental library (§5.2), a library containing the same range of scriptural texts as HC1, but supplemented by a broader range of literary authors (Homer, Menander, Hesiod, Euripides, Aratus, Herodotus, and Plato). On the basis of HC2's expanded mental library, his preferred cosmological template consists of a Platonic, seven-planetary spheres design, ornamented by the Aratean constellations – a template which diverges sharply from the tripartite cosmos of the Apocalypse (§5.3). HC2's exegetical method is informed by his *encyclical* studies: the vivid verbal description of the abyssal locusts in Rev 9:7-9 is perceived to be an ἔκφρασις requiring decoding by a wise interpreter, with the result that HC2 adopts an allegorical method, which resolves the surface-level dissonance with his preferred cosmological template (§5.4). HC2's allegorical interpretation of the hybrid locusts of Rev 9:1-12 is then outlined (§ 5.5): HC2 re-interprets these figures as a constellational composite, comprised of Λέων, Παρθένος, and Σκορπίος (cf. Aratus, *Phaenomena*). The plausibility of HC2's hypothetical interpretative approach is then supported by an appeal to extant evidence: a 3rd-century CE Christian grammarian's allegorical interpretation of the Aratean constellations by means of scriptural figures (cf. 'Hippolytus', ἔλεγχός IV.46-50) (§5.6). The chapter concludes by reflecting upon the viability of the hearer-construct reading proposed (§5.7).

5.2 HC2: Definition and Mental Library

The focus of the second exegetical study, hearer-construct two (HC2), is defined as a late first-century CE/early second-century CE resident of a major urban centre in Asia Minor. The principal distinguishing characteristic of HC2, compared with HC1, is that he is presumed to have received a tertiary level Greek *encyclical* education, which included exercises in prose composition (προγυμνάσματα) and close study of verse and prose authors (including some philosophical study) (cf. §2.2-3). As a consequence of HC2's tertiary-level education, he is able to read fluently and write in a 'rapid hand'.[1] HC2 is a member of an early Christian community in Asia Minor that possesses a copy of the Apocalypse, which is frequently read aloud (perhaps most likely in short extracts) and commented on in this group's liturgical assemblies.

The contents of HC2's mental library, like that of HC1 (§4.2), is restricted to two streams of influence for the purposes of the present study. In order to isolate the influence of HC2's relatively more extensive educational attainment, the range of scriptural texts with which he is familiar will precisely correspond to the eleven booklets known also to HC1: a core group of five prophetic authors, Isaiah, Ezekiel, Daniel, Jeremiah and David (i.e. Psalms), supplemented by portions of Exodus, Hosea, Amos, Joel, Jonah, Zechariah, plus I Enoch (1-36). On the basis of HC2's extended *encyclical* studies this range of scriptural texts is supplemented by a limited selection of poets: Homer, *Iliad* and *Odyssey*, Menander, Hesiod, *Theogony* and *Works and Days*; Euripides, Aratus, *Phaenomena* (studied with the aid of a celestial globe cf. §2.3), and prose authors: Herodotus, *History*, and Plato, *Timaeus, Republic*. The 'core' and 'periphery' of HC2's mental library is set out in figure 5.1.

5.3 HC2's Mental Map

The dominant cosmological model presupposed by this tertiary-educated hearer-construct (HC2) is a Hellenistic, seven-planetary sphere system, shaped and informed by his philosophical study of portions of Plato's *Timaeus* (cf. §3.2). The relative positioning, and mythological representations, of the standard set of 48 Greek constellations that are displayed on the outer firmament of a celestial globe are familiar to HC2 from an acquaintance with Aratus' *Phaenomena* studied at the grammatical stage of his education (cf. §2.3).[2] HC2's principal cognitive map of the cosmos sharply deviates from the archaic triple-decker universe (single heaven, disc-earth, underworld abyss) displayed in the Apocalypse (§3.4). The description of the cosmos recounted in the

---

1   Cribiore 1996: 112: '"The rapid hand"...is the hand of an advanced student. It is fluent and can be trusted to do lots of writing. Often it cannot be distinguished from a personal and well-developed hand...'. Characteristic examples of this fourth grade of handwriting are provided by papyri 345, a prose summary of *Iliad* XVIII.45–49, and 371 an extract from a prose compositional treatise, comparable to Dionysius' Τέχνη; Cribiore 1996: 259, 267.

2   Kidd 1997.

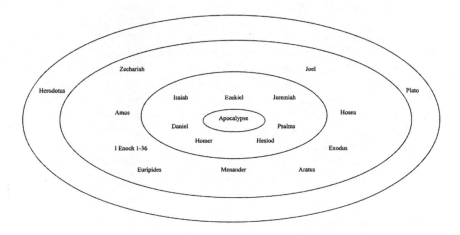

Fig. 5.1 The Contents of HC2's Mental Library

Apocalypse on the basis of the seer's privileged ascents to the celestial Holy Place, undercuts HC2's anticipated picture of the structure of the κόσμος. Celebrated accounts of heavenly ascents, familiar to first-century CE tertiary-educated readers, in either Greek or Latin, such as the 'Myth of Er' in Plato's *Republic* (10.613ff), or the 'Dream of Scipio', in Cicero's *De republica* VI.9-26, presuppose that a vision of the universe from the vantage point of the firmament will correspond to the Platonic system, portraying a multiplicity of planetary spheres (cf. Plato, *Republic*, 10.616D–E).[3] The Apocalypse, by contrast, makes no mention of the planets or planetary spheres when the seer peers down onto the earth from the firmament, and the earth itself is confusingly described as a four-cornered square (Rev 7:1) rather than a spherical orb.[4] In Rev 9:1-2 an archaic tripartite cosmos is described: sun, moon and stars in heaven (οὐρανὸς), earth (γῆ) beneath, and watery abyss (ἄβυσσος) under the earth (cf. Rev 5:3, 13; 14:7).

---

3   Albinus 1998; Halliwell 2007.
4   In the Apocalypse the heavenly bodies (sun, moon and stars) are usually closely related as a group (cf. Rev 6:12-13; 8:12) that are loosely located in the (upper) air (cf. Rev 9:2), rather than assigned to distinct spheres.

HC2's resolution of the dissonance between his predominant Platonic cosmological model and alternative sets of mental maps of the heavens contained within his mental library (e.g. Homeric template texts) is to conform the aberrant cognitive maps to his principal cosmological model. HC2's interpretative method is consistent with the approach of contemporary Hellenistic/Roman Stoic intellectuals who allegorically reinterpreted passages deemed ethically dubious in the Homeric epics to conform to their philosophical presuppositions.[5] Perhaps the closest analogy, however, is Philo's celebrated allegorical reinterpretation of the archaic cosmology of the Genesis creation narratives (*De Opificio Mundi*), under the influence of his Middle-Platonic cognitive map of the cosmos.[6] Interpreted 'correctly', using an allegorical exegetical approach, HC2 will also endeavour to re-read Rev 9:1ff in conformity with a Middle Platonic, seven-planetary spheres cosmology, ornamented with the Aratean constellations.

5.4 HC2's Interpretative Method

5.4.1 ἔκφρασις [7]

For a tertiary-educated ancient hearer, the detailed depictions of the locust-hybrids (Rev 9:7-9) correspond, in large measure, to a familiar component of ancient narrative: the descriptive passage (ἔκφρασις).[8] As noted in §2.2, ἔκφρασις constitutes one of the core components for use in preparatory exercises in prose composition (προγυμνάσματα), as defined and explained in ancient rhetorical handbooks. According to Aelius Theon (*c.* 1st century CE), '*ekphrasis* is descriptive language, bringing what is portrayed clearly before the sight' (ἔκφρασίς ἐστι λόγος περιηγηματικὸς ἐναργῶς ὑπ' ὄψιν ἄγων τὸ δηλούμενον) (Theon, 118.7-8), such that the primary virtue (ἀρετή) of this compositional form is 'most of all, clarity and a vivid impression of all-but-seeing what is described' (σαφήνεια μὲν μάλιστα καὶ ἐνάργεια τοῦ σχεδὸν ὁρᾶσθαι τὰ Ἀπαγγελλόμενα) (Theon, 119.31-33).[9] Among the conventional topics that were considered suitable for detailed narrative descriptions Theon lists persons, events, places and periods of time (Theon, 118). Under the first of these categories, 'persons' (προσώπων),

---

5   Lamberton 1986: 1–54.

6   Runia 1986; Runia 2001.

7   This section was inspired by Aune 1998b: 919–28: Rev 17 as a literary ἔκφρασις of an image of *Dea Roma*, interpreted allegorically.

8   In Graeco-Roman rhetorical handbooks ἔκφρασις was not restricted to a description of a work of art (e.g. the Shield of Achilles, Homer, *Iliad*, xviii), but denoted descriptive narration in general. According to Hermogenes, *Progymnasmata* (10.49), the aim of such descriptive passages is 'to bring about seeing through hearing'; cf. Elsner 2002.

9   Kennedy 2003: 45, 47; Patillon 1997: 66, 69; (cf. §4.3 for the affective use of ἔκφρασις by orators).

Theon includes descriptions of various (exotic) animals recounted by Herodotus, namely the ibis (Herodotus 2.76), the hippopotamus (Herodotus 2.71) and the crocodile (Herodotus 2.68), (Theon 118.15-17).[10]

The choice of subject matter (exotic animals) and depth of visual detail (emphasizing anomalous features with a vivid use of auditory and ocular similes) in Rev 9:7-9 is comparable to many types of ἔκφρασις recounted across a diverse range of ancient genres: from epic to tragedy and history to novels.[11] The undoubted descriptive skill of the implied author of the Apocalypse in recounting visionary details does not require that he received a tertiary-level Greek education, however, as such talent is not restricted to rhetorically educated writers, but it is nonetheless instructive to consider how a *tertiary-educated hearer* may have responded to such a passage.[12]

One prominent method of interpreting descriptive narrative (ἔκφρασις), evidenced within descriptive narratives themselves and perhaps best represented by the Πίναξ of Cebes (*c.* 1st century BCE), involves a two-stage interpretative process.[13] The narrative commences with a detailed description of an object by the narrator, which in Cebes' case is a painting, whose meaning is initially enigmatic or elusive to both the narrator and the implied audience that is dependent upon his description.[14] The hidden meaning is subsequently

---

10   Kennedy 2003: 45; Patillon 1997: 66.
Later rhetoricians will include 'animals' (ζῷα) as a separate topic alongside persons. Graeco-Roman novelists delight in this compositional skill: Heliodorus, *Aethiopica* 10.27.1-4 provides a description of the exotic 'cameleopard' (giraffe), whilst Achilles Tatius, *Leucippe* and *Clitophon*, includes descriptions of exotic animals such as the elephant (4.4.2-5.2) and the phoenix (3.25.1-7); cf. Reardon 2008.

11   Cf. Bartsch 1989; Bartsch and Elsner 2007; Becker 1995.

12   As noted above, the primary technical skill that students were encouraged to demonstrate when composing an ἔκφρασις was visual clarity: to bring the object described before the hearer's eye (Theon, 118–19). Such a skill cannot be artificially restricted to writers who had received a tertiary-level Greek education, as it was an equally prized ability of oral composition (cf. Homer's *Shield of Achilles*). Whilst Theon recommends following a chronological structure when narrating an ἔκφρασις of an event (cf. Theon, 119.16ff), the guidance for composing an ἔκφρασις of a 'person' (or animal) is ostensibly limited to relating the description to the narrative context (Theon, 119.24–30), and matching the style to the content (Theon, 119.31–120.2).
Studies of the compositional techniques of the author of Acts, notably the chronological structuring of ἔκφρασις of events, provides supporting evidence that this author had been trained in *progymnastic* compositional techniques, in view of the close correspondence with the structural guidance provided for these types of ἔκφρασις and the overlap with text-book examples; cf. Parsons 2003; Penner 2003.

13   Fitzgerald and White 1983. For the possible literary influence of the Πίναξ of Cebes on the ἔκφρασεις recounted in the *Shepherd of Hermas* (cf. especially the description of the κῆτος (Vision IV.1–3; Ehrman 2003: 226–35), possibly based on the image of a ceramic sculpture), see Taylor 1901; Taylor 1903.

14   Cf. Bartsch 1989: 14-39, (28): '...a painting is described that contains a hidden and allegorical meaning that neither is simple enough to be immediately apparent nor is decoded by the author in the course of his description of it. Instead, the personage of the narrator-

provided by a wise character who appears within the narrative, a role undertaken by an elderly man (πρεσβύτερος) in Cebes' Πίναξ, who informs the
puzzled narrator (and implied audience) of the *allegorical* meaning of each
of the various details described previously.[15] A comparable two-stage interpretative process is widely attested in Graeco-Roman dream interpretation,
a classic example of which is Artemidorus' *Oneirocritica* (2nd century CE),
in which the narrator provides his own wise (allegorical) exegesis.[16] Closely
related parallels are found in Graeco-Roman dream-vision and heavenly-
ascent narratives (e.g. Zech 1:7–6:15; Daniel 7; I Enoch 83-84; IV Ezra
9:26–10:59) in which an enigmatic (dream-)vision is decoded for the puzzled
seer/narrator by an interpreting angel.

This same exegetical technique is present in Rev 17, where the narrator
provides a detailed description (ἔκφρασις) of a vision of the personified figure
of Babylon sitting on a scarlet Beast (Rev 17:3-6), which the narrator claims
to have experienced whilst in an altered state of consciousness (ἐν πνεύματι)
(17:3).[17] Having explicitly voiced his perplexity (Rev 17:6 ἐθαύμασα) as to its
meaning, the narrator (and implied audience) are then afforded an allegorical
interpretation of various aspects of the vision / ἔκφρασις by an interpreting
angel (Rev 17:7-18). The appearance of the stock interpretative device of
a 'wise interpreter' to decode allegorically an enigmatic ἔκφρασις/vision to
a puzzled narrator (and implied audience) is surprisingly rare, however, in
the Apocalypse. One possible reason for the marked absence of an *angeles
interpres* is that the implied author may have considered that the visionary
material was, in the main, straightforward rather than enigmatic, such that
an interpreting angel was not required as the visions describe the predicted
events just as they will occur.[18] Alternatively, the implied author may be

viewer is introduced into the text to voice explicitly his confusion about the meaning of the
painting. In so doing, he inevitably acts as a proleptic model for the confusion of the reader
or listener, who likewise cannot be sure of the hidden significance of what is described.'

15　For other examples of allegorical interpretations of descriptive narratives see Lucian's
Slander and *On Salaried Posts*, and contrast this with Philostratus' omniscient narrator who
interprets the paintings directly to a minor character within the narrative (including 'intertextual' references to ancient narratives, notably in Homer); cf. Bartsch 1989: 14–39.

16　For the text of Artemidorus' *Oneirocritica* cf. Pack 1963 (Greek); White 1975
(English). For an analysis of his oneirocritical method see Husser 1999: 32–4; Miller 1994:
77–91.

Artemidorus divides revelatory significant dreams (ὄνειροι) into two broad types
(*Oneirocritica* I.2): theorematic, or direct dreams, which 'come true just at they are seen',
and *allegorical* dreams, in which the dream-vision is enigmatic, 'signifying one thing by
means of another', and which requires a skilled dream-interpreter (like Artemidorus) to
decode them.

17　Cf. Aune 1998b: 919–28, who suggests that the ἔκφρασις may be a parody of
the static depiction of the Goddess Roma, seated on the seven hills of Rome. A comparable image is extant on coins minted in the Roman province of Asia during the reign of
Vespasian (*c*.71 CE), cf. Plate 1, p.920.

18　To use Artemidorus' later (2nd century CE) category, the visions are 'direct'
(θεωρηματικός) rather than allegorical (ἀλληγορικός) (cf. *Oneirocritica* I.2), and consequently a dream-interpreter is not required.

encouraging the implied audience to undertake for themselves the role of a wise interpreter, utilizing their own prophetically inspired interpretative capabilities in response to the oral performance of this revelatory text (cf. I Cor 14:26-30). The distinction, in the end, hinges on the extent to which a particular hearer (or group of hearers) considers the visions/descriptions in the Apocalypse to be transparent or enigmatic.

As already noted, for HC2 the cosmology of Rev 9 is disjunctive and opaque, jarring with his dominant mental map of the cosmos. Accordingly HC2 will adopt an allegorical approach to interpret the ἔκφρασις of Rev 9:7-9, analogous to Philo's treatment of Genesis 1 (*De Opificio Mundi*).

5.4.2 Allegory

A consideration of Philo's allegorical re-interpretation of the abyssal chaos waters of Gen 1:2 LXX (ἄβυσσος) will afford constructive insights into how a tertiary-educated hearer of Rev 9 may similarly attempt to reconfigure the archaic cosmology of this vision to accord with his dominant Platonic worldview. Although Philo is keen not to negate a 'literal' sense of scripture at the expense of a 'deeper' meaning revealed through an allegorical method (cf. *Migr.* 89–93), he is nonetheless not averse to privileging the latter component over the former in his interpretative commentaries.[19]

Philo explicitly refers to ἡ ἄβυσσος on four occasions in his exegetical writings (*Opif.* § 29, 32; *Fug.*192; *QG* 2:64a), with two of the references occurring in his extended commentary on Genesis 1:2 LXX in *De Opificio Mundi*.[20]

Opif. §29

First, therefore, the maker made an incorporeal heaven and an invisible earth and a form of air (ἀήρ) and the void (χάος). To the former he assigned the name darkness (σκότος), since the air (ἀήρ) is black by nature, to the latter the name abyss (ἄβυσσος), because the void (χάος) is indeed full of depths and gaping (ἀχανές).[21]

Philo interprets the first creation narrative (Gen 1) as an account of the creation of the incorporeal, intelligible cosmos (§§16–25), corresponding to the Platonic Form of the universe which functions as a plan for the material copy.[22] In this context the corporeal abyssal chaos waters of Gen 1:2 are re-imagined, identified with the second of seven generative elements of the incorporeal universe, the first of which is air (equated

---

19   On Philo's allegorical exegetical method, which he associated with the disclosure of heavenly mysteries (cf. *Fug.* 179), see Amir 1988; Borgen 2003.

20   As listed in the *Philo Index*, Borgen, Fuglseth and Skarsten 2000.

21   Translation, Runia 2001: 53; Greek text, Colson 1929.

22   Runia 2001: 163–4;

with non-illuminated darkness (σκότος) (cf. *QE* 2.85)).[23] The abyss here denotes the gaping void (χάος), the space which the corporeal cosmos will occupy completely (in line with Platonic thought (cf. *Plant* 6–8; *QE* 2.68)).[24] Philo further explicates the relationship between air and abyss, a few lines later, citing Gen 1:2 LXX 'καὶ σκότος ἐπάνω τῆς ἀβύσσου':

Opif. §32
Well said too is the statement that 'there was darkness above the abyss' (καὶ σκότος ἐπάνω τῆς ἀβύσσου), for in a way the air (ἀήρ) is over the void (χάος), since it is mounted on and has filled up the entire gaping, empty and void space that extends from the region of the moon to us.[25]

Philo's exegetical comment in §32 praises Moses' description of the darkness above (ἐπάνω) the abyss, by demonstrating how this corresponds with a Platonic-Aristotelian conception of the cosmos that envisages 'air' as the element that fills the entire sub-lunar region characterized by transitoriness and change (in contrast to the orderly aetherial tier above). Philo suggests that this is analogous to an idea of air being mounted upon a base of χάος (in the sense of χάος as an incorporeal element that has been pushed down and displaced by the air which fills the sub-lunar region).

In *Opif.* §§29 and 32, therefore, Philo reinterprets ἡ ἄβυσσος of Gen 1:2 LXX, where it refers to the primeval deep (תהום), to denote the cosmological 'void' (χάος) of the universe which is filled by the material κόσμος.[26] Philo reconfigures the description of the abyssal chaos waters of a tripartite cosmos in Gen 1:2ff to conform to the Platonic conception of the void (χάος) as the container of the physical universe.

Philo's allegorical interpretations of ἡ ἄβυσσος are not restricted to cosmological re-readings. In *De Fuga et Inventione* §§188–93 the Platonic conception of the human body as a microcosm of the universe (cf. *Timaeus*, 44D–45B) and the ANE *topos* of a close correspondence between the workings of the earth and human bodies (e.g. eye/spring (עין)), underlie Philo's allegorical treatment of 'the fountain (πηγή) of folly' (Lev 20:18 LXX). Philo takes 'fountain', in this context, to refer to a person's external senses pouring forth without the control of

---

23   In Hesiod, *Theogony* 116, χάος is the first of the gods to be generated: 'In truth, first of all Chasm came to be (πρώτιστα Χάος), and then broad-breasted Earth...' (Most 2006: 12-13); cf. Clay 2003: 15–16; Mondi 1989.

24   Runia 2001: 165–6 notes that Philo generally assents to the Platonic and Aristotelian position that the physical cosmos completely fills the 'void', such that it ceases to exist, in contrast to Stoic thought which requires the presence of a void outside the living cosmos to enable the cosmos to increase in size (cf. *Her* 228; *Prov.* 2.55-56).

25   Translation, Runia 2001: 53; Greek text Colson: 1929.

26   As Runia 2001: 170 notes, although Philo is describing the incorporeal plan of the cosmos, there is a certain slippage in many instances which suggest that he is often thinking more about the physical cosmos.

reason, which he links with the description of the flood-waters in Gen 7:11 LXX:

Fug. §§192–193[27]
This is the great deluge in which 'the cataracts of heaven were opened' – by heaven I here mean the mind – and the fountains of the bottomless pit were revealed (αἱ πηγαὶ τῆς ἀβύσσου) that is to say of the outward sense; for in this way alone is the soul overwhelmed, iniquities being broken up and poured over it from above, as from the heaven of the mind, and the passions irrigating it from below, as from the earth of the outward senses.

Philo's anthropology here envisages a human person as a microcosm of the universe, assailed from 'above' by an uncontrolled mind, and from 'below' by unrestrained external senses. The cosmological significance of αἱ πηγαὶ τῆς ἀβύσσου as the terrestrial mouths of the subterranean abyss, is transposed into an anthropological key, descriptive of a person's external senses.[28]

Philo is cognizant that in the context of the cosmology of the Pentateuch, the abyss (ἡ ἄβυσσος), and especially 'the fountains of the deep' (αἱ πηγαὶ τῆς ἀβύσσου) (Gen 7:11 LXX) refer to the subterranean waters that spring forth at the surface of the (disc-)earth (cf. *QG* II.64). Philo, considers, however, that correctly understood, Moses' account of the creation prefigures the best of contemporary cosmological thought, as delineated in Middle Platonic exegesis of Plato's *Timaeus*. As a consequence, Philo allegorically interprets references to ἡ ἄβυσσος in Gen 1:2 LXX to denote not archaic subterranean chaos waters, but rather the cosmological 'void' (χάος), the elemental 'space' occupied by the material κόσμος (*Opif.* §§29 and 32; cf. Plato, *Timaeus* 48E–52D).[29]

Philo's allegorical reinterpretation of ἡ ἄβυσσος, bringing it into conformity with his dominant cosmological worldview (Middle Platonic planetary spheres), will serve as a model for this study's tertiary-educated hearer-construct (HC2) when he is faced with the archaic cosmology of Rev 9:1-12 and its obscure ἔκφρασις of abyssal locusts. HC2 will allegorically reinterpret the hybrid locusts from the abyss as constellational figures, as opposed to subterranean δαιμόνια, under the influence of his dominant Middle Platonic cosmology and Aratean constellational knowledge.

---

27 Yonge 1993: 338.
28 Philo, *QG* II.64 similarly alludes to Gen 7:11 LXX (αἱ πηγαὶ τῆς ἀβύσσου) in passing when discussing the meaning of the rainbow in Gen 9:13, specifically refuting a connection with the belt of Jupiter. The phrase is understood literally in this brief mention, as an example of the breaking-up of 'all things' that occurred as a result of the deluge.
29 On the 'Receptacle' of Becoming in the *Timaeus*, see Cornford 1937: 177–97.

5.4.3 Rejoinder: Previous Astronomical Interpretations of Rev 9:1-12

Before proceeding with HC2's exegesis of Rev 9:1ff it is important to distinguish clearly the method and aims of the present study from previous astronomical readings of this passage, notably by Boll, Farrer, Malina and Chevalier.[30]

Franz Boll's *religionsgeschichtliche* approach to the Apocalypse sought to uncover the latent presence of astrological imagery in the text, on the basis of proposed parallels with ancient Mesopotamian astrological figures. ANE constellational analogues were suggested for the four living beings (Rev 4), the woman clothed with the sun and the dragon (Rev 12) and the locust-hybrids (Rev 9).[31] Boll proposed that opaque elements in the verbal depiction of the hybrid locusts (Rev 9), which bore no parallel to Joel 1–2, were derived instead from a single source: ancient Babylonian depictions of the zodiacal constellation Archer, portrayed as a hybrid winged-centaur replete with a scorpion-tail (a remnant of an earlier fusion of the constellations Archer and Scorpion) (cf. Kudurru boundary stone (*c.* 1186–1172 BCE); Dendera Zodiac (planisphere), Upper Egypt *c.*50 BCE).[32]

Identifying the hybrid-locusts as a constellational figure was seen to provide an interpretative key to the a-typical time reference of five months (Rev 9:5, 10), equated with the last five zodiacal signs of the sidereal year (Scorpion–Fishes; Oct–Mar).[33] Boll's theories, subsequently adopted and expanded by Malina (who identifies ten constellational figures in the Apocalypse), understood the eschatological subject matter of Rev 9:1ff to be transposed into a zodiacal register, depicting a five-month period of tribulation for unrighteous humanity, symbolized by the torturous authority of the constellation Archer/Scorpion, at the conclusion of a symbolic year, culminating in the Lord's return in judgment as the Lamb (= Aries/ ἀρνίον) (Rev 5:6).[34]

---

30   Boll 1914; Chevalier 1997; Farrer 1949, 1964; Malina 1995; Malina and Pilch 2000; cf. Hegedus 2005, Hegedus 2007: 231–60.

31   Boll 1914: 35, equated the four living beings with the four constellations that marked the solstices and equinoxes (Leo, Taurus, Scorpio and Pegasus) and identified the woman and the Dragon with Virgo and Hydra, respectively (103ff).

32   Boll 1914: 69ff.

33   Πέντε, Rev 9:5, 10, 17:10 (re. heads of the beast – 'five have fallen').
A number of commentators refer to the approximate five-month life-span of a locust (cf. Charles 1920a: 243; Aune 1998a: 530; Beale 1999: 497), but as Prigent aptly states 'this would be to forget that our author is talking of supernatural locusts' (Prigent 2004: 314). Alternatively, a vaguer symbolic resonance is detected, as 'five' is interpreted as a stock number to denote 'a few' (Aune 1998a: 530), or more pertinently, by Swete, as an indicator of 'incompleteness' (5/12ths of a year), such that it does not constitute the final judgement (Swete 1906: 114).

34   Malina 1995: 144ff. On the equation of τὸ ἀρνίον (Rev 5:6ff) with the constellation Aries/Lamb cf. Johns 2003: 68–75, who is cautiously open to the use and knowledge of zodiacal imagery among Graeco-Roman Jews/Christians (cf. 4Q 318; later *Beth Aleph* synagogue, zodiac mosaic (4th–6th century CE)), but remains unconvinced that an astrological resonance is present in the Apocalypse's use of the figure.

An elegant variation on the astronomical theme is furnished by Austin Farrer's interwoven liturgical/seasonal/zodiacal macrostructure of the Apocalypse.[35] Farrer retains a zodiacal interpretation of the four living creatures (Rev 4:6b-7): Bull (= Ταῦρος) (spring equinox), Lion (= Λέων) (summer solstice), Eagle (= ᾿Αετός in place of Σκορπίος) (vernal equinox) and Man (= Ὑδρηχόος) (winter solstice), but stops short of equating the locust hybrids with a constellational equivalent.[36] Instead, according to Farrer's liturgical template, the seventh trumpet in the trumpet-cycle (Rev 11:15ff) culminates in the Jewish festival of Trumpets/New Year (cf. Lev 23:23-25), whilst the weekly units of the preceding trumpets in the series cover the period from mid-summer onwards.[37] For Farrer, the first six trumpets (Rev 8–9), which run from mid- to late summer, are to be situated principally under the sign of Λέων (cf. verbal echoes, Rev 9:8, 17; 10:3), although there is a degree of overlap with the sign of ᾿Αετός (autumn) which explicitly precedes the three woes (Rev 8:13), such that trumpets five and six are also intimately connected with the autumnal indicator, trumpet seven (New Year).[38]

Chevalier is persuaded by the evidence amassed by Boll and Malina, and considers that the combined imagery of darkness (Rev 9:2), scorpions (Rev 9:3, 10) and above all 'five months' (Rev 9:5, 10), '…can hardly fail to evoke the *five-month period it takes the sun to reach the vernal equinox after its passage through the late-October sign of Scorpio.*'[39] Like Boll and Malina, Chevalier does not negate latent resonances of Joel's eschatological locust-swarm, and even tries to emphasize possible calendrical connections between autumnal harvest festival imagery in Joel 1–2 (Tishri, Feast of Trumpets, Day of Atonement, and Feast of Tabernacles) (cf. Joel 2:23) with an autumnal

---

35   Farrer 1949.

36   The proposal that the four living beings/cherubim of Ezekiel 1, 10 (which informed Rev 4:6-7) derive from archaic Mesopotamian constellations (Bull, Lion, Scorpion and Ea (Aquarius)) is based on an hypothesis that these constellations contain four first magnitude royal stars (Aldebaran, Regulus, Antares and Fomalhaut), that marked the four cardinal points. Cf. Boll 1914: 35ff; Charles 1920a: 122–3; Hegedus 2005: 72–5; and Malina 1995: 97ff. In view of the extreme antiquity of such Mesopotamian zodiacal conceptions I would side with Charles who considers it highly unlikely that the (implied) author of Ezekiel, let alone the (implied) author of the Apocalypse, was aware of such origins (Charles 1920a: 122).

37   Farrer 1949: 198–201.

38   Farrer 1949: 199–201. Farrer 1964: 116–22 emphasizes the controlling influence of the Eagle over the series of woes, at the expense of the Lion. Implicit allusions to the autumnal quarter are also signalled by latent resonances of the Scorpion (for whom the Eagle is merely a surrogate) in trumpets five and six (cf. Rev 9:5, 10 and Farrer's interpretation of the colour/stone ὑακίνθινος (Rev 9:17, 21:20) as a gemstone correlating to the zodiacal sign of Scorpion).

39   Chevalier 1997: 298–300 (298, author's own italics). A neglected weakness, however, is that Boll identifies the hybrid-locusts with an archaic form of the constellation 'Archer', not Scorpion, and the noun μήν designates a lunar month, not the duration of a zodiacal sign (cf. Geminos, *Phaenomena*).

context for Rev 9:1-12.[40] Yet, much of the imagery is considered to resonate more strongly with Egyptian and Babylonian representations of the southern hemisphere constellations of Archer, Scorpion, Centaur and Altar.[41] Ultimately, for Chevalier, this text supports his deconstructive thesis that the implied author of the Apocalypse appropriates astrological imagery in order implicitly to subordinate it within his grander revelatory scheme:

> In retrospect, what needs to be explained is not the intended meaning of the scorpion motif as much as John's silence, his refusal to mention the 'nearly obvious' – the lunisolar and astral contextuality of his imagery.[42]

Viewed in isolation from the expansive astronomical meta-narratives that Boll, Malina and Chevalier discern in the structure of the Apocalypse, the evidence of a zodiacal layer of meaning in Rev 9:1-12 has much to commend it. A cluster of otherwise obscure elements in the ἔκφρασις of the abyssal locusts (Rev 9:7-9), complicating the simpler similes of Joel 1–2, are illuminated, with allusions to 'five months', 'scorpions' and darkness conceivably pointing to an implicit zodiacal undertone. But what of the more specific iconographic proposal, that the abyssal locusts represent the fused Archer-Scorpion of Egyptian planispheres (Boll, Malina)? The single biggest obstacle to this proposal concerns the *accessibility* of the imagery. One of the recurrent methodological flaws in both Boll's and Malina's astronomical research is a systemic failure to filter-out alleged astronomical parallels that post-date the composition of the Apocalypse and/or originate in a distant geographical context with no evidence of dissemination in the province of Asia Minor.[43] As a consequence the elaborate network of astronomical parallels that are uncovered frequently serve to weaken, rather than to support, a cumulative argument for the prevalence of astronomical imagery.[44] The artificial, and procrustean, character of many of the constellational analogues suggested, notably in the case of the Woman (Virgo) and the Dragon (Hydra, Scorpion), is an attendant deficiency, starkly highlighted by the coherent, and spatially consistent, iconography of contemporary Mithraic Tauroctonies (depicting a comparable series of zodiacal constellations of Bull, Scorpion, Lion, etc.).[45]

---

40   Chevalier 1997: 300.
41   Chevalier 1997: 300–1.
42   Chevalier 1997: 300.
43   Cf. Pearson 1997.
44   Another recurrent weakness is the exalted claims that astronomy is the predominant, if not exclusive, hermeneutical key to the Apocalypse, rather than, at most, an additional resonant layer; cf. DeSilva 1997.
45   Cf. Beck 2004: 251–66; 2006a: chapter 7 for detailed plans of the Mithrauem of the Seven Spheres, Ostia.

On balance, therefore, proposed identifications of various images in the Apocalypse with constellational figures, including the scorpion-locusts of Rev 9, remain unpersuasive, in view of the lack of direct connection between the ancient Mesopotamian analogies and the date and provenance of the Apocalypse, coupled with the deviations and dissonances between the iconographic images and the verbal depictions in the text. Farrer's ambitious superstructure, plotting the visionary narrative of the Apocalypse onto the contours of a liturgical/lectionary cycle proved similarly unsound, even in the author's own opinion, suffering from a similar evidential gap, as serious doubts were cast on the very existence of a Jewish lectionary cycle in the 1st century CE.[46]

The present study differs markedly from those that precede, in that it does not propose or require that the implied author of the Apocalypse either knew, or alluded to, astrological/zodiacal symbolism in Rev 9 (or indeed any other passage). Instead, this exegesis aims creatively to imagine how a tertiary-educated hearer of the Apocalypse may *allegorically* (re-) interpret the verbal description of hybrid-locusts (Rev 9:7-9) through the lens of constellational iconography known to him through his studies of Aratus' *Phaenomena* (with the aid of a celestial globe). How might HC2 (re-)interpret the verbal description of these figures in conformity with his dominant Platonic/Aratean cosmological template?

5.5 HC2's Interpretation of the Fifth Trumpet (Rev 9:1-12)

5.5.1 The Well of the Abyss (Rev 9:1-2)

One of the most significant aspects of HC2's reinterpretation of Rev 9:1-12 relates to the altered cosmological significance of ἡ ἄβυσσος (Rev 9:1). Where Philo equated ἡ ἄβυσσος (Gen 1:2 LXX) with the 'void' (χάος) (*Opif.* §§29, 32), HC2 will correlate ἡ ἄβυσσος in Rev 9 with the 'celestial sea' in the southern hemisphere of the celestial globe. An equation of stellar regions of the southern hemisphere of the celestial globe with watery regions/the Deep is plausible on the basis of HC2's knowledge of the Aratean constellations. One cluster of southern-hemisphere constellations in particular, namely the grouping of Sea-monster (Κῆτος) (Aratus 353-66), River (Ποταμός) (Aratus 360-2), Fishes ('Ιχθύες) (Aratus 362-4), the ship Argo ('Αργώ) (Aratus 342-52), the Southern Fish

---

46   Farrer 1964: v–vi; cf. Goulder 1981. For critical evaluations of the existence of Jewish lectionary cycles in the first century CE see Bradshaw 2002: 21–72; Goodacre 1996: Part III; and Perrot 1998.

The use of the *Songs of the Sabbath Sacrifice* in yaḥad sabbath worship (13 sabbaths, first quarter of the year) suggests, however, that the potential presence of a 'liturgical' pattern, latent in the Apocalypse's design, merits renewed investigation (cf. Rev 1:10); cf. Kavanagh 1984; Vanni 1991.

(Νότιος Ἰχθὺς) (Aratus 386-8), and Water ("Ὕδωρ) (from the Water-bearer's jar) (Aratus 389–401), emphatically suggest an extensive 'watery' region in the southern sky.[47]

In accordance with his Platonic-Aratean cosmology HC2 understands ἡ ἄβυσσος to denote the 'celestial sea', broadly conceived as the region to the south of the zodiacal constellations of Capricorn, Water-bearer and Fishes, in the southern-hemisphere of the celestial globe (cf. fig. 5.2). This astronomical context is perceived to be consistent with attendant references to the fixed stars on the celestial firmament (Rev 9:1β, ἀστέρες), the planetary sphere of the sun (Rev 9:2β), and the sub-lunar region of air (Rev 9:2β, ἀήρ) above the central planetary sphere of the earth (Rev 9:1β, γῆ) that are all understood by HC2 to be described in the immediate context of Rev 9:1-2. In this altered cosmological context the topographical feature, 'the well of the abyss' (τὸ φρέαρ τῆς ἀβύσσου) (Rev 9:1γ, 2α), refers not to a shaft that connects the terrestrial disc with the subterranean Deep (cf. αἱ πηγαὶ τῆς ἀβύσσου, Gen 7:11, 8:2 LXX) but rather its functional equivalent, the Hadean region of the firmament (cf. Ps 68:16 for τὸ φρέαρ as an image of the throat of Hades).[48]

5.5.2 The Abyssal Locusts (Rev 9:3-12)

As discussed in the previous chapter (§4.4.2), there are persuasive indications that a first-century hearer of Joel 1–2 would be predisposed to interpret Joel's locust-army as an eschatological re-envisioning of the Egyptian locust plague (Exod 10) aligned with the mythological enemy from the north (cf. Joel 2:20 LXX (τὸν ἀπὸ βορρᾶ)) of Ezek 38–39. This latter connection may have been further elaborated by a distinctive interpretative tradition represented by Amos 7:1 LXX, which identified one of these locusts as Gog the king (Γωγ ὁ βασιλεύς).

HC2, like HC1, associates the Apocalypse's re-envisioned locust-cavalry with the Lord's eschatological agents of judgment (cf. Joel 2:25), now commissioned to torture unsealed humanity rather than devastate the vegetation (Rev 9:4-5). The verbal echoes of the 'enemy from the north' tradition (cf. Amos 7:1 LXX) are distorted, however, as a consequence of HC2's altered cosmological perspective. In HC2's allegorical reinterpretation of the locust-cavalry, detailed below, allusions to the 'northern' foe are realigned, removed from the 'land of Magog' at the northern edge of the οἰκουμένη (Ezek 38:2 LXX) and transposed onto the northern hemisphere of the celestial globe.

47   Cf. Kidd 1997: 98–103; 314-26; Rogers 1998b: 86: '…the southern sky was filled with watery images – rivers, fishes and sea monsters. It was already called "the Water" by Aratus.'

48   Boll 1914: 72–3 and Malina 1995: 141–4 cite an eclectic range of Graeco-Roman authors who allude to a celestial Hades or Celestial Sea in the southern hemisphere of the firmament (e.g. Firmicus Maternus, *Mathesis* 8.12.2; Plutarch, *On the Genius of Socrates* 590B–592E). Such references are allusive, however, and lie outside the narrow parameters of HC2's mental library, and so will not be pressed to validate HC2's allegorical reading.

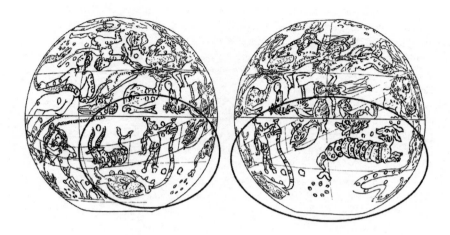

Fig. 5.2. The 'Celestial Sea' in the Southern Hemisphere of the Celestial Globe (Mainz Globe)[49] (Ringed regions)

HC2 allegorically reinterprets the hybrid abyssal locusts of the fifth trumpet as a constellational composite comprised of three closely related zodiacal signs: Lion (Λέων), Young woman (Παρθένος) and Scorpion (Σκορπίος). HC2's constellational reinterpretation of this hybrid creature connects the repeated temporal reference to five months (μῆνας πέντε) (Rev 9:5, 10) with associative images of the seasonal shift from summer (Λέων) to autumn (Σκορπίος).

The extended description (ἔκφρασις) of the hybrid locusts (Rev 9:7-10) combines a cluster of similes (ὅμοιος, ὡς) that depict an army of composite creatures with conflated human and animal attributes. The hybrids have human hair and faces (9:7γ, 8α), leonine teeth (9:8β), equine legs and chest (9:7α, 9), and scorpion tails with sting (9:10). Verbal echoes of the locust characteristics (wings, Rev 9:9β) and equine attributes (legs and chest, Rev 9:7α, 9) of these hybrids are evocative of the non-constellational locust-cavalry of Joel 1–2, envisaged as the Lord's eschatological agents of judgment, the enemy from the north.[50]

---

49   Künzl 2000: 496, Abb. 1a and 1b. Drawing/Römisch-Germanisches Museum Mainz, J. Ribbeck.

50   The equine attributes of the locust-cavalry (Rev 9:7-10) could also be interpreted astronomically with reference to the northern-hemisphere constellation of Horse (ἵππος). HC2 chooses not to make such a connection, however, in view of the distance separating this constellation from Lion, Young Woman and Scorpion on the ecliptic.

HC2's allegorical reinterpretation of these composite creatures take its impetus from the elements which *diverge* from Joel's former vision, to offer an astronomical re-envisioning of the 'enemy from the north'. The leonine, human and scorpion attributes of the locust-cavalry are linked, by HC2, with the constellational figures of Λέων, Παρθένος and Σκορπίος, with which he is familiar from Aratus' verbal description and illustrated celestial globes, and which accords with his cosmological perspective, which identifies ἡ ἄβυσσος as the 'celestial sea' in the southern-hemisphere of the celestial globe. The result is an interpretation of the locust-cavalry of Rev 9:7-10 as a composite constellation, conflating three zodiacal signs (Lion, Young woman, Scorpion) (fig. 5.3).

The first constellation, Λέων, supplies the fearsome jaws of this celestial *Mischwesen* (Rev 9:8β, καὶ οἱ ὀδόντες αὐτῶν ὡς λεόντων ἦσαν). The human head, specifically its face (Rev 9:7γ, τὰ πρόσωπα αὐτῶν ὡς πρόσωπα ἀνθρώπων) and hair (Rev 9:8α, καὶ εἶχαν τρίχας ὡς τρίχας γυναικῶν), derive from the succeeding constellation on the ecliptic, Παρθένος. This identification provides an especially close match for the gender-specific coiffure.[51] The tail-end of this constellational hybrid is provided by the infamous tail replete with sting (κέντρον) of the constellation Σκορπίος (Rev 9:10α, καὶ ἔχουσιν οὐρὰς ὁμοίος σκορπίοις καὶ κέντρα). The zodiacal constellation Claws (Χηλαί) (cf. Aratus 89-90), which precedes the celestial Scorpion on Hellenistic star-maps, is passed over in silence in the description of this constellational composite (Rev 9:7-10); but the lack of a specific reference to Claws is not unparalleled, as it was originally conceived of as an integral component of the constellation Scorpion, and was occasionally still depicted as such in 1st/2nd century CE literature (cf. Pseudo-Eratosthenes, *Catasterismi* 7).[52]

---

51   The stars that formed the tail of Λέων were also sometimes separated from the lion's body by some Greek and Latin μαθήματικοι to denote a separate constellation, created in Hellenistic Alexandria (3rd century BCE) and referred to as Berenice's Hair (in honour of Queen Berenice II of Egypt) and/or Ariadne's Hair (cf. Hyginus, *De Astronomia* 2.24; Ptolemy, *Almagest*, 7.5; Pliny, *Nat. Hist.* II. 178; Catullus, *Carmina*, 66).

If a tertiary-educated hearer of Rev 9 was inclined to add non-zodiacal star-groups to such a constellational composite, and was cognizant of such traditions, Berenice's Hair would be an ideal candidate to equate with αἱ τρίχες γυναικῶν (Rev 9:8a) in view of its spatial position at the tail-end of Λέων.

52   Cf. Aratus, *Phaenomena* 88–90; Kidd 1997: 78–9; 211–13.

Λέων   Παρθένος   Σκορπίος

Fig 5.3. The Zodiacal Constellations Λέων, Παρθένος *and* Σκορπίος
(Mainz Celestial Globe)[53]

The position of the constellation Σκορπίος, in the southern-hemisphere of the celestial globe, is consistent with HC2's cosmological interpretation of ἡ ἄβυσσος as the 'celestial sea', the functional equivalent of Hades in the heavenly firmament. The Hadean origin of Σκορπίος hints at the severity of the eschatological judgment that it triggers, which causes unsealed humanity to seek Death in preference (Rev 9:6) and which accords with the appellations of its ruler, Ἀβαδδών and Ἀπολλύων (Rev 9:11) – personifications of the realm of Death (cf. Prov 15:11, 27:20, Job 26:6). The northern hemispherical positioning of the first two components, Λέων and Παρθένος, substantially inform HC2's cosmological reinterpretation of the 'enemy from the north' traditions that coalesce around Joel's locust-cavalry (Joel 2:20; Ezek 38–39; Amos 7:1 LXX). HC2's transformation of Joel's eschatological locust-cavalry, into a composite constellational figure, results in the

53   Künzl 2000: 498, Abb. 3a. Drawing/Römisch-Germanisches Museum Mainz, J. Ribbeck.

transposition of the northern foe from the northern rim of the οἰκουμένη in a tripartite cosmos, to the northern hemisphere of the celestial globe in a Platonic-Aratean universe.

The repeated temporal reference to 'five months' (μῆνας πέντε) (Rev 9:5, 10) may be interpreted by HC2 as indicative of the approximate duration of this constellational creature's astronomical authority, from Λέων to Σκορπίος (approximately four months, if Scorpion is counted as a double sign, Claws-Scorpion, alongside Lion and Young woman). The heliacal rising of the constellations of Λέων and Σκορπίος formerly corresponded with the summer solstice and autumn equinox, respectively, in archaic Sumerian zodiacs (c. 3rd millennium BCE), and continued to serve as seasonal indicators (of summer and autumn) in the Hellenistic and Roman eras.[54] Aratus explicitly refers to the heliacal rising of Λέων as a sign of summer:

> ...the Lion shines brightly (καλὰ φαείνει). This is where the sun's track is hot-test, and the fields are seen bereft of their corn-ears when the sun first comes into conjunction with the Lion (ἠελίου τὰ πρῶτα συνερχομένοιο Λέοντι).
>
> (Aratus, *Phaenomena*, 148–51)[55]

Although the summer solstice had shifted backwards to the constellation of the Crab since the Sumerian era (as a consequence of precession), the hottest time of the year remained in the sign of Λέων.[56] The seasonal significance of the constellation Λέων is as an indicator of the burning heat of high summer in the Roman month of *Julius*, with its threatened destruction of vegetation and crops by drought. The jaws of the celestial-hybrid, as allegorically interpreted by HC2, evoke the constellational sign of Λέων with its associative connections with fiery heat and drought.[57] Such an expectation is explicitly undercut in the text, however, by divine command (Rev 9:4), owing to the express warning to the locust-cavalry *not* to harm any vegetation (καὶ ἐρρέθη αὐταῖς ἵνα μὴ ἀδικήσουσιν τὸν χόρτον τῆς γῆς οὐδὲ πᾶν χλωρὸν οὐδὲ πᾶν δένδρον). Accordingly, the leonine teeth of this hybrid constellational figure play a muted role in the fifth trumpet plague; its fiery destruction is curtailed, as instead the figure's primary weapon is its scorpion sting (Rev 9:5, 10).

---

54   Cf. Rogers 1998a: 24–5.

55   Kidd 1997: 82–5.

56   Kidd 1997: 237; cf. Beck 2004: 286. Rogers 1998a: 9: 'Precession is the gradual circling of the Earth's axis around the pole of the ecliptic. It alters the zodiac's relation to the seasons at a rate of one constellation every 2160 years (1° every 72 years).' The cardinal points shifted by one constellation in approx 2220 BCE and again in 60 BCE.

57   Cf. Rev 9:17γδ, where the lions' heads of the hybrid creatures (ie. Chimaera, cf. Homer, *Iliad* VI.181-2; Hesiod, *Theogony*, 319-24) emit fire.

The second zodiacal component of HC2's allegorical creation is the constellation Παρθένος, which 'follows' Λέων along the ecliptic.[58] The iconographic representation of the constellation Παρθένος in Aratus, and Graeco-Roman celestial globes, is as follows:

> Beneath the two feet of Bootes you can observe the Maiden (Παρθένος) who carries in her hand the radiant Spica.
>
> (Aratus, *Phaenomena*, 96–7)[59]

The zodiacal sign of Παρθένος was represented very simply in the Greek astrological tradition (cf. fig. 5.3) as a horizontally orientated young woman, flying across the ecliptic, clutching an ear of corn (i.e. Spica, the brightest star in the constellation).[60] In later Roman tradition (cf. Pseudo Eratosthenes, *Catasterismi* 9; the Mainz celestial globe) Παρθένος/Virgo is additionally depicted as winged (cf. Rev 12:14).[61] The heliacal rising of the constellation Παρθένος was a seasonal indicator of the September harvest, indicated by the ear of corn (Spica) that she clutches in her hand. Aratus offers a further layer of resonant meaning, for HC2 to recall, by his identification of Παρθένος with the goddess of Justice (Δίκη) (Aratus 100–136), revisiting and combining Hesiod's former accounts of Δίκη (*Works and Days*, 220–262) with the first three ages (gold, silver and bronze) of humanity's degradation (*Works and Days*, 109–155).[62] Young woman's / Justice's prediction of the future bloodshed that would characterize the bronze generation of humanity, which proves the catalyst for her own departure from the earth and ascent to the stars (catasterism as the constellation Παρθένος) (Aratus 133–4), affords associative connections with humanity's physical suffering in Rev 9:5ff (cf. Mk 13:7) for HC2 to explore:

---

58   Strictly speaking it is the apparent path of the sun that proceeds eastward along the ecliptic, passing through the zodiacal signs in the order Λέων, Παρθένος, Σκορπίος. The outer sphere of the stars, on which the zodiacal constellations were imagined to be affixed, was itself envisaged as rotating in a westward motion (cf. Plato, *Timaeus* 36ff, regarding the motions of the Same and the Different).

59   Kidd 1997: 78–81.

60   Cf. Kidd 1997: 215–16.

61   Boll 1914: 103ff and Malina 1995: 155–60 equate the heavenly sign (σημεῖον) – in the sense of constellation (cf. Aratus, *Phaenomena* 10) – of the Woman (γυνή) (Rev 12:1ff) with the constellation Παρθένος. The marked divergences in the iconographic depiction of the celestial Woman in Rev 12:1ff compared with standard Graeco-Roman depictions of Παρθένος seriously weaken such a suggested identification (which collapses entirely on account of the difficulties in identifying the sign Dragon, once the polar Δράκων is dismissed). The σημεῖον that is described in Rev 12:1, whilst having resonances with prominent constellational signs such as Παρθένος, is not portrayed as one of the zodiacal signs, but rather as one having dominion over the whole zodiac.

62   Cf. Beall 2005/6; Kidd 1997: 216–31; Solmsen 1966.

What an inferior generation your golden fathers have left! And you are likely to beget a still more evil progeny. There will surely be wars (πόλεμοι), yes, and unnatural bloodshed (ἀνάρασιον αἷμα) among men, and suffering from their troubles will come upon them (κακῶν δ' ἐπικείσεται ἄλγος).

(Aratus, *Phaenomena*, 124–7)[63]

The bronze generation of humanity is held responsible for introducing war and murder on the earth (cf. *Works and Days*, 143–55), a greater descent into wickedness (κακότητος, Aratus 121) than was apparent even in the silver age that preceded. If HC2 recalls the Hesiodic passage that Aratus here re-expressed, he may detect even closer verbal parallels between Παρθένος / Δίκη and the torturous effects of the fifth trumpet plague:

But to those who care only for evil outrageousness and cruel deeds, far-seeing Zeus, Cronus' son, marks out justice (δίκη)...Upon them, Cronus' son brings forth woe from the sky (οὐρανόθεν...ἐπήγαγε πῆμα), famine (λιμός) together with pestilence (λοιμός), and the peoples die away (ἀποφθινύθουσι δὲ λαοί)...

(Hesiod, *Works and Days*, 238-44)[64]

The presence of the second constellational component (Παρθένος) in HC2's allegorical reading of Rev 9:7-10 evokes a female personification of Justice (Δίκη) (cf. Aratus 100–136), which is consistent with the function of the fifth trumpet blast as an eschatological woe (οὐαί) (Rev 9:12). The future suffering (ἄλγος) of the unjust members of humanity has been predicted by Παρθένος / Δίκη (Aratus 124–7), and comes to pass as Hesiod earlier described in verse: 'misery from heaven' (πῆμα οὐρανόθεν) (*Works and Days*, 242).[65] Despite the close association of Παρθένος with the grain-harvest, the predicted woe does not take the expected form of a famine or pestilence (λιμός or λοιμός), but rather as the direct torture of unsealed humanity (Rev 9:5, 10). The unexpected aspect of torture (βασανίζω) is supplied by the third and final component of HC2's constellational composite, Σκορπίος.

The zodiacal constellation Σκορπίος is positioned by Aratus directly underneath the gigantic human-configured constellation of Ophiuchus: one foot is upon the eyes of the 'great beast' (μέγα θηρίον), and the other upon its chest/thorax (θώραξ), pressing it firmly down (ἐπιθλίβω) onto the ecliptic (Aratus 81-86) (cf. fig. 5.4).

---

63   Kidd 1997: 80–3.
64   Most 2006: 106–7.
65   LSJ. ἄλγος pain of body (pl. sufferings) or of mind (grief); πῆμα misery, calamity (of persons: bane, calamity).

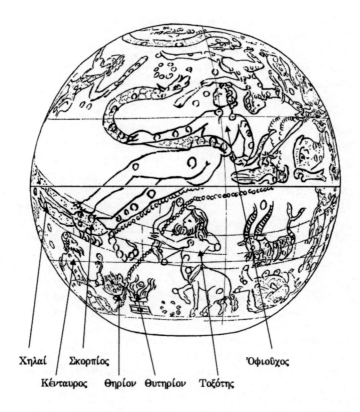

Χηλαί   Σκορπίος   Ὀφιοῦχος

Κένταυρος   Θηρίον Θυτηρίον   Τοξότης

Fig 5.4. Scorpion and Surrounding Constellations (Southern Hemisphere):
Mainz Celestial Globe[66]

HC2's allegorical identification of the scorpion-tailed locust-cavalry as
a composite constellation, which includes Σκορπίος, offers a neat reversal of this image: the human-figure's subjection of the scorpion will be
inverted by a sustained period of torturous retribution directed against
unsealed humanity on the planetary sphere of the earth (Rev 9:4βff).[67]
The most characteristic attribute, and identifying feature, of the constellational Scorpion is its venomous sting (κέντρον) (cf. Rev 9:10), frequently mentioned by Aratus as a fixed-point for his hearers to identify
in order to locate other constellations in its vicinity (cf. Aratus 305,

66   Künzl 2000: 498, Abb. 3b. Drawing/Römisch-Germanisches Museum Mainz,
J. Ribbeck.
67   The fearsome character of the locust-cavalry is more akin to the ἐξουσία of the
constellation Scorpion as viewed from the perspective of the earth (cf. Aratus 634–47)
rather than from an external position beyond the celestial firmament (Aratus 85, 304–7,
402–3, 438).

402, 505). The heliacal rising of Σκορπίος is itself a seasonal indicator of Autumn (November), although Aratus does not describe this aspect directly. Instead, the pre-dawn rising of Σκορπίος is cited as a visible sign of the onset of winter, which is used as a practical guide to identify the heliacal rising of the next sign, Archer (Τοξότης) (whose rising is itself invisible to an observer), as an indication that night-sailing is no longer viable (Aratus 300–308).[68]

The most resonant verbal and visual parallel between Rev 9:7-10 and Aratus' description of Σκορπίος concerns the sustained fable (λόγος) that is recounted to explain the coincidence in the rising and setting of the constellations of Orion and Scorpion.[69] From the perspective of a viewer positioned on the earth's surface (specifically, a viewer located in the Mediterranean region) each night, as the constellation Scorpion rises above the eastern horizon, the celestial hunter, Orion, descends into the subterranean realm in the west. Aratus relates 'an earlier tale' (προτέρων λόγος, Aratus 637) that provides the motivation for Orion's fearful retreat:

> [The arrival of the Scorpion]... also puts great Orion to flight (φοβέει μέγαν Ὠρίωνα) at its coming (ἐπερχόμενος). May Artemis be gracious! It is a tale of the ancients (προτέρων λόγος), who said that stalwart Orion seized her by the robe, when in Chios he was smiting all the wild creatures (θηρία πάντα) with his stout club, striving to secure a hunting gift for Oenopion there. But she immediately summoned-up against him another creature (ἐπετείλατο θηρίον ἄλλο), breaking open the centre of the island's hills (νήσου ἀναρρήξασα μέσας ἑκάτερθε κολώνας) to left and to right, a scorpion (σκορπίον) that stung (ῥά) and killed him (ἔκτανε) for all his size, emerging even more massive, because he had outraged Artemis herself. That is why they say that when the Scorpion comes over the horizon (περαιόθεν ἐρχομένοιο Σκορπίου), Orion flees round the earth's boundary ('Ὠρίωνα περὶ χθονὸς ἔσχατα φεύγειν) [lit. Orion flees to the ends of the earth/ underworld]

> (Aratus, *Phaenomena*, 636–47)[70]

---

68   Kidd 1997: 94–5.

69   On the definition of a fable (μῦθος) that a tertiary-educated hearer may be familiar with, see Theon, *Progymnasmata*, 4.72 'A fable is a fictitious story giving an image of truth'. Theon, *Progymnasmata*, 4.73 notes that such fables are elsewhere described as αἶνος or λόγος. For a full discussion of the development of this genre in antiquity see van Dijk 1997: 79–90, 124–37.

70   Kidd 1997: 118–21.

The constellation of Orion was one of the foremost Greek star-groups, referred to as early as the 6th century BCE as a seasonal indicator (cf. Hesiod, *Works and Days*, 597, 609, 615; cf. Homer, *Iliad* XVIII.486), and its eponymous hero, the Boetian hunter Orion, was equally famed in the Homeric era (cf. *Odyssey*, XI.309–10, 572–7 where Orion is a shade in Hades). Aratus' version is the earliest extant report (*c.* 276 BCE) of the conflict between Orion and a scorpion, although Aratus himself describes his story as based on 'an earlier account' (πρότερων λόγος) (Aratus 637), one that most likely coincided with the creation of the Greek constellations in the 5th/4th centuries BCE.[71] Evidence for the posited origin of the tale is provided by the existence of alternative ancient versions of Orion's demise, in which he is killed directly by Artemis (ε 121–4), traditions which the tale recounted by Aratus modifies (by describing the scorpion as an agent of Artemis) or in other versions wholly replaces.[72] The function of the fable recounted by Aratus is explicitly stated to provide an explanation as to why the constellation Orion sets just as Scorpion rises (Aratus 645).

In the tale Artemis dispatches a giant, chthonic scorpion to sting Orion fatally, as a punishment for laying hands upon her (seizing her robe, Aratus 639), whilst hunting on the island of Chios. Interestingly, given the astrological origins of the account, the giant Scorpion is described as emerging from beneath the earth, after Artemis had first violently ripped apart (ἀναρρήγνυμι) the centre of the island's hills (νῆσοι) (Aratus 642).[73] The gigantic size of the scorpion corresponds to the relative size of the constellation Scorpion in comparison with the constellation of Orion (Aratus 643). The terrestrial conflict between Orion and the Scorpion is now played out in the heavens, with an altered conclusion, as Orion *eternally escapes* ('flees to the ends of the earth', περὶ χθονὸς ἔσχατα φεύγειν), descending to the earth (χθών), from whence the Scorpion rises, whenever his assailant ascends from its subterranean abode.

Rev 9:1-12 contains a cluster of verbal echoes which would prompt HC2 to recall this 'former tale', notably shared references to a scorpion/scorpions (Rev 9:3, 10; Aratus 635, 643, 646) and an emphasis on the creature's sting (κέντρον) as its primary offensive weapon (cf. Rev 9:10; Aratus 643).[74] The

---

71   Cf. Kidd 1997: 396–7. Later, modified retellings, are provided by Pseudo-Eratosthenes, *Catasterismi* 7 and Hyginus, *De Astronomia* 2.26; cf. Condos 1997: 187–8.

72   In Hyginus' version Artemis is entirely absent, replaced by the goddess Gaia to prevent Orion killing all the animals on the earth (Hyginus, *De Astronomia* 2.26).

73   Note that the verb ἀναρρήγνυμι is used elsewhere of the violent rupture of earthquakes and volcanoes (cf. Aristotle, *De Mundi* 400a25, *Iliad* xx.62-3, Kidd 1997: 400), which is consistent with the volcanic origins, and activity, of the island of Chios.

74   Aratus, *Phaenomena* 643 *implicitly* refers to the barbed tail of the scorpion with which he fatally stings (ῥά) the Boetian hunter. Compare Aratus 305, 402 and 505 which explicitly refer to the sting (κέντρον) of the constellational Scorpion as one of its most prominent characteristics (used to describe the relative position of other constellations in its vicinity).

most pertinent connection of all, however, concerns a shared methodological interest in transposing the scorpion's subterranean origins into a celestial register. For Aratus, the chthonic origins of the giant Scorpion (cf. Aratus 646), emerging from the fiery, volcanic depths of the island of Chios, is correlated with the nightly ascent of the constellation Scorpion above the eastern hemisphere of the earth.[75] In a similar vein, HC2 allegorically reinterprets the ascent of the hybrid locusts through the well of the subterranean abyss (τὸ φρέαρ τῆς ἀβύσσου) (Rev 9:1-2), as the motion of a composite constellational figure, which includes Σκορπίος, along the ecliptic, bisecting the Hadean portion of the southern hemisphere of the celestial globe.

Drawing the various threads together, HC2's distinctive interpretative response to Rev 9:1-12 can be succinctly summarized as follows. The locust-cavalry formerly envisioned by the prophet Joel (cf. Joel 1:6, 2:4-5), and which, by the Hellenistic era, had increasingly come to be associated with the mythical 'enemy from the north' under the leadership of their ruler Gog (cf. Joel 2:20; Ezek 38–39; Amos 7:1 LXX) in Jewish exegetical tradition, is re-envisioned in Rev 9:1-12 as the ascent of hybrid locusts from the subterranean abyss under the direct control of the personified ruler of Hades. HC2 responds to the discordant cosmology of this text by offering an allegorical interpretation of three major components of these hybrid locusts: the leonine teeth (Rev 9:8β), the human faces and hair (Rev 9:7γ-8α), and the scorpion tails and sting (Rev 9:10). The controlling force of HC2's allegorical reading is his dominant Platonic-Aratean cosmology, by means of which he relocates the text's spatial reference to the subterranean abyss (ἄβυσσος) of a disc-earth (Rev 9:1-2) to the southern-hemisphere of the celestial globe (specifically the 'celestial sea'). Refracted through this altered cosmological viewpoint, informed by verbal echoes of Aratus' *Phaenomena* and visual correspondences with celestial globes, HC2 offers a constellational reading of Rev 9:7-10. The leonine teeth correspond to the constellation Λέων, a seasonal indicator of fiery heat and crop-destruction. The female face and hair correspond to the constellation Παρθένος, resonant with the retributive justice of the goddess Δίκη against the injustices of humanity. The precise form that this retribution takes is signalled by the final component, the scorpion-tail, which corresponds to the torturous sting (κέντρον) of the constellation Σκορπίος, an earlier catasterized retelling of a monstrous subterranean scorpion, that resonantes in HC2's mental library.

75   The goddess Artemis tears apart (ἀναρρήγνυμι) the centre of a hill (μέσος νῆσος) on the island of Chios, enabling the scorpion to ascend to the surface through a newly created fissure (Aratus 642).

The burning effects of the poisonous sting of the scorpion is consistent with its origins in *fiery* realms beneath the earth: the abyssal locusts emerge from a subterranean realm that resembles a furnace (κάμινος), whilst the Aratean scorpion is released like lava from the crater of a volcano on Chios.

5.6 Evidence of Early Christian Astronomical Exegesis: 'Hippolytus', ἔλεγχός IV.46-50

How plausible is it to propose that an early Christian, with a sound *encyclical* education, may have offered an astronomical exegesis of scripture, informed by Aratus' *Phaenomena*? Intriguingly, there is some fragmentary evidence that at least one 3rd-century CE Christian exegete adopted a method akin to that ascribed to HC2, allegorically interpreting the constellations described in Aratus' *Phaenomena* by means of scripture.[76]

Extracts from an unnamed Christian author's allegorical exegesis of Aratus' *Phaenomena*, are cited by 'Hippolytus' in ἔλεγχός κατὰ πασῶν αἱρέσεων (*Refutation of all Heresies*), book IV, chapters 46–50 (3rd century CE).[77] Before we proceed, a brief note is required on the designation 'Hippolytus'. The ascription of the vast corpus of commentaries and studies attributed to 'Hippolytus' in antiquity, notably various exegetical studies engaging with the Apocalypse (*Commentary on the Apocalypse, On Christ and Antichrist*) as well as the ἔλεγχός (cf. Jerome, *Lives of Illustrious Men*, 61) remains a subject of sustained critical enquiry in contemporary scholarship.[78] Scholars continue to debate whether the Hippolytean corpus is the work of one, two or more authors (or perhaps even a Hippolytean tradition), such that the author of the ἔλεγχός can no longer be presumed to be the same author as one or both of the Apocalypse studies mentioned.[79] Fortunately, for our present purposes, it is not necessary to resolve such an intricate puzzle, only to acknowledge the lack of clarity as to the authorship or provenance of the ἔλεγχός, save for its accepted 3rd-century CE date of composition.[80]

---

76   For studies of the exegesis of Aratus' *Phaenomena* referred to in ἔλεγχός IV.46-50, see Beck 2006a: 170–5; Hegedus 2007: 279–86.

77   For the text of the ἔλεγχός cf. Marcovich 1986 (Greek); MacMahon 1995 (English). For the ascription of the work to 'Hippolytus' see Brent 1995: 127–44.

78   Kannengiesser 2006: 529. 'In current scholarship, Hippolytus is probably the most controversial writer of the early church.'

For the attribution of another work to 'Hippolytus', a dialogue in which the character of Hippolytus defends the authenticity of the Apocalypse against Gaius ('Heads against Gaius' (κεφάλαια κατὰ Γαίου)) (possible fragments of which are contained in the 12th-century Syriac Commentary of Dionysius Bar Salibi), cf. Brent 1995: 144–84.

79   Cf. Brent 1995 (especially regarding the list of works on the extant statue of 'Hippolytus') and Cerrato 2002, and the extensive bibliographies provided by these studies.

80   Cf. Cerrato 2002: 4–5 for the range of possible options as to authorship and provenance (Rome, Palestine, Egypt, Asia Minor, etc.) for some or all of the items in the Hippolytean corpus. Cf. Jerome, *Lives of Illustrious Men* 61: 'Hippolytus, bishop of a church in some city, the name of which I could not discover'; Halton 1999: 87.

'Hippolytus' is highly critical of his subject's methodological approach, which he characterizes as allegorizing (ἀλληγορέω) the Aratean constellations with representations (ἀπεικονίζω) derived from scripture in order to arrive at artificial catasterisms (καταστερίζω) of the author's own composition. Interestingly, 'Hippolytus'' refutation involves direct appeal to Aratus' *Phaenomena*, to undermine the artificiality of the exegesis he disputes:

> In order that what I am going to say may appear clearer to my readers, I have decided to discuss the thoughts of Aratus (τὰ τῷ Ἀρατῷ πεφροντισμένα) on the disposition of the stars in heaven (περὶ τῆς κατὰ τὸν οὐρανὸν ἄστρων διαθέσεως ἐξειπεῖν), how certain people allegorize those thoughts by transferring (μετάγειν) the celestial likenesses [i.e. the constellation figures] to what is said in holy scripture (ὥς τινες εἰς τὰ ὑπὸ τῶν γραφῶν εἰρημένα ἀπεικονίζοντες αὐτὰ ἀλληγοροῦσι)...showing a strange marvel, how their own sayings have been 'catasterized' (κατηστερισμένων τῶν ὑπ' αὐτῶν λεγομένων)
>
> (ἔλεγχός IV.46.2)[81]

The selected excerpts that 'Hippolytus' includes in his study to demonstrate, and devalue, such an astronomical exegesis of scripture provide some indication of the generic and methodological characteristics of the source-text. The work functions, in part, as a running commentary on Aratus' *Phaenomena*, not dissimilar to the educational commentaries and *scholia* produced by ancient grammarians and astronomers (μαθηματικοί) on this influential astronomical text book.[82] 'Hippolytus'' source often deviates from the literary structure of Aratus' epic poem, however, by bringing together clusters of constellations to present a series of interconnected 'astronomical myths', with a distinctive Christian spin.[83] Three of these λόγοι are extant in the extracts cited by 'Hippolytus':[84] the eternal struggle between Αδαμ and ὁ διάβολος catasterized in the revolutions of ἐν γόνασιν and Δράκων (ἔλεγχός IV. 46.6-48.6); the superiority of the second creation over the first, catasterized in the revolutions of μικρὰ Ἀρκτος versus μεγάλη Ἀρκτος (ἔλεγχός IV.48.9-14); and the deliverance of the soul (of Adam and Eve) by

---

81   Beck 2006a: 170–1; Marcovich 1986: 130.

82   Cf. §2.3, above.

83   For example, the extract author discusses the Lyre (A. 268–74) in connection with Engonasin (A. 63–70), diverging markedly from Aratus' structural arrangement.

84   It is plausible that the extract author had written a more extensive work, from which 'Hippolytus' selected a few examples:

Cf. Hegedus 2007: 280 'It should be noted that this system need not have been restricted to only those constellations found in the report of Hippolytus. The group may well have utilized all the constellations discussed in Aratus' *Phaenomena*; cf. the mention of "crabs and bulls and lions and rams and goats and kids and whatever other animals are named throughout the stars" (καρκινοι δε και ταυροι και λεοντες και κριοι και αιγες και εριφοι και οσα αλλα θηρια δια των αστρων ονομαζεται), evidently a reference to the zodiacal signs, at the end of the discussion of the group in the *Refutation* (49.4).'

the Logos, overwriting the myth of Perseus' rescue of Andromeda from the Sea-monster (cf. Pseudo-Eratosthenes Καταστερισμοί 17 and Hyginus' *De astronomia*) (ἔλεγχός IV.48.14–49.3).[85]

My suspicion is that 'Hippolytus'' source-text may have been composed by a Christian grammarian, endeavouring to utilize a standard text-book of Greek ἐγκύκλιος παιδεία for use by his students, but in such a way as to re-appropriate the pedagogical content to affirm specifically Christian as opposed to 'Greek' values.[86] The live debate as to the use, if any, that Christian students and teachers should make of the classic texts of Greek παιδεία in the third and fourth century CE received a wide spectrum of responses.[87] The extract-author would be aligned with the perspective of writers such as Clement of Alexandria (*c.* 150–215 CE) and Basil of Caesarea (*c.* 330–379 CE) who advocated the continued use of *encyclical* studies, provided that the positive benefits are extracted, and the negative components discarded:

> But he who culls what is useful for the advantage of the catechumens, and especially when they are Greeks...must not abstain from erudition, like irrational animals; but he must collect as many aids as possible for his hearers.
>
> (Clement of Alexandria, *Stromateis* 6.11/89.13)[88]

> It is, therefore, in accordance with the whole similitude of the bees, that we should participate in pagan literature. For these neither approach all flowers equally, nor in truth do they attempt to carry off entire those upon which they alight, but taking only so much of them as suitable for their work, they suffer the rest to go untouched. We ourselves too, if we are wise, having appropriated from this literature what is suitable to us and akin to the truth will pass over the remainder.
>
> (Basil of Caesarea, *Ad adolescentes*, 4:8-9)[89]

A brief overview of the first 'astrological-myth' recounted in the surviving extracts (ἔλεγχός IV.47.1–48.6) will give a flavour of the character of this work (cf. fig. 5.5).

---

85   Ps-Eratosthenes; cf. Pàmias and Geus 2007 (Greek and German); Hyginus; cf. Viré 1992 (Latin); Condos 1997 (English).

86   Cf. The pejorative characterization of Greek education as circling in on itself as a helix, that is as 'ἀνακύκλωσις' rather than 'ἐγκύκλιος' education, indicating the allegedly fruitless goal towards which the Greeks are being disciplined (παιδεύω) (IV.48.8).

87   Cf. Sandnes 2009: 81–243.

88   Sandnes 2009: 135.

89   Sandnes 2009: 178.

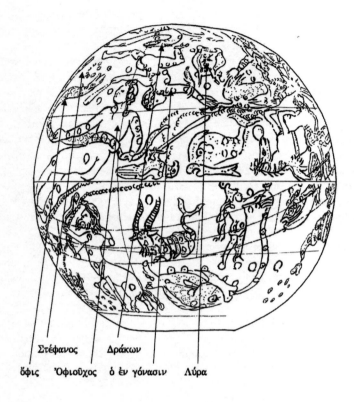

Στέφανος   Δράκων

ὄφις   'Οφιοῦχος   ὁ ἐν γόνασιν   Λύρα

Fig. 5.5 The Constellations: Δράκων, ὁ ἐν γόνασιν, Λύρα, Στέφανος, ὄφις and 'Οφιοῦχος *(Mainz celestial globe); cf. Hippolytus, Refutatio IV. 46.6-48.6 (3rd century CE)*[90]

The cluster commences with a description of the northern polar location of Δράκων, alluding to Aratus (ll. 45–46, 61), and draws out the significance of this constellation's position which enables it to survey all of creation, both the eastern and western hemispheres, unceasingly (as it never sets) (ἔλεγχός IV.47.1-4). On the basis of Job 1:7 LXX the extract author catasterizes the Devil (ὁ διάβολος), equating his stated wanderings with the polar revolutions of the constellation Δράκων: 'I have been wandering to and fro under heaven and going round about' (ἐμπεριπατήσας τὴν ὑπ' οὐρανὸν και περιελθὼν). The extract author omits the Accuser's reference to *terrestrial wanderings* (τὴν γῆν) in the LXX, and adds an explanatory clause to emphasize his revolutionary

90   Künzl 2000: 496, Abb. 1a. Drawing/Römisch-Germanisches Museum Mainz, J. Ribbeck.

motion: 'that is, spinning around and observing what is occurring (τουτέστι περιστραφεὶς καὶ περισκοπήσας τὰ γινόμενα)' (ἔλεγχός IV.47.2).[91]

The second constellational character described, following Aratus' order, is the unidentified figure of 'the one on his knees' (ὁ ἐν γόνασιν) (ἔλεγχός IV.47.4-5). The extract-author delights in Aratus' lack of knowledge as to this constellation's identity (cf. Aratus 71–3), and fills the gap with his own suggestion of Αδαμ, once again corroborated by means of scripture, alluding on this occasion to Genesis 3:15 LXX.[92] Aratus' description of the relative spatial locations of Δράκων and ἐν γόνασιν, the latter holding his foot above the dragon's head, is equated with the scriptural reference to Adam[s' offspring] 'guarding' (τηρέω) the serpent's head with his heel. The extract-author, like other Aratean commentators of the 2nd and 3rd centuries CE, sought to identify the unnamed figure catasterized by the constellation ἐν γόνασιν but differed from most in failing to select a noted 'monster-slayer' (e.g. Hercules, Prometheus, Theseus).[93]

The adjacent constellations of Στέφανος (cf. Aratus, 71–3) and Λύρα (cf. Aratus, 268–74) are brought in to develop further this astronomical-myth of celestial conflict between Αδαμ and ὁ διάβολος (ἐν γόνασιν / Δράκων) (ἔλεγχός IV. 48.1-6).[94] The outstretched arms of ἐν γόνασιν are equated with his making a 'confession of sins' (ἁμαρτίας ἐξομολογούμενον), as he strives to obey the divine will. At one hand is the constellation Λύρα, a seven-stringed instrument fashioned by Hermes/Logos (cf. Aratus, 268), and an image of the divine harmony of the created world, which the extract-author relates to the seven days of creation (alluding to Gen 2:2 LXX). If Αδαμ lives in harmony with this divine order, by obeying the divine command, then he will attain his celestial reward of a crown (Στέφανος).

The striking identification of the Logos with Hermes ('...the Logos is the same as he who is denominated Hermes among the Greeks' (Λόγον δὲ εἶναι παρὰ τοῖς Ἑλλησιν ἀκούομεν τὸν Ἑρμῆν)) (ἔλεγχός IV.48.2) is indicative of the extract-author's emphasis on the continuity between Greek epic and scriptural witness, an emphasis reflecting his ultimate aim of embellishing his Aratean base-text with a scriptural overlay.

The extract-author appears unable to restrain himself, however, from drawing in yet more constellational characters to the cast of this astronomical-myth (ἔλεγχός IV.48.4-6), despite the incoherence it adds

91   Marcovich 1986: 131; Hegedus, 2007: 281.

92   'Hippolytus' here provides his own summary, in third person speech, so the citation of Gen 3:15 LXX presumably utilized by the extract-author is not provided.

93   Cf. Kidd 1997: 200–1.

94   Note that Λύρα and Στέφανος are not usually positioned according to the placement of the hands of Ἐν γονασιν. The Crown (Στέφανος) is more usually described as lying close to the 'back' of Ἐν γονασιν (cf. Aratus, 71–3), whilst the Lyre (Λύρα) is usually described as close to his 'knee' (Cf. Aratus, 271–2).

to his catasterism. The interrelated constellations of Ὄφις and Ὀφιοῦχος (cf. Aratus, 74–87) further complicate the celestial conflict between Αδαμ and ὁ διάβολος (Ἐν γόνασιν / Δράκων). Ὄφις, somewhat obscurely, is identified as an 'offspring' (γεννήμα) of Δράκων, who aims to prevent Αδαμ from attaining the crown (Στέφανος), but he is restrained by Ὀφιοῦχος, equated with the Λόγος, rendering this aspect of the conflict somewhat futile.

For the extract-author the revolutions of this small cluster of northern polar constellations animate a simple tale of pedagogical significance: if one (Αδαμ) strives to obey the divine command, and live in harmony with the cosmic order, then a celestial reward (στέφανος) is within one's grasp, despite the machinations of demonic forces.

Ultimately, the Aratean commentator excerpted by 'Hippolytus' and the hypothetical hearer-construct of this chapter (HC2) differ in the use each makes of the content of his *encyclical* education. The former overlays his Aratean base text with Christian catasterisms, whilst the latter utilizes Aratus' *Phaenomena* as a reading-grid to efface a discordant scriptural cosmology. Yet, the very survival of a Christian grammarian's commentary on Aratus endorses this study's focus on the potential impact of *encyclical* education on early scriptural interpretation.

5.7 Conclusion

The focus of this chapter has been creatively to re-imagine how a hypothetical, tertiary-educated hearer of Rev 9:1ff may have responded to the discordant cosmology of the text, on the basis of the rich contents of his mental library. It was proposed that HC2 might choose to reinterpret the archaic tripartite cosmology of Rev 9:1ff allegorically in line with his own cosmological preference for a Platonic multiple-spheres design.

Adopting a comparable method to Philo, in his allegorical reinterpretation of ἡ ἄβυσσος in *De Opificio Mundi*, HC2 equates the abyssal origins of the hybrid cavalry of Rev 9:1-12 with the celestial sea in the southern hemisphere of the celestial globe. In such an altered context, the Apocalypse's hybrid locusts are reconfigured to conjure up a tripartite constellational composite, comprising Λέων, Παρθένος and Σκορπίος, evocative of constellational imagery from Aratus' *Phaenomena*. This zodiacal hybrid repositions the 'enemy from the north' evoked by Joel's former vision, (cf. Ezek 38–39; Joel 2:20, Amos 7:1 LXX), onto the northern hemisphere of the celestial globe. The extensive resonances of prophetic visions, notably by Joel, Ezekiel and Amos, continue to guide HC2's interpretative reading, but new voices can also be detected, most notably the astronomical 'mythology' of Aratus, transposing the temporal myths of Hesiod, from a previous age, into an eternal key, recurrently played out on the celestial firmament (cf. Aratus 636–47).

The plausibility of this hypothetical reading was supported by fragmentary extracts from a 3rd-century CE Christian author's allegorical interpretation of Aratus' *Phaenomena* in 'Hippolytus', ἔλεγχός IV.46-50, who transposed Christian catasterisms (Adam, Eve, Logos, etc.) onto a classical template of the heavens. Although the hermeneutical flow is reversed in the case of HC2, such that the scriptural text is allegorically re-read in the light of Aratus' *Phaenomena*, the intimate connection envisaged in ἔλεγχός IV.46-50 between the Aratean constellations and scriptural images serves to corroborate the viability of such a hypothetical model.

Chapter 6

VICTORINUS, TYCONIUS AND OECUMENIUS: INTERPRETATION OF THE COSMOLOGY OF REV 9

6.1 Introduction

The study now turns from the hypothetical responses of ancient hearers (Chapters 4–5), to focus upon the evidence of the early reception-history of Rev 9:1-21. This chapter has two principal aims: first, to consider how the cosmology of Rev 9 was interpreted by the authors of the earliest extant exegetical *Commentaries* on the Apocalypse: Victorinus (3rd century CE) (§6.2), Tyconius (4th century CE) (§6.3), and Oecumenius (6th century CE) (§6.4). The second, related, aim is to reflect on this evidence as a means of testing the validity of the exegeses of the hearer-construct models detailed in Chapters 4 and 5.

Each of the ancient authors' exegetical commentaries will be considered on its own terms, and thus each sub-section will begin by situating the relevant commentators' work in its unique historical context. Attention will then be paid to the contents of each author's mental library, as far as this can be reconstructed on the basis of his extant writings, paying particular attention to the extent of each author's formal, literary education (ἐγκύκλιος παιδεία). Next, each writer's exegetical method will be discussed, as well as his understanding of the structural organization of the Apocalypse. Particular attention will be paid to the position of Rev 9 in each commentator's analysis of the structural design of the text. Finally, each author's exegetical understanding of the cosmological imagery of Rev 9 will be scrutinised. How do Victorinus, Tyconius, and Oecumenius respond to the cosmological referents in this passage (star, abyss, Euphrates)? To what extent is each author's interpretation shaped by the contents of his mental library, particularly those contents derived from his *encyclical* studies?

The chapter will conclude (§6.5) by reflecting on the significance of this evidence for the hearer-construct models proposed in this study. To what extent does the evidence of the earliest extant reception of the cosmological imagery of Rev 9, by Victorinus, Tyconius and Oecumenius, support the validity of the hearer-construct models proposed, which emphasize the significance of the extent of an ancient hearer's *encyclical* education on his interpretation of cosmological imagery?

6.2 Victorinus (fl. c.250–280 CE)

6.2.1 Introduction –Victorinus' Life and Work

Victorinus was bishop (*episcopus*) of Poetovio (modern day Ptuj, Slovenia), a prominent city in the Roman province of Pannonia Superior, during the second half of the third century CE.[1] According to Jerome (*De virus illustribus 74* (*c.* 392/3 CE)), Victorinus was a prolific exegete and apologist who wrote commentaries, in Latin, on the Pentateuch (Genesis, Exodus, Leviticus), prophets (Isaiah, Ezekiel, Habakkuk) and wisdom literature (Ecclesiastes, Song of Songs), a *Commentary on the Apocalypse*, a treatise *Against All Heresies* (*adversum omnes haereses*), and 'many other' works.[2] Despite publishing in Latin, Victorinus' cultural frame of reference and mother-tongue were evidently Greek, as is apparent from his faltering Latin syntax and grammar, and his marked dependence on Greek language sources. 'Victorinus...did not know Latin as well as he did Greek (*non aeque Latine ut Graece noverat*); as a result, his works, which are excellent in content, seem inferior in composition' (*Unde opera ejus grandia sensibus, viliora videntur compositione verborum*) (*De virus illustribus 74*).[3] Jerome concludes his short biography with a reference to Victorinus' death ('At the end he received the crown of martyrdom'), but the event itself is not precisely dated, although Jerome does position Victorinus' *vita* chronologically between Anatolius who died in 283 CE and Pamphilus who died in 309/10. Whilst Victorinus' martyrdom is generally dated to the 'Great Persecution' under Diocletian (*c.*304 CE), Dulaey persuasively argues that Jerome's lack of precise information may be better accounted for if Victorinus' execution occurred during an earlier, lesser-known, period of state prosecution in the region *c.*283–4 CE under Numerian.[4] Such a date is consistent with the internal evidence of Victorinus' own extant writings, which lack any reference to Manichaeism or Arianism, which 'tends to suggest a writer of the second half of the third century'.[5]

Victorinus' city, the Roman colony (*colonia*) of Poetovio on the river Drava, was a customs centre at the hub of a network of trade routes, notably the Amber trade from Gaul to the Baltic as well as river-traffic to the cities of the Danube basin.[6] Little is known of the Christian communities of Poetovio in the second half of the third century CE, beyond what can be gleaned from Victorinus' own extant writings, due to the absence of

---

1   Cf. Dulaey 1993, vol. I: 11–19, 221–33; Weinrich 2011b: xviii–xxiv.
2   Halton 1999: 105–6. One of the notable works, not listed by Jerome, was a *Commentary on Matthew*; cf. Dulaey 1993, vol. I: 51–68.
3   Halton 1999: 105.
4   Dulaey 1993, vol. I: 11–12.
5   Dulaey 1993, vol. I: 11. 'Comme notre auteur ignore tout du manicéisme et de l'arianisme, cela tend à en faire un écrivain de la deuxième moitié du IIIe siècle.'
6   Cf. Mócsy 1974: 118.

archaeological evidence for this period.[7] Nonetheless, as will be noted below, the rich mercantile links of this administrative city are reflected in Victorinus' preserved writings, particularly traces of Greek-speaking influence from the east, Illyricum and Asia Minor, as well as Syria.[8]

Only one of Victorinus' scriptural commentaries is extant, his *Commentary on the Apocalypse* (*in Apocalypsin Joannis*), plus a short treatise, not listed by Jerome, 'On the Creation of the World' (*De Fabrica Mundi*).[9] In addition there are fragmentary remains of a Chronological treatise, and an exegesis on the Parable of the Ten Virgins (Mt 25:1-13).[10] The present study will focus on the major extant writings of Victorinus, *in Apocalypsin* and *De Fabrica Mundi*.

6.2.2 *Victorinus' Mental Library*

On the basis of explicit citations and implicit allusions to scriptural and other literary texts in Victorinus' *Apocalypse Commentary* and *De Fabrica Mundi*, the parameters of Victorinus' mental library can be tentatively sketched as follows.[11] Commenting on the significance of the twenty-four elders and the twenty-four wings of the living creatures (6 x 4) around the divine throne (Rev 4:4-8), Victorinus explicitly refers to twenty-four books of the OT, although without listing their titles:

> The books of the Old Testament (*testimonia ueteris*) which are received (*excipiuntur*), are twenty-four, which we find in the *Epitomies of Theodore* (*quos in epitomis Theodori inuenimus*), just as there are twenty-four patriarchs and apostles as we said.
>
> (*In Apoc.* 4.5)[12]

---

7   Cf. Mócsy 1974: 322–36. In addition to worship of the gods of the Roman pantheon, and various local deities, the Mithras cult was particularly prominent in Poetovio, especially among customs officials, with five Mithraic sanctuaries excavated in the city (cf. Beck 2006b).

8   Cf. Dulaey 1993, vol. I: 14–15.

On the basis of the evidence of Christian grave inscriptions in Pannonia and Upper Moesia of the 3rd–4th centuries CE, Mócsy concludes that the majority of members of these small Christian communities were Greek-speaking immigrants from the eastern provinces (Mócsy 1974: 322–3).

9   Cf. Dulaey 1997 (Latin/French), Wallis 1994 (English), Weinrich 2005 (English, extracts) and Weinrich 2011b (English, full-text of the Apocalypse Commentary).

10   *Chronological Fragment*, Dulaey 1997: 133–5; *De decem uirginibus*, Wilmart 1958: 172–4. On Victorinus' authorship of both fragments cf. Dulaey 1993, vol. I: 37–42.

11   See Dulaey 1993, vol. I: 69–88 for a discussion of the range of scriptural texts cited by Victorinus, supplemented by the Scripture Index that accompanies Victorinus' extant texts (Dulaey 1997: 235–9). For Victorinus' use of earlier patristic sources see Dulaey 1993, vol. I: 271–307.

12   Dulaey 1997: 70–71.

Victorinus specifies twenty-four books of OT scripture, comparable to the twenty-four books that are 'made public' (*in palam pone*) in IV Ezra 14:44-47 (in contrast to the seventy books which are to be retained (*conservabis*) for the wise).[13] Strikingly, Victorinus also cites his (otherwise unknown) source for this information: the 'Epitomes of Theodore'. This reference may indicate that Victorinus utilized ancient scriptural *testimonia*, as had Justin, a view supported by occasional errors of referencing by Victorinus, e.g. erroneously attributing a citation of Ezek 31:3-4 to Isaiah (*In Apoc.* 11.4).[14] Significantly, however, as noted by Dulaey, Theodore's collections are stated to be *epitomae*, abridgements, not (Christologically arranged) extracts (*eclogae*) as in Melito of Sardis' Ἐκλογαις (ἐκλογὰς ἐκ τε τοῦ νόμου καὶ τῶν προφητῶν περὶ τοῦ σωτῆρος)) (Eusebius, *Hist. Eccl.* IV.26).[15] Furthermore, Victorinus' publication of a series of commentaries is weighty evidence in support of his first-hand knowledge of the Septuagint. In his extant exegetical writings, Victorinus alludes to sixteen Septuagintal books (Pentateuch, Joshua, I Maccabees, Psalms, Proverbs, Ecclesiastes, Wisdom, Sirach, Isaiah, Jeremiah, Ezekiel, Daniel, and the Twelve).[16]

Victorinus, drawing upon the earlier exegesis of Irenaeus (*Adv. Haer.* 3.11.8), equates the four Gospels with the faces of the four living beings of Rev 4:6-8 (*In Apoc.* 4.3-4), although in an unusual order, placing the Gospels of John and Matthew first, the apostolic pair whom Victorinus cites most frequently in his extant publications.[17] Interestingly, Victorinus also specifies the structural organization of the Pauline epistles, dividing them into two sets: letters to churches and letters to individuals, the former group comprising letters to precisely *seven* churches (Rome, Corinth, Ephesus, Thessalonica, Galatia, Philippi, and Colossae), viewed as having a comparable universal significance to the letters to the seven churches in Rev 2–3 (*In Apoc.* 1.7). No further details of the contents of the set of letters to individuals is provided, save for a citation of I Tim 3:15.[18] That Victorinus is here dependent on an earlier source, perhaps 'Hippolytus',[19] or even the

13   Compare the twenty-two volume Judean ἀναγραφαί referred to by Josephus (*Against Apion* I.37-42); cf. Mason 2002: 113–15 (§2.5.2, above).

14   For a reconstruction of Justin's scriptural *testimonia* see Skarsaune 1987: 228–45; Skarsaune 2007.

15   Lake 1926: 390–3. Cf. Dulaey 1993, vol. I: 69–71, 271–2.

16   Cf. Dulaey 1997: 235–7.

17   An order of the Gospels also found in some *Vetus Latina* manuscripts, cf. Dulaey 1997: 237–8. On the four living creatures in patristic exegesis, see Stevenson 2001.

18   The structural division of the Pauline epistles is comparable to that found in the *Muratorian Canon*, although the letters are listed in a different order. On the disputed date (2nd?/4th?century CE) and provenance of the *Muratorian Canon* see Hahneman 1992, 2002.

19   For Dionysius Bar Salbi's 12th-century reference to the comparable enumeration of 'Hippolytus' (13 Pauline Epistles, minus Hebrews, with letters addressed to precisely seven churches) see Armstrong 2008: 14–15. On the problematic status of the identity of 'Hippolytus' in patristic scholarship see Brent 1995 (cf. §5.6 above).

Epitomes of Theodore (*In Apoc. 4.5*), is apparent from the marked discrepancies with his own exegetical practice, as he alludes to Hebrews on three occasions (*In Apoc.* 5.2, 6.4, 21.5) despite its failing to fit either sub-category (neither addressed to an individual nor one of the seven churches).[20] Victorinus' own extant exegesis engages with a narrower range of Pauline epistles (Rom, I Cor, Col, Eph, II Thess, I Tim, II Tim, Heb), with a marked preference for I Cor and II Thess.

In addition to Victorinus' extensive engagement with the Apocalypse in his *Commentary*, he also alludes to passages in Acts, I and II Peter and Jude.[21] There is little or no evidence of Victorinus' knowledge of non-Septuagintal Second Temple Jewish or Early Christian literature, aside, perhaps, from the *Apocalypse of Peter*, but this reference occurs in a short fragment from *De decem uirginibus*, for which Victorinus' authorship is uncertain, and so will be set aside in the present study.[22]

The scriptural versions that Victorinus utilizes are distinctive, indicative of the marked influence that Greek witnesses exert on Victorinus' thought.[23]

> For the OT, Victorinus used a Greek translation closer to the original Hebrew than the LXX, such as the translation by Theodotion. For the NT, his Latin text is strictly local, characterized by a certain attempt at a harmonization of the Gospels, but without any parallels in the *Vetus Latina*. For both, OT and NT, he occasionally corrected the Latin translation at his disposal by checking the Greek text.[24]

Victorinus is heavily dependent on a range of earlier patristic authors, most significantly, for the present study, Irenaeus (*fl.* late 2nd century), 'Hippolytus' (3rd century CE), and Origen (185–253 CE), whose exegetical methods and conclusions colour Victorinus' *Apocalypse Commentary*.[25] According to Jerome, Victorinus' principal merit had

---

20   It is not possible to engage in detail with the insightful and detailed case that Armstrong presents in favour of Victorinus' authorship of the *Muratorian Canon* (Armstrong 2008), save to raise one significant concern. The parallels cited resonate more strongly with passages where Victorinus is citing from a source (e.g. the enumeration of the Pauline epistles minus Hebrews, *In Apoc* 1.7) but cohere less with the author's own exegetical practice (e.g. his citations of Hebrews, *In Apoc.* 5.2, 6.4, 21.5). Accordingly, the *Muratorian Canon* has interesting resonances with Victorinus' sources (*In Apoc* 1.7), perhaps indicative of a related provenance, but is less likely to be directly authored by Victorinus himself.

21   Dulaey 1997: 239.

22   Cf. Armstrong 2008: 27–8, *De decem uirginibus* 58–60: '...there is a river of fire that separates the impious from the kingdom of God, as it is written (*scriptum est*) in Daniel and Peter – in his Apocalypse (*in Apocalypsi eius*).'

23   Cf. Dulaey 1993, vol. I: 77–88.

24   Kannengiesser 2006: 639.

25   For more detail on the subjects mentioned here, and an evaluation of the potential influence of a more extensive range of patristic sources, both Greek and Latin authors (Papias, Theophilus of Antioch, Justin, Clement of Alexandria, Tertullian, Minucius Felix, and Cyprian), see Dulaey 1993, vol. I: 271–307.

been to make known to a Latin-speaking audience the exegesis of the Greek east, specifically Origen and Hippolytus.[26]

Victorinus was profoundly influenced by Irenaeus, evidencing a deep knowledge of both Irenaeus' *Against Heresies* and *Demonstration of the Apostolic Preaching*.[27] The bishop of Poetovio appropriated Irenaeus' characteristic emphasis on the significance of the incarnation of the Word, and the antithetical parallelism between Adam and Christ. Perhaps most significantly, as will be noted below, Victorinus was influenced by Irenaeus' rich and complex theory of the 'recapitulation' (ἀνακεφαλαίωσις, cf. Eph 1:10) of 'all things' (τὰ πάντα) in Christ, analogously ascribing this function to the NT as scriptural prophecy, and allowing it to inform his understanding of the Apocalypse's structural design.[28]

As noted by Jerome, the exegetical content of Victorinus' *Commentary on the Apocalypse* is richly informed by 'Hippolytus'' earlier exegetical studies on the *Apocalypse* (*Commentary on the Apocalypse, On Christ and Antichrist*, cf. Jerome, *De virus illustribus* 61), as far as these are recoverable on the basis of the surviving treatise *On Christ and Antichrist* plus exegetical comments on the Apocalypse attributed to 'Hippolytus', preserved in the sixth-century Greek commentary of Andrew of Caesarea and the twelfth-century Syriac commentary of Dionysius Bar Salibi.[29] A number of elements of Victorinus' exegesis are indebted to 'Hippolytus', notably the interpretation of the golden belt, the eyes of flame, and the seven stars, in the opening vision of the Son of Man (Rev 1:9-20), as well as the significance of the opening of the seven seals.[30]

Origen's influence upon Victorinus is readily apparent in his emphasis upon the 'spiritual sense' (*spiritalis sensus*) of scripture that has been given to the churches (*In Apoc.* 1.4), a distinctive turn of phrase, reminiscent

---

26 Dulaey 1993, vol. I: 271.

27 Cf. Dulaey 1993, vol. I: 280–88.

28 Irenaeus employed the term ἀνακεφαλαίωσις in an intricate fashion, as a way of encapsulating the multi-faceted significance of Christ's summing-up, consummating and restoring the divine plan of salvation. For detailed studies of the complex nuances of 'recapitulation' in Irenaeus see Bouteneff 2008: 73–85, Osborn 2001: 97–140 and Smith 1994.

29 Cf. Dulaey 1993, vol. I: 288–93 and Weinrich 2005: xxi. For the complexities surrounding sources and referent(s) that frustrate attempts to reconstruct the exegetical comments on the Apocalypse by 'Hippolytus' see Allen 1995: 144–84 (cf. §5.6 above).

For 'Hippolytus' treatise *On Christ and Antichrist* see Achelis 1897: 1–47 (Greek); Salmond 1995 (English). On the excerpts attributed to 'Hippolytus' by Andrew of Caesarea, see Schmid 1955 (Greek); Weinrich 2011a (English). Dionysius Bar Salibi's Commentary (Syriac) preserves extracts from a dialogue between 'Hippolytus' and 'Gaius' which may derive from a 3rd-century CE defence of the authenticity of the Apocalypse written to refute Gaius of Rome (cf. Epiphanius, *Panarion* 51; Williams 1994: 26–66), known as 'Heads against Gaius' (κεφάλαια κατὰ Γαίου), or perhaps a *florilegium* dependent on this work; see Prigent 1972 (French) and Prigent and Stehly 1973 (French).

30 Cf. Dulaey 1993, vol. I: 288–91.

of Origen.[31] Whilst Victorinus does not enumerate a threefold sense of scripture, as did Origen, he nonetheless assimilated a central aspect of his thought, namely, the conflation of two central images: scripture is veiled and obscure, like the veil of Moses and the sealed book of the Apocalypse (*In Apoc.* 5.2), until Christ unseals/unveils it.[32]

Evidence of Victorinus' literary education (ἐγκύκλιος παιδεία) is much more difficult to trace. In his extant writings (*In Apocalypsin, De Fabrica Mundi*) there is no explicit citation or allusion to any literary authors, whether Latin or Greek. As noted above, one of Victorinus' early readers, Jerome, highlighted the deficiencies in Victorinus' Latin grammar and syntax, indicative, perhaps, of an author who was a primary bilingual (i.e. he learnt Latin informally, rather than receiving a literary education in Latin).[33] Although Victorinus was a native Greek-speaker, there are no traces of Greek literary authors either, whether poets, historians, or philosophers, in his extant writings. The absence of any trace of a formal literary education (ἐγκύκλιος παιδεία), coupled with Victorinus' heavy dependence on patristic writers and traditions, notably liturgical traditions, especially regarding fasts, that derive from an Asia Minor or Syrian Greek tradition,[34] have led Martine Dulaey to propose that Victorinus may have instead received an 'in-house' education:

> If he [Victorinus] did not follow the cycle of classical studies, as suggested by Jerome ('*licet desit eruditio*'), he may well have received an education of a Semitic type, possibly through a church tradition linked with a Judaeo-Christian milieu.[35]

The absence of allusions to Greek literary authors, coupled with the lack of technical vocabulary or traces of the exegetical methods taught by a grammarian, strongly suggest that Victorinus did not receive a formal Greek literary education. Such an assessment is consistent with the

31   Dulaey 1997: 157.
32   Cf. Dulaey 1993, vol. I: 295.
33   Cf. Bruce 1938: 353 'Jerome's witness to his [Victorinus'] imperfect Latin is decidedly justified by his writings that remain. While his meaning is usually quite plain, his grammatical constructions are the reverse. In many places they conform to no known rule of Latin syntax, classical or postclassical.'
On primary and secondary bilingualism in antiquity see Horsley 1989: 24.
34   Cf. Dulaey 1993, vol. I: 225–33; 271–7.
35   Dulaey 1993, vol. I: 36. 'S'il n'a pas suivi le cycle des études classiques, comme le suggère Jérôme ("licet desit eruditio…"), il pourrait bien avoir bénéficié d'une formation de style sémitique, peut-être à travers une tradition ecclésiale d'ascendance judéochrétienne'.
For extant manuscript evidence of early Christian writing exercises using scriptural texts (especially Psalms) in place of extracts from Homer, see the overview in Römer 2003 and the specific test-case of P. Oxy II. 209/*P* [10] = Rom 1:1-7 as a writing exercise, contained in the archive of Aurelius Leonides, a flax merchant from Oxyrhyncus (4th century CE) discussed by Lujendijk 2010.

concerted emphasis on scriptural study as an *alternative* to ἐγκύκλιος παιδεία in a Christian treatise on education, written in Greek-speaking Syria during this era, a provenance which has strong resonances with Victorinus' own writings (notably his discussion of fasts).[36] *Didascalia Apostolorum* 2 proposes that Christian students should read the Pentateuch, the Book of Kings and the prophets as alternatives to Homeric epic, Greek historians, and philosophers.[37] Even if it is hypothesized that Victorinus received a minimal literary education as a child, perhaps basic literacy with the aid of extracts from Homer, then such knowledge and insights have been effaced, in his extant writings, by his subsequent extensive studies of the scriptures in Greek and Greek patristic authors (notably Irenaeus, 'Hippolytus', Origen). In one of the few traces of erudition in Victorinus' extant writings, the opening line of *De Fabrica Mundi*, the recollection of a 'Ciceronian expression', is deemed by Dulaey to be a secondary echo, derived from Victorinus' recollection of a Christian author (Minucius Felix, *Octavius* 1.1 (early 3rd century CE)).[38] Accordingly, in the absence of any concrete evidence to the contrary, the contents of Victorinus' mental library are limited to a combination of scriptural texts and early patristic commentaries and treatises.

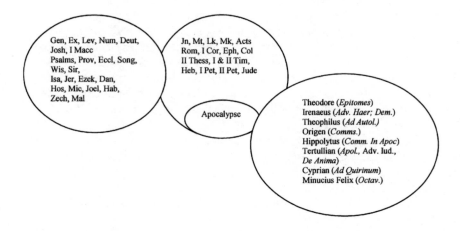

Fig 6.1. Victorinus' Mental Library

36   Cf. Dulaey 1993, vol. I: 27–8, 225–31.
37   Cf. Sandnes 2009: 102–10 cf. Connolly 1929; Stewart-Sykes 2009.
38   Dulaey 1997: 215.

6.2.3 Victorinus' Interpretative Method

Two interrelated facets of Victorinus' exegetical method merit discussion: the spiritual sense of scripture and recapitulation.[39] Both traits emerge from Victorinus' reflective engagement with Irenaeus and Origen, and together underpin his interpretation of the content, structure, and significance of the Apocalypse.

Scriptural prophecy, its images and figures, are obscure and indecipherable, akin to the veiled face of Moses (Ex 34:33; cf. II Cor 3:13-16) or the sealed scroll of the Apocalypse (Rev 5–8) – until the Passion of Christ.[40] For Victorinus, the sealed scroll of Rev 5:1 is to be identified with the Old Testament,[41] that Christ alone could open. It is because Christ, by his death and resurrection, fulfilled the scriptural prophecies, as priest victim, and new temple (*In Apoc.* 5.1-2, cf. Heb 4:14-10:39, Jn 2:13-22), that the sealed-scroll of scripture has been opened, in the figurative sense of disclosing its previously veiled meaning.[42]

The exegete's task, according to Victorinus, is to discern the 'spiritual sense', that is, the revealed meaning of scripture, centred on Christ, disclosed through the Spirit. Victorinus refers to this in his interpretation of the 'golden sash' (Rev 1:13) that he equates with 'the pure spiritual sense given to the churches' (*purus spiritalis sensus traditus est ecclesiis*) (*In Apoc.* 1.4). The task of the third-century exegete, as Victorinus perceives it, is to function as a prophet, in the restricted sense of *interpreting the prophetic scriptures* (cf. I Cor 12:28, 14:29; *In Apoc* 10.2), a task enabled by prophetic gifts bestowed on the Church by the Spirit in the post-apostolic era. True as opposed to false prophecy (i.e. correct discernment of the spiritual sense) is determined by the extent to which the interpretation 'coheres with the prophetic testimony' (*interpretatio cum testimoniis congruat dictionis propheticae*) (*In Apoc.* 10.2). Accordingly, the task of the exegete is to bring out the coherence and harmony between the two testaments, centred on Christ as the fulfilment of prophetic scripture, in order to unveil the 'spiritual sense' of scripture disclosed by the Spirit.[43]

Just as for Irenaeus, Christ is the 'recapitulation' of all things, so, for Victorinus, the NT is the 'recapitulation' of all prophetic scripture, whose

---

39   For a more detailed analysis of Victorinus' exegetical presuppostions and principles see Dulaey 1993, vol. I: 89–128.

40   For Origen's earlier conflation of these same two images (Moses' veil and the sealed scroll of the Apocalypse) in his homilies on Exodus and Ezekiel, see Dulaey 1993, vol. I: 295.

41   The lemma of Victorinus' text of Rev 5:1 describes the scroll as 'written on the inside' (*scriptum deintus*), with no reference to it being written on the outside. This differs from the text and interpretation provided by Origen, who interprets the image as the two basic senses of scripture: the inner, spiritual meaning, and the outward, literal sense; cf. Dulaey 1993, vol. I: 296; Dulaey 1997: 174.

42   Cf. Dulaey 1993, vol. I: 95.

43   Cf. Dulaey 1993, vol. I: 98.

harmonious coherence with the OT enriches and clarifies its full import (cf. *In Apoc.* 4.1). Central to this task is the Apocalypse itself, which Victorinus equates with the open scroll of Rev 10 (*In Apoc.* 10.1), visualized as the direct counterpart to the sealed scroll of Rev 5 (= OT). 'For the Pannonian, the Apocalypse is not primarily a prophecy of the last things...it is the perfect revelation of the meaning of scripture by Christ'.[44] This is strikingly evident in Victorinus' exegesis of the throne-room vision of Rev 4–5, which functions as a visual illustration of his *hermeneutical understanding* of prophetic scripture, and the 'coherence' (*cohaereo*) of the two testaments (*In Apoc.* 5.2).[45]

Formerly, the meaning of scripture was veiled and obscure, analogous to the closed heavens, but now, as a result of Christ's death, resurrection, and ascent, the heavens are open and the content of scripture disclosed (*In Apoc.* 4.1). Accordingly, the image of the open heaven (Rev 4:1) is a figure of the prophecies of the New Testament, which recall those things 'which had been foretold in the law by means of similitudes' (*recolit quae per legem in similitudinibus praenuntiata erant*) and by connecting with 'all the previous prophets' (*coniungit omnes priores prophetas*) 'opens the Scriptures' (*adaperit scripturas*) (*In Apoc.* 4.1).[46] Victorinus stresses the harmony and coherence between the earlier prophecies of the OT and the newly revealed prophecies of the NT, in such a way that the latter draw out and illuminate the obscurities of the former by their Christological key. The two testaments *together* afford the vision of God, equated with the two precious stones (jasper (*iaspis*) and sardis (*sardius*)) seated on the divine throne of judgement (Rev 4:3, *In Apoc.* 4.2).

Victorinus, engaging with the rich imagery of Irenaeus, envisages the divine throne-room as a depiction of the interplay between the multifaceted components of the prophetic scriptures. The four living creatures fuse the fourfold Gospel (faces) with the prophetic witness of the OT (24 wings) by means of the spiritual sense of the NT (eyes), whilst the twenty-four elders combine the content of the OT with its mode of dissemination (twelve patriarchs and twelve apostles) (*In Apoc.* 4.3-5). Touchingly, Victorinus interprets the antiphonal worship of the elders and living creatures as an expression of all the scriptures harmoniously rejoicing at their fulfilment in Christ (*In Apoc.* 4.7).[47]

---

44   Dulaey 1993, vol. I: 103 'L'Apocalypse n'est pas essentiellement, pour le Pannonien, une prophétie des fins dernières...elle est révélation parfaite du sens de l'Ecriture par le Christ lui-même...'.

45   In *Apoc.* 5.2 'Therefore, the diligent person ought to be attentive to the fact that the totality of preaching comes together into a unity (*in unum cohaerere*)'; Weinrich 2011b: 9.

46   Cf. Lk 24:32, 24:45; Dulaey 1997: 167; Weinrich 2011b: 6.

47   Dulaey 1997: 72–3; Weinrich 2011b: 8–9.

6.2.4 Victorinus' Structural Organization of the Apocalypse

Victorinus' sense of the 'recapitulative' function of NT scripture, centred on Christ, informs and controls his understanding of the structural design of the Apocalypse. Integral to Victorinus' plan of the text's structure is his interpretation of the unsealing of the seven seals (Rev 6:1–8:1):[48]

> The breaking of the seals ... is the disclosing of the prophecies of the Old Testament (*apertio est ueteris testamenti praedicatorum*) and the foretelling of those things that will happen at the end of time (*et praenuntiatio in nouissimo tempore futurorum*). Although our prophetic writing expresses the events to come by way of the individual seals (*per singula sigilla dicat*), yet, it is with all the seals being opened simultaneously (*omnibus tamen simul apertis sigillis*), that the prophecy has its order (*ordinem suum habet praedicatio*).
>
> (*In Apoc.* 6.1)[49]

Victorinus stresses that the seals are opened all at once (*simul*) in the death and resurrection of Christ, as Christ's Passion functions as the hermeneutical key to scripture. The events of Christ's victory (cf. *In Apoc.* 4.7), both those already accomplished (incarnation, death/resurrection), and those awaiting fulfilment (parousia, messianic kingdom) (cf. *In Apoc.* 5.3), are the locus of scriptural prophecy. Whilst disavowing a strict chronological progression in the narrative order of the seven seals, Victorinus nonetheless continues to search for a sense of 'order' (*ordo*) in the collective content of the end-time events enumerated.

Victorinus' reconstruction of the 'order' of the eschatological events is heavily influenced by the Matthean Apocalypse (Mt 24) which he explicitly cites with reference to the opening of the first four seals (*In Apoc.* 6.1–3 / Mt 24:14, 7b, 6–7a, 9). Rather than offering a strict verse-by verse commentary on the Apocalypse,[50] Victorinus instead 'blocks-together' eschatological imagery contained in Rev 6–21 in order to construct an organized three-stage schema of end-time events, influenced by previous schematic readings, notably in connection with the advent of the Antichrist (cf. 'Hippolytus', *On Christ and Antichrist*) (3rd century CE).[51] In this regard, Victorinus' tripartite schematization of the Apocalypse resonates

---

48   Cf. Lumsden 2001: 15–32, especially his discussion of the first seal. '[Victorinus] established the exegesis of the rider of the white horse as a symbol representing the successful expansion of the church over all parts of the world' (16).

49   Dulaey 1997: 78–9; Weinrich 2011b: 10 (altered).

50   Cf. Cassiodorus, *Institutes on Divine and Secular Learning*, 1.9.2, '[Victorinus] interpreted certain difficult passages [of the Apocalypse] in concise form': Weinrich 2011b: xxii. Victorinus' interpretation of the letters to the seven churches (Rev 2–3) is similarly schematic, as he reorganizes and selects textual data in order to outline seven different 'classes' of saints (*classis sanctorum*).

51   Cf. Cerrato 2009; Tsirpanlis 1990.

with 19th-century theories that similarly sought to uncover the presence of a tripartite structural framework embedded within the Synoptic Apocalypse (Mk 13 pars.), informed by its alleged use of portions of a Jewish(-Christian) 'apocalypse' source:

   i. 'beginning of the labour pains' (ἀρχὴ ὠδίνων) (cf. Mk 13:7-8);
   ii. 'tribulation' (θλῖψις) (cf. Mk 13:14-20);
   iii. 'end' (τὸ τέλος) (cf. Mk 13:24-27, (cf. 13:7)).[52]

Stage I. End-Time (*novissimus tempus futurus*) (cf. *In Apoc.* 6.1)	Christian Preaching in the context of famine, war, and death (Mt 24:4-14)
Stage II. Final Persecution (*novissimus persecutio*) (cf. *In Apoc.* 6.5)	Final persecution of the righteous Return of Elijah Reign of Antichrist (cf. Mt 24:15-29; II Thess 2:1-12; Mal 4:5-6)
Stage III. Eternal Rest (*quies aeternus*) (cf. *In Apoc.* 6.7)	Parousia First resurrection Millennial Kingdom (cf. Mt 24:30-31; I Thess 4:15-17; I Cor 15; Isa 60-61, Dan 2, 7)

Fig. 6.2 Victorinus' Structural Organization of Rev 6–22

Victorinus' guiding principle differs markedly from 19th-century historical-critics, however, in that his goal is to elucidate the 'coherence' of scripture with regard to the 'order' of end-time events, rather than striving to uncover the influence of hypothetical sources that may influence the text's structural design. Accordingly, Victorinus selects material that he considers relevant from Rev 6–22, adding mutually illuminating scriptural prophecies (from OT and NT) with which these events *cohere*, and arranges them according to the 'order' (*ordo*) of the simplified schema outlined in fig. 6.2. Of the

52 For an overview of the history of research relating to the source(s) potentially underlying the Markan Apocalypse (Mk 13), notably the 'Little Apocalypse' theory of Colani, refined by Weizsacker to comprise three structurally significant fragments (birth-pangs, tribulation, coming of the Son of Man), see Beasley-Murray 1993; Marcus 2009: 864–923; Yarbro Collins 2007: 591–619. For an analysis of the variety of organizational arrangements used to schematise eschatological events in Jewish apocalyptic literature, see Yarbro Collins 1996b.

three septets in the Apocalypse, the seven seals are afforded by far the fullest treatment (*In Apoc.* 6.1-7), with seals one to five illustrating stage one (*In Apoc.* 6.1-4), seal six illustrating stage two (*In Apoc.* 6.5), and seal seven illustrating stage three (*In Apoc.* 6.7).

Victorinus' central interest is in the events of the 'final persecution', which dominate his exegesis in the middle section of the Apocalypse (*In Apoc.* 7–15). Victorinus fills out the content of the 'final persecution', detailing the return of Elijah and the malevolent reign of the Antichrist, with only the briefest of references to the opening of the seventh seal (Rev 8:1; *In Apoc.* 6.7), or the contents of the seventh trumpet (Rev 11:15-19; cf. *In Apoc.* 11.6), so as to produce a *reorganized summary* of the final persecution based on the text of Rev 6–16. Accordingly, the angel descending from the rising sun (Rev 10:1) and the two witnesses (Rev 11:3-13) are combined to produce an account of the eschatological role of Elijah *rediturus* (*In Apoc.* 7.1, citing Mal 4:5-6; *In Apoc.* 11.2-5), whilst Rev 13 and 17 are conflated to provide a composite image of the Beast/Antichrist (= Nero *rediturus*) (*In Apoc.* 13).[53] Victorinus' interpretation of the parousia, first resurrection and millennial kingdom, is organized into its own coherent block in the final chapters of his *Commentary* (*In Apoc.* 19–21).[54]

On the basis of this simplified schema, Victorinus omits and conflates passages to produce his more systematic account.[55] Passages within the central section of the Apocalypse (Rev 7–16) are recounted only where Victorinus deems that they provide additional, 'fuller', detail of material already covered. As a result, he wholly omits the septet of bowls (Rev 16), and retains only a select extract from the sixth trumpet (Rev 9:13–11:14) passing over the remainder of the trumpet septet because he considers that this material has already been sufficiently covered in the septet of seals (*In Apoc.* 6.1-5).[56]

Victorinus grounds his selection decisions on the *repetitive* structure of the Apocalypse itself, comprised of a series of *internal coherences* that resonate with broader scriptural harmonies. Discussing a series of *coherences* between the role of the trumpet archangels as eschatological agents of judgement in Rev 8:6 and Mk 13:27 pars./Mic. 5:5-6 (*Latin*)/

---

53   On Victorinus' interpretation of the Antichrist, and the influence of 'Hippolytus' on his exegesis, see Dulaey 1993, vol. I: 192–207.

54   On the chiliastic interpretation of the millenial kingdom in Victorinus, set against the context of the writings of Papias and Irenaeus, see Dulaey 1993, vol. I: 255–70 and Hill 2001: 11–44.

55   Victorinus also notes lines of continuity between stages, notably stage I and II, for example in relation to the famine that commences with the black horse (= seal 2 for Victorinus), but which 'is also properly extended to the time of the Antichrist' (*Proprie autem extendit se uerbum usque ad Antichristum*) (*In Apoc.* 6.2), Dulaey 1997: 80; Weinrich 2011b: 11.

56   Cf. Dulaey 1997: 33.

Mt 13:27-30, Victorinus highlights a similar set of *internal coherences* with the septet of bowls:

> And although there is a repetition of scenes by means of the bowls (*licet repetat per fialas*) [Rev 16:1-20] [i.e. archangels as eschatological agents of judgement], this is not spoken as though the events occurred twice (*non quasi bis factum esse dicat*). Rather, since those events that are future to them have been decreed by God to happen, these things are spoken twice. And therefore, whatever he said rather briefly by way of the trumpets (*Quicquid igitur in tubis minus dixit*), he said more completely by way of the bowls (*id in fialis propensius dixit*). Nor ought we to pay too much attention to the order of what is said (*Nec aspiciendus ordo dictorum*). For the sevenfold Holy Spirit, when he has passed in review the events to the last time, to the very end (*ubi ad nouissimum temporis finemque percurrit*), returns again to the same times and supplements what he had said incompletely (*redit rursus ad eadem tempora et supplet quae minus dixit*). Nor ought we inquire too much into the order of the Revelation (*Nec requirendu est ordo in Apocalypsi*). Rather, we ought inquire after the meaning (*sed intellectus requirendus*), for there is also the possibility of a false understanding [lit. false prophecy] (*pseudopropheteia*).
>
> (*In Apoc.* 8.1-2)[57]

Victorinus' reading-strategy privileges the prophetic *coherence* detected between the trumpet and bowl cycles over the chronological order of these units in the plot of the narrative. As a consequence, for Victorinus, the bowl cycle is placed in an analogous relationship to other passages of scripture which *cohere* on this topic (Mk 13:27 pars./Mic. 5:5-6 (*Latin*)/Mt 13:27-30). Yet, the distinctiveness of each passage is not simply collapsed, as variation as well as repetition is acknowledged. Each scriptural passage that treats of the same topic offers its own insights – some more fully than others: the trumpets (*minus*), the bowls (*propensius*). What is of central importance for Victorinus is not the order of what is said in the Apocalypse itself (*ordo dictorum*), but rather the meaning of the text in relation to the *coherence* of scripture as a whole, discernment of which is the task of true- as opposed to false-prophecy (*pseudo-propheteia*). This is the task that Victorinus sets himself in his *Commentary* and results in his *reordering* of the material in the Apocalypse to bring out its true meaning, both in relation to other sections within the Apocalypse itself, as well as other parts of scripture, that he understands treat of the same topic.

As a consequence of Victorinus' principle of selection, he makes only a passing reference to Rev 9 in his exegetical comments, restricted to a remark on the bound angels at the river Euphrates:

---

57   Dulaey 1997: 86–9; Weinrich 2011b: 12.

> *The four angels at the four corners of the earth* [Rev 7:1], or *the four* winds
> (*quattuor uentos*) *across the Euphrates River* [Rev 9:13] are four nations
> (*gentes sunt quattuor*), because to every nation (*omni genti*) an angel is
> assigned by God (*deputatus...angelus*), as the Law said: *He established them*
> *according to the number of angels of God* [Deut 32:8]. While the number of
> saints is being completed, they do not leave the boundaries assigned to them
> (*suos non egrediuntur termino*), because in the end they will come with the
> Antichrist (*quia in nouissimo cum Antichristo uenient*).
>
> (*In Apoc. 6.6*)[58]

Victorinus' exegesis of Rev 9:13-15 is heavily dependent on 'Hippolytus''
exegesis of the same passage.[59] Victorinus accepts, but abridges, 'Hippolytus''
fuller identification of the four bound angels with four nations (omitting
'Hippolytus'' enumeration of the four nations as the Danielic quartet of
Persians, Medes, Babylonians, and Assyrians) and imitates his citation of
Deut 32:8 in support of this reading.[60] 'Hippolytus'' exegesis functioned
as an apologetic defence of the authenticity of the Apocalypse in the 3rd
century CE, directly responding to Gaius of Rome's questioning of the
scriptural status of the Apocalypse on the basis of the perceived dissonance between Rev 9:15 (angels as eschatological agents of judgement)
and Mt 24:7 (nation rising against nation).[61] Hippolytus resolved the
alleged scriptural contradiction by an appeal to Deut 32:8, with its
notion of guardian angels appointed to each nation, to argue that Rev
9:15 coheres with Mt 24:7 as the four bound angels refer to four nations
that will function as eschatological agents of judgement.[62]

Victorinus retains this passage, and 'Hippolytus'' interpretation of
it, as it expands on a significant aspect of his stage II, namely the role
of the nations, allied to the Antichrist, in the period of the final persecution (cf. *In Apoc.* 13.2, 19.1). Strikingly, Victorinus himself softens
the alleged dissonance with Mt 24:7 by referring to the bound angels
as 'four *winds*' (*quattuor uentos*) across the Euphrates river, which he

58   Dulaey 1997: 84.
59   Cf. Dulaey 1993, vol. I: 291; Dulaey 1997: 180.
60   For the extract, extant in the 12th century Commentary of Dionysius Bar Salibi
see Sedlaček and Chabot 1906: 10.28.11, also referred to in Hippolytus' *Commentary*
on Daniel 3.9.10 'For all the nations were handed over to the angels, as John says in the
Apocalypse, "And I heard one saying, 'Release the four angels who reside on the great
river Euphrates'" who are Persians, Medes, Assyrians, and Babylonians'; Schmidt 2010;
cf. Bonwetsch 2000.
61   Cf. Brent 1995: 162–4; (cf. Epiphanius, *Panarion* 51.34).
62   Further evidence of the problematic status of this clause in Rev 9:15 in the 3rd–
4th centuries is provided by disturbances to the manuscript tradition, specifically in the
singular reading of the 4th-century CE Codex Sinaiticus, which includes a μή that negates
such an assigned role to the bound angels: 'καὶ ἐλύθησαν οἱ τέσσαρες ἄγγελοι...ἵνα μὴ
ἀποκτίνωσιν τὸ τρίτον τῶν ἀνθρώπων', 'and the four angels were released...so as *not* to kill
a third of humanity'; cf. Hernandez 2006: 185-8.

does on the basis of the 'coherence' that he perceives with Rev 7:1-3, as the latter passage describes the four angels (τέσσαρας ἀγγέλους) holding back the four winds (τέσσαρας ἀνέμους) at the four corners of the earth. Victorinus may perhaps be influenced by Ps 103:4 LXX, 'ὁ ποιῶν τοὺς ἀγγέλους αὐτοῦ πνεύματα', and the use made of this passage in early Christian exegesis (cf. Heb 1:7) to describe elemental forces as messengers of the Deity.[63]

Victorinus' truncated exegesis of the trumpet septet, notably his omission of trumpet five (Rev 9:1-12), reduces the viability of Rev 9 as a test-case. Accordingly, it is necessary to consider Victorinus' extant writings more broadly (*In Apoc., Fabr.*) to assess the impact of the contents of Victorinus' mental library on his choice of preferred cosmological model.

6.2.5 Victorinus' Cosmology

Victorinus held to a three-tier cosmology of heaven-earth-underworld (= Hades (*inferno*)) (cf. *In Apoc.* 5.1, 6.4) and envisaged the heavens as containing multiple tiers, specifically, seven-tiers (cf. *De Fabrica Mundi* 7). The aim of this section is to delve a little more deeply into the details of Victorinus' hybrid-cosmology (cf. §3.2) and to ascertain its relationship with the contents of his mental library.

In his exegetical comment upon Rev 5:3, Victorinus discloses the broad topography of his tripartite cosmos. He glosses each of the three tiers recounted in Rev 5:3 (heaven-earth-under the earth), briefly enumerating the relevant inhabitants of each tier in turn: angels in heaven (*angelis in caelo*), people on earth (*in hominibus in terra*) and 'the souls of the saints in rest' (*neque inter animas sanctorum in requie*).[64] Victorinus here focuses on the netherworld in its function as the abode of the *righteous dead*, discounting the unrighteous dead or other malevolent Hadean powers as self-evidently unworthy of opening the scroll.[65] Yet, even amongst the righteous inhabitants of Hades, none was worthy to unseal the scroll, only Christ, who defeated Hades, and rose from among the dead (*et debellato inferno primus resurrexit a mortuis*) (*In Apoc.* 1.1).[66]

Greater clarity with regard to Victorinus' topography of Hades is provided by his innovative exegesis of the golden altar of Rev 6:9-11 (fifth seal):

'And he saw the souls of the slain under the altar (*sub ara*)', that is, under the earth (*sub terra*). For both the heaven (*caelum*) and the earth (*terra*) are called 'altar' (*ara*). And so the law, prefiguring by way of images the form of

---

63   On the terrestrial significance of the number 'four' in Victorinus' numerical symbolism, see Dulaey 1993, vol. I: 117, and *De Fabrica Mundi* 3, where Victorinus relates it to the four elements, the four seasons, and the four rivers in paradise.

64   Dulaey 1997: 74.

65   Cf. Hill 2001: 35–6.

66   An image of Christ engaged in combat (*debellare*) against personified Hades, cf. Dulaey 1997: 154.

the truth, presented two altars, one that is gold within and one that is bronze without. [cf. Ex 30:3, 27:2]

...heaven is understood to be the altar that was gold within (*Sicut ergo caelum intellegitur ara aurea quae erat interior*) [Mt 5:23-4; Heb 9:7, Lev 16]...

And parallel to this, the bronze altar is to be understood as the earth (*sic et aerea terra intellegitur*), under which exists Hades, a region removed from pains and fire (*sub qua est infernum, remota a poenis et ignibus regio*), a place for the repose of the saints (*requies sanctorum*), in which to be sure the just are seen and heard by the impious, but these cannot go across to those (*in qua quidem uidentur ab impiis et audiuntur iusti, sed neque illi ad illos transire possunt*). [cf. Lk 16:26] ...

(*In Apoc.* 6.4)[67]

Victorinus here fuses a figurative reading of the *sensus spiritalis* of the text, with a concrete, cosmological interpretation of Hades. Victorinus endeavours to hold in tension two, apparently contradictory, propositions: i. *only* those who have ascended bodily to heaven (Christ, Elijah, Jeremiah) (cf. *In Apoc.* 11.3) reside in the heavenly realm with the angels, prior to the parousia;[68] ii. executed witnesses to the faith, the righteous 'martyrs', reside 'under the altar' (Rev 6:9).[69] Victorinus' decisive exegetical move is made on the strength of an appeal to Mt 5:23-24, informed by the thought-world of the Epistle to the Hebrews (cf. Heb 4:14-10:25), whereby the 'similitudes' of the sacrificial cult are fulfilled in Christ (*In Apoc.* 5.2). Accordingly, the golden altar of incense (Ex 30:3) denotes the golden altar in the heavenly temple, the focal-point of believers' gifts of prayer to the Deity (Mt 5:23-24, cf. Rev 8:3). Furthermore, the architectural relationship between the two altars, the golden altar inside the sanctuary, and the bronze altar outside, is transposed into a cosmological key: the golden altar denotes the interior of the heavens, and the bronze altar its exterior, the earth. On this basis, Rev 6:9-11 can be seen to validate Victorinus' understanding of the locale of the executed righteous (the 'martyrs') who reside under the earth (*sub terra*) in Hades (*inferno*).

Nonetheless, Victorinus is keen to demarcate distinct territories within Hades itself, lest his readers misapprehend the character of the interim abode of the righteous. The place of rest of the righteous (*requies sanctorum*) in Hades (*inferno*) is spatially removed (*remota*) from the unrighteous, who reside in a place of subterranean 'punishment and fire' (*poenis et ignibus*

67　Dulaey 1997: 80–82; Weinrich 2011b: 11.

68　Victorinus idiosyncratically identifies the two witnesses of Rev 11:3-13 as Elijah and *Jeremiah*, discounting more popular alternatives (Elisha and Moses 'are both dead' (*In Apoc.* 11.3)), owing to Jeremiah's unfulfilled mission to be 'a prophet to the Gentiles' (Jer 1:5).

69　Hill 2001: 36–7 '...Victorinus makes no allowance for the martyrs, as a special class of saints, to rise beyond the confines of the underworld...'.

regio) (cf. Lk 16:19-31).[70] The negative connotations of a Hadean repose are further weakened by Victorinus' modifications of the traditional imagery: the righteous in Hades receive the Spirit (symbolized by their white garments) and continue to live a life of prayer.[71]

Victorinus comments on the locale of the abyss (*abyssus*) in his interpretation of Rev 11:7, with reference to the beast that ascends from the abyss (*ascendisse bestiam de abysso*) to kill the two witnesses (*In Apoc.* 11.4). In line with Victorinus' supposition of the *coherence* of scripture, he cites a catena of scriptural witnesses in support of this prediction (Ezek 31:3-4, II Thess 2:7-11, Isa 59:9). It is likely that Victorinus is here drawing upon a pre-existing *testimonium*, as he erroneously ascribes Ezek 31:3-4 to Isaiah, whilst utilizing a series of texts that are commonly equated with the Antichrist in antiquity.[72] Despite his mislabelling of the passage, the most revealing text that Victorinus cites remains Ezek 31:3-4 LXX, with its reference to the abyss (ἡ ἄβυσσος) 'raising up' (ὕψωσεν) Assour [= Antichrist]. The Latin lemma of Victorinus' text renders ὑψόω by the translation equivalent *augeo*, which contains comparable resonances of physical and metaphorical exaltation. The crucial step is Victorinus' own interpretative gloss, '*id est ructuauit eundum*', which metaphorically describes the personified abyss 'vomiting-out' (*ructuo*, 'belch-forth') the Antichrist from its innards. That Victorinus essentially equates the abyss (*abyssus*) with Hades (*inferno*) is apparent from his recapitulation of this passage (Ezek 31:4), again incorrectly ascribed to Isaiah, in his exegesis of Rev 13:2-3, as a comment on the Antichrist [= Nero] coming forth from Hades (*De inferno autem illum resurgere*) (*In Apoc.* 13.3).[73]

In line with Victorinus' intricate mental map of the interior of Hades, his visualization of the celestial realm is similarly complex. Although Victorinus predominantly refers to the heavens in the plural in his *Apocalypse Commentary* (cf. *In Apoc.* 1.2, 5.3, 12.3),[74] his most detailed description of its multiple tiers is extant in his (earlier) treatise on the creation of the cosmos, *De Fabrica Mundi*.[75] *De Fabrica Mundi* is a short treatise on the primordial week as outlined in Genesis, with a particular focus on the fourth, sixth and seventh days, and the symbolism and chronological significance of those same numbers.[76] The treatise lacks sufficient focus on each day in

70   Cf. *De decem uirginibus* 58–60 cited above.
71   Cf. Dulaey 1993, vol. I: 182.
72   Cf. 'Hippolytus', *Antichrist* 57; Jerome, In *Ezekiel* 10.
73   Dulaey 1997: 108; Weinrich 2011b: 18.
74   There are also one or two references in the singular (e.g. *In Apoc.* 6.4, *merismus*, heaven and earth), usually in line with the lemma of the text being interpreted.
75   Dulaey 1993, vol. I: 23 plausibly argues that *De Fabrica Mundi* predates Victorinus' *Apocalypse Commentary*, as his exegesis of the twenty-four elders of Rev 4:4 is in line with inherited tradition in *Fabr.* 10, but a more original interpretation is offered in his *Apocalypse Commentary*.
76   For a more detailed discussion of the genre, structure and content of *De Fabrica Mundi* see Dulaey 1993, vol. I: 24–36; Dulaey 1997: 23–28, 215–31; and Kannengiesser 638.

the primordial week to plausibly be identified as a fragment of Victorinus' lost *Commentary on Genesis*; it displays other concerns, notably providing a rationale for certain liturgical fasts on the fourth and sixth days (*Fabr. 3, 4, 5*).[77] There are some parallels with treatises on the creation, culminating in the creation of humanity in the image of God on the sixth day, known as *Hexameron*, which began to be published in the third and fourth centuries (e.g. 'Hippolytus', *On the Hexameron* (fragments) (3rd century CE), Basil of Caesarea, *Hexameron* (*c*.330–379 CE), Ambrose of Milan, *Hexameron* (*c*.339–397 CE)), albeit that Victorinus' distinctive emphasis on the seventh day serves to differentiate it somewhat from this genre.[78]

The passage in *De Fabrica Mundi* that most concerns us occurs in Chapters 6–7, where Victorinus is meditating on the significance of the divine number seven, specifically the 'true' sabbath of the seventh millennium of history, when Christ will reign on earth with the righteous (cf. *In Apoc.* 20-21; Irenaeus, *Adv. Haer.* 4.16.1, 'Hippolytus', *In Daniel* 4.23) (*Fabr.* 6).[79] Victorinus appeals to the structure of the created cosmos in support of the well-established theory that the world is designed to endure for a total span of seven thousand years (6 x 1000 years, culminating in the millennium (+ 1000)) in line with the primordial week itself (six days followed by the sabbath), given that a thousand years are as one day to the Lord (Ps 89:4, II Pet 3:8; cf. 'Hippolytus', *In Daniel* 4.23.5-6).

> Moreover, the seven heavens (*septem...caeli*) agree with those days; for thus we are warned:
> 'By the word of the Lord (*verbum*) were the heavens made, and all the pow-ers of them by the spirit (*spiritus*) of His mouth.' [Ps 32:6]
> There are seven spirits (*septem spiritus*). Their names are the spirits which abide on the Christ of God, as was intimated in Isaiah the prophet:
> 'And there rests upon Him the spirit of wisdom and of understanding, the spirit of counsel and might, the spirit of wisdom and of piety, and the spirit of God's fear hath filled Him.' [Isa 11:2-3]
> Therefore the highest heaven (*summum...caelum*) is the heaven of wisdom;
> the second, of understanding;
> the third, of counsel;
> the fourth, of might;
> the fifth, of knowledge;
> the sixth, of piety;
> the seventh, of God's fear.
>
> (*De Fabrica Mundi* 7)[80]

77   On the parallels with the liturgical calendar and fasts, especially fasting on the Sabbath, with Syrian (i.e. Antiochene) traditions of the 4th century (e.g. *Didascalia Apostolorum*), see Dulaey 1993, vol. I: 27–8, 225–31.

78   Cf. Giet 1950; Savage 1961; Dulaey 1993, vol. I: 27.

79   On Victorinus' interpretation of the millennium, in the context of second and third century CE chiliast thought, see Daley 1991: 20–68, Dulaey 1993, vol. I: 264–7, Hill 2001: 11–44.

80   Dulaey 1997: 144; Wallis 1994: 342.

Victorinus is here heavily dependent upon Irenaeus, *Demonstration of the Apostolic Preaching* 5 and 9.[81] The first passage cited by Victorinus in this unit, Ps 32:6, echoes the earlier usage made of this same text by Theophilus of Antioch, *Ad Autolycum* 1.7 (second half of 2nd century CE) and Irenaeus, *Dem.* 5, to affirm that Son (λόγος) and Spirit (πνεῦμα) together functioned as divine agents of creation.[82]

The Spirit, co-creator of the cosmos, is comprised of 'seven spirits' (cf. Rev 1:4, 3:1, 4:5, 5:6; cf. Fabr. 8), which Victorinus equates with the sevenfold spirit of Isa 11:2-3 that came to rest upon Christ.[83] As a result, the cosmos created by the divine agency of Son and Spirit fashioned a seven tiered heaven, with each tier equating to one of the seven spirits, listed in descending order according to the enumeration of Isa 11:2-3: the highest heaven, heaven one, is wisdom, and the lowest, heaven seven, is fear of God. Victorinus derives this idea directly from Irenaeus' earlier treatise (*Dem* 9), including his proof-text of Isa 11:2-3.[84]

How does Victorinus envisage these multiple-tiered heavens? Victorinus' principal source, Irenaeus *Dem.* 9, certainly portrays *seven planetary spheres*, in view of Irenaeus' description of *nested* heavens. The largest, outermost sphere 'encircles' or 'contains' (*continetur*/περιέχω) the world within, containing within itself (*continet*/ἐμπεριέχω) the other (*alios*) six nested spheres (*Dem.* 9).[85] As a result, the innermost sphere constitutes 'our firmament' (*nos firmamentum*) (*Dem.* 9). Irenaeus' recourse to a Platonic template of seven, nested planetary spheres is congruent with his advanced grammatical-level education, which included close study of poetic authors, and at least some engagement with prose authors of rhetoric and philosophy:

> Irenaeus elegantly claims to have no rhetoric or excellence of style, but shows some rhetorical skill and a knowledge of the works of Plato, Homer, Hesiod and Pindar. Although he does not confront the philosophical tradition as do Clement and Origen, his account of God reveals his awareness of the Middle Platonic and Stoic philosophies of the day.[86]

81 Cf. Behr 1997: 42–3; Dulaey 1993, vol. I: 225–6; MacKenzie 2002: 2–3, 81–100.

82 Grant 1970: 10–11; Behr 1997: 42–3.

83 Victorinus interprets the seven spirits of Rev 1:4, again with reference to Isa 11:2-3, as the 'sevenfold spirit' (*septiformi spiritu*), that is the seven 'gifts' (*dona*) of the Spirit (*In Apoc.* 1.1). For Victorinus, the seven spirits are the sevenfold form of the one Spirit, that he closely associates with the spirit of Christ. For Victorinus' reflection on the Spirit/ seven spirits see Dulaey 1993, vol. I: 151–2, 243–5, Dulaey 1997: 153–4, 159–60.

84 Irenaeus' version is a modification of a multiple-tiered cosmos in which each heaven is ruled over by an angelic 'spirit' or 'power' ('... this world is encompassed by seven heavens, in which dwell <innumerable> powers and angels and archangels ...') (*Dem* 9, Behr 1997: 42). Irenaeus utilises Isa 11:2-3 to refute speculation regarding angelic hierarchies; cf. McKenzie 2002: 96–7, Bucur 2006: 254–60.

85 Rousseau 1995: 96–7.

86 Osborn 2001: 3–4.

For evidence that Irenaeus attained at least an upper secondary-level literary education, in view of his evident grammatical skills, notably his manipulation and use of a *cento*

Victorinus' version, by contrast, contains no such reference to nested planetary spheres. Instead, perhaps more akin to Theophilus of Antioch's scripturally informed single-heaven cosmos (*Ad Autolycum* 2.13), Victorinus' focus is more limited, conceiving of the firmament of the terrestrial realm as a 'ceiling' that keeps the inhabitants of the world enclosed (*clausi*), *De Fabrica Mundi* 1; cf. Theophilus, *Ad Autolycum* 2.13.[87] Accordingly, whilst appropriating a seven-tiered heavenly model, the conception is underdeveloped in Victorinus' thought, as is evidenced by its limited presence in his *Apocalypse Commentary*. Ultimately, Victorinus' conception of the heavens is a hybrid model, ostensibly a biblically informed celestial vault (akin to Theophilus, *Ad Autol.* 2.13/Isa 40:22), that Victorinus extends to include higher heavenly tiers (Isa 11:2-3).

6.2.6 Conclusion

On the basis of Victorinus' extant exegetical writings, there is little evidence that he received a formal Greek literary education. Instead, Victorinus' mental library is dominated by scriptural texts (in both Latin and Greek), and the treatises of earlier scriptural exegetes, notably those from an eastern, Greek-speaking milieu (Irenaeus, 'Hippolytus', Origen). Lacking direct contact with Plato and Ptolemy, Victorinus' cosmological template conforms to its literary antecedents, but in a modified form. The Homeric-style tripartite cosmos that dominates Victorinus' scriptural sources is modified into a hybrid model, under the influence of Irenaeus, such that Victorinus' preferred cosmological template is a hybrid cosmos, comprising seven-tiered heavens, atop a tripartite universe (seven tiered heavens – earth – bipartite Hades/*abyssus*). Victorinus' seven-heaven system echoes Isa 11:2-3, yet differs from the Platonic model of seven nested planetary spheres explicated in his source, Irenaeus (*Dem.* 9), to present a simpler, tripartite universe ornamented with additional heavenly tiers.

(κέντρων) of lines from Homer's *Iliad* and *Odyssey* in *Adv. Haer.* 1.9.4, see Grant 1949, Osborn 2001: 158, and Wilken 1967.

87   Grant 1970: 48–9; cf. Nautin 1973: 168–70.

Despite Theophilus' reference to a wide range of literary authors, especially in Book II, Grant suggests that most citations derive from second-hand anthologies (*doxographi*) in popular handbooks, and his first-hand reading was more likely limited to extracts from Homer and Hesiod at school, with perhaps a smattering of Plato (cf. Grant 1970: xi–xii). For the possible structural influence of Hesiod's *Theogony* on Theophilus' *Ad Autolycum* see Curry 1988.

6.3 Tyconius (fl. 370–390 CE)

6.3.1 Introduction –Tyconius' Life and Work

Little is known of Tyconius' life (*fl.* 370–390 CE), beyond the brief references to his background noted by Augustine and Gennadius.[88] Augustine characterizes Tyconius as an anomalous member of the Donatist movement in North Africa: 'A certain Tyconius, who although a Donatist himself wrote against the Donatists with irresistible power – and thereby stands convicted of having a split personality since he was unwilling to make a clean break with them...' (*De Doctrina Christiana* III.30.42).[89] The Donatists were a rigorist wing of the church that had opposed the readmittance of *traditores* ('surrenderers'), notably clergy, who had yielded to the authorities' demands to surrender sacred writings or face prosecution and potential execution, in line with various edicts of Diocletian (*c.*303–305 CE). The hard-line stance of such communities, grounded on the witness of executed 'martyrs' (cf. *The Passion of Saints Maxima, Donatilla and Secunda*, and *Acts of the Abitinian Martyrs*) and steadfast in its non-acceptance of '*traditor*' clergy (or those consecrated by them) was held to be schismatic by the Catholic church and opposed by the (post-)Constantinian state, intermittently with violence, throughout the 4th century.[90]

Tyconius' early writings, referred to by Gennadius in his 5th-century CE *De viris illustribus 18*, entitled 'On the Civil War' (*De bello intestino*) (*c.* 370s CE) and 'Explanations of Various Legal Cases' (*Expositiones diversarum causarum*) (*c.* 370s CE), are no longer extant, but appear to have been concerned with disunity in the church.[91] The writings were not well received, however, as Tyconius was excommunicated from the Donatist church at the Council of Carthage (380 CE) by the bishop of the city, Parmenian, perhaps principally for his controversial ecclesiology.[92] 'Rather than seeing the Catholic attackers of the Donatist church to be outside the church, he perceived them also to be part of the one church'.[93]

Tyconius' distinctive ecclesiology was intertwined with his scriptural hermeneutics,[94] as is readily apparent from the extant remains of his own writings, written in the decades of his isolation from the Donatist church

---

88   Cf. Kannengiesser 2006: 1139–1148 and Vercruysse 2004: 11–34, 70–82, 117–28.

89   Green 1997: 89.

90   For a more nuanced analysis see Frend 1952: 1–24 and Tilley 1997: 18–76. On Donatist martyr stories, see Tilley 1996. The pejorative labelling Donatist/Catholic is retained for the sake of brevity, but its distorting imposition of external categories onto the subject is noted.

91   Harvey 1999: 151 (Appendix 2); cf. Richardson 1896: 68 (Latin).

92   Cf. Tilley 1997: 112–14; (Augustine *Epistle* 93.10.43-44).

93   Kugler 1999: 131.

94   On Tyconius' ecclesiology see Hahn 1900: 57–116; Ratzinger 1956.

(*c.* 380s–390s CE). Principal among these writings is the complete text of Tyconius' *libellus regularis* 'essay on rules', more commonly referred to as the *Book of Rules* (*Liber Regularum*) under the influence of Augustine's influential appropriation of the work as a manual of scriptural hermeneutics in *De Doctrina Christiana* III.30.42-37.56 (*c.* 427 CE).[95] Tyconius' *libellus regularis* is closely correlated with his *Commentary on the Apocalypse*, which survives in fragmentary, revised, manuscript copies (10th century CE Bobbio fragments, 9th century CE Budapest Fragments),[96] and extended citations and summaries embedded in the writings of later commentators on the Apocalypse (notably Caesararius of Arles (6th century CE), Primasius of Hadrumentum (6th century CE) Cassiodorus' *Complexiones* (6th century CE), Beatus of Liebana (8th century CE), and Bede of Northumbria (8th century CE)).[97] On the basis of a painstaking critical study of the extant sources, Roger Gryson has recently produced a standard critical edition of Tyconius' *Apocalypse Commentary*, for the complete span of Rev 1–22, as far as this is recoverable.[98]

Close scrutiny of Tyconius' two extant writings reveal that there is an intimate, interlocking relationship between them: the first, the *libellus regularis*, delineates the *ratio* of seven mystical rules that underlie the compositional principles of inspired scripture, and the latter, the *Apocalypse Commentary*, provides both the source and the goal of these seven hermeneutical 'keys' and 'lamps'.[99] Tyconius identified prophetic scripture with the seven-sealed heavenly scroll of Rev 5:1ff, as explicated in his *Apocalypse Commentary*: 'And I saw in the right hand of him who was seated upon the throne a book written on the inside and the outside, that is both testaments (*utrumque testamentum*), on the outside the old, and on the inside the new, because it lay hidden within the old, but consequently one book... (*a foris uetus, ab intus nouum, quod intra uetus latebat, propeterea autem unus liber*).'[100] Tyconius identifies the seven 'seals' with the seven *regulae mysticae* which function to *conceal* the hidden meaning of scripture (cf. *libellus regularis*, Rule VI.1), from interpreters who lack insight into the Spirit's compositional principles.

95   Cf. Babcock 1989 (Latin/English); Vercruysse 2004 (Latin/French).

96   For the Latin text of the Budapest Fragments (containing parts of Rev 6) see Gryson 1997 and for the Latin text of the Turin fragments (Bobbio Codex 62, containing Rev 2:18–4:1, and 7:16–12:6) see Lo Bue 1963 and Gryson 2011a: 347–86.

97   '[Tyconius'] commentary on the Apocalypse no longer exists – or perhaps more accurately, it lives on obscured in the penumbra of the later Catholic commentaries that drew on Tyconius even as they repudiated him'; Fredriksen 1992: 25.

98   Gryson 2011a: 20–73 (sources); 74–102 (source-critical method); 103–228 (text); 229–338 (critical notes); cf. Gryson 2011b (French translation).

99   Cf. Kanengiesser 1999: 160–1, Vercruysse 2004: 36–7.

100   Gryson 2011a: 133. Compare Victorinus who identifies the sealed scroll more narrowly with the OT (*uetus testamentum*), whose opaque 'similtudes' are unveiled as a result of Christ's death and resurrection (*In Apoc.* 5.1).

6.3.2 Tyconius' Interpretative Method and Mental Library

The prologue of the *libellus regularis* serves as a programmatic guide to Tyconius' hermeneutical project:

> Above everything else that came to mind, I considered it necessary to write (*scribere*) a book of rules [lit. an essay about the rules (*libellum regularem*)] and so to fashion (*fabricare*) keys and lamps (*claues et luminaria*), as it were, to the secrets of the Law (*secretorum legis*). For there are certain mystic rules (*regulae mysticae*) which obtain in the inner recesses (*recessus*) of the entire law and keep the rich treasures of the truth (*veritatis thesauros*) hidden (*invisibiles faciunt*) from some people. But if the sense of these rules (*ratio regularum*) is accepted without ill will, as we impart it, whatever is closed will be opened and whatever is dark will be illumined; and anyone who walks the vast forest of prophecy (*prophetiae immensam siluam perambulans*) guided by these rules, as by pathways of light, will be kept from straying into error.
>
> (Tyconius, *libellus regularis*, Prologue)[101]

Tyconius' essay presupposes that there are certain 'mystical rules' (*regulae mysticae*) that underlie scriptural prophecy (both OT and NT), whose function is to deny access, for some, to the inner secrets, or 'recesses' (*recessus*) of those divine mysteries. The purpose of Tyconius' essay is not to create (*fabricare*) a set of 'mystical rules', but rather to outline the 'logic' of the rules (*ratio regularum*) that are inherent in scripture itself, knowledge of which will serve as 'keys' to open what is closed, and 'lamps' to illuminate what is dark in scriptural prophecy.[102] The *regulae* are *mysticae* because they are integral to scripture itself, they are the compositional principles of the author of scripture, the Spirit, by means of which the Spirit both reveals, and conceals, the mysteries it discloses.[103]

Given Tyconius' stated hermeneutical goal of illuminating the *ratio* of the compositional principles of Scripture, it is unsurprising that his mental library is dominated by *scriptural texts*, both OT and NT, all of which he

---

101 Babcock 1989: 2–3.

102 Kannengiesser 2002: 301 'It is as if the author [Tyconius] stated: "This is what I have read in scripture, and these are my conclusions about its inner consistency; there are structural principles at work in the living reality of sacred scripture, which, after a patient investigation, I succeeded in identifying".'

Cf. Bright 1988: 119–27; Kannengiesser 1999: 155–7; Kugler 1999: 132–3; Tilley 1997: 115–16. As Bright and Kannengiesser emphasize, Augustine collapsed the distinction between 'mystical rules' and 'keys' and 'lamps', such that he interpreted Tyconius' work as an hermeneutical essay that develops seven hermeneutical principles to interpret scripture. Accordingly, Augustine incorrectly understood the 'mystical rules' to render visible what is invisible, not to purposefully *keep hidden* the inner secrets of scripture.

103 Cf. Bright 1988: 133, Vercruysse 2004: 38. Kannengiesser 1999: 166 likens Rule IV to a treatise 'On Style' in which the Spirit is the author under scrutiny. Tyconius' *libellus regularis* functions, in part, as a 'style guide' to the compositional principles of the Spirit.

deems to be prophetic.[104] Aside from the notable exception of Hebrews, and some of the shorter epistles (II Jn, III Jn, II Pet, James, Jude), Tyconius engages closely with the dominant core of an emerging NT canon in the fourth century.[105] His knowledge of Septuagintal texts, in Latin translation, is similarly broad, such that he includes Sirach, Wisdom, I and II Maccabees, and each of the Twelve prophets, amongst the dense range of texts he cites.[106] On the basis of Tyconius' citation of, and allusions to, scriptural texts in his extant writings, aside from the Apocalypse itself, it is apparent that his thought is particularly shaped by Isaiah (175) and Ezekiel (159) (cf. Rule VII), Psalms (83) and Genesis (57), from the OT, and Matthew (140) and the Pauline corpus (notably Romans (87) (cf. Rule III) and Ephesians (27)) from the NT.[107]

Tyconius' exegetical method is outlined in detail in his carefully structured hermeneutical essay, *libellus regularis*, that arranges his insights into a neat chiasm of seven *regulae*, centred on rule IV:[108]

I. The Lord and his Body (*De Domino et corpore eius*)
   II. The Lord's Bipartite Body (*De Domini corpore bipertio*)
      III. The Promises and the Law (*De promissis et lege*)
         IV. The Particular and the General (*De specie et genere*)
      V. Times (*De temporibus*)
      VI. Recapitulation (*De recapitulatione*)
   VII. The Devil and His Body (*De diabolo et eius corpore*)

                  (Tyconius, *libellus regularis*, Prologue)[109]

Tyconius' essay is intended to shed light on apparent obscurities (*obscura*) or contradictions in prophetic scripture. Such apparent obscurities reflect the Spirit's deliberate employment of opaque or shifting referents, aimed at concealing the full meaning of scripture.[110]

---

104 See Bright 1988: 35–51 for an analysis of the range of scriptural texts cited by Tyconius in the *libellus regularis*, both OT and NT, plus the scripture indices in Babcock 1989: 147–52 and Vercruysse 2004: 393–9. For the citations of scripture in Tyconius' *Apocalypse Commentary* see the scripture index in Gryson 2011a: 339–45. For a discussion of the text type of the Greek and Latin versions known to Tyconius see Vercruysse 2004: 82–91.

105 Cf. McDonald and Sanders 2002.

106 Few Septuagintal texts are passed over in silence, aside from shorter historical books (e.g. Ruth, Tobit, Judith).

107 Cf. Babcock 1989: 147–53 and Gryson 2011a: 339–45. The indicative figures refer to the combined total of verses cited in the *libellus regularis* and *Apocalypse Commentary*. On Tyconius' exegesis of Pauline literature see Babcock 1982; cf. LR Rule III.

108 On the chiastic structure of the *libellus regularis*, see Bright 1988: 89–119 and Vercruysse 2004: 66–9.

109 Babcock 1989: 2–3.

110 On the 'logic' (*ratio*) of the mystical rules see Bright 1988: 53–87. Compare Origen, *De Principiis* IV.ii–iii for an earlier methodological approach to handle apparent 'stumbling blocks' (σκάνδαλα) and contradictions in scripture.

Integral to Tyconius' hermeneutics is his *ecclesiological* insight that the Body of Christ, the church (Rule I),[111] and the Devil and his Body (i.e. the Devil's adherents, notably the Antichrist) (Rule VII)[112] are intermingled and *bipartite* prior to the eschaton (Rule II). As a result, apparently mutually exclusive statements that are ultimately aimed at the one church, of both praise and blame, approval and disapproval, are comprehensible when it is understood that the Body of Christ is *bipartite*, comprising both good (right-side) and bad (left-side) members.[113] Praise of Israel or Jacob, for example, as God's chosen, coupled with explicit references to God's disapproval of the same subject (e.g. Isa 42:16-17, 45:3-5), are to be interpreted not as contradictory statements, but rather signals of internal shifts of referent, between the right-hand and the left-hand side of the Body of Christ. Tyconius' emphasis on the presence of evil within the true church of the Donatists, comprising both good and evil members (right and left side), differed from the characteristic emphasis of his Donatist contemporaries focused on the external contrast with the Catholic church of the *traditores*, and clearly signalled the distinctiveness of Tyconius' ecclesiology that distanced him from his peers.[114]

The full extent of Tyconius' mental library is much more difficult to establish, however, as '...with the exception of the Bible Tyconius never cites, indeed never even mentions, another author or book.'[115] Nonetheless, there are strong grounds for proposing that Tyconius had received a tertiary-level education, in view of his command of exegetical and rhetorical skills and technical terminology characteristic of an oratorical education.[116] At the heart of Tyconius' chiastically structured hermeneutical treatise, *libellus regularis*, beats rule IV *De specie et genere*.[117] Despite conventional claims of rhetorical innocence, citing I Cor 1:17,[118] Tyconius' terminology, and the use he makes of it, indicate that he was nonetheless cognizant of rhetorical categories of thought, and

111 Rule I is concerned to aid an exegete to use his own logic (*ratio*) to distinguish referents in scriptural passages, noting shifts between clauses that refer to Christ (Head) and clauses that are addressed to the Church (Christ's Body) (cf. Eph 4:15-16, Col 2:19), attentive to shifts in number and gender even within a single passage; cf. Tilley 1997: 118.

112 Rule VII applies the principles of Rule I to an extended exegesis of Isa 14:12-21 and Ezek 28:2-19, disentangling the elements that refer to the Devil and the Antichrist.

113 On the central significance of the figure of the 'man of lawlessness' in II Thess 2:3-4, 7 (cited eight times, at the conclusion of all but one of the rules of the *libellus regularis*) as integral to Tyconius' understanding of the presence of evil in the midst of the Church until the eschaton, see Bright 1988: 43–51, 85–7, and Hughes 2005: 82–94.

114 Cf. Tilley 1997: 96–112.

115 Steinhauser 1993: 394.

116 Cf. Dulaey 1989: 99–103; Kannengiesser 1999: 165–72; Kannengiesser 2002; Vercruysse 2006.

117 Cf. Bright 2010; Bright 1988: 69–76.

118 On the recurrent appeal to I Cor 1–2 in Christian debates on the appropriate response to ἐγκύκλιος παιδεία see Sandnes 2009: 124–40.

wrote with an educated audience in mind who are presumed to share this intellectual background.

> I am not referring to the particular and the general as they are used in the rhetorical art devised by human wisdom (*De specie et genere loquimur, non secundum artem rhetoricam humanae sapientiae*). Although better able than anyone, Paul did not use that art – for fear that he would make 'the cross of Christ empty' [I Cor 1:17] if, like falsehood, it needed the aid and ornament of eloquence (*auxilio atque ornamento sermonis*). Rather I am speaking with reference to the mysteries of heavenly wisdom in relation to the teaching of the Holy Spirit. Making faith the price of truth, the Spirit produced an account marked by mysteries, concealing the general in the particular (*in speciem genus abscondens*)...
>
> (Tyconius, *libellus regularis*, IV.1)[119]

Oratorical students were taught to carefully define and distinguish between a 'class' or 'group' (*genus*) and a representative of a class or group (*species*) when devising an argument based on definition, to prove or refute a point (cf. Quintilian, *Inst. Or.* v.10.56-7, Cicero, *De inventione* i.22.32, i.28.42; *De oratore* ix.39-40). Crucially, the order in which *genus* and *species* are defined may differ in a rhetor's speech and students are taught that subtlety is required to distinguish them: '...A little subtlety (*subtilitar*) will see a little further; as species comes after genus, so genus precedes species' (Quintilian, *Inst. Or. vii.1.59*).[120] A similar concern is evident throughout rule four, where Tyconius encourages his audience to be attentive to the subtle shifts and transitions between *species* and *genus* prophecies in scripture.[121] A *species* prophecy is one which refers, in part, to the person (e.g. Jacob) or place (e.g. Babylon) denoted in the text, whilst a *genus* prophecy has wider resonance for the 'group' as a whole, that is, for the church.[122] Tyconius encourages his readers to be similarly attentive to the numerous subtle shifts (*transitus*) of referent, from genus to species and back again, even within a single sentence, in scriptural texts.

Tyconius' emphasis on the interpretative value of 'synecdoche' in rule V *De temporibus* similarly draws upon his rhetorical training. Tyconius defines synecdoche as a figure of speech in which 'a part represents the whole, or a whole represents the part' (*synecdoche vero est aut a parte totum, aut a*

---

119 Babcock 1989: 54–5.

120 Russell 2001: II.392–5.

121 Cf. Kannengiesser 1999: 171 on the description of the subtle (*subtile*) Spirit, and the shifting movements from the particular to the general and back again.

122 A *species* prophecy concerns the subject named (e.g. David) which then also functions typologically as a figure (*figura*) for the Church, whilst a genus prophecy was never intended for the subject named (i.e. it remains unfulfilled), but refers exclusively to the present and future of the Church; cf. Bright 1988: 71–4.

tot pars).[123] Synecdoche is one of a range of 'ornaments of speech' (*ornatu orationis*) discussed by Quintillian in book VIII of his *Institutia Oratoria*, which he closely relates to shifts between genus and species:

> Synecdoche has the power to vary the discourse, enabling the hearer to understand many things from one, the whole from the part (*ex uno plura intellegamus parte totum*), the genus from the species (*specie genus*), the consequences from the antecedent, and vice versa. Poets have more scope for it than orators...In prose it is liberty of number (*numerorum...libertas*) which will be most useful. Livy often says, 'The Roman was victor in the battle', when he means that the Romans won...
>
> (Quintilian, *Institutia Oratoria viii.6.19-22*)[124]

Tyconius encourages his erudite audience to be similarly attentive to the Spirit's use of the rhetorical ornament of synecdoche in his temporal referents, like other educated (prose) authors, by which the Spirit may indicate a whole (or perfect) number by means of a part, and vice versa.

In addition to Tyconius' evident rhetorical expertise, there are also allusive echoes of Latin poetic authors, notably Virgil and Ovid, whom Tyconius plausibly studied under a grammarian, most memorably in the poetic figure of the 'immense forest of prophecy' (*prophetiae immensam silvam*) with which the *libellus regularis* begins (prologue).[125]

> From a literary point of view Tyconius' *immensam silvam* echoes the sixth book of the *Aeneid* where Aeneas, directed by the prophetess of the Cave of Cumae, is seeking for the Golden Bough. In answer to his prayer, two doves lead him through the *silvam immensam* that clothes the slopes of the mountain near the Sibyl's cave...In the *Book of Rules*, the traveller walking through the forest of prophecy, following the *ratio* of the 'mystical rules' will [similarly] be guarded from going astray...from the maze.[126]

Further evidence of Tyconius' tuition by a grammarian is provided by his meticulous exegesis of scriptural texts, both the Apocalypse (*Apocalypse Commentary*) and extended passages of Isaiah 14:12-21 and Ezekiel 28:2-19 (*libellus regularis*, Rule VII). The painstakingly close reading of these texts, his undertaking line-by-line, and even word-by-word analysis, highlighting variant readings, rare or difficult words, and poetic turns of phrase, are consistent with an author trained in the exegetical technique of exposition (*enarratio*) (cf. Quintilian, *Inst. Or.* i.8.13-21; Cicero, *De. Orat.* i.187).[127]

---

123 Babcock 1989: 88–9.
124 Russell 2001: III.434–7.
125 Babcock 1989: 2–3. Cf. Bright 1988: 134–6.
126 Bright 1988: 134, 135. Cf. Kannengiesser 2002: 305–8 for further resonances of Ovid (*Metamorphoses*, 6.521, 7.20) and Virgil (*Aeneid*, 6.131, 139, 186, 270, 450).
127 Cf. Vercruysse 2006: 515 and Marrou 1956: 279–80.

The full extent of Tyconius' ἐγκύκλιος παιδεία is ultimately irrecoverable, but on the basis of his extant writings, it can be plausibly reconstructed as having *included* a study of Latin poetic authors (notably Virgil and perhaps Ovid) and Latin rhetoricians (akin to Quintilian and Cicero), consistent with a grammatical and oratorical education in the criticism and composition of poetry and prose.[128]

The final component of Tyconius' mental library, complementing the scriptural texts and literary and oratorical authors, are early Christian exegetical writers, notably Origen and Victorinus. Despite evident correspondences between Tyconius' hermeneutical project and that of Origen in *De Principiis*, it is a matter of continued debate among patristic scholars whether Tyconius read and was influenced by Origen's earlier treatise, not least because of Tyconius' much greater emphasis on typology and lack of any clear citation of the Alexandrian. Perhaps the most plausible inference of influence may lie in the two exegetes' common interest in probing the inner compositional principles (ἀρχαὶ/*regulae mysticae*) of scripture.[129] Tyconius' knowledge and use of Victorinus' *Apocalypse Commentary*, however, is not in dispute, as Tyconius frequently draws upon and develops Victorinus' exegetical insights in his own scriptural expositions.[130] A particularly striking example is Tyconius' engagement with Victorinus' interpretation of the seventh seal, as a partial glimpse of eternal rest (cf. Victorinus, *In Apoc.* 8.1/Tyconius, *Apoc.* II.58).[131]

The major components of Tyconius' mental library can now be tentatively sketched, fusing scriptural texts and attendant exegetical commentaries, with the rich interpretative tools and techniques drawn from his grammatical and oratorical studies.

128   Cf. Gennadius, *De viris illustribus* 18 'Tyconius, an African by nationality was, it is said, sufficiently learned in sacred literature, *not wholly unacquainted with secular literature*, and zealous in ecclesiastical affairs' (trans. Hughes 2005: 84).

129   Cf. Vercruysse 2010. If Tyconius had read Origen, it would necessarily have been in Greek, as Tyconius' own writings predate Rufinus' Latin translation of *De principiis* (*c*.398 CE). On Tyconius' likely bilingualism see Steinhauser 1993, corroborated by Tyconius' references to the Greek text of the Apocalypse in his *Apocalypse Commentary* (e.g. III.38, Gryson 2011a: 159–60).

130   Cf. Dulaey 1993, vol. I: 339–43.

131   Cf. Dulaey 1997: 85; Gryson 2011a: 152.

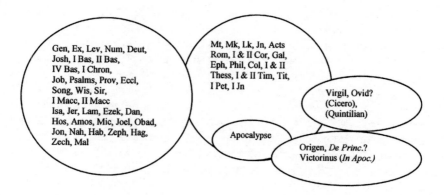

Fig 6.3. Tyconius' Mental Library[132]

6.3.3 Tyconius' Structural Organization of the Apocalypse

Tyconius traces a subtle 'recapitulative' structure across the pulsing fabric of the Apocalypse. Undoubtedly cognizant of Victorinus' prototype, Tyconius refined and reshaped the rudimentary plan sketched by the Pannonian, to track the almost imperceptible movements of the Spirit as it shuttles amid the interweaving threads of the visionary narrative.[133] Tyconius' multifaceted understanding of 'recapitulation' is sketched in his succinct treatment of the topic in Rule VI (*De recapitulatione*) of *libellus regularis*, building on Rule V (*De temporibus*) which precedes, and informed by Rule II (*De Domini corpore bipertio*), its paired rule in the treatises' chiastic design.[134] Tyconius directly warns his reader that the 'seal of recapitulation', one of the seven seals that conceal the full meaning of scripture, is deceptive and must be teased out by an interpreter with the Spirit's aid:

> Among the rules with which the Spirit has sealed the law (*legem signavit*) so as to guard the pathway of light, the seal of recapitulation (*recapitulationis sigillum*) guards some things with such subtlety (*subtilitate*) that it seems more a continuation (*continuatio...narrationis*) than a recapitulation (*recapitulatio*) of the narrative.

> (*libellus regularis*, Rule VI.1)[135]

---

132 Cicero and Quintilian are placed in brackets as Tyconius received a Latin rhetorical education that coheres with the content of their treatises, but it cannot be verified that Tyconius actually read either author.

133 Cf. Bright 2010: 161 for the image of the 'loom of the Spirit' that she applies to Tyconius' hermeneutics.

134 See the insightful analysis of Dulaey 1989: 84–9, 95–9.

135 Babcock 1989: 108–9.

Central to Tyconius' idea of 'recapitulation' is a sense of repetition with variation, of saying the same thing but using different words or images (*eadem aliter dicere*). Accordingly, a reader needs to be attentive to subtle shifts (*transitus*) in scriptural narrative, where chronological progression is broken off, and the Spirit circles back to an earlier point and reiterates the narrative by means of variant imagery.[136]

Yet, awareness of patterned repetition is highly sophisticated in Tyconius' understanding of *recapitulatio* (Rule VI) due to its intimate interconnection with *synecdoche* (Rule V).[137] By means of *synecdoche*, a whole can be represented by a part (and vice versa), that is, for Tyconius, the *whole* history of the church can be represented by a *part* of Scripture (as well as by Scripture in its totality). As a result, he envisages the whole history of the church to be encapsulated in multiform ways in numerous *subsections* within Scripture (cf. Rule V.8.2-3: 'For these are parts of a recapitulation (*partes recapitulationis*) that goes from the beginning to the end' (*ab initio usque in finem*)).[138]

This more developed sense of *recapitulatio* underlies Tyconius' subtle structural subdivision of the Apocalypse into a *septet* of recapitulative 'sections' (περιοχαὶ) in his *Apocalypse Commentary*.[139] Tyconius uses a Latinized form (*periocha* II.43.80) of the Greek noun περιοχή (circumscribed portion, section of a book; cf. Acts 8:32) to refer to the major sub-sections within the Apocalypse.[140] For Tyconius the Apocalypse comprises a series of seven recapitulative *periocha*, each one focusing upon some, or all, of the entire span of the history of the church, from Christ's birth to the parousia. Tyconius' analysis is attentive and nuanced, exemplified by the variety of internal transitions and shifts that he notes within sections (e.g. the presence of an internal recapitulation within an overarching περιοχή (cf. περιοχή 2: seal septet, Rev 4:1–8:1); successive series (*capitulae*) that individually, and collectively, recapitulate the whole history of the church (cf. περιοχή 4: Rev 11:19–14:5); paired-diptychs that each narrate the same period (cf. περιοχή 6: Fall of Babylon, Rev 17:1–19:10). The broad outlines of Tyconius' structural design may be sketched as follows (fig. 6.4).

---

136 Cf. Augustine, *De Doctrina Christiana* III.36.52 (Green 1997: 96); Augustine's definition emphasizes this aspect of Tyconius' rule, to the exclusion of other facets.

137 Cf. Dulaey 1989: 100–101.

138 Babcock 1989: 108–9.

139 Cf. Gryson 2011a: 93–102 and Dulaey 1989: 95–9.

140 Gryson 2011a: 145.

Section 1:   **Vision of the Son of Man and Seven Letters**
Rev 1:1–3:22   Temporal Period: ⎯⎯⎯⎯⎯⎯⎯⎯⎯⎯⟶
                  Christ's birth   Christ's parousia
                  [No Internal Recapitulation]

Section 2:   **Seven Seals**
Rev 4:1–8:1   Temporal Period: ⎯⎯⎯⎯⎯⎯⎯⎯⎯⟶
                  Christ's birth   Christ's parousia
                  Internal recapitulation: Rev 7:1-17
                  Rev 8:1 (half-an hour of eternal rest) conclusion to internal
                  recapitulation (7:1-8:1) and whole section (Rev 4:1–8:1)

Section 3:   **Seven Trumpets**
Rev 8:2–11:18   Temporal Period: ⎯⎯⎯⎯⎯⎯⎯⎯⎯⟶
                  Christ's birth   Christ's parousia
                  Trumpet Six   Rev 9:13-21   + 11:14
                  Internal Recapitulation   Rev 10:1-11:10 + 11:11-13
                  (little scroll and two witnesses)
                  Trumpet Seven   Rev 11:14-18

Section 4:   **Opening of Temple to Lamb on Mt Zion**
Rev 11:19–14:5   Temporal Period: ⎯⎯⎯⎯⎯⎯⎯⎯⎯⟶
                  Christ's birth   Christ's parousia

Ten-subsections (*capitulae*)
1) The temple of God is opened in heaven (Rev 11:19) [= birth of Christ]
2) A great sign appeared in heaven a woman clothed with the sun (Rev 12:1-2).
3) Another sign appeared in heaven, a great fiery-coloured dragon (Rev 12:3-4a).
4) The dragon was posted in front of the woman who gave birth (Rev 12:4b-6).
5) War in heaven, Michael and his angels fighting the dragon (Rev 12:7-8).
6) Defeated dragon cast unto the earth, and where it is shown pursuing the woman (Rev 12:9-14)
7) The serpent spewed from his mouth a torrent of water behind the woman (Rev 12:15-18).
8) The beast rising from the sea (Rev 13:1-10).
9) Another beast coming up from the earth (Rev 13:11-18).
10) The Lamb standing on Mount Zion surrounded by the 144,000 (Rev 14:1-5) [= parousia]

[The whole period is recapitulated in each of the *capitulae*, and across the span of ten *capitulae*]

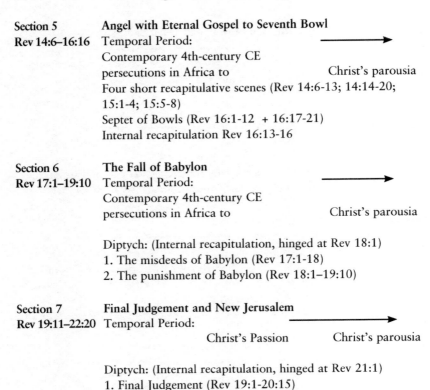

Section 5   **Angel with Eternal Gospel to Seventh Bowl**
Rev 14:6–16:16   Temporal Period:
Contemporary 4th-century CE
persecutions in Africa to   Christ's parousia
Four short recapitulative scenes (Rev 14:6-13; 14:14-20;
15:1-4; 15:5-8)
Septet of Bowls (Rev 16:1-12 + 16:17-21)
Internal recapitulation Rev 16:13-16

Section 6   **The Fall of Babylon**
Rev 17:1–19:10   Temporal Period:
Contemporary 4th-century CE
persecutions in Africa to   Christ's parousia

Diptych: (Internal recapitulation, hinged at Rev 18:1)
1. The misdeeds of Babylon (Rev 17:1-18)
2. The punishment of Babylon (Rev 18:1–19:10)

Section 7   **Final Judgement and New Jerusalem**
Rev 19:11–22:20 Temporal Period:
Christ's Passion   Christ's parousia

Diptych: (Internal recapitulation, hinged at Rev 21:1)
1. Final Judgement (Rev 19:1-20:15)
2. New Jerusalem (Rev 21:1-22:20)

Fig. 6.4 Tyconius' Structural Outline of the Apocalypse

Space constraints preclude a detailed analysis of the complex and subtle structuration of the Apocalypse outlined by Tyconius, so I restrict my comments to the immediate context of Rev 9, namely περιοχαὶ 2–3 (Rev 4:1–11:18, septet of seals and trumpets).

Commenting upon the transition from the seven letters to the seals (Rev 3:22–4:1), Tyconius describes how the narrative shifts backwards to recapitulate events from the birth of Christ (*recapitulat a Christ natiuitate*), indicated by the open door in heaven (II.1-2).[141] Innovatively, for Tyconius, the interval in narrative time relates not to the events described, which are the same, but to their visionary expression (*Diuersum tempus non gestorum, sed uisionum est*) – the same period, namely the whole span of the church, is re-described using 'various figures' (*dieursis figuris*) (II.1-2). Within the second περιοχή (Rev 4:1–8:1) the narrative progression is reversed by the

---

141 Gryson 2011a: 129. Compare Rev 11:19 describing the open temple in heaven, which Tyconius similarly equates with the birth of Christ and the beginning of a subsequent recapitulation (IV.1-2).

presence of an internal recapitulation (Rev 7:1-17), between the sixth and seventh seals, which begins again from the beginning, reaching a combined conclusion in Rev 8:1. In discussing this internal recapitulation, Tyconius indicates to his reader the general principles on which they operate:

> Sed et ipsa recapitulatio pro locis intellegenda est: aliquando enim ab origine passionis, aliquando a medio tempore, aliquando de sola ipsa nouissima pressura aut non multo ante dicturus recapitulat; illud tamen fixum seruat ut a sexto recapitulet.

> The recapitulation itself must be understood from the context: sometimes he [the Spirit] recapitulates from the starting point of the passion, at others from an intermediate period, and at others only from the final persecution or a little earlier; but he keeps to a rule of recapitulating from the sixth.
>
> (Tyconius, Expositio Apocalypseos, II.43.83-87)[142]

In sequences comprising seven components (seals, trumpets, bowls), Tyconius indicates that an internal recapitulation regularly occurs at the sixth item, but the point to which the visionary narrative returns differs in each context. Once both of these visionary paths have converged and concluded (Rev 4:1-6:17 and 7:1-17), with a glimpse of eternal rest in Rev 8:1 (seventh seal), the narrative begins again from the beginning 'so that many things are revealed more clearly' (et ut ei apertius multa ostenderentur) (II.58.7).[143]

The third περιοχή, in which Rev 9 is situated, runs from Rev 8:2–11:18. The first four trumpets return to the beginning of the visionary narrative (§III.1–18), equating Christ's first coming (adventus) with the coming (venit) of the 'other angel' (Rev 8:3), and linking the trumpet blasts to the universal preaching of the church and attendant end-time testing. As already signalled by Tyconius, this septenary comprises an internal recapitulation, between the sixth and seventh trumpets (Rev 10:1–11:10). This sub-unit, containing the little scroll and the two witnesses, does not return the visionary narrative to the beginning, but only jumps back as far as the final period of history. Interestingly, Tyconius distinguishes two conclusions in this περιοχή: one for the internal recapitulation itself (Rev 11:11-13) and one for the broader series of trumpets/woes as a whole (Rev 11:14-18) (cf. III.49).

Tyconius' deft understanding of the multifaceted recapitulative structural design of the Apocalypse, notably its framework of a septet of recapitulative περιοχαὶ, is richly informed by his grammatical and rhetorical training in close exegesis with an attentive ear to subtle shifts between genus and species and the role of synecdoche. Tyconius' application of the term recapitulatio owes much to its use in fourth-century CE Latin rhetoric, where it was used to describe partial recapitulations (summaries) at the end of each topic

142 Gryson 2011a: 146.
143 Gryson 2011a: 152.

or chapter of an argument, as well as outlines of the argument to follow. Irenaeus' theological use of the concept of 'recapitulation' (ἀνακεφαλαίωσις), which so influenced Victorinus, sounds a much more muted note in Tyconius' hermeneutical symphony.[144]

Tyconius' advanced grammatical-level education has manifestly informed and enriched his nuanced interpretation of scripture in both the *libellus regularis* and *Apocalypse Commentary*. The focus of the next section will be to determine whether, or to what extent, Tyconius' tertiary-level education has left its traces upon his extended comments on the cosmic geography of Rev 9:1-21 (star, abyss, Euphrates) (*Apocalypse Commentary* §§III.19-49).[145]

6.3.4 Tyconius' Interpretation of the Cosmology of Rev 9:1-21 (Commentary III.19-49)

Tyconius, in line with his consistent focus throughout the *libellus regularis*, transposes the imagery of the trumpet-cycle (Rev 8:2-11:18, §§III.1–III.84) into an *ecclesiological* key, centred on the Lord's bipartite body (see *libellus regularis* Rules I, II and VII). Accordingly, the cosmological framework of the Apocalypse is consistently re-envisioned in the *Apocalypse Commentary*, in the light of the cosmological significance of the church (cf. Eph 1:22). Silence in heaven (*silentium in caelo*) (Rev 8:1, §II.58) denotes silence in the church (*id est in ecclesia*).[146] This accords with Tyconius' interpretation of Isa 14:12, referring to the Morning Star who has fallen from 'heaven', that is, fallen from 'the church' (*libellus regularis*, Rule VII).[147] Similarly, the heavenly bodies, sun, moon, and stars which are darkened by a third (Rev 8:12, fourth trumpet, §III.17) are interpreted as a figure for the bipartite church (Rule II): 'Sun, moon, and stars are the church (*Sol, luna, stellae ecclesia est*), a third part of which are struck. 'Third' is a designation (*nomen*), not a quantity (*quantitas*). There are two parts in the church, one day and the other night...'.[148] Terrestrial referents are afforded a similar treatment, with the third part of the earth and trees struck by the first trumpet (Rev 8:7, § III.10) interpreted as a reference to humanity (*homines*) as a whole divided into three parts: gentiles, false-brethren (within the church), and the good (within the church) (cf. *libellus regularis*, Rule II).

144 Cf. Dulaey 1989: 99-103. In Tyconius' Latin version of Eph 1:10 the verb *restaure* is used (*libellus regularis* Rule III.11), not *recapitulare*, indicative of Tyconius' disinterest in an Irenean sense of Christ as the recapitulation of all things (cf. Osborn 2001: 95–140).

145 Gryson 2011a: 156–63.

146 Gryson 2011a: 152.

147 Cf. *Libellus regularis* VII.3.2, Babcock 1989: 116–17: 'As we shall see as scripture proceeds, it is the church that he calls "heaven" (*caelum ecclesiam*). And it is from this heaven (*hoc caelo*) that the morning daystar falls.'

148 Gryson 2011a: 157.

For Tyconius, the fifth and sixth trumpets (Rev 9:1-21) principally function as *genus* prophecies (*libellus regularis*, Rule IV), directly applicable to the *present* and *future* history of the Church. The contemporary relevance of the torturous activities of the hybrid locusts is signalled, for Tyconius, by the temporal significance of 'five months' (*mensibus quinque*) (Rev 9:5, 10), according to a hermeneutical principle already outlined in *libellus regularis* Rule V (*De temporibus*) (V. 6.1). In this prophecy 'months' stand for 'years' (*menses pro annis*), which as a result 'indicates the whole five-year duration of the persecution, which was intense in Africa' (*mensibus quinque pro toto tempore persecutionis annorum quinque dixit, quae facta est maxime in Africa*) (§III.25, cf. §III.35).[149] Whilst the precise historical referent is difficult to determine, Tyconius is perhaps most plausibly referring to the intense period of state prosecution initiated by the edicts of Diocletian (*c*.303–305 CE), which led to the inception of the Donatist church in North Africa (cf. περιοχή V: Rev 14:6-16:16).[150] The apparent eschatological force of the temporal referents in Rev 9:5, 10 is retroverted by Tyconius onto the present, or more precisely the living, recurring, history, of the Donatist church in Roman North Africa (cf. *libellus regularis* VI.3.1, '...what Daniel mentioned [Dan 9:27, 11:31] is happening now in Africa, not at the time of the end' (*Quod autem Danihel dixit in Africa geritur, neque in eodem tempore finis*)).[151]

Whilst Tyconius' ecclesiological hermeneutic enables him to 'exorcise' texts such as Daniel of their apparent eschatological referents,[152] his aim was not to evacuate all eschatological content from scriptural prophecy. This is strikingly verified by Tyconius' interpretation of the tri-morphic cavalry of Rev 9:17-19 (trumpet six) as a prediction of the 'final battle' (*nouissimo bello*) (§III.29). In this regard, the hybrid locusts of the fifth trumpet are interpreted *both* as a type of present persecutors in Africa and a typological figure (*figura*) of the final eschatological forces of evil.[153] Both the horses like locusts and the horses like lion-headed serpents 'describe a single reality in different ways' (*unam rem dissimiliter describit*) (§III.43), the sixth trumpet *recapitulating* the former in its more detailed eschatological portrayal.

The Well of the Abyss (Rev 9:1-2/§§ III.19-21, III.36)
Ps 68:15-16 LXX envisages the Deep (βυθός), or the Well (φρέαρ), as a subterranenan beast, that closes its mouth (τὸ στόμα αὐτοῦ) after swal-

---

149   Gryson 2011a: 158, 159.

150   Cf. Frend 1952: 1–24 and Tilley 1997: 18–76. This is more plausible than the later state prosecution of Donatists under Constantine (c.317–21 CE) which was more narrowly focused on North Africa, whereas the persecution mentioned by Tyconius is implicitly more wide-ranging, given its particular severity in Africa (*maxime in Africa*).

151   Babcock 1989: 111.

152   Fredriksen Landes 1982: 65–6.

153   'The horses are men (*homines*), while their riders are evil spirits (*spiritus nequam*), §III.41 (Rev 9:17), Gryson 2011a: 161.

lowing its victim whole.[154] Tyconius offers an anthropological twist on this cosmological image, by visualizing the well of the abyss (*puteus abyssi*, Rev 9:1) as a *human mouth*, whose opening releases the imprisoned 'devil' within, to be enthroned over a sinner's life (cf. Rev 9:11).

> *abyssus enim populus est, in quo diabolus in occulto cordi eorum ligatus tenetur, et rex huius saeculi perspicuae principatur*

> For the abyss is the people in whom the devil is tied and held in the secret of their hearts, and the ruler of this age reigns conspicuously
>
> (Tyconius, *Commentary on the Apocalypse*, 9:11, §III.36)[155]

Tyconius supports his anthropological reading by an explicit citation of Ps 68:16:

> Sic Dauid, cum ab inimicus ne comprimeretur orauit, ne contineat,[156] inquit, super me puteus os sum

> So David, when he prayed not to be overcome by his enemies, said, 'Let not the Pit hold fast her mouth upon me'
>
> (Tyconius, *Commentary on the Apocalypse*, 9:1, §III.20)[157]

For Tyconius, the cosmological referents of star and abyss (Rev 9:1) are reinterpreted as a corporate representation of sinful humanity (*homines*), receiving 'the power of the heart' (*potestatem cordis*), represented by the key (*clavis*), to release the confined diabolic force within.[158] Accordingly, for Tyconius, Rev 9:1ff affords an anthropological dissection of the human will, a textbook example of the human body as microcosm, rather than a topographical sketch of the unchartered boundaries of the οἰκουμένη.[159] The image affords an insight into the captive will of sinners, whether in or out of the church, subject to the interior devil who rules their heart (§§III.20, III.36), whom they have returned to power by their lips (§III.20), especially in their assent to false-prophecy (§III.35).

---

154 For a discussion of the influence of Ps 68:15-16 LXX on the cosmic geography of HC1 see §4.4.1, above.

155 Gryson 2011a: 159.

156 Gryson 2011a: 283 suggests that the unusual reading of *contineat* (from the verb *contineo* hold or keep together, keep, hold fast, enclose) may be derived from an African version of the Psalter.

157 Gryson 2011a: 156.

158 Tyconius, *Commentary on the Apocalypse*, 9:1, §III.19-21; Gryson 2011a: 156.

Tyconius applies the logic of *synecdoche* (a part representing the whole, cf. *libellus regularis* Rule V.1) to argue that the one star (*una stella*) of Rev 9:1 represents 'the whole body' (*corpus...multarum*) – the body of the Devil/left-hand side of the body of Christ (Rules I and VII) – of falling sinners; §III.19.

159 Tyconius, *Commentary on the Apocalypse*, 9:1, §III.19; Gryson 2011a: 156. '*Stella, abyssus, puteus hominess sunt*' (Star, abyss, well, are human beings).

In line with Rule II of Tyconius' *libellus regularis* the identity of such sinners is carefully nuanced, owing to the mystery of the bipartite nature of the church. Tyconius eschews a simplistic division into outsiders and insiders, those sealed and those unsealed (Rev 9:5), recognizing instead the presence of sinners within the church. For Tyconius, the divine seal indicates the 'double-character' (*duplex persona*) of insiders, comprising both the good (right-hand side) and the bad (left-hand side) members of the body of Christ (§III.24).

Euphrates (Rev 9:14/§III.38)
Tyconius' ecclesiological preoccupation continues in his exegesis of the geographical referent of the river Euphrates (Rev 9:14, §3.38), in line with principles already enunciated in rule IV (*De specie et genere*) of *libellus regularis*:

> It is also very important to know this: that every one of the cities or provinces of Israel and of the nations (*omnes omnio civitates Israhel et gentium uel prouincias*) that scripture mentions or in which it reports some event is a figure of the church (*figuram esse Ecclesiae*). Some are figures of the evil part (*partis malae*), some of the good (*aliquae bonae*), and some of both (*utriusque*).
>
> (*libellus regularis* IV.11)[160]

The crucial issue for Tyconius, therefore, is to determine which aspect of the church the Euphrates denotes. The interpretative lens is provided by Tyconius' exegesis of Jer 26:10 (LXX enumeration) which serves to associate the Euphrates with 'Babylon' (*Eufrates autem fluuius est Babylonis, sicut per Ieremiam*) (§III.38), the land of the 'north'.[161]

Tyconius has previously discussed the ecclesiological significance of Babylon at length in *libellus regularis* Rule IV.18-20, as a test-case example of a scriptural city, like Sodom (LR IV.17), that represents the negative, left-hand side of the church.[162] Babylon's central typological function in scripture is to serve as a figure of 'the whole world' (*totus mundus*) (LR IV.18), or more precisely 'all the nations' (*omnes gentes*) (LR IV.19.1), in their offensive military role as enemies of Jerusalem/Israel. Given that the membership of the church, the body of Christ, is itself comprised of 'all the nations' (*omnes gentes*) (LR IV.20.3), Tyconius argues that the most acute battle between the church and 'all the nations' does not take the form of an external military threat, but rather *internal dissension* between the right and left sides of the body of Christ (exegesis of Jer 32:1-15 (LXX enumeration)):

---

160   Babcock 1989: 68–9.
161   Gryson 2011a: 160.
162   Babcock 1989: 82–7. Other cities, for example Egypt, are bipartite (cf. LR IV.14.1, Babcock 1989: 72–3). See also *libellus regularis* VII for Tyconius' interpretation of the King of Babylon (= Antichrist, the Devil's body) in the context of an exegesis of Isa 14:12–21; Babcock 1989: 117–29; cf. Bright 1988: 84.

But if both then and now, he [Jeremiah] spoke in the church (*in Ecclesiam*), it is also manifest that all the nations (*omnes gentes*) are represented in their preeminent part (*in principipali eorum parte*) in the place where Jeremiah does speak [= the church]. For if Satan holds anything of excellence in his body (*in corpore suo*), anything of the right-hand (*si quid dextrum*), anything of eminence (*si quid graue habet*), he mingles it with the heavens (*caelestibus miscuit*)... [= the church]

(*libellus regularis*, IV.20.3)[163]

In this visual image the two bodies overlap: the right-hand side of the body of the Devil (Rule VII) overlaps with the left-hand side of the body of Christ (Rule II), such that the negative forces within the Church are comprised of the élite forces under the Devil's military command.[164]

This emphasis upon Babylon as constitutive of the left-hand side of the church dovetails neatly with Tyconius' alternative visualization of the bipartite church as split into 'north' and 'south', previously delineated in *libellus regularis* Rule VII.4.2-3.[165]

There are two parts in the church, one of the south and one of the north. The Lord abides in the southern part, as it is written: 'Where you graze your flocks, where you abide in the south (*in meridiano*)' [Song of Songs 1:7]. But the devil abides in the north, as the Lord says to his people: 'The invader from the north (*ab Aquilone*) I will drive away from you... [Joel 2:10]

(*libellus regularis*, VII.4.2)[166]

The topographical division of the earth into a positive southern region contrasted with a negative northern one appears to have been a characteristic emphasis of Donatist exegesis, privileging the African continent as the locus of the church, and appealing to Song of Songs 1:7 as a proof-text.[167] What is striking about Tyconius' exegesis is that he reorientates this characteristic Donatist exegetical move, citing the same text (Song of Songs 1:7) in support of his nuanced understanding of the bipartite church: the church is not restricted to Africa, but is present 'in all the world' (*in toto mundo*) (LR VII.4.3), only the body of Christ is mixed, containing both good and bad members (south/right/good; north/left/bad).[168]

---

163 Babcock 1989: 88–9.

164 Vercruysse 2004: 273 n.3–4 comments that this is the sole reference to Satan, rather than the Devil in the *libellus regularis*, but that the resulting image is nonetheless a variant on the familiar one of the bipartite church.

165 Babcock 1989: 120–25.

166 Babcock 1989: 120–21.

167 Cf. Tilley 1997: 148–9; Vercruysse 2004: 333–4 n.4. Whereas Catholics, such as Augustine, interpreted *meridies* in Song of Songs 1:7 to mean 'mid-day', Donatists, with whom he disputes, read it as 'the south', indicative of Africa (Augustine, *Ep. ad Cath.* 16:40-41).

168 Cf. *libellus regularis* I.4.1 'For it is not that the Lord *filled the whole earth* [Dan 2:34-5] with his power rather than with the fullness of his body. Some make this claim –

The Euphrates, as a river of Babylon, the land of the north (§III.38, Jer 26:10 (LXX enumeration)) consequently functions as a *figura* for the body of the Devil, not least those false-brethren within the left-hand side of the church: 'the river Euphrates is the name it gives to the persecuting people, among whom Satan and his will have been bound (*Flumen enim Eufraten populum persecutorem dixit, in quo Satanas et propria uoluntas ligata est*).' In this way the Euphrates (*Eufraten*) and the well (*puteus*), in trumpets five and six, are interpreted as variant images of the same sinful human beings (*homines*), which includes those on the left-hand side of the body of Christ, within whom the Devil is 'bound' (*ligo*) and who accordingly do his 'will' (*voluntas*) (§§III.36 and III.20; III.38).

Tyconius' interpretation of the Euphrates is further supported by his elucidation of the four angels bound within its banks (Rev 9:14). Implicitly agreeing with Victorinus' prior exegetical decision to equate the four-bound angels (Rev 9:14) with the four angels restraining the winds (Rev 7:1) (Victorinus, *In Apoc.* 6.6),[169] Tyconius moves to resolve the resultant topographical disparity between a location at the river Euphrates compared to 'the four corners of the earth' (*in quattuor angulis terrae*) (Rev 7:1) (§III.38). On the basis of the principle of *synecdoche* (*libellus regularis* V.1), whereby a part represents the whole (*parte totum*), the four corners of the earth indicate that the Euphrates is 'in the whole earth' (*in omni terra esse*) (§III.38). This exegetical move coheres with Tyconius' interpretation of the Euphrates, akin to Babylon/the land of the north, as 'all the nations' (*omnes gentes*) 'in all the world' (*in toto mundo*), that is as contemporary 4th-century CE sinners fulfilling the *typological* role of the hostile nations against Jerusalem/Israel.

6.3.5 Conclusion

On the basis of Tyconius' ecclesiological hermeneutic the fallen star and the well of the abyss (Rev 9:1-2) are divested of mundane cosmological content, and transposed into an anthropological register, to serve as an image of sinners. The latter is more evocatively sketched: the well of the abyss becomes the interior human shaft – stomach, throat and mouth – through which inner desires are expressed, and the inner devil released to reign over the seat of the emotions. New life is breathed into the monstrous conceit of Ps 68:16 as the anthropomorphized well-shaft becomes fully human, but only on a microcosmic scale (§§III.36, III.20). The topography of the Euphrates (Rev 9:14) is similarly distorted, dug-up from its position as a marginal boundary

which I do not report without sorrow – to the dishonour of God's kingdom and of Christ's unvanquished inheritance' (Babcock 1989: 4–5).

169 Dulaey 1997: 84–5.

marker, it appears to flood the whole terrestrial plain (*in omni terra esse*) (§III.38), with a noted rage and swell in Babylon, the land of the north (Jer 26:10 (LXX)). Once more, however, apparent geopolitical signposts are internalized, serving as diagnostic terms that chart the health of the ecclesial body, and its bipartite membership. Star, abyss, and Euphrates each function as interchangeable images for sinful humanity (*eadem aliter dicere*), providing little or no indication of Tyconius' preferred cosmological template, whether Homeric, Platonic/Ptolemaic, or hybrid.[170]

Yet the preferred cosmological template of our tertiary-educated exegete is explicitly and evocatively expressed: 'This world was constructed in the likeness of the church' (*Ad instar Ecclesiae fabricatus est iste mundus*) (*libellus regularis*, VII.4.2).[171] For Tyconius, the poles of imitation are reversed as humanity is not envisaged as a microcosm of the universe, but rather the world itself is created as an image (*instar*) of the body of Christ, the church (cf. Eph 1:22 κεφαλὴ ὑπὲρ πάντα τῇ ἐκκλησίᾳ). Accordingly, all geographical and topographical referents in scripture function as typological figures (*figurae*) of the bipartite church (*libellus regularis,* IV.11). All spatial terms take their meaning from Christ (left/right, north/south), whose body fills the entire earth (*libellus regularis*, I.4.1), and whose birth signals the opening of the heavens (Rev 4:1, 11:19; §§II.1, IV.1). To speak of heaven (§II.58), earth (LR VII.4.2), or abyss (§III.20, 36) is to speak of Christ's body, the church.

Tyconius' christological/ecclesiological template of the cosmos is fashioned from the dominance of scriptural texts in his mental library, almost to the exclusion of all other influences. Tyconius does not retain the outmoded Homeric template that dominates his scriptural sources, but rather wholly refashions his model of the cosmos in the light of his (Deutero-Pauline) ecclesiological blueprint, which presents Christ as the head of the cosmos, that is, the church (cf. Eph 1:22).

170   Cf. §3.2 (above).
171   Babcock 1989: 120–21.

6.4 Oecumenius (c. 6th century CE)

6.4.1 Introduction – Oecumenius' Life and Work

Oecumenius' *Commentary on the Apocalypse*[172] is the earliest extant full-length exegetical study of the Apocalypse in Greek.[173] The *Commentary* was a formative influence on Andrew, bishop of Caesarea, whose own complete *Commentary on the Apocalypse* (c. 6th/7th century CE) '...often ...mentions or summarizes the views of Oecumenius, usually to disagree and to offer his own comments.'[174] The precise date of Oecumenius' *Commentary*, and the identity of its author, remain keenly disputed issues, with the debate polarized by the presence of conflicting data in the scant internal and external evidence.[175] The most direct internal evidence is provided by Oecumenius' comment on ἃ δεῖ γενέσθαι (Rev 1:1):

> But what does he mean by adding *what must soon take place* (ἃ δεῖ γενέσθαι), since those things which were going to happen have not yet been fulfilled, although a very long time has elapsed since these things were said (ἤδη πλείστου δεδραμηκότος χρόνου ἐξ οὗ ταῦτα εἴρηται), more than five hundred years (ἐτῶν πλειόνων ἢ πεντακοσίων;)?
>
> (Oecumenius, *Commentary on the Apocalypse*, 1.3.6)[176]

Given that Oecumenius dates the composition of the Apocalypse to the reign of Domitian (81–96 CE) (1.21.1),[177] this rhetorical question suggests that Oecumenius' *Commentary* is unlikely to predate the closing decades of the 6th century CE.[178] Few other indications of temporal context are discernible in Oecumenius' *Commentary*, although it has been proposed, by Castagno and De Groote in particular, that certain facets of Oecumenius' defence of the 'orthodoxy' of the Apocalypse's

---

172   Cf. De Groote 1999 (Greek); Suggit 2006 (English); Weinrich 2011a (English).

173   The earliest extended exegeses of the Apocalypse in Greek date from the 3rd century CE; cf. McGinn 2009. For the surviving fragments of 'Hippolytus'' *Commentary*, cf. Prigent 1972 (French); Prigent and Stehly 1973 (French), (and cf. §5.6); for Methodius' partial exegesis of Rev 20–21 (*Symposium*, dialogue 9), cf. Bonwetsch 1917 (Greek); Musirillo 1958 (English).

174   Weinrich 2011a: xxxii. For the text of Andrew of Caesarea's *Commentary* see Schmid 1955 (Greek); Weinrich 2011a (English). For a list of citations/allusions to Oecumenius' *Commentary* by Andrew, although Andrew never refers to Oecumenius by name, see De Groote 1999, Index III.

175   Cf. Castagno 1980; De Groote 1996; De Groote 2009: 13-20; Diekamp 1901; Durousseau 1984; Lamoreaux 1998; Pétridès 1903; Spitaler and Schmid 1934; Suggit 2006: 3–6; Weinrich 2011a: xix–xxv.

176   De Groote 1999: 68; Suggit 2006: 22 (alt.).

177   Oecumenius explicitly bases this date on the testimony of Eusebius of Caesarea, (*Chronicon Paschale* 250C); cf. Suggit 2006: 28; De Groote 2003: 255–6.

178   So Diekamp 1901.

theology corroborate a date in the *latter half* of the sixth century CE.[179] Although influenced by Origen's thought, Oecumenius never refers to the Alexandrian by name, and whilst broadly sympathetic to Origen's idea of the restoration of all things at the *eschaton* (ἀποκατάστασις),[180] he nonetheless attempts to conflate this concept with what he understands to be the agreed teaching (δόγμα) of the church, that the punishment of the unrighteous will be eternal (5.19.1-4 with reference to Rev 9:5-6).[181] Such a stance, it is argued, may reflect the author's knowledge of the edicts of the Fifth Ecumenical Council (Constantinople, 553 CE), at which Origen and the concept of ἀποκατάστασις were formally condemned.[182]

At variance with such intimations of a late 6th-century CE date, however, are crucial strands of external evidence. An extract from the eleventh λόγος of Oecumenius' *Commentary* is contained among a catena of citations from twenty-five different authors, in a 7th-century CE manuscript in Syriac.[183] The extract is introduced as follows: 'From Oecumenius, a careful man who is very orthodox, as the letters of Patriarch Mar Severus written to him show, from the sixth discourse which he composed on the Revelation of the Evangelist John.'[184] Substantiation of the claim that a certain 'Oecumenius' was a correspondent of Severus, the Monophysite bishop of Antioch (*c*.465–538 CE) are provided by a series of nine extant letters, dating from 508–18 CE, which are either addressed directly to Oecumenius, or refer to him by name, among Severus' voluminous correspondence.[185] The Oecumenius who corresponded with Severus, bishop of Antioch, in

---

179   Oecumenius endeavours to verify the 'orthodoxy' of the Apocalypse against detractors (cf. 1.1.4-6; 12.20.1-6), an 'orthodoxy' which Oecumenius equates with certain Christological formulae of Chalcedon (451 CE), interpreted in a Cyrilline fashion (cf. 1.3.1-3); cf. Lamoreaux 1998: 95–100; Suggit 2006: 6–9.

180   Cf. Ramelli 2007.

181   Oecumenius (5.19.1-2) 'One must combine the opinions of both [i.e. eternal punishment and restoration]. I say this as a suggestion and not as an affirmation; for I associate myself with the teaching of the church (ἐγὼ γὰρ τῷ δόγματι τῆς ἐκκλησίας προστίθεμαι) in meaning that the future punishments will be everlasting...'; De Groote 1999: 148; Suggit 2006: 89.

Oecumenius shows a marked tendency throughout his *Commentary* to emphasize divine mercy over divine vengeance (cf. 3.5.8; 5.15.2; 8.13.1-7); cf. De Villiers 2009.

182   It could equally be argued, however, that Oecumenius' *retention* of the idea, which he 'blends' (κεράννυμι) (5.19.1) with the agreed teaching, to suggest a lessening severity during the course of the eternal punishment, is indicative of a date prior to the concept's formal condemnation.

183   Cf. Diekamp 1901; Spitaler and Schmid 1934.

184   Spitaler and Schmid 1934: 209–10. On the Monophysite provenance of the catena, signalled by its choice of authors and value judgements (notably its critique of Theodore of Mopsuestia), see Lamoreaux 1998: 92; Weinrich 2011a: xxi n.14.

185   Cf. Pétridès 1903; Lamoreaux 1998: 100–102. For details of the letters see Lamoreaux 1998: 100 n.56, and for a sample of Severus' correspondence see Brooks 1904 (123 letters out of a total corpus in excess of 4000 letters); cf. Kannengiesser 2006: 924–7.

the early decades of the 6th century CE, was a married layman (cf. *Epistle* 1), who is referred to by the official title of 'count' (κόμης) (*Select Epistle* 1.2; *Epistle* 1 and 2), a rank, of varying grade, within the imperial civil service, often denoting a military official.[186] As an official in the imperial bureaucracy of Isauria, count Oecumenius had close contacts with Severus, bishop of Antioch, assisting him in matters of clerical discipline, notably in the process of acquiring the Emperor's assent when depriving a bishop of his see.[187] As an imperial bureaucrat and administrator, Oecumenius is likely to have received at least a προγύμνασματα education, which afforded him the requisite reading, exegetical, and prose compositional skills to administer his post effectively.[188] In count Oecumenius' case, however, it is plausible that he received a full tertiary-level oratorical education, as Severus refers to him on one occasion as a *scholasticus*,[189] a designation for someone who has completed the full circle of ἐγκύκλιος παιδεία and is qualified to practise law.[190]

Is the author of the *Commentary on the Apocalypse* to be identified with Severus' correspondent, the rhetorically educated count of Isauria? The debate is finely balanced. Scholars who separate the two figures (e.g. Castagno, De Groote) distinguish a Neo-Chalcedonian Oecumenius, writing at the close of the 6th century (1.3.6), from a Monophysite Oecumenius, who corresponded with Severus (*c*.508–18 CE). The confusion is attributable to the author of the Syriac catena (7th century CE), who mistakenly conflated the Apocalypse commentator with an earlier namesake.[191] Scholars who attempt to hold the conflicting strands together (e.g. Spitaler and Schmid, Lamoreaux, Suggit, Weinrich) lessen the adjudicating function of 1.3.6 to

186   The civil service rank of κόμης was first formalized by Constantine (whilst sole Emperor, 324-37 CE) and divided into three grades: Cf. Eusebius, *Life of Constantine* IV.1.1 '[Constantine] did not neglect secular affairs...he would honour those known to him with special promotions...some acquired posts as prefects, others senatorial rank, others that of consuls; very many were designated governors; some were appointed comites of the first order, others of the second, others of the third...for in order to promote more persons the Emperor contrived different distinctions'; Cameron and Hall 1999: 154, (cf. 309–10); cf. also Suggit 2006: 5 n.12.

187   On Isauria in late antiquity see Feld 2005, and for Severus of Antioch's episcopal oversight of this province within his patriarchate (491–518 CE), intertwined with matters of imperial bureaucracy, see Frend 1981: 214–15.

188   Cf. Morgan 1998: 197–226 on the significance of a *progymnastic* education for 'bureaucratic middlemen in a variety of posts' (225).

189   Lamoreaux 1998: 101.

190   Cf. Dijkstra 2003: 137 n.10 with reference to the education of the 6th-century CE Egyptian lawyer/rhetorician Dioscorus: 'The term *scholasticus*, Greek σχολαστικός, denotes both a man of letters and a lawyer'.

191   Oecumenius may also be the author of certain portions of a *scholia* on the Pauline epistles (whilst other sections are falsely ascribed to him), cf. Lamoreaux 1998: 89. For the purposes of the present debate, however, it is preferable to set this disputed material aside to focus on the authorship of the *Apocalypse Commentary*.

determine dating, and highlight the broad coherence of the remainder of Oecumenius' *Commentary* with an early to mid-6th-century CE date.[192]

The significance of this issue for the present study is restricted to its impact upon the educational attainment of the author of the *Apocalypse Commentary*. Whilst the present study does not claim to resolve this debate, the contents of Oecumenius' mental library that are identified are consistent with an author who has attained at least a *progymnastic* level of education, and consequently does not preclude an identification of the implied author of the text with the Count of Isauria.

6.4.2 Oecumenius' Mental library

On the basis of explicit citations of named literary authors and extracts in Oecumenius' *Commentary on the Apocalypse*, the scope of its implied author's mental library can be tentatively sketched as follows. Oecumenius offers his own, broadly independent, interpretation of the Apocalypse, save for some limited engagement with the earlier Greek exegeses of 'Hippolytus' and Methodius. Oecumenius' exegesis is principally informed by a diverse range of scriptural texts, most prominently Psalms, Isaiah, Genesis, Exodus and Daniel from the LXX, and the Pauline epistles (Romans, I and II Corinthians, Hebrews) and Gospels (principally Mt and Jn) from the NT.[193] These scriptural sources are supplemented by a wide knowledge of the 'fathers' (πατέρες) (1.1.4), often cited in defence of the authoritative status of the Apocalypse,[194] with a particular influence exerted on his thought by the writings of Cyril of Alexandria, Eusebius, Gregory of Nyssa, 'Hippolytus', and Methodius.[195] Oecumenius had firsthand knowledge of Josephus (*Antiquities*, *War*), and also cites the *Shepherd of Hermas*, although not as a scriptural witness, most likely in dependence on Clement of Alexandria.[196]

---

192   Spitaler and Schmid 1934 suggested that 1.3.6 may mean 500 years since the birth of Christ, but more recent studies reject this argument as unpersuasive in the context of the passage; cf. Lamoreaux 1998: 102–6 'perhaps five-hundred was just a round number, not to be taken too literally...' (106); Weinrich 2011a: xxiii–xxiv.

193   Cf. Durousseau 1984: 30–31. For more details of Oecumenius' citation of scripture, consult Index I in De Groote 1999: 310–19; Suggit 2006: 211–16.

194   See especially the dense citations of patristic authorities in defence of the authoritative status of the Apocalypse at the beginning and end of the *Commentary* (1.1.4-7; 12.20.1-6); cf. Index II in De Groote 1999: 326–36.

195   See the detailed analysis of Oecumenius' citations and allusions to patristic sources by De Groote 2003.

196   Josephus, *Antiquities* iv.126–40 (*Commentary* 2.7.3); Josephus, *Antiquities* xviii. 63–4 (*Commentary* 4.10.7-8); Josephus, *War* v.567–9 (*Commentary* 4.17.3, 8).

Oecumenius cites *Shepherd of Hermas*, Sim. 9.16.4 (*Commentary* 2.11.2), but this is likely to be indirect knowledge based on Clement of Alexandria's reference to the same passage in *Stromateis* VI.46.5; cf. De Groote 2003: 262.

The extent of Oecumenius' ἐγκύκλιος παιδεία is more difficult to pinpoint, as he refers only intermittently to Greek literary authors. Nonetheless, there are sufficient allusions to indicate a familiarity with poetic authors (Homer, Hesiod) and the requisite exegetical and prose compositional skills of someone with at least a sound προγύμνασματα education.

Oecumenius' ambivalent attitude towards Greek poetic literature is neatly encapsulated in the preface to his *Commentary*:

> So his [John's] present treatise, insofar as it contains both plain and polished mysteries (περὶ μυστηρίων ἰσχνῶν καὶ ἀπεξεσμένων ἔχει), could be rightly considered the most mystical (μυστικωτάτην). For he does not only speak to us about present events (παρόντων), but also about those which have happened (παρεληλυθότων) and those which are still to come (μελλόντων πραγμάτων). For this is the mark of consummate prophecy (ἐντελοῦς προφητείας), to encompass the three periods (περὶ τῶν τριῶν διαλαμβάνειν καιρῶν). For even those who are not Christians [lit. 'outsiders' (οἱ ἔξωθεν)] introduce their own seers (μάντεις) who knew 'the events of the present, the future and the past,' (τά τ' ἐόντα τά τ' ἐσσόμενα πρό τ' ἐόντα) [Homer, *Iliad* I. 70; Hesiod, *Theogony*, 38] though they have, I think, been held in disdain by our prophets. For their diviners never had knowledge of everything (οἱ παρ' αὐτοῖς χρησμολόγοι τὴν ἁπάντων γνῶσιν ἔσχον ποτέ), nor did even the demonic powers (δαίμονες) at work in them.

(Oecumenius, *Commentary on the Apocalypse*, 1.1.2)[197]

For Oecumenius, the Apocalypse is 'complete' or 'full' prophecy (ἐντελοῦς προφητείας) as the mysteries that it discloses fully encompass the three periods of time: past, present, and future.[198] This interpretation is supported by an allusion to the classical definition of prophetic insight provided by Homer (*Iliad* I.70) and Hesiod (*Theogony* 38), the former text from the popular opening section of the *Iliad* (books I–II), widely studied under a grammarian's tuition. In response to Achilles' request for a seer (μάντις) or priest (ἱερεύς) or reader of dreams (ὀνειροπόλος) to divine the reason for Apollo's anger, Calchas arose, the foremost diviner who had guided the ships to Ilios, 'who had knowledge of all things that were, and that were to be, and that had been before (τά τ' ἐόντα τά τ' ἐσσόμενα πρό τ' ἐόντα)'.[199] Hesiod's parallel phrase (*Theogony* 38) is ascribed to the Heliconian Muses who inspire his poetic composition.[200] Nonetheless, 'divinely voiced' (θέσπεσιος, cf. *Iliad* II. 600; *Odyssey* XII. 158) John's prophetic insight exceeds that of all previous seers

---

197 Suggit 2006: 19; De Groote 1999: 64.

198 On the prominence of the language of 'mystery' in Oecumenius' *Commentary* see De Villiers 2007.

199 Murray/Wyatt 1999: 16–19. The 2nd-century BCE Alexandrian scholar, Aristarchus, in an extant *scholia* on this passage of the *Iliad*, classified μάντις as the genus (prophecy), with ἱερεύς and ὀνειροπόλος as the two species, the former indicating divination from sacrifices, and the latter from dreams; cf. Kirk 1985: 59.

200 Most 2006: 4–5.

and oracles (μάντεις, χρησμολόγοι), in Oecumenius' opinion, by the *scope* of his divinely disclosed visions which encompasses 'all things' (ἅπαντα) – a level of knowledge withheld from all rival seers and their *daemons*.[201]

Evidence of Oecumenius' tuition in the poetic interpretative skills of γραμματική (cf. Dionysius Thrax, Τέχνη Γραμματική) is evident throughout the *Commentary* in his use of technical terminology to describe the compositional, structural and stylistic traits of the Apocalypse. For example, Oecumenius discusses the syntax (σύνταξις) (*Commentary* 1.1.3.1) of a sentence,[202] in order to tease out its meaning (cf. Apollonius Dyscolus, *Syntax*), and labels Rev 11:3-14, the account of the two witnesses, as an 'aside' (παρέξοδος, literally 'off-road' (excursion)) in the path of the narrative (cf. Cicero, *De inventione* 1.5.1.97; *De oratore* 2.19.80-3; Quintilian, *Inst. Or.* iv.3).[203] Furthermore, Oecumenius uses a number of expressions to denote the metaphorical language of this visionary narrative, notably the adjective τροπικῶς (cf. *Commentary* 5.9.3-4), which is a technical grammatical term used to denote a figure of speech (cf. Longinus, *On the Sublime* 32.6).

Whilst Oecumenius' poetic exegetical skills and prose compositional expertise are abundantly in evidence, traces of tertiary-level philosophical study are harder to identify. Speculation that Oecumenius had read Plato's *Timaeus* arises from his novel interpretation of the four living creatures around the divine throne (τέσσαρα ζῷα) (Rev 4:6-9) as the four primal elements – fire, earth, air, water – (*Commentary* 3.9.3; cf. Plato, *Timaeus* 32A).[204] Yet such an interpretation did not originate with Oecumenius, but rather derives from Methodius, *On the Resurrection* 2.10.4 (d. *c*.311 CE), a treatise that Oecumenius explicitly refers to as a source at 1.1.4-5.[205]

The same source, Methodius, *On the Resurrection*, may also account for Oecumenius' nuanced understanding of the fifth element, *aither* (*Commentary* 8.25.5).[206] Oecumenius' description of *aither* as the fifth element, which is eternal, because of its circular motion (Aristotle, *De Caelo* 270b16-25), appears to reflect Methodius' discussion of this element in his parody of Origen's understanding of the disembodied body of those raised, as ethereal/'spherical' (*On the Resurrection* 3.1.1-3).[207]

---

201   There is also an echo of the Homeric epithet used to characterize Ares, as 'baneful' and 'bloodthirsty' (βροτολοιγέ, μιαιφόνε) (cf. *Iliad* V. 31, 455, 844, 846), in the ascription of Ares as a national god of the 'baneful' (βροτολοιγός) and 'bloodthirsty' (μιαιφονος) Scythians (Oecumenius, *Commentary*, 10.11.5-6); cf. De Groote 1999: 332.

202   Oecumenius, *Commentary* 1.13.1 'The syntax (ἡ σύνταξις) of these words goes from the end to the beginning'; Suggit 2006: 25; De Groote 1999: 72.

203   On the variety of terms used to describe a 'digression' (παρέκβασις) in a speech/narrative in ancient rhetorical theory see Perry 2009: 29–30.

204   Suggit 2006: 57–8.

205   For Methodius' influence on Oecumenius consult De Groote 2003: 259–60 (although this passage is not discussed); for Oecumenius' dependence on Methodius here see Stevenson 2001: 487.

206   Suggit 2006: 139.

207   Cf. Wright 2006: 109–25. For Methodius' critique of Origen in *On the Resurrection* see Patterson 1997: 170–86.

Correspondences between Oecumenius' conception of the celestial bodies with Ptolemy's nuanced design (cf. *Almagest* 9.1), with both authors positioning the sun in the centre of the seven planets (*Commentary* 10.15.2), are equally striking, not least because such an arrangement differs from Plato's earlier influential account (*Timaeus*, 38D). The planetary order outlined by Ptolemy (*Almagest* 9.1) was, from lowest to highest: Moon, Mercury, Venus, Sun, Mars, Jupiter, Saturn, which positioned the sun at the centre of the seven planets.[208] Plato, by contrast, whilst only enumerating the order of the first four planets, had placed the Sun just above the Moon (Moon, Sun, Venus, Mercury) (*Timaeus*, 38D).[209] Oecumenius' simpler description of the central position of the sun – 'the sun is firmly fixed in the middle of the seven planets' (ὁ γὰρ ἥλιος ἐν μέσῳ τῶν ἑπτὰ πλανητῶν κατεστήρικται), with three above it and three below it' (10.15.2) – betrays no verbal echoes of Ptolemy's complex astronomical treatise, however, but instead has closer affinities with Philo (cf. *Heres.* 221–4), who placed the sun in central position, with reference to the image of the seven lamps of the Temple *menorah* as an image of the seven planets (cf. Irenaeus, *Dem.* 9).[210]

Accordingly, it is difficult to determine whether Oecumenius' philosophically informed cosmological insights derive from direct knowledge of Plato, Aristotle, and Ptolemy, or rather represent indirect knowledge mediated through patristic sources (notably Methodius of Olympus, *On the Resurrection*) or *doxographies*. On the basis of the available evidence, Oecumenius' educational attainment is consistent with a writer who received *at least* a προγύμνασματα level of tuition (supported by allusive references to Homer and Hesiod, coupled with technical exegetical analytical skills and prose compositional acumen), but whose philosophical studies of Plato's *Timaeus*, etc. may be more limited, perhaps mediated through secondary sources and summaries. The author's tertiary level tuition may perhaps have been concentrated on oratorical texts and techniques in preference to philosophical study.[211]

The contours of Oecumenius' cosmology, inferred from his *Commentary*, may be sketched as follows: Oecumenius' cosmological template is Homeric in design, founded on his close exegetical study of Homer and Hesiod under a grammarian and enriched by his wide reading of scriptural texts. This tripartite cosmos of heaven-earth-Hades (cf. *Commentary* 3.13.12; 4.15.2) is nuanced by further study and reading, perhaps principally of

208   Toomer 1984: 419–20.
209   Cf. Taub 1995: 105–9. Whilst Ptolemy was not the first to position the sun at the centre of the seven planets (cf. Pliny, *Natural History* 2.6; Cicero, *On Divination* 2.43, *Dream of Scipio*) his cosmological model was the most influential explication in antiquity.
210   Behr 1997: 42.
211   Such an interpretation is consistent with an author who studied law, ie. rhetoric, (perhaps in preference to philosophy). Consider the designation *scholasticus* applied to count Oecumenius by Severus, discussed above.

patristic authors, by means of which Oecumenius is cognizant of certain philosophical principles. The visible creation was fashioned by the Deity (δημιουργός) (3.3.4) out of the four primal elements (air, fire, earth, water, 3.9.3-4; 8.25.5), whilst the heavens, beyond the fixed stars, are comprised of *aither* (8.25.5). The seven planets are arranged in ascending order, with the sun in the central position (10.15.2), although there is no explicit reference to planetary spheres in this design.

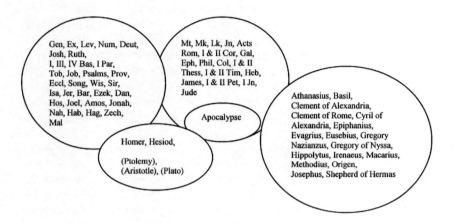

Fig 6.5. Oecumenius' Mental Library[212]

6.4.3 Oecumenius' Interpretative Method and Structural Organization of the Apocalypse

Oecumenius' exegetical method was informed by the tools of literary analysis that he had gained from his own grammatical education (γραμματική),[213] enriched and honed by his study of a range of patristic commentaries and treatises on scripture (notably by Eusebius, Hippolytus and Methodius).[214] Oecumenius, like Origen, paid close attention both to the 'literal', lexical meaning of a word or clause (πρὸς τὸ γράμμα) (cf.

212 Aristotle, Plato, and Ptolemy are placed in brackets as it cannot be verified that Oecumenius had read these sources directly.

213 For the appropriation of exegetical tools of literary analysis originally applied to classical poets, notably Homer, subsequently reapplied to scriptural texts by educated Jews and Christians, (e.g. Philo, Clement of Alexandria, Origen) see especially Young 1989; 1997: 76–96, 161–85; 2003.

214 Cf. De Groote 2003: 255–6 (Eusebius, particularly his *Chronicle*); 257–8 (Hippolytus, notably his *Commentary on Daniel* and treatment of the Antichrist, *On Christ and Antichrist*); 259–60 (Methodius, especially his discussion of the resurrection body in *De resurrectione*).

Commentary 5.11.3) as well as more figurative nuances (cf. *De Princ.* 4.2.4/Oecumenius, *Commentary* 1.15.2; 4.11.5; 5.9.3-4 (τροπικῶς)).[215] Inconsistencies, or disharmonies (ἀδύνατα) (cf. *De Princ.* 4.2.9), within and between passages of scripture at the lexical level were regarded as indicative of the interpretative significance of a 'figurative' or 'allegorical' sense. Where Oecumenius principally differed from Origen was not in the range of exegetical tools he used, nor in a preference for 'literal' over 'spiritual' interpretation, but rather in his preferred choice of *referent*. Where Origen sought the allegorical sense of (prophetic) scripture primarily in the realm of the soul and the heavens,[216] Oecumenius was more often concerned to discern a multivalent historical fulfilment of prophecy in the events of Christ's life, death and resurrection (cf. seven seals, *Commentary* 4.1–5.5) or the ongoing history of the people of God (cf. seven-headed beast, *Commentary* 9.12-15).[217]

Oecumenius divides his *Commentary* into twelve discourses (λόγοι), although these subdivisions appear to play a minimal role in the interpretative process.[218] On a number of occasions Oecumenius' comments on a particular vision are simply broken off at the end of one λόγος and resumed at the opening of the next section (e.g. the vision of the woman clothed with the sun (Rev 12:1ff, λόγοι 6-7); bowls one to three (λόγος 8), four to seven (λόγος 9)).[219] On one occasion (*Commentary* 6.1), Oecumenius indicates that the subdivisions aim at ease of reading, by breaking the material into proportionate sections.[220]

Of greater interpretative significance is Oecumenius' assessment of the nature of the Apocalypse and its prophetic content. The Apocalypse is a prophetic text that discloses 'mysteries' (μυστήρια) pertaining to the three periods of time: past, present, and future (*Commentary* 1.1.2, cited above). Central to Oecumenius' structural organization of his *Commentary* is his understanding that the Apocalypse is *not* primarily a sequential narrative, but rather it alternates between past, present, and future in its visionary sections.

---

215   Cf. Butterworth 1936; De Villiers 2007: 319–25; Suggit 2006: 9–14.

216   Cf. Weinrich 2011a: xxviii who is critical of Suggit for identifying Oecumenius' approach too closely with Origen in this regard.

217   In this sense Oecumenius' hermeneutical approach is often closer to Eusebius of Caesarea than Origen; cf. Hollerich 1992, 1999: 67–102; Young 1997: 120–22.

218   Contrast this with the slightly later *Commentary* of Andrew of Caesarea, and the theological conceit that underlies its structural arrangement: 'He [Andrew] divides Revelation into twenty-four books (βίβλοι) corresponding to the twenty-four elders. Each book is further divided into three chapters (κεφάλαια) corresponding to the threefold nature of a person, body, soul, and spirit. There are, therefore, seventy-two chapters in all' (Weinrich 2011a: xxxii).

219   It is possible that Oecumenius deliberately separates seals one to six and trumpets one to six from the climactic seventh item in each series (cf. λόγοι 2-3; 4-5), but if this is the case the logic breaks down in the case of the bowl cycle (bowls one to three, λόγος 8; bowls four to seven, λόγος 9).

220   Suggit 2006: 95.

The overarching temporal framework is set out in Oecumenius' innovative interpretation of the seven seals (Rev 6:1–8:1) as a sequential series of events in the life of Christ, stretching from his incarnation (seal 1) to the parousia (seal 7).[221]

> The successive removal of the seals...symbolizes the resumption, little by little of the openness and intimacy towards God that the Only-begotten by his incarnation made possible for us...the undoing of each seal denotes one of the works of the Lord effected for our salvation (ἰστέον δὲ ὅτι ἑκαότης σφραγῖδος λύσις ἕν τι τῶν ὑπὸ Κυρίου ἐνεργηθέτων εἰς ἡμετέραν σωτηρίαν)...
>
> (Oecumenius, *Commentary on the Apocalypse*, 4.7.1)[222]

The content of the seals, each resulting in a 'benefit' (εὐεργεσία) or 'mercy' (ἐλεημοσύνη) for humanity, is outlined as follows: 1. the physical birth of the Lord (4.7.3); 2. the temptation of the Lord and his conquering of the tempter (4.8.1); 3. Christ's saving teaching and the benefits effected through his divine miracles (4.10.1); 4. the 'blows' that Christ received (in his passion) (4.11.2); 5. the bonds and wounds that the Lord received at the hands of Pilate (4.13.1); 6. the cross of the Lord and his death followed by the resurrection and ascension (4.15.1); 7. the second coming of the Lord and the consequent gift of his benefits (5.5.4).

Having reached the eschatological pinnacle of the visionary narrative at the opening of the seventh seal (Rev 8:1), the bulk of the remaining chapters (Rev 8:2–22:21) are understood by Oecumenius to visualize events that will occur in the (imminent) future, that is between seals six (death/resurrection/ ascension of Christ) and seven (parousia), spanning the present age of tribulation until the final eschatological judgement (cf. *Commentary* 5.5.1-3).

Yet within these eschatologically orientated chapters (Rev 8–22), there are also significant temporal shifts, where the visionary narrative runs backwards to focus once again on the events of Christ's incarnation (Rev 12 woman clothed with the sun; Rev 20 millennium), or stretches back even further to the time before Christ's incarnation (the expulsion of Satan from heaven, Rev 12:7-12).[223] The major temporal blocks that Oecumenius envisages within the narrative may be set out as follows (fig. 6.6):

---

221 Weinrich 2011a: xxx.

222 Suggit 2006: 66; De Groote 1999: 120.

223 In addition, Oecumenius interprets the seven heads of Rev 17:9-14 as referring to events of the past: the seventh head is identified as Diocletian (284–305 CE), and the infamous, climactic period of Roman state prosecution of Christians during his reign, succeeded by the 'pious' Constantine (*Commentary* 9.13.1-6).

Past	Past (Seals 1–6)	Present → Future (Seals 6–7)
(pre-Incarnation)	(Incarnation, Life and Death of Christ)	(Eschatological Tribulations/Parousia)
	Seals 1–6 (Rev 6:1–7:17) Christ's life, death and resurrection (cf. *Commentary* 4.6-15)	Seal 7 (Rev 8:1) Christ's parousia (cf. *Commentary* 5.5.1-3) Trumpets 1 →7 (Rev 8:2–11:19)
Expulsion of Satan from heaven (Rev 12:7-12) (cf. *Commentary* 7.5.1)	Woman Clothed with the Sun and the Dragon (Rev 12:1-6) (cf. *Commentary* 6.19.1)	Antichrist (Rev 13) Bowl cycle 1–7 (Rev 15-16) Fall of Babylon/Rome (Rev 17–19)
	Millennial Kingdom Thousand years = 1 day (II Pet 3:8) = day of the Lord's Incarnation (Isa 49:8) (Rev 20) (Cf. *Commentary* 10.17.5-6)	New Jerusalem (Rev 21–22)

Fig. 6.6. Oecumenius' Structural Organization of the Apocalypse (Temporal Periods)

Within these shifting temporal sections, the trumpet cycle (Rev 8:2–11:19) constitutes a future-orientated series of judgements that will be directed against the *unrighteous*, occurring in-between the opening of the sixth seal (past: Christ's death/resurrection/ascension) and the seventh seal (future: Christ's parousia), after the saints have been removed from the earth:[224]

> The righteous (οἱ δίκαιοι) had been considered worthy of their share in blessedness, as I said at the end of the breaking of the sixth seal [Rev 7:9-17,

224 Cf. *Commentary* 4.15.2, 5.5.4.

Commentary 5.1.1-2], being caught up before the coming of the Lord 'in the clouds into the air' [I Thess 4:17] so that they might meet the Lord as he came, according to the testimony of the apostle which was there presented to me. The vision (ἡ ὀπτασία) then goes on to indicate the end of the rest of humankind (τῷ τέλει τῶν λοιπῶν ἀνθρώπων), and the punishment of sinners (καὶ τῇ τῶν ἁμαρτωλῶν κολάσει)...The same trumpets which bring about death for those on earth will also raise the dead after this.

(Oecumenius, *Commentary* 5.9.1-2 [= Rev 8:7])[225]

Accordingly, trumpets one to six recount the eschatological punishment of sinners in the tribulation that precedes the parousia, culminating in the second coming itself and the reward of the righteous at the blowing of the seventh trumpet (cf. *Commentary* 6.11.1). An 'aside' (παρέξοδος) occurs at Rev 11:3-13 in which the two witnesses (identified as Elijah and Enoch) in their role as precursors of the parousia of Christ are described (*Commentary* 6.11.1).[226]

6.4.4 Oecumenius' Interpretation of the Cosmology of Rev 9:1-21

This section focuses on Oecumenius' response to the cosmic-geography of Rev 9, specifically the text's positioning of 'the well of the abyss' (τὸ φρέαρ τῆς ἀβύσσου) (Rev 9:1-2) in a tripartite cosmos, and its plotting of the river Euphrates on a four-cornered mental-map (Rev 9:13-19; cf. 7:1-6). How did Oecumenius' modified mental-map, informed by his grammatical education, affect his interpretation of these topographical referents?

The Well of the Abyss (Rev 9:1-2; *Commentary* 5.16-21)
In view of the broad coherence between the mental map of Rev 9:1-2 and Oecumenius' own dominant Homeric cosmological template (heaven-earth-Hades (ᾅδης)) (cf. 3.13.12; 4.15.2), Oecumenius might be expected to identify 'the well of the abyss' (τὸ φρέαρ τῆς ἀβύσσου) with the subterranean abode of the dead, Hades (ᾅδης). Interestingly, however, Oecumenius avoids the term ᾅδης in this context, preferring instead to evoke the scripturally resonant designation, Gehenna:

He calls Gehenna *a shaft of a bottomless pit.*
(φρέαρ ἀβύσσου τὴν γέενναν καλεῖ)
That is why *there also came up from the shaft smoke* as of abundant fire, which was clearly lurking in the shaft.

(Oecumenius, *Commentary* 5.17.3)[227]

---

225   Suggit 2006: 84; De Groote 1999: 141.
226   Cf. Perry 2009: 29–30.
227   Suggit 2006: 87; de Groote 1999: 146.

Gehenna (γέεννα) occurs a dozen times in the NT, principally in the Synoptics (Mt 5:22, 29, 30; 10:28; 18:9; 23:15, 33; Mk 9:43, 45, 47; Lk 12:5; Ja 3:6), as a fiery locale of post-mortem punishment.[228] Oecumenius' choice of this term is influenced by two interrelated factors. First, his concern is to focus solely on the punishment of the *unrighteous* (non-baptised sinners, cf. *Commentary* 5.17.7-9), and accordingly he selects a designation for the underworld that refers solely to its function as a place of punishment, Gehenna (γέεννα), distinct from the more general term, Hades (ἅδης), which is indicative of the subterranean abode of the dead, both for righteous and unrighteous.[229] Secondly, Gehenna evokes images of 'fiery' punishment (cf. Mt 5:22, 18:9 'into the Gehenna of fire' (εἰς τὴν γέενναν τοῦ πυρός); Mk 9:43 'into Gehenna, into the inextinguishable fire' (εἰς τὴν γέενναν, εἰς τὸ πῦρ τὸ ἄσβεστον); cf. James 3:6) that resonate strongly with the description of the well-shaft in Rev 9:1-2.

As a consequence, Oecumenius considers that a temporal shift occurs at this point in the visionary narrative (trumpet five), projecting forward from the tribulations that precede the parousia, to the post-mortem judgement that succeeds it (trumpet seven):

> Up to now the vision was describing for us the way and the kind of plagues with which the [elements] of earth and heaven, and with them human beings, were being consummated or changed. But now as though the consummation has already come about (νῦν δέ γε, ὡς ἤδη τῆς συντλείας γεγενημένης) and the resurrection has been effected (καὶ τῆς ἀναστάσεως ἐνεργεθείσης), he describes the punishments accorded to sinners (τὰς κατὰ τῶν ἁμαρτωλῶν διηγεῖται κολάσεις).
>
> (Oecumenius, *Commentary*, 5.17.1)[230]

Oecumenius appears to recall the phrasing of Mk 9:47-48, with its injunction to tear out an eye rather than enter Gehenna (γέεννα), which concludes with an allusion to Isa 66:24 'Their worm shall not die, and their fire shall not be quenched', as he goes on to cite this same passage in his interpretation of the locusts (*Commentary* 5.17.5; 5.19.2). Given that the fifth trumpet has made a temporal shift forward to the post-parousia punishment of sinners, Oecumenius makes an interpretative link with the eternal biting pain of Isaiah's 'worm' (σκώληξ), which he

---

228 For the transformation of Gehenna (γέεννα), originally a Greek transliteration of 'valley of Hinnom' (גי־הנם) cf. Josh 15:8; 18:16, Neh 11:30), into an eschatological locale of punishment in Second Temple Jewish literature see Milikowsky 1988.

229 For this distinction between Hades and Gehenna in patristic authors, notably Origen, see Crouzel 1978.

230 Suggit 2006: 87; De Groote 1999: 145.

metaphorically interprets as 'the biting sting of the soul' (τὴν δῆξιν τῆς ψυχῆς) of those eternally punished (*Commentary* 5.17.5).[231]

The dominance of the scriptural components of Oecumenius' mental library in sketching the topography of the post-mortem place of punishment, Gehenna, in Rev 9, differs from Oecumenius' concern, elsewhere in his *Commentary*, to offer a more nuanced, philosophical perspective on post-mortem existence.[232] On other occasions the patristic components of Oecumenius' mental library exert a much stronger influence, notably Methodius' *On the Resurrection* 238.8-31, a philosophical dialogue, which aims, in part, to refute Origen's views on the resurrection body.[233] Oecumenius draws upon Methodius' attempt to defend the philosophical logic of bodily resurrection in Rev 20:13–21:2 (*Commentary* 11.10.1-9), by arguing that the reference to Death, Hades, and the sea giving up the dead in them, is a figurative description of the reconstitution of matter which has dispersed to its four, constituent, elements on death (Sea = water, Death = earth (cf. Ps 21:16 'dust of death'), Hades air and fire). 'So the resurrection takes place when each of the elements has rendered back all of the human composition they contained' (*Commentary* 11.10.9).[234]

Euphrates (Rev 9:13-16; *Commentary* 5.22-23)

As noted above, Oecumenius draws a sharp contrast between the events signalled by the opening of each of the six seals (Rev 6:1–7:17) and the events triggered by the first six trumpet-blasts (Rev 8:7–11:14). Whereas seals one to six refer back to *past* events in the life, death and resurrection/ascension of the incarnate Christ, trumpets one to six portray *future* eschatological plagues directed against the unrighteous. Accordingly, Oecumenius makes no direct connection between the four angels of Rev 7:1, located at the four corners of the earth (τέσσαρας ἀγγέλους ἑστῶ τας ἐπὶ τὰς τέσσαρας γωνίας τῆς γῆς), and the four angels bound at the river Euphrates (Rev 9:14) (λῦσον τοὺς τέσσαρας ἀγγέλους τοὺς δεδεμένους ἐπὶ τῷ ποταμῷ τῷ μεγάλῳ Εὐφράτῃ).

In his reading of the former passage, Oecumenius neatly side-steps the anachronistic four-point border map of Rev 7:1, interpreting it not as a reference to the οἰκουμένη, but rather limiting it to the political territory (γῆ) of Judea. In line with his reading of the sixth seal as a description of

---

231   Cf. 5.19.1-4 in which Oecumenius attempts to combine 'eternal' punishment with Origen's idea of the ἀποκατάστασις of all things, including sinners, whom Oecumenius describes as 'people deserving our sympathy' (ἀνθρώπων δὲ ὅμως συμπαθῶν) (5.17.8).

232   Oecumenius also makes a brief reference to the point on the tripartite earth at which the star (= angelic functionary) descends (Rev 9:1), namely 'the valley of Jehoshaphat' (Joel 3:2) – but without any further discussion of its geographical location (*Commentary* 5.17.2); cf. Crenshaw 1995; Wolff 1977.

233   Cf. De Groote 2003: 260; Bonwetsch 1917; Patterson 1997: 141–99.

234   Suggit 2006: 182.

the death/resurrection of Christ, and attendant circumstances, Rev 7:1ff is interpreted, historically, as the Jewish revolt against Rome (c.66-70 CE), which Oecumenius closely aligns with the cross:

> Here all that happened to the Jews in the war against the Romans (ἐν τῷ πρὸς ῾Ρωμαίους πολέμῳ) is clearly shown to the evangelist. These things happened to them because of the cross and their madness (παροινίας) against the Lord. The four angels controlling *the four corners* of *the land* of the Jews (τὰς τέσσαρας γωνίας τῆς Ἰουδαίων γῆς) were on guard lest any of the Jews deserving of death should escape...These are indicated figuratively (τροπικῶς) by their control of the four corners of Judea (τὰς τέσσαρας γωνίας τῆς Ἰουδαίας). The control of the four winds, that they should not blow *on earth or sea or against any tree*, indicates that the Jews found no relief in the war, nor any consolation for their disasters, whether they were fighting on foot on land, or fighting on ships at sea – for they fought many naval battles according to Josephus – ...
>
> (Oecumenius, *Commentary* 4.17.1-3 [= Rev 7:1-6])[235]

In the absence of any connection back to the four angels of Rev 7:1, and lacking any sense that the οἰκουμένη is depicted as a four-cornered square in the Apocalypse's mental-map, Oecumenius' interpretation of the river Euphrates in Rev 9:14ff is reconfigured on the basis of his interpretation of its angelic inhabitants.

Oecumenius begins by dismissing a surface-level interpretation of this passage, in view of its inconsistency with other scriptures that treat of this topic, notably Jude 6, II Peter 2:4 and Job 41:25. Oecumenius understands II Peter and Jude to describe how Satan and his rebel angels are in fact bound in the 'nether gloom' (ζόφος), not in the river Euphrates as suggested by Rev 9:14.

> Yet no one ever told us that they had been bound in the river Euphrates, or that they would ever be released, nor even that human beings were to be punished by them. For Jude, in saying that they had been bound 'with eternal chains', denied that they would ever be released.
>
> (Oecumenius, *Commentary on Revelation*, 5.23.7)[236]

Oecumenius continues by proposing his own preferred interpretation:

> I suspect that the words are figurative (τροπολογίαν), in line with the manner of the whole vision (πάσης ὀπτασίας). I think he means by the angels those who had been spiritually bound to the joyful contemplation of God (τοὺς ἀγγέλους τοὺς προσδεδεμένους τῇ τοῦ Θεοῦ νοητῶς εὐφραινούσῃ). For *the river* (ποταμός) is used allegorically (ἀλληγορεῖται) by Isaiah to refer

---

235 Suggit 2006: 76–7; De Groote 1999: 132.
236 Suggit 2006: 92.

to the divine (τὸ θεῖον): 'See, I am turning to them as a river (ποταμός) of peace, and as a torrent enveloping the glory of the nations.' [Isa 66:12]

(Oecumenius, *Commentary on Revelation*, 5.23.8)[237]

In this extract, Oecumenius' guiding exegetical principle is evident. The cogency of a non-figurative reading of a scriptural passage is first tested by its harmony with other scriptural passages that are understood to treat of the same topic. The concordance perceived between the other pertinent witnesses, here Jude and II Peter, is in discord with Rev 9:14, and thus a literal, lexical understanding of the latter is rejected. Once a figurative sense is detected (τροπολογίαν), Oecumenius feels entitled to make interpretative connections between passages even where only one word is in common (in this instance the word 'river' (ποταμός) shared with Isa 66:12). The minimal verbal resonance is unproblematic for Oecumenius, as it is ultimately his prior interpretative choice, namely that the river refers to the divine, which guides his selection of parallel passages (Isa 66:12, Ps 45:5 LXX, Jn 7:38) from the vast range of possible candidates contained in his mental library.[238] Unusually Oecumenius' selection is aligned with Origen's favoured choice of referent, as Oecumenius describes how the figurative sense of the passage refers to heavenly realities, namely the contemplation of God.[239] As a result, the river Euphrates is imaginatively transposed from the eastern limits of the οἰκουμένη, to visually ascend to the celestial realm, where it accords with the waters above the firmament as a visual evocation of the living God.

On the basis of Oecumenius' figurative interpretation of this passage, informed by a verbal parallel with Isa 66:12, he is able to invert completely the identification of the bound angels, as they might initially have been perceived:

He says, 'Release them from the contemplation of God (λύσας ἐκ τῆς τοῦ θεοῦ θεωρίας) and send them to punish the impious.' He means that these are those who have been appointed for the day of his presence (εἰς τὴν παρουσίαν ἡμέραν). But who does he say the four angels are? Perhaps they are those designated in the Scripture: Michael, Gabriel, Uriel and Raphael.

(Oecumenius, *Commentary on Revelation*, 5.23.9)[240]

---

237   Suggit 2006: 92–3; de Groote 1999: 152.

238   Compare Oecumenius' interpretation of the 'waters' (τὰ ὕδατα) and 'the rivers' (οἱ ποταμοί) of the third trumpet as a figurative (τροπικῶς) reference *not* to the divine, but to human beings (citing Ps 92:3-4 LXX) (*Commentary* 5.13.1-2); Suggit 2006: 85–6; De Groote 1999: 143–4.

239   Cf. Eusebius, who in his *Commentary on Isaiah* 66:12-13, interprets the 'river of peace' as the eternal peace that the nations will enjoy in the new Jerusalem, and similarly draws in Ps 45:5 with its supporting reference to the 'city of God' (ἡ πόλις τοῦ θεοῦ); cf. Hollerich 1999: 169–70.

240   Suggit 2006: 93; de Groote 1999: 152.

The four angels who are bound at the Euphrates are *not* to be identified with the rebel angels of Satan, as II Peter and Jude demonstrate that such figures are bound at a different location on Oecumenius' mental-map, namely the netherworld. Instead, on the basis of a single verbal parallel with Isa 66:12 (ποταμός), Oecumenius inverts the cosmological template, interpreting Rev 9:14 as a reference to angels whose bound duty is to *contemplate God* (θεωρία θεοῦ), that is, the four archangels, the angels of the presence, who are engaged in contemplation of the divine in the celestial realm. As a result, the river Euphrates is transposed to the celestial temple, affording a glimpse of the eternal peace (Isa 66:12) of the heavenly Jerusalem (cf. *Commentary* 12.7.3-4 on Rev 22:1-2).

6.4.5 Conclusion

Oecumenius' cognitive map of the cosmos is closely aligned with the contents of his mental library: a modified Homeric template comprised of four-elements, and ornamented by the seven planets in motion in the *aither*. Scriptural texts and patristic studies (notably Methodius, *On the Resurrection*) exert the greatest pressure on Oecumenius' cosmological world-view. The contents of Oecumenius' literary education play a supporting role, either as quiescent chorus in the scriptural choir that affirms a tripartite universe (Homer, Hesiod), or providing scientific rigour, as (indirect) knowledge of Platonic, Aristotelian, and Ptolemaic insights, are filtered through patristic sources.

Oecumenius' exegesis of the cosmic-geography of Rev 9 is similarly dominated by the major strands in his mental library: the prophetic voices of Isaiah, David (Psalms), the Evangelists, and Joel are combined to neatly position the imagistic mysteries within Oecumenius' existing cosmological template. The 'well of the abyss' (Rev 9:1-2) is equated with Gehenna, the shadow-side of Oecumenius' Hadean topography and exclusive site of punishment for the unrighteous – albeit recipients of Oecumenius' concerted sympathy and merciful ingenuity (cf. 5.17.8; 5.19.3). The Euphrates (Rev 9:13-14), figuratively (τροπικῶς) re-imagined, provides an image of the Divine, a locus of celestial contemplation, spatially translated from the perimeters of the οἰκουμένη to the heavenly temple, yet never breaking the boundaries of Oecumenius' existing cosmological template (heaven-earth-Hades (ἄδης)) (cf. 3.13.12; 4.15.2).

The principal impact of Oecumenius' literary education upon his cosmology is made by the tools of literary exegesis honed in his grammatical studies, which enable him to render the imagery of Rev 9 sufficiently malleable to re-shape it into his existing cosmological template.

6.5 Conclusion

The evidence gained from a close scrutiny of the earliest strata in the reception-history of Rev 9 broadly supports, yet also nuances, the validity of the principles that inform the hearer-construct models proposed in this study. The basic tenet of these models avers that the extent of an ancient hearer's *encyclical* studies will play a significant – but not a determinative – role in an ancient hearer's choice of preferred cosmological template, and thus his/her interpretation of cosmic-geographical referents.

Victorinus functions as a control-sample in this experiment, as there is little discernible evidence that he had received even a cursory level of *encyclical* education. Accordingly, his mental library was free of any direct influence from Homer, Hesiod, Aratus, or Plato, such that his cosmological template was almost wholly shaped by his knowledge of scriptural texts and patristic commentaries and studies. Accordingly, Victorinus' preferred cosmological model was a scripturally fashioned tripartite cosmos (heaven-earth-abyss/Hades), and whilst Rev 9 received only a brief treatment in his *Commentary*, it was apparent from his exegesis of Rev 11:4 that he identified the abyss with the netherworld of Hades. Despite Victorinus' 'control' function, his exegesis still affords some important insights, due to the subtle kink in his cosmological template, by which the heavens are extended by seven, spiritually designated tiers (Isa 11:2-3). Victorinus supports the caveat that the absence of an *encyclical* education does not necessarily entail that a subject adheres to a simple single-heaven, tripartite design (cf. II Cor 12:1ff; §3.2.3). Intriguingly, Victorinus also points to an area of research that merits continued careful scrutiny in tandem with the subject of this study: the extent of an early Christian exegete's *catechetical* education, supplemented by the use of scriptural texts as writing exercises, signalled in Victorinus' case by the marked influence that Irenaeus' *Demonstration of the Apostolic Preaching* had in reshaping his cosmological template.[241]

Oecumenius' adherence to a standard 'Homeric' template (heaven-earth-Hades/Gehenna) is initially more surprising. The recipient of a προγύμνασματα education, or perhaps even a full circle of oratorical studies if he is to be identified with the *scholasticus* of Isauria, yet Oecumenius' exegesis lacks any trace of the expected Platonic planetary spheres, or Aratean constellations. On closer inspection, however, the precise contents of his reconstructed mental library cohere quite precisely with the exegesis that results. As the recipient of a grammatical-level education, Oecumenius' preferred cosmological template coheres with his close exegetical study of Homer and Hesiod, and conforms with the dominant cosmological template in his scriptural sources. Despite Oecumenius' extended circuit around the perimeter of the *encyclical* circle, evidence of his direct study of philosophical

---

241   Cf. Römer 2003; Wilken 2004: 48–62.

authors is muted, perhaps filtered through patristic studies and *doxographies*, suggestive of an author whose rhetorical training exceeded his philosophical tuition. As a result, Oecumenius' cosmological exegesis represents a fusion of Homeric grounding with a philosophical veneer, perhaps most evocatively expressed in his allegorical reinterpretation of Sea, Death, and Hades (Rev 20:13ff) as the four elements, leaning on Methodius of Olympus. Oecumenius reminds an interpreter to closely scrutinize the contents of an ancient hearer's mental library: a direct correlation between preferred cosmological template and extent of *encyclical* education requires an attentiveness to the range of authors circumscribed by the circle, not merely a calculation of its circumference.

Tyconius is the most enigmatic and elusive of the commentators assessed. Although he is the recipient of a rich oratorical education, yet he never mentions any literary author by name and he barely breathes a word of the memorized verse of Virgil or Ovid, save for the odd enduring locution that drops, unbidden, from his tongue. The Homeric, Platonic, and Ptolemaic templates that were impressed upon his memory are refashioned in the light of Christ, and his body, the church. All spatial referents, heaven, earth, abyss; north or south; left or right, take their meaning from Christ and serve as *figurae* for his Head or Body. The wax-tablets of Tyconius' memory on which the φαντάσματα of the seven planetary spheres or the tripartite cosmos were impressed have become a *tabula rasa*, wholly effaced by his Christological/ecclesiological hermeneutic. Tyconius' originality precludes procrustean attempts to call upon him as a witness in support of the validity of this method. Tyconius represents the revaluation of ἐγκύκλιος παιδεία, the point at which, by a conscious choice, the direct correlation between educational attainment and preferred cosmological template is irrevocably snapped. Yet the significance of the exegetical tools that Tyconius attained remain, albeit in an altered form, transferred from the exegete to the author of scripture, the Spirit, who is deemed to utilize the compositional traits of *synecdoche* and *specie et genere* in his transcription of the heavenly mysteries.

Chapter 7

CONCLUSION

This chapter reflects on the results of the investigation by surveying some of the major findings, before indicating promising lines of further research that emerge from this study.

7.1 Principal Findings

The principal aim of this study was to consider the impact that variations in educational-level may have had on an ancient hearer's reception of the cosmology of the Apocalypse. More specifically, this study focused on the correlation between an individual's attainment in Greek literary education (ἐγκύκλιος παιδεία) and the extent of his/her cosmological knowledge. The initial investigation (Chapters 2–3) scrutinized the connection between *encyclical* education and cosmology, commencing with a careful survey of the progressive cycles of Greek *encyclical* education, on the basis of extant Graeco-Roman school-text papyri from Egypt and treatises by ancient educational theorists (Philo, Pseudo-Plutarch, Cicero, Quintilian). Particular attention was paid to the manner in which a Graeco-Roman student's cosmological knowledge increased as he progressed along this circle of learning, attentive to variations due to gender and ethnicity. Two notable boundary-markers were highlighted: the close literary study of Aratus' *Phaenomena* under a grammarian, which exposed the student to Greek constellational signs, and Plato's *Timaeus*, indicative of the student's tertiary-level engagement with a sophisticated seven-planetary spheres cosmological design. The evidence provided by the contents of ἐγκύκλιος παιδεία (Chapter 2), postulated a *direct correlation* between the extent of a student's literary education, and the breadth and depth of her cosmological knowledge.

This proposition was nuanced by a closer scrutiny of the diversity of cosmological models represented in Graeco-Roman literature (Chapter 3), with particular attention paid to three prominent cosmological templates: tripartite (single heaven, disc-earth, underworld); Platonic (geocentric universe with seven planetary spheres); and hybrid (tripartite cosmos with multiple heavenly tiers). These templates were scrutinized with reference to three test-cases (I Enoch 1–36, Philo, II Cor 12:1ff), each functioning as a representative example of a respective template. The direct correlation hypothesized between educational attainment and cosmological sophistication was corroborated by Philo, who privileged a Platonic cosmological template on the basis of his tertiary level education. Yet the subtle variations evident within and between test-cases, notably Paul's ascription to a hybrid cosmology (II Cor 12:1ff), highlighted the significance of non-literary sources in shaping an ancient hearer's cosmological worldview. Accordingly, on the basis of Chapters 2–3, the proposition was reformulated: the extent of an ancient student's Greek literary education (ἐγκύκλιος παιδεία) has a direct impact – although not a determinative one – on her choice of preferred cosmological template.

The significance of educational attainment as a variable, affecting an ancient hearer's reception of the cosmology of the Apocalypse, was then assessed with reference to a test-case passage (Rev 9). Rev 9 was chosen principally on the basis of its rich cosmological imagery: it depicts all three tiers of a tripartite cosmos (heaven-earth-abyss), contains a unique reference to 'the well of the abyss', and suggests an intriguing geo-political function for the Euphrates. The reception of this passage was analysed in two ways: i. two hypothetical hearer-construct models (*c.* 1st–2nd centuries CE), each with a differing level of *encyclical* education (Chapters 4–5); and ii. early evidence of the reception-history of this passage, provided by the *Commentaries* of Victorinus, Tyconius, and Oecumenius (3rd–6th centuries CE) (Chapter 6).

Hearer-construct one (HC1), the recipient of a minimal Greek *encyclical* education (Homer, *Iliad* I–II, extracts from Menander and Euripides), corroborated the close correlation proposed. The nominal expanse of her formal study of literary authors had little discernible impact upon her interpretation of Rev 9, which was predominantly shaped by evocative resonances of Joel's locust-cavalry, refracted through the prism of Ezekiel's 'northern' foe (Ezek 38–39, Amos 7:1 LXX) – affective φαντάσματα that are recalled from the verbal images impressed upon her mental library. The muted presence of Homer is discernible only as supporting cast, principally in its conformity to her dominant tripartite cosmological template.

Hearer-construct two (HC2), the recipient of a προγυμνάσματα education, further affirmed the direct correlation, but in subtler shades, as the contents of his richer *encyclical* education interacted with his scriptural knowledge. HC2's allegorical interpretation of Rev 9:7-9 as an ἔκφρασις, depicting a constellational composite of Λέων Παρθένος and Σκορπίος (cf. Aratus, *Phaenomena*) represented a plausible fusion of literary education with pre-existing interpretative traditions, that served to reposition the northern foe on the celestial firmament. Strikingly, HC2's interpretation of the cosmological imagery of Rev 9 is shaped by his *encyclical* education in two ways: the breadth of his cosmological knowledge (Aratus, Plato), and his choice of exegetical method (allegorical interpretation of an ἔκφρασις). The plausibility of such a hypothetical reading was validated by analogues in Philo's allegorical re-reading of the abyss as the non-material void (*De Opificio Mundi*), and extant 3rd-century CE evidence of a Christian grammarian's interplay between Aratus' *Phaenomena* and scripture, forging innovative Christian catasterisms (cf. 'Hippolytus', ἔλεγχός IV.46-50).

The evidence of the early reception-history of Rev 9 (Chapter 6) both confirmed and refined the correlation proposed between *encyclical* education and cosmological knowledge. Victorinus (3rd century CE), lacking appreciable evidence of formal Greek literary studies, functioned as a 'control' sample. His cosmology lacked any traces of Plato or Aratus, yet, like II Cor 12:1ff, he held to a 'hybrid' model that modified a basic Homeric template, with its extension of the heavenly vault by seven tiers. Victorinus' refinement highlights the significance of *non-literary sources*, in his case the catechetical tuition afforded by Irenaeus (*Demonstration of the Apostolic Preaching*). Oecumenius similarly corroborated the proposition by his close adherence to a Homeric template, nuanced by additional philosophical insights, consistent with a grammatical level education refined by further rhetorical, rather than philosophical, studies at tertiary level. Oecumenius emphasizes the importance of scrutinizing the precise contents of each student's *encyclical* education, in view of the gradations of study within each cycle. Tyconius, by contrast, demarcates the boundaries of this study: the close correlation between the extent of an ancient student's *encyclical* education and preferred cosmological template does not invariably hold – a subject may choose to *reject* his acquired expertise in favour of an alternative model, for ideological reasons. Yet the influence of *encyclical* education on cosmological reception is multifaceted, as it may affect not merely the range of cosmological sources to which a student has been exposed, but also her choice of *exegetical method* to interpret cosmological imagery (cf. Philo, HC2, Tyconius).

7.2 Further Research

In the course of this study three trajectories for further research have emerged that offer the potential to enhance and enrich the findings of the present monograph.

The first strand involves creatively opening-up the definition of 'education' to include non-literary sources of influence. This study chose to limit its range of enquiry in order to focus on one variable: the potential impact of ἐγκύκλιος παιδεία upon an ancient hearer's reception of cosmological imagery. This narrow definition of education is methodologically defensible, but also signals the potential to expand the scope of this project, in further research studies, to assess the significance of non-literary education, specifically early Christian catechetical education, including the use of scriptural (Septuagintal) texts as alternatives to the contents of ἐγκύκλιος παιδεία.[1] Support for such a development is signalled most strongly by Victorinus, whose hybrid cosmology was shaped by his knowledge of Irenaeus'

---

1   Consider the informative studies of Sandnes 2009 and Wilken 2004.

catechetical study, *Demonstration of the Apostolic Preaching*, to a much greater degree than any (potential) *encyclical* schooling.

The second strand concerns the use and refinement of 'hearer-construct models', as a valuable method to engage creatively with the earliest reception of the Apocalypse (and other scriptural texts). Close interplay between such interpretative models and the extant evidence of the earliest reception of the Apocalypse offers rich potential for a refined and nuanced (re-)construction of the diversity of responses to the Apocalypse in the earliest decades of its reception.[2] In this regard, the shadowy, fragmentary remains of 'Hippolytus'' Apocalypse studies merit renewed critical interest, given the recurrent traces of this author's (or authors') presence within the earliest sustained exegeses of Victorinus, Tyconius and Oecumenius.[3]

The third proposal is to scrutinize further the significance of memory and recollection as principally *visual* processes in Graeco-Roman antiquity, relating to the evocation of affective mental pictures (φαντάσματα) (cf. Aristotle, *On Memory and Recollection*, Quintilian, *Inst. Or.* VI.2.8, 20-36).[4] Greater appreciation of the role of verbal imagery (ἔκφρασις), in emotionally engaging an audience, may further enhance our understanding of the persuasive significance of vivid verbal imagery in the Apocalypse, and its power to move its audience to act. I leave the final word to Quintilian, on the affective force of vivid verbal imagery:

> It is a great virtue to express our subject clearly and in such a way that it seems to be actually seen (*videantur*). A speech does not adequately fulfil its purpose, or attain the total domination it should have, if it goes no further than the ears, and the judge feels that he is merely being told the story of the matters he has to decide, without their being brought out and displayed to his mind's eye (*non exprimi et oculis mentis ostendi*).
>
> (Quintilian, *Inst. Or.* VIII.3.62-3)[5]

---

2   This includes close scrutiny of the text's reception discernible in the variant readings of extant papyri and Majescule manuscripts, notably Sinaiticus and Alexandrinus (4th/5th century CE); cf. Hernández 2006; 2009.

3   Cf. Brent 1995: 144–184 on *Heads Against Gaius*; Cerrato 2002: 147–157, 221–235 on the *Antichrist* treatise; Prigent 1972; Prigent and Stehly 1973.

4   Cf. Carruthers 1998; 2008; Small 1997; Vasaly 1993; Yates 1966.

5   Russell 2001: 374–7.

BIBLIOGRAPHY

Achelis, Hans, (ed.) (1897) *Hippolyt's kleinere exegetische und homiletische Schriften* (Leipzig, Hinrichs) [GCS 1, 2]

Achtemeier, Paul J. (1990) '"Omne verbum sonat": The New Testament and the Oral Environment of Late Western Antiquity', *JBL 109*, pp.3–27

Adams, Edward (2007) *The Stars Will Fall From Heaven: 'Cosmic Catastrophe' in the New Testament and its World* [Library of New Testament Studies 347] (London and New York, T&T Clark, Continuum)

Adams, Edward (2008) 'Graeco-Roman and Ancient Jewish Cosmology', in Jonathan T. Pennington and Sean M. McDonough (eds), *Cosmology and New Testament Theology* [Library of New Testament Studies 355], (London and New York, T&T Clark, Continuum), pp.5–27

Ahlström, Gösta W. (1971) *Joel and the Temple Cult of Jerusalem* [Vetus Testamentum Sup 21] (Leiden, Brill)

Albinus, Lars (1998) 'The Katabasis of Er. Plato's Use of Myths, Exemplified by the Myth of Er', in Erik Nis Ostenfeld (ed.), *Essays on Plato's Republic* [ASMA II] (Aarhus, Aarhus University Press), pp.91–105

Alexander, Loveday (1992) 'Schools, Hellenistic', in David Noel Freedman (ed.), *The Anchor Bible Dictionary, Volume 5* (New York, Doubleday), pp.1005–11

Alexander, Loveday (1995) 'Narrative Maps: Reflections on the Toponymy of Acts', in M. Daniel Carroll R., David J. A. Clines and Philip R. Davies (eds), *The Bible in Human Society: Essays in Honour of John Rogerson* [JSOT Sup 200] (Sheffield, Sheffield Academic Press), pp.17–58

Alexander, Philip S. (1992) 'Geography and the Bible (Early Jewish)', *The Anchor Bible Dictionary, Volume 2*, (New York, Doubleday) pp.977–88

Alexander, Philip S. (1997) 'Jerusalem as the Omphalos of the World: On the History of a Geographical Concept', *Judaism 46*, pp.147–58.

Alexander, Philip (2006) *Mystical Texts* (London and New York, T&T Clark/Continuum) [LSTS 61]

Alföldy, Geza (1984) *Römische Sozialgeschichte* (Wiesbaden, Steiner)

Allison, Dale C. (1986) '4Q403 Fragm. 1, col. I, 38–46 and the Revelation to John', *RevQ 12*, pp.409–14

Amir, Y. (1988) 'Authority and Interpretation of Scripture in the Writings of Philo', in M. J. Mulder and H. Sysling (eds), *Mikra: Text, Translation, Reading and Interpretation of the Hebrew Bible in Ancient Judaism and Early Christianity* (Assen, van Gorcum/Philadelphia, Fortress), pp.421–53

Andersen, R. Dean (1999) *Ancient Rhetorical Theory and Paul* (Leuven, Peeters)

Andiñach, Pablo R. (1992) 'The Locusts in the Message of Joel', *VT* 62, pp.433–41

Arcari, Luca (2007) 'A Symbolic Transfiguration of a Historical Event: The Parthian Invasion in Josephus and the Parables of Enoch', in Gabriele Boccaccini (ed.), *Enoch and the Messiah Son of Man: Revisiting the Book of Parables* (Grand Rapids MI, Eerdmans), pp.450–68

Armstrong, Jonathan J. (2008) 'Victorinus of Pettau as the Author of the Canon Muratori', *VC* 62, pp.1–34

Arnott, W. G., ed. and trans. (1979, 1997, 2000) *Menander* (3 vols) (LCL) (Cambridge MA, Harvard)

Ascough, Richard S., (ed.) (2005) *Religious Rivalries and the Struggle for Success in Sardis and Smyrna* (Toronto, Wilfred Laurier Press)

Aune, David E. (1989) 'The Prophetic Circle of John of Patmos and the Exegesis of Revelation 22:16', *JSNT* 37, pp.103–16

Aune, David E. (1997) *Revelation 1–5* (WBC 52) (Dallas TX, Word Books)

Aune, David E. (1998a) *Revelation 6–16* (WBC 52B) (Nashville, TN, Thomas Nelson)

Aune, David E. (1998b) *Revelation 17–22* (WBC 52C) (Nashville, TN, Thomas Nelson)

Aune, David E. (1999) 'Qumran and the Book of Revelation', in Peter W. Flint and James C. VanderKam (eds), *The Dead Sea Scrolls after Fifty Years: A Comprehensive Assessment, Volume 2.* (Leiden, Brill)

Aune, David E. (2006) 'The Apocalypse of John and Palestinian Jewish Apocalyptic', in *Ibid.* (ed.), *Apocalypticism, Prophecy and Magic in Early Christianity: Collected Essays* [WUNT 199], (Tübingen, Mohr Siebeck), pp.150–74

Babcock, William (1982) 'Augustine and Tyconius: A Study in the Latin Appropriation of Paul', *SP* 17, pp.1209–15

Babcock, William S. (1989) *Tyconius: The Book of Rules* (Atlanta GA, Scholars Press)

Bagnall, Roger S. and Cribiore, Raffaella (2006) *Women's Letters from Ancient Egypt 300 BC–AD 800* (Ann Arbor, University of Michigan Press)

Bal, Mieke (1997) *Narratology: Introduction to the Theory of Narrative* [2nd edn] (Toronto, University of Toronto Press)

Balme, Maurice, ed. and trans. (2001) *Menander/ The Plays and Fragments* (Oxford, OUP)

Barclay, John M. G. (1996) *Jews in the Mediterranean Diaspora: From Alexander to Trajan (323 BCE–117 CE)* (Edinburgh, T&T Clark)

Barclay John M. G. (2007) *Flavius Josephus Translation and Commentary*, (ed.) Steve Mason, *Volume 10. Against Apion* (Leiden, Brill)

Bar-Ilan, Meir (1988) 'Writing In Ancient Israel and Early Judaism, Part Two: Scribes and Books in the Late Second Commonwealth and Rabbinic Period,' in Martin Jan Mulder (ed.), *Mikra: Text, Translation, Reading and Interpretation of the Hebrew Bible in Ancient Judaism and Early Christianity* (Assen, van Gorcum/Philadelphia, Fortress), pp.21–38

Bar-Ilan, Meir (1992) 'Illiteracy in the Land of Israel in the First Centuries CE', in S. Fishbane, S. Schoenfeld and A. Goldschlaeger (eds), *Essays in the Social Scientific Study of Judaism and Jewish Society*, II (New York: Ktav), pp.46–61

Barker, Margaret (1991) *The Gate of Heaven: The History and Symbolism of the Temple In Jerusalem* (London, SPCK)

Barker, Margaret (1998) 'Beyond the Veil of the Temple: The High Priestly Origin of the Apocalypses', http://www.margaretbarker.com/Papers/BeyondtheVeil.pdf (accessed 8/4/2010)

Barker, Margaret (2000) *The Revelation of Jesus Christ: Which God Gave Him to Show his Servants what must Soon Take Place* (London, T&T Clark)

Barr, David L. (1986) 'The Apocalypse of John as Oral Enactment', *Int 40*, pp.243–56

Barton, John (2001) *Joel and Obadiah* [OTL] (Louisville KY, WJK Press)

Bartsch, Shadi (1989) *Decoding the Ancient Novel: The Reader and the Role of Description in Heliodorus and Achilles Tatius* (Princeton, Princeton University Press)

Bartsch, Shadi and Elsner, Jaś, (eds) (2007) 'Special Issue on Ekphrasis', *CP 102*, pp. i–138

Bauckham, Richard (1993) *The Climax of Prophecy* (Edinburgh, T&T Clark)

Bautch, Kelley Coblentz (2003) *A Study of the Geography of I Enoch 17–19: 'No One Has Seen What I Have Seen'* [JSJ Sup. 81] (Leiden, Brill)

Beale, G. K. (1984) *The Use of Daniel in Jewish Apocalyptic Literature and the Revelation of St John* (Lanham MD, University Press of America)

Beale, G. K. (1997) 'Solecisms in the Apocalypse as Signals for the Presence of Old Testament Allusions: A Selective Analysis of Revelation 1–22', in Craig A. Evans and James A. Sanders (eds), *Early Christian Interpretation of the Scriptures of Israel: Investigations and Proposals* [JSNT Sup 148] (Sheffield, Sheffield Academic Press), pp.421–46

Beale, G. K. (1998) *John's Use of the Old Testament in Revelation* [JSNT Sup 166] (Sheffield, Sheffield Academic Press)

Beale, G. K. (1999) *The Book of Revelation* [NIGTC] (Grand Rapids MI, Eerdmans)

Beall, E. F. (2005/6) 'Hesiod's Treatise on Justice: "Works and Days 109–380"', *CJ 101*, pp.161–82

Beasley-Murray, G. R. (1993) *Jesus and the Last Days: The Interpretation of the Olivet Discourse* (Peabody MA, Hendrickson)

Beck, Roger (2004) *Beck on Mithraism. Collected Works with New Essays* (Aldershot, Ashgate)

Beck, Roger (2006a) *The Religion of the Mithras Cult in the Roman Empire – Mysteries of the Unconquered Sun* (Oxford, OUP)

Beck, Roger (2006b) 'On Becoming a Mithraist: New Evidence for the Propogation of the Mysteries', in Leif E. Vaage (ed.), *Religious Rivalries in the Early Roman Empire and the Rise of Christianity* (Waterloo Ont, Wilfred Laurier Press), pp.175–94

Becker, Andrew Sprague (1995) *The Shield of Achilles and the Poetics of Ekphrasis* (Lanham MD, Rowman and Littlefield)

Beckwith, Roger T. (1985) *The Old Testament Canon of the New Testament Church* (London, SPCK)

Behr, John, trans. (1997) *St Irenaeus of Lyon. On the Apostolic Preaching* (Crestwood NY, St Vladimir's Seminary Press)

Betz, Hans Dieter (1972) *Der Apostel Paulus und die sokratishe Tradition* (Tübingen, Mohr Siebeck)

Betz, Hans Dieter (1983) 'The Problem of Apocalyptic Genre in Greek and Hellenistic Literature: The Case of the Oracle of Trophonius', in David Hellholm (ed.), *Apocalypticism in the Mediterranean World and the Near East* (Tübingen, JCB Mohr), pp.577–59

Bietenhard, Hans (1951) *Die himmlische Welt im Urchristentum und Spätjudentum* [WUNT 2] (Tübingen, Mohr/Siebeck), pp.161–86

Bivar, A. D. H. (1983) 'The Political History of Iran under the Arsacids', in E. Yarshater (ed.), *The Cambridge History of Iran: Volume 3. The Seleucid, Parthian and Sasanid Periods* (Cambridge, CUP), pp.21–99

Black, Matthew, (ed.) (1970) *Apocalypsis Henochi Graece. Fragmenta Pseudepigraphorum Quae Supersunt Graeca* (Leiden, Brill)

Black, Matthew, VanderKam, James C. and Neugebauer, Otto, (eds) (1985) *The Book of Enoch or I Enoch: With Commentary and Textual Notes and an Appendix on the 'Astronomical' Chapters 72–82 by Otto Neugebauer* (Leiden, Brill)

Bloch, David (2007) *Aristotle on Memory and Recollection: Text, Translation, Interpretation and Reception in Western Scholarship* (Leiden, Brill)

Block, Daniel I. (1998) *The Book of Ezekiel Chapters 25–48* [NICOT] (Grand Rapids MI, Eerdmans)

Boccaccini, Gabriele, (ed.) (2007) *Enoch and the Messiah Son of Man: Revisiting the Book of Parables* (Grand Rapids MI, Eerdmans)

Bøe, Sverre (2001) *Gog and Magog. Ezekiel 38–39 as Pre-text for Revelation 19.17-21, 20.7-10* [WUNT 135] (Tübingen, Mohr Siebeck)

Boll, Franz J. (1914) *Aus der Offenbarung Johannis: Hellenistische Studien zum Weltbild der Apokalypse* (Berlin, Teubner)

Bonner, Stanley F. (1977) *Education in Antiquity: From the Elder Cato to the Younger Pliny* (London, Methuen & Co.)

Bonwetsch, G. N. (1917) *Methodius* (Leipzig, Hinrichs) [GCS 27]

Bonwetsch, Georg N., (ed.) (2000) *Hippolyt/Kommentar zu Daniel* (Berlin, Akademie Verlag)

Booth, Alan D. (1979) 'Elementary and Secondary Education in the Roman Empire', *Florilegium 3*, pp.1–20

Borgen, Peder (1993) 'Heavenly Ascent in Philo: An Examination of Selected Passages', in James H. Charlesworth and Craig A. Evans (eds), *The Pseudepigrapha and Early Biblical Interpretation* [JSP Sup 14] (Sheffield, Sheffield Academic Press), pp.246–68

Borgen, Peder (1984) 'Philo of Alexandria', in Michael Stone (ed.), *Jewish Writings of the Second Temple Period* (Assen van Gorcum/ Philadelphia, Fortress Press), pp.233–82

Borgen, Peder (1997) *Philo of Alexandria, An Exegete for His Time* [Novum Testamentum Sup. 86] (Leiden, Brill), pp.14–16

Borgen, Peder (2003) 'Philo of Alexandria as Exegete', in Alan J. Hauser and Duane F. Watson, *A History of Biblical Interpretation: Volume 1: The Ancient Period* (Grand Rapids MI, Eerdmans), pp.114–43

Borgen, Peder, Fuglseth, Kåre and Skarsten, Roald, (eds) (2000) *The Philo Index: A Complete Greek Word Index to the Writings of Philo of Alexandria* (Grand Rapids, MI, Eerdmans)

Bousset, Wilhelm (1901) 'Die Himmelsreise der Seele', *ARW 4*, pp. 136–69, 229–73

Bouteneff, Peter C. (2008) 'Recapitulation: The Second-Century Apologists', in *Ibid.*, *Beginnings. Ancient Christian Readings of Biblical Creation Narratives* (Grand Rapids MI, Baker Academic), pp.55–87

Boxall, Ian (2006) *The Revelation of Saint John* (London, A & C Black)

Bradshaw, Paul F. (2002) *Search for the Origins of Christian Worship: Sources and Methods for the Study of Early Liturgy* [2nd edn] (London/New York, SPCK/OUP)

Bréguet, Esther, ed. and trans. (1980) *La république/Cicéro* (Paris, Les belles lettres)

Brent, Allen (1995) *Hippolytus and the Roman Church in the Third Century: Communities in Tension Before the Emergence of a Monarch-Bishop* (Leiden, Brill) [VC Sup 31]

Briggs, Robert A. (1999) *Jewish Temple Imagery in the Book of Revelation* [Studies in Biblical Literature 10] (New York, Peter Lang)

Bright, Pamela (1988) *The Book of Rules of Tyconius: Its Purpose and Inner Logic* (Notre Dame In, University of Notre Dame Press)

Bright, Pamela (2010) 'Scripture, the Loom of the Spirit: Genre and Species in the *Book of Rules* of Tyconius at Carthage', in *SP 46*, pp.161–6

Brooks, E. W., ed. and trans. (1902–4) *The Sixth Book of the Select Letters of Severus, Patriarch of Antioch, in the Syriac Version of Athanasius of Nisibus* (London, Williams & Norgate) (2 vols)

Bruce, F. F. (1938) 'The Earliest Latin Commentary on the Apocalypse', *EvQ* 10, pp.352–66

Bruce, F. F. (1972) 'The Earliest Old Testament Interpretation', *OTS* 17, pp.37–52

Bucur, Bogdan G. (2006) 'The Other Clement of Alexandria: Cosmic Hierarchy and Interiorized Apocalyptisicm', *VC* 60, pp.251–68

Butterworth, G. W. (1936) *Origen: On First Principles* (London, SPCK)

Cameron, Averil and Hall, Stuart G. trans. and intro (1999) *Eusebius: Life of Constantine* (Oxford, Clarendon)

Campbell, Gordon (2004) 'Findings, Seals, Trumpets and Bowls: Variations Upon the Theme of Covenant Rupture and Restoration in the Book of Revelation', *WTJ* 66, pp.71–96

Caplan, Harry, ed. and trans. (1954) *Cicero / Ad C. Herennium* (Cambridge MA and London, Harvard) [LCL]

Carone, Gabriela Roxana (2005) *Plato's Cosmology and its Ethical Dimensions* (Cambridge, CUP)

Carruthers, Mary (1998) *The Craft of Thought: Meditation, Rhetoric and the Making of Images, 400–1200* (Cambridge, CUP)

Carruthers, Mary J. (2008) *The Book of Memory: A Study of Memory in Medieval Culture* (Cambridge, CUP) [2nd edn]

Castagno, Adele Monaci (1980) 'Il problema della datazione dei Commenti all' *Apocalisse* di Ecumenio e di Andrea di Caesarea', *Atti della Accademia della Scienze di Torino: II. Classe di Scienze Morali, Storiche e Filologiche* 114, pp.223–46

Cerrato, J. A. (2002) *Hippolytus Between East and West: The Commentaries and the Provenance of the Corpus* (Oxford, OUP)

Cerrato, J. A. (2009) 'Hippolytus and Cyril of Jerusalem on the Antichrist: When did an antichrist theology first emerge in early Christian baptismal catechesis?', in Robert J. Daly (ed.) *Apocalyptic Thought in Early Christianity* (Grand Rapids MI, Baker Academic), pp.154–59

Charles R. H. (1920a) *A Critical and Exegetical Commentary on the Revelation of St John* [ICC] *Volume 1* (Edinburgh, T&T Clark)

Charles R. H. (1920b) *A Critical and Exegetical Commentary on the Revelation of St John* [ICC] *Volume 2* (Edinburgh, T&T Clark)

Charlesworth, James H. and Newsom, Carol A., (eds) (1999) *The Dead Sea Scrolls: Hebrew, Aramaic and Greek Texts with English Translations, Volume 4B, Angelic Liturgy: Songs of the Sabbath Sacrifice* (Tübingen, Mohr Siebeck)

Chatman, Seymour (1978) *Story and Discourse: Narrative Structure in Fiction and Film* (Ithaca, Cornell University Press)

Chatman, Seymour (1990) *Coming to Terms: The Rhetoric of Narrative in Fiction and Film* (Ithaca and London, Cornell University Press)

Cheon, Samuel (1997) *The Exodus Story in the Wisdom of Solomon: A Study in Biblical Interpretation* [JSP Sup 23] (Sheffield, Sheffield Academic Press)

Chevalier, Jacques M. (1997) *A Postmodern Revelation: Signs of Astrology and the Apocalypse* (Toronto, University of Toronto Press)

Childs, Brevard S. (1959) 'The Enemy from the North and the Chaos Tradition', *JBL 78,* pp.187–98.

Chyutin, Michael (2006) *Architecture and Utopia in the Temple Era* [Library of Second Temple Studies 58] (London and New York, T&T Clark/Continuum)

Clarke, Katherine (1999) *Between Geography and History: Hellenistic Constructions of the Roman World* (Oxford, Clarendon)

Clay, Jenny Strauss (2003) *Hesiod's Cosmos* (Cambridge, CUP)

Cole, Susan G. (1981) 'Could Greek Women Read and Write?', in Helen P. Foley (ed.), *Reflections of Women in Antiquity* (Philadelphia, Gordon & Breach), pp.219–45

Collard, Christopher and Cropps, Martin, eds and trans. (2008) *Euripides: Fragments* [Vol. VII] (LCL) (Cambridge MA, Harvard)

Collins, John J. (1974) *The Sibylline Oracles of Egyptian Judaism* (Missoula MT, SBL)

Collins, John J. (1998) *The Apocalyptic Imagination: An Introduction to Jewish Apocalyptic Literature* [2nd edn] (Grand Rapids MI, Eerdmans)

Colson, F. H. (1916–17) 'Philo on Education', *JTS 18*, pp.151–62

Colson, F. H., ed. and trans. (1962) *Philo X. On the Embassy to Gaius;* General Indexes (J. W. Earp) [LCL] (Cambridge MA, Harvard)

Colson, F. H. and Whittaker, G. H. trans. (1929) *Philo I. On the Creation. Allegorical Interpretation of Genesis 2 and 3* [LCL] (Harvard, Loeb)

Condos, Theony (1997) *Star Myths of the Greeks and Romans: A Sourcebook* (Grand Rapids MI, Phanes Press)

Connolly, R. Hugh ed. and trans. (1929), *Didascalia Apostolorum: the Syriac version translated and accompanied by the Verona Latin fragments,* (Oxford, Clarendon)

Cornford, Francis Macdonald (1937) *Plato's Cosmology: The Timaeus of Plato translated with a running commentary* (London, Kegan Paul)

Crawford, Sidnie White (2000) *The Temple Scroll and Related Works* [Companion to the Qumran Scrolls 2] (Sheffield, Sheffield Academic Press)

Crenshaw, James L. (1995) *Joel: A New Translation with Introduction and Commentary* [AB 24C] (New York, Doubleday)

Crenshaw, James L. (1998) *Education in Ancient Israel: Across the Deadening Silence* [ABRL] (New York, Doubleday)

Cribiore, Raffaella (1996) *Writing, Teachers and Students in Graeco-Roman Egypt* (Atlanta GA, Scholars Press)

Cribiore, Raffaella (1999) Review of Teresa Morgan, *Literate Education in the Hellenistic and Roman Worlds* (Cambridge CUP, 1998):

BMCR 22.05.1999, http://bmcr.brynmawr.edu/1999/1999-05-22. html (accessed 17/07/2007)

Cribiore, Raffaella (2001) *Gymnastics of the Mind: Greek Education in Hellenistic and Roman Egypt* (Princeton, Princeton University Press)

Cribiore, Raffaella (2001a) 'The Grammarian's Choice: The Popularity of Euripides' *Phoenissae* in Hellenistic and Roman Education', in Yun Lee Too (ed.), *Education in Greek and Roman Antiquity*, (Leiden, Brill), pp.241–59

Cribiore, Raffaella (2001b) 'Windows on a Woman's World: Some Letters From Roman Egypt', in André Lardinois and Laura McClure (eds), *Making Silence Speak: Women's Voices in Greek Literature and Society* (Princeton, Princeton University Press), pp.223–39

Crouzel, Henri (1978) 'Hadìs et la géhenne selon Orìgene', *Gregorianum* 59, pp.291–331

Curry, Carl (1988) 'The Theogony of Theophilus', *VC 42*, pp.318–26

Cuvigny, Hélène (2004) 'Une sphère céleste antique en argent ciselé', *in Gedenkschrift Ulrike Horak*, Hrsg.: Hermann Harrauer; Rosario Pintaudi (Florence, Gonnelli)

Dahood, Mitchell (1968) *Psalms II. 51–100* [AB 17] (New York, Doubleday)

Daley, Brian E. (1991) *The Hope of the Early Church: A Handbook of Patristic Eschatology* (Cambridge, CUP)

Dalley, Stephanie (1989) *Myths from Mesopotamia: Creation, the Flood, Gilgamesh and Others* (Oxford, OUP)

Danby, Herbert (1933) *The Mishnah* (Oxford, Clarendon)

Davila, James R. (2000) *Liturgical Works* (Grand Rapids MI, Eerdmans)

De Groote, Marc (1996) 'Die Quaestio Oecumeniana', *SE 36*, pp.67–105

De Groote, Marc, (ed.) (1999) *Oecumenii. Commentarius in Apocalypsin* (Leuven, Peeters)

De Groote, Marc (2003) 'Die Literatur der Kirchenväter im Apokalypse-kommentar des Oecumenius', *ZAC 7*, pp.251–62

De Groote, Marc (2009) *Oecumenius/Verklaring van de Apocalyps* (Ghent, Academia Press)

De Jonge, H. J. (1975) 'The earliest traceable stage of the textual tradition of the Testaments of the Twelve Patriarchs', in M. de Jonge (ed.), *Studies on the Testaments of the Twelve Patriarchs* (Leiden, Brill), pp.63–86

De Jonge, Marinus and Tromp, Johannes (1997) *The Life of Adam and Eve and Related Literature* (Sheffield, Sheffield Academic Press)

DeSilva, David Arthur (1995) Review: 'Bruce J. Malina, *On the Genre and Message of Revelation: Star Visions and Sky Journeys* (Peabody MA, Hendrickson, 1995), *PRSt 23*, pp.91–5

De Villiers, Pieter G. R. (2007) 'History, Mysticism and Ethics in Oecumenius: A Hermeneutical Perspective on the Earliest Extant Commentary on Revelation', *SHE 33*, pp.315–36

De Villiers, Pieter G. R. (2009) 'The Understanding of Violence in Oecumenius' Greek Commentary on Revelation', *APB 20*, pp.232–45

Dewey, Joanna (1989) 'Oral Methods of Structuring Narrative in Mark', *Int 43*, pp.32–44

Diekamp, Franz (1901) 'Mittheilungen über den neuaufgefundenen Commentar des Oekumenius zur Apokalypse', *Sitzungsberichte der Königlich Preussischen Akademie der Wissenschaften zu Berlin*, pp.1046–56

Dieterich, Albrecht (1893) *Nekyia: Beiträge zur Erklärung der neuentdeckten Petrusapokalypse* (Leipzig, Teubner)

Diggle, James, ed. and trans. (2004) *Theophrastus: Characters* (New York, CUP)

Dijkstra, Jitse H. F. (2003) 'A World Full of the Word: The Biblical Learning of Dioscorus', in Alasdair A. MacDonald, Michael W. Twomey and Gerrit J. Reinink (eds), *Learned Antiquity: Scholarship and Society* (Leuven, Peeters), pp.135–46

Dillon, J. (1977) *The Middle Platonists: A Study of Platonism 80 BC to AD 220* (London, Duckworth)

Dines, Jennifer M. (1992) *The Septuagint of Amos: A Study in Interpretation* (unpublished thesis, University of London)

DiTommaso, Lorenzo (2007a) 'Apocalypses and Apocalypticism in Antiquity (Part 1)', *CBR 5.2*, pp.235–86

DiTommaso, Lorenzo (2007b) 'Apocalypses and Apocalypticism in Antiquity (Part 2)', *CBR 5.3*, pp.367–432

Dueck, Daniela, Lindsay, Hugh and Pothecary, Sarah, (eds) (2005) *Strabo's Cultural Geography: The Making of a Kolossourgia* (Cambridge, CUP)

Duff, Paul Brooks (2001) *Who Rides the Beast? Prophetic Rivalry and the Rhetoric of Crisis in the Churches of the Apocalypse* (Oxford, OUP)

Duke, D. (2006) 'Analysis of the Farnese Globe', *JHA 37*, pp.87–100

Dulaey, Martine (1986) 'L'Apocalypse: Augustin et Tyconius', in Anne-Marie La Bonnardiere (ed.), *Saint Augustin et la Bible* (Paris, Editions Beauchesne), pp.369–86

Dulaey, Martine (1989) 'La sixième Règle de Tyconius et son résumé dans le "De doctrina Christiana"', *REAug 35*, pp.83–103

Dulaey, Martine (1993) *Victorin de Poetovio: premier exégète latin* (Paris, Institut d'Études Augustiniennes) (2 vols)

Dulaey, Martine (1997) *Victorin de Poetovio. Sur l'Apocalypse et autres écrits* (Paris, Les Éditions du Cerf) [SC 423]

DuRousseau, Cliff (1984) 'The Commentary of Oecumenius on the Apocalypse of John: A Lost Chapter in the History of Interpretation', *BR 29*, pp.21–34

Eagleton, Terry (2008) *Literary Theory: An Introduction* (Minneapolis, University of Minnesota Press)

Ebner, Eliezer (1956) *Elementary Education in Ancient Israel During the Tanaaitic Period (10–220 CE)* (New York, Bloch)

Edmonds III, Radcliffe G. (2004) *Myths of the Underworld Journey: Plato, Aristophanes and the 'Orphic' Gold Tablets* (Cambridge, CUP)

Edwell, Peter M. (2008) *Between Rome and Persia: The Middle Euphrates, Mesopotamia and Palmyra under Roman Control* (New York, Routledge)

Ehrman, Bart D. (2003) *The Apostolic Fathers II.* [LCL] (Cambridge MA, Harvard)

Eldridge, Michael D. (2001) *Dying Adam with his Multiethnic Family: Understanding the Greek Life of Adam and Eve* (Leiden, Brill)

Elgvin, Torleif (2009) 'Priests on Earth as in Heaven: Jewish Light on the Book of Revelation', in Florentino García Martínez (ed.), *Echoes from the Caves: Qumran and the New Testament* (Leiden, Brill) [STDJ 85], pp.257–78

Elsner, Jaś (2002) 'Introduction: The Genres of Ekphrasis', in *Ibid.* (ed.), *Ramus Volume 31. The Verbal and the Visual: Cultures of Ekphrasis in Antiquity* (Bendigo Vic, Aureal Publications), pp.1–18

Eshel, Hanan and Eshel, Esther (2003) 'Separating Levi from Enoch: Response to "Enoch, Levi and Peter: Recipients of Revelation in Upper Galilee"', in Jacob Neusner and Alan J. Avery-Peck (eds), *George W. E. Nickelsburg in Perspective: An Ongoing Dialogue of Learning. Volume Two* [JSJ Sup 80] (Leiden, Brill), pp.395–408

Evans, James and Berggren, J. Lennart (2006) *Geminos' Introduction to the Phaenomena: A Translation and Study of a Hellenistic Survey of Astronomy* (Princeton, Princeton University Press)

Exum, J. Cheryl (2005) *Song of Songs. A Commentary* [OTL] (Louisville KY, WJK Press)

Farrer, Austin (1949) *A Rebirth of Images: The Making of St John's Apocalypse* (London, Dacre Press)

Farrer, Austin (1964) *The Revelation of St John the Divine: Commentary on the English Text* (Oxford, Clarendon)

Fekkes, Jan (1994) *Isaiah and Prophetic Traditions in the Book of Revelation: Visionary Antecedents and their Development* [JSNT SS 93] (Sheffield, JSOT Press)

Fekkes, Jan (2006) 'Isaiah and the Book of Revelation: John the Prophet as a Fourth Isaiah?', in Claire Matthews McGinnis and Patricia K. Tull (eds), *'As Those who are Taught': The Interpretation of Isaiah from the LXX to the SBL* [SBL Symposium 27] (Leiden, Brill), pp.125–43

Feld, Karl (2005) *Barbarische Bürger: die Isaurier und das Römische Reich* (Berlin, de Gruyter)

Feldman, Louis H. (1997) 'Josephus' *Jewish Antiquities* and Pseudo-Philo's *Biblical Antiquities*', in Louis H. Feldman and Gohei Hata (eds), *Josephus, The Bible and History* (Leiden, Brill), pp.59–80

Feldman, Louis H. (1998) *Josephus' Interpretation of the Bible* (Berkeley, University of California Press)

Feldman, Louis H. (2006) 'The Influence of the Greek Tragedians on Josephus', in *Ibid.*, *Judaism and Hellenism Reconsidered* (Leiden, Brill), pp.413–43

Ferrari, G. R. (ed.), Griffith, Tom, trans. (2000) *Plato, The Republic* [Cambridge Texts in the History of Political Thought] (Cambridge, CUP)

Fish, Stanley (1980) *Is There a Text in This Class? The Authority of Interpretative Communities* (Cambridge MA, Harvard)

Fitzgerald, John T. and White, L. Michael, trans. (1983) *The Tabula of Cebes* (Chico CA, Scholars Press)

Foster, Robert L. (2008) 'Reoriented to the Cosmos: Cosmology and Theology in Ephesians Through Philemon', in Jonathan T. Pennington and Sean M. McDonough (eds), *Cosmology and New Testament Theology* [Library of New Testament Studies 355] (London and New York, T&T Clark, Continuum), pp.107–24

Fowler, Richard (2007) 'Kingship and Banditry: The Parthian Empire and its Western Subjects', in Tessa Rajak (ed.), *Jewish Perspectives on Hellenistic Rulers* (Berkeley CA, University of California Press), pp.147–64

Fowler, Robert M. (2008) 'Reader-Response Criticism: Figuring Mark's Reader', in Janice Capel Anderson and Stephen D. Moore, *Mark and Method: New Approaches in Biblical Studies* [2nd edn] (Minneapolis, Fortress Press), pp.59–93

Fox, Michael V. (2000) *Proverbs 1–9* [AB 18A] (New York, Doubleday)

Fredriksen Landes, Paula (1982) 'Tyconius and the End of the World', *REAug 28*, pp.59–75

Fredriksen, Paula (1991) 'Apocalypse and Redemption: From John of Patmos to Augustine of Hippo', *VC 45*, pp.151–83

Fredriksen, Paula (1992) 'Tyconius and Augustine on the Apocalypse', in Richard K. Emmerson and Bernard McGinn (eds), *The Apocalypse in the Middle Ages* (Ithaca NY, Cornell University Press), pp.20–37

Frend, W. H. C. (1952) *The Donatist Church: A Movement of Protest in Roman North Africa* (Oxford, Clarendon Press)

Frend, W.H.C. (1981) 'Isauria: Severus of Antioch's Problem Child, 512–518', *TU 125*, pp.210–16

Friesen, Steven J. (2001) *Imperial Cults and the Apocalypse of John: Reading Revelation in the Ruins* (Oxford, OUP)

Friesen, Steven J. (2005) 'Satan's Throne, Imperial Cults and the Social Settings of Revelation', *JSNT 27*, pp.351–73

Furnish, Victor Paul (1984) *II Corinthians* [AB] (New York, Doubleday)

Galil, Gershon and Weinfeld, Moshe, (eds) (2000) *Studies in Historical Geography and Biblical Historiography: Presented to Zechariah Kalai* [VT Sup 81] (Leiden, Brill)

García Martínez, Florentino (1992) *Qumran and Apocalyptic. Studies on the Aramaic Texts from Qumran* [STDJ IX] (Leiden, Brill)

García Martínez, Florentino (1994) *The Dead Sea Scrolls Translated: The Dead Sea Scrolls in English* (Leiden, Brill)

Garrow, A. J. P. (1997) *Revelation* [New Testament Readings] (London and New York, Routledge)

Gerhardsson, Birger (1961) *Memory and Manuscript: Oral Tradition and Written Transmission in Rabbinic Judaism and Early Christianity* (Lund, Gleerup)

Giblin, Charles Homer (1994) 'Recapitulation and the Literary Coherence of John's Apocalypse', *CBQ 56*, pp.81–95

Giet, Stanislas, ed. and trans. (1950) *Basil / Homélies sur l'Hexaéméron* (Paris, Les Éditions du Cerf) [SC 26]

Gilfillan Upton, Bridget (2006) *Hearing Mark's Endings: Listening to Ancient Popular Texts through Speech Act Theory* [Biblical Interpretation Series 79] (Leiden, Brill)

Gilliard, Frank D. (1993) 'More Silent Reading in Antiquity: "*Non omne verbum sonabat*"', *JBL 112*, pp.689–94

Gillingham, Susan (1999) 'The Exodus Tradition and Israelite Psalmody', *SJT 52*, pp.19–46

Goodacre, Mark S. (1996) *Goulder and the Gospels: An Examination of a New Paradigm* [JSNT Sup 133] (Sheffield, Sheffield Academic Press)

Gooder, Paula (2006) *Only the Third Heaven? 2 Corinthians 12:1-10 and Heavenly Ascent* (New York/ London, Continuum/T&T Clark)

Gordis, Robert (1948) 'Homeric Books in Palestine', *JQR 38*, pp.359–68

Gould, Peter and White, Rodney (1986) *Mental Maps* (London, Allen & Unwin)

Goulder, Michael D. (1981) 'The Apocalypse as an Annual Cycle of Prophecies', *NTS 27*, pp.342–67

Goulder, Michael (1994) 'Vision and Knowledge', *JSNT 56*, pp.53–71

Grabbe, Lester L. (2003) 'Prophetic and Apocalyptic: Time for New Definitions – And New Thinking', in Lester L. Grabbe and Robert D. Haak (eds), *Knowing the End from the Beginning: The Prophetic, the Apocalyptic and their Relationships* [JSP Sup 46] (London and New York, T&T Clark/Continuum), pp.107–33

Grafton, Anthony and Williams, Megan (2006) *Christianity and the Transformation of the Book: Origen, Eusebius and the Library of Caesarea* (Cambridge MA and London, Belknap Press)

Grant, Robert M. (1949) 'Irenaeus and Hellenistic Culture', *HTR 42*, pp.41–51

Grant, Robert M., trans. (1970) *Theophilus of Antioch. Ad Autolycum* (Oxford, Clarendon Press)

Gray, Rebecca (1992) *Prophetic Figures in Late Second-Temple Judaism: The Evidence From Josephus* (Oxford, OUP)

Green, R. P. H. (1997) *Saint Augustine/On Christian Teaching* (Oxford, Oxford University Press)

Grelot, Pierre (1958) 'La géographie mythique d'Hénoch et ses sources Orientales', *RB 65*, 33–69

Gryson, Roger (1997) 'Fragments inédits du commentaire de Tyconius sur l'Apocalypse', *RBén 107*, pp.189–226

Gryson, Roger (2011a) *Tyconii Afri. Expositio Apocalypseos* (CCSL 107A) (Turnhout, Brepols)

Gryson, Roger (2011b) *Tyconius. Commentaire de l'Apocalypse* (Turnhout, Brepols)

Gumerlock, Francis X. (2008) 'Patristic Commentaries on Revelation', *K:JNWTS 23*, pp.3–13

Hahn, Traugott (1900) *Tyconius-Studien: ein Beitrag zur Kirchen- und Dogmengeschichte des 4. Jahrhunderts* (Leipzig, Dieterich)

Hahneman, Geoffrey (1992) *The Muratorian Fragment and the Development of the Canon* (Oxford, Clarendon Press)

Hahnemann, Geoffrey (2002) 'The Muratorian Fragment and the Origins of the New Testament Canon', in Lee Martin McDonald and James A. Sanders (eds), *The Canon Debate* (Peabody MA, Hendrickson), pp.405–15

Haines-Eitzen, Kim (1998) '"Girls Trained in Beautiful Writing": Female Scribes in Roman Antiquity and Early Christianity', *JECS 6*, pp.629–46

Hall, R. G. (1990) 'Living Creatures in the Midst of the Throne: Another Look at Revelation 4:6', *NTS 36*, pp.609–13

Halliwell, Stephen, ed. and trans. (1995) *Aristotle, Poetics* (LCL) (Cambridge MA, Harvard)

Halliwell, Stephen (2007) 'The Life-and-Death Journey of the Soul: Interpreting the Myth of Er', in G. R. F. Ferrari (ed.), *The Cambridge Companion to Plato's Republic* (Cambridge, CUP), pp.445–73

Halperin, David (1988) *The Faces of the Chariot: Early Jewish Responses to Ezekiel's Vision* [TSAJ 16] (Tübingen, Mohr/Siebeck)

Halton, Thomas P., trans. (1999) *St Jerome. On Illustrious Men* (Washington DC, Catholic University of America Press) [FOTC 100]

Hamilton, Alastair (1999) *The Apocryphal Apocalypse: The Reception of the Second Book of Esdras (4 Ezra) from the Renaissance to the Enlightenment* (Oxford, Clarendon)

Harley, J. B. and Woodward, David, (eds) (1987) *The History of Cartography. Volume 1. Cartography in Prehistoric, Ancient and Medieval Europe and the Mediterranean* (Chicago, University of Chicago Press)

Harlow, Daniel C. (1996) *The Greek Apocalypse of Baruch (3 Baruch) In Hellenistic Judaism and Christianity* (Leiden, Brill)

Harris, William V. (1989) *Ancient Literacy* (Cambridge MA, Harvard)

Harvey, Paul B. (1999) 'Approaching the Apocalypse: Augustine, Tyconius and John's Revelation', in Mark Vessey, Karla Pollmann and Allan D. Fitzgerald (eds), *History, Apocalypse and the Secular Imagination: New Essays on Augustine's City of God* (Bowling Green OH, Bowling Green State University), pp.133–51

Havelock, Eric A. (1984) 'Oral Composition in the *Oedipus Tyrannus* of Sophocles', *NLH* 16, pp.175–97

Hawley, Richard (1994) 'The Problem of Women Philosophers in Ancient Greece', in Leonie Archer (ed.), *Women in Ancient Societies: An Illusion of the Night* (Basingstoke, Macmillan), pp.70–87

Hays, Richard B. (1989) *Echoes of Scripture in the Letters of Paul* (New Haven and London, Yale University Press)

Hegedus, Tim (2005) 'Some Astrological Motifs in the Book of Revelation', in Richard S. Ascough (ed.), *Religious Rivalries and the Struggle for Success in Sardis and Smyrna* [ESCR 14] (Waterloo Ont., Wilfred Laurier Press), pp.67–85

Hegedus, Tim (2007) *Early Christianity and Ancient Astrology* [Patristic Studies 6] (New York, Peter Lang)

Heine, Ronald E. (2004) 'Hippolytus, Ps.-Hippolytus and the Early Canons', in Frances Young, Lewis Ayres and Andrew Louth (eds) *The Cambridge History of Early Christian Literature* (Cambridge, CUP), pp. 142–151

Hemelrijk, Emily A. (1999) *Matrona Docta: Educated Women in the Roman Élite From Cornelia to Julia Domna* (London and New York, Routledge)

Hemer, Colin J. (1986) *The Letters to the Seven Churches in their Local Setting* [JSNT Sup 11] (Sheffield, JSOT Press)

Hengel, Martin (1974) *Judaism and Hellenism. Studies in their Encounter in Palestine during the Early Hellenistic Period* (London, SCM) (2 vols)

Hernández, Juan, Jr. (2006) *Scribal Habits and Theological Influences in the Apocalypse: The Singular Readings of Sinaiticus, Alexandrinus and Ephraemi* [WUNT 218] (Tübingen, Mohr Siebeck)

Hernández, Juan, Jr. (2009) 'Codex Sinaiticus: The Earliest Greek Commentary on John's Apocalypse?' Unpublished Conference Paper: *Codex Sinaiticus: Text, Bible, Book*: British Library, London, 7 July 2009

Hett, W. S., ed. and trans. (1935) *Aristotle/On the Soul, Parva Naturalia, On Breath* (Cambridge MA and London, Harvard) [LCL]

Hezser, Catherine (2001) *Jewish Literacy in Roman Palestine* [TSAJ 81] (Tübingen, Mohr Siebeck)

Hill, Charles E. (2001) *Regnum Caelorum: Patterns of Future Hope in Early Christianity* (Grand Rapids MI, Eerdmans) [2nd edn]

Himmelfarb, Martha (1983) *Tours of Hell: An Apocalyptic Form in Jewish and Christian Literature* (Philadelphia, University of Pennsylvania Press)

Himmelfarb, Martha (1987) 'Apocalyptic Ascent and the Heavenly Temple', *Society of Biblical Literature 1987 Seminar Papers*: (SBLSP 26) (Atlanta GA, Scholars Press), pp.210–17

Himmelfarb, Martha (1991) 'The Temple and the Garden of Eden in Ezekiel, the Book of the Watchers, and the Wisdom of Ben Sira', in Jamie Scott and Paul Simpson-Housley (eds), *Sacred Places and*

Profane Spaces: Essays in the Geographics of Judaism, Christianity, and Islam (New York: Greenwood Press), pp.63–78

Himmelfarb, Martha (1993) *Ascent to Heaven in Jewish and Christian Apocalypses* (New York, OUP)

Hock, Ronald F. (2001) 'Homer in Greco-Roman Education', in Dennis R. McDonald (ed.), *Mimesis and Intertextuality in Antiquity and Christianity* (Harrisburg, Trinity Press International, 2001), pp.56–77

Hock, Ronald F. (2003) 'Paul and Greco-Roman Education', in J. Paul Sampley (ed.), *Paul in the Greco-Roman World: A Handbook* (London & New York, TPI/Continuum), pp.198–227

Hock, Ronald F. (2005) 'The Educational Curriculum in Chariton's *Callirhoe*', in Jo-Ann Brant, Charles W. Hedrick, and Chris Shea (eds), *Ancient Fiction: The Matrix of Early Christianity and Jewish Narrative* [Symposium Series 32] (Atlanta GA, SBL), pp.15–36

Hollander, H. W. and De Jonge, Marinus (1985) *The Testament of the Twelve Patriarchs: A Commentary* (Leiden, Brill)

Hollerich, Michael J. (1992) 'Eusebius as a Polemical Interpreter of Scripture', in H. W. Attridge and G. Hata (eds), *Eusebius, Christianity and Judaism* (Leiden, Brill), pp.585–615

Hollerich, M. J. (1999) *Eusebius of Caesarea's Commentary on Isaiah* (Oxford, Clarendon)

Horowitz, Wayne (1998) *Mesopotamian Cosmic Geography* (Winona Lake IN, Eisenbrauns)

Horsley, G. H. R. (1989) 'The Fiction of Jewish Greek', in *Ibid.*, *New Documents Illustrating Early Christianity*, [vol. V] (Sydney, Macquarrie University), pp.5–40

Horsley, Richard A. (2007) *Scribes, Visionaries and the Politics of Second Temple Judea* (Louisville KY, WJK Press)

Hort, A. F., ed. and trans. (1916) *Theophrastus II., Enquiry into Plants, Books 6–9: Treatise on Odours, Concerning Weather Signs* [LCL] (Cambridge MA, Harvard)

Houtman, Cornelis (1993) *Der Himmel im Alten Testament. Israels Weltbild und Weltanschauung* (Leiden, Brill)

Howell Chapman, Honora (2005) 'By the Waters of Babylon: Josephus and Greek Poetry', in Joseph Sievers and Gaia Lembi (eds), *Josephus and Jewish History in Flavian Rome and Beyond* [JSJ Sup 104] (Leiden, Brill), pp.121–46

Hughes, Kevin L. (2005) *Constructing Antichrist: Paul, Biblical Commentary, and the Development of Doctrine in the Early Middle Ages* (Washington DC, Catholic University of America Press)

Humphrey, J. H. (1991) *Literacy in the Ancient World* (Ann Arbor MI, University of Michigan)

Husser, Jean-Marie (1999) *Dreams and Dream-Narratives in the Biblical World* (Sheffield, Sheffield Academic Press)

Iser, Wolfgang (1974) *The Implied Reader: Patterns of Communication in Prose Fiction from Bunyan to Beckett* (Baltimore and London, Johns Hopkins University Press)

Jastrow, M. (1926) *A Dictionary of the Targumim, the Talmud Babli and Yerushalmi and the Midrashic Literature* (New York/Berlin, Verlag Choreb)

Jauhiainen, Marko (2003) 'Recapitulation and Chronological Progression in John's Apocalypse: Towards a New Perspective', *NTS* 49, pp.543–59

Jauhiainen, Marko (2005) *The Use of Zechariah in Revelation* [WUNT 199] (Tübingen, Mohr Siebeck)

Jeffers, Ann (2007) '"Nor by Dreams, nor by Urim, nor by Prophets": The Story of the Woman at the Pit in I Samuel 28', in Patrick Curry and Angela Voss (eds), *Seeing with Different Eyes: Essays in Astrology and Divination* (Newcastle, Cambridge Scholars Publishing), pp.129–40

Jenson, Philip Peter (1992) *Graded Holiness: A Key to the Priestly Conception of the World* [JSOT Sup 106] (Sheffield, Sheffield Academic Press)

Jeremias, Joachim 'ἄβυσσος', *TDNT I*, p.9

Jeremias, Joachim 'ᾅδης', *TDNT I*, pp.146–9

Johns, Loren L. (2003) *The Lamb Christology of the Apocalypse of John: An Investigation into its Origins and Rhetorical Force* (Tübingen, Mohr Siebeck) [WUNT 167]

Jones, Alexander (2003) 'The Stoics and the Astronomical Sciences', in Brad Inwood (ed.), *The Cambridge Companion to the Stoics* (Cambridge, CUP), pp.328–44

Jones, W. H. S., ed. and trans. (1935) *Pausanius, Description of Greece IV* (Books VIII.22–X) [LCL] (Cambridge MA, Harvard)

Kaizer, Ted, (ed.) (2008) *The Variety of Local Religious Life in the Near East* [Religions in the Graeco-Roman World 164] (Leiden, Brill)

Kannengiesser, Charles (1999) 'Augustine and Tyconius: A Conflict of Christian Hermeneutics in Roman Africa', in Pamela Bright (ed.), *Augustine and the Bible* (Notre Dame IN, University of Notre Dame Press), pp.149–77

Kannengiesser, Charles (2002) 'Tyconius of Carthage, the earliest Latin theoretician of biblical hermeneutics: the current debate', in Mario Maritano (ed.), *Historiam perscrutari* (Roma, Editrice LAS), pp.297–311

Kannengiesser, Charles (2006) *Handbook of Patristic Exegesis: The Bible in Ancient Christianity* (Leiden, Brill)

Kavanagh, Michael A. (1984) *Apocalypse 22:6-21 as Concluding Liturgical Dialogue* (Rome, Pontifical Gregorian University)

Keel, Othmar, trans. Timothy J. Hallett (1978) *The Symbolism of the Biblical World: Ancient Near Eastern Iconography and the Book of Psalms* (London, SPCK)

Kennedy, George A. (1994) *A New History of Classical Rhetoric* (Princeton, Princeton University Press)

Kennedy George A., trans. (2003) *Progymnasmata: Greek Textbooks of Prose Composition and Rhetoric* (Atlanta GA, SBL)

Kennedy, George A., intro., notes and trans. (2007) *On Rhetoric: A Theory of Civic Discourse/ Aristotle* (Oxford, OUP)

Kern, Philip H. (1998) *Rhetoric and Galatians: Assessing an Approach to Paul's Epistles* (Cambridge, CUP)

Keyes, Clinton W., ed. and trans. (1928) *Cicero XVI. Philosophical Treatises. On the Republic. On the Laws* [LCL] (Cambridge MA, Harvard)

Kidd, Douglas, ed., intro., trans. and commentary (1997) *Aratus: Phaenomena* (Cambridge, CUP)

Kirk, G. S. (1985) *The Iliad: A Commentary. Volume I: Books 1–4* (Cambridge, CUP)

Kirk, G. S., Raven, J. E. and Schofield, M. (1983) *The Presocratic Philosophers: A Critical History with a Selection of Texts* [2nd edn] (Cambridge, CUP)

Klauck, Hans-Josef (2001) 'Do they Never Come Back?: Nero *Redivivus* and the Apocalypse of John', *CBQ 63*, pp.683–98

Knight, Jonathan (1999) *Revelation* [Readings] (Sheffield, Sheffield Academic Press)

Köstenberger, Andreas (2006) 'The Use of Scripture in the Pastoral and General Epistles and the Book of Revelation' in Stanley E. Porter (ed.), *Hearing the Old Testament in the New Testament* (Grand Rapids MI, Eerdmans), pp.230–54

Kovacs, David, ed. and trans. (1994–2003) *Euripides* (6 vols) [LCL] (Cambridge MA, Harvard)

Kovacs, Judith and Rowland, Christopher (2004) *Revelation* [Blackwell Bible Commentaries] (Oxford, Blackwell)

Kowalski, Beate (2004) *Die Rezeption des Propheten Ezechiel in der Offenbarung des Johannes* (Stuttgart, Katholisches Bibelwerk)

Kraus, Hans Joachim, trans. Hilton C. Oswald (1989) *Psalms 60–150. A Commentary* (Minneapolis, Fortress Press)

Kreitzer, L. Joseph (1988) 'Hadrian and the Nero *Redivivus* Myth', *ZNW* 79, pp.92–115

Kretschmar, Georg (1985) *Die Offenbarung des Johannes: Die Geschichte ihrer Auslegung im 1. Jahrtausend* (Calwer Theologische Monographien, B9. Stuttgart: Calwer Verlag)

Kugler, Robert A. (1999) 'Tyconius' Mystic Rules and the Rules of Augustine', in Pamela Bright (ed.), *Augustine and the Bible* (Notre Dame IN, University of Notre Dame Press), pp.129–48

Künzl, Ernst (2000) 'Ein römischer Himmelsglobus der mittleren Kaiserzeit. Studien zur römischen Astralikonographie', in *Jahrbuch des Römisch-Germanischen Zentralmuseum* 47.2, pp.495–594

Künzl, Ernst (2005) *Himmelsgloben und Sternkarten. Astronomie und Astrologie in Vorzeit und Allertum* (Stuttgart, Theiss)

Lake, Kirsopp, trans. (1926) *Eusebius / Ecclesiastical History Books I–IV* (Cambridge MA, Harvard) [LCL]

Lallot, Jean, trans. (1998) *La Grammair de Denys le Thrace* [2nd rev. edn] (Paris, CNRS)

Lambert, W. G. (2008) 'Mesopotamian Creation Stories', in Markham J. Geller and Mineke Schipper (eds), *Imagining Creation* (Leiden, Brill), pp.15–59

Lamberton, Robert (1986) *Homer the Theologian: Neoplatonist Allegorical Reading and the Growth of the Epic Tradition* (Berkeley, University of California Press)

Lambrecht, Jan (1980) 'A Structuration of Revelation 4, 1–22, 5', in Jan Lambrecht (ed.), *L'Apocalypse johannique et l'Apocalyptique dans le Nouveau Testament* [BETL LIII] (Leuven, Leuven University Press), pp.77–104

Lamoreaux, John C. (1998) 'The Provenance of Ecumenius' Commentary on the Apocalypse', *VC 52*, pp.88–108

Law, Vivien and Sluiter, Ineke, (eds) (1995) *Dionysius Thrax and the Techne Grammatike* (Münster, Nodus Publikationen)

Lawrence, John M. (1978) 'Nero Redivivus', *Fides et Hist. 11*, pp.54–66

Lee, Archie C. C. (1990) 'The Context and Function of the Plagues Tradition in Psalm 78', *JSOT 48*, pp.83–9

Leiman, Sid Z. (1989) 'Josephus and the Canon of the Bible', in Louis H. Feldman and Gohei Hata (eds), *Josephus, the Bible and History* (Leiden, Brill), pp.50–58

Lieu, Judith (2006) 'Letters', in J. W. Rogerson & Judith M. Lieu (eds), *The Oxford Handbook of Biblical Studies* (Oxford, OUP), pp.445–58

Linton, Gregory L. (2006) 'Reading the Apocalypse as Apocalypse: The Limits of Genre', in David L. Barr (ed.), *The Reality of Apocalypse: Rhetoric and Politics in the Book of Revelation* (Atlanta GA, Scholars Press), pp.9–42

Lo Bue, Francesco (1963) *The Turin Fragments of Tyconius' Commentary on Revelation* (Cambridge, Cambridge University Press)

Longenecker, Bruce W. (1995) *2 Esdras* [GAP] (Sheffield, Sheffield Academic Press)

Lössl, Josef (2004) 'When is a Locust Just a Locust? Patristic Exegesis of Joel 1:4 in the Light of Ancient Literary Theory', *JTS 55*, pp.575–99

Ludlow, Jared W. (2002) *Abraham Meets Death: Narrative Humor in the Testament of Abraham* [JSP Sup 41] (London, Sheffield Academic Press/Continuum)

Luijendijk, AnneMarie (2010) 'A New Testament Papyrus and its Documentary Context: An Early Christian Writing Exercise from the Archive of Leonides (P.Oxy. II 209/$\mathcal{P}^{10}$)', *JBL 129*, pp.575–96

Lumsden, Douglas W. (2001) *And then the End will Come: Early Latin Christian Interpretations of the Opening of the Seven Seals* (London, Garland)

Macaskill, Grant (2007) *Revealed Wisdom and Inaugurated Eschatology in Ancient Judaism and Early Christianity* [JSJ Sup 115] (Leiden, Brill)

MacDonald, Dennis R. (2000) *The Homeric Epics and the Gospel of Mark* (New Haven and London, Yale University Press)

MacKenzie, Iain (2002) *Irenaeus' Demonstration of the Apostolic Preaching: A Theological Commentary and Translation* (Aldershot, Ashgate)

MacMahon, J. H. (1995) 'The Refutation of all Heresies', in Alexander Roberts and James Donaldson (eds), *The Ante-Nicene Fathers, Volume 5*, pp.9–162 (Edinburgh, T&T Clark, 1995) [repr.]

McDonald, Lee and Sanders, James A., (eds) (2002) *The Canon Debate* (Peabody MA, Hendrickson)

McDonough, Sean M. (2008) 'Revelation: The Climax of Cosmology', in Jonathan T. Pennington and Sean M. McDonough (eds), *Cosmology and New Testament Theology* [Library of New Testament Studies 355] (London and New York, T&T Clark/Continuum), pp.178–88

McGinn, Bernard (2009) 'Turning Points in Early Christian Apocalypse Exegesis', in Robert J. Daly (ed.), *Apocalyptic Thought in Early Christianity* (Grand Rapids MI, Eerdmans), pp.81–105

Maier, Johann (1985) *The Temple Scroll: An Introduction, Translation and Commentary* [JSOT Sup 34] (Sheffield, Sheffield Academic Press)

Mair, G. R., ed. and trans. (1921) *Callimachus, Lycophron, Aratus* [LCL] (Cambridge MA, Harvard)

Malina, Bruce J. (1995) *On the Genre and Message of Revelation: Star Visions and Sky Journeys* (Peabody MA, Hendrickson)

Malina, Bruce J. and Pilch, John J. (2000) *Social-Science Commentary on the Book of Revelation* (Minneapolis, Fortress Press)

Manitius, Carolus (1894) *Hipparchi in Arati et Eudoxi Phaenomena commentariorum libri tres ad codicum fidem recensuit Germanica interpretatione et Commentariis instruxit Carolus Manitius* (Teubner)

Marcovich, Miroslav (1986) *Refutatio omnium haeresium/Hippolytus* (Berlin/New York, de Gruyter)

Marcus, Joel (2009) *Mark 8–16: A New Translation with Introduction and Commentary* (New Haven/London, Yale)

Marrou, Henry I. (1956) *A History of Education in Antiquity* (New York, Sheed & Ward)

Martin, Jean (1974) *Scholia in Aratum Vetera* (Stuttgart, Teubner)

Martin, Ralph P. (1986) *2 Corinthians* [WBC 40] (Waco TX, Word)

Mason, Steve (2002) 'Josephus and His Twenty-Two Book Canon', in Lee Martin McDonald and James A. Sanders (eds), *The Canon Debate* (Peabody MA, Hendrickson, 2002), pp.110–27

Mason, Steve (2003a) *Josephus and the New Testament* [2nd edn] (Peabody MA, Hendrickson)

Mason, Steve, ed., trans. and comment. (2003b) *Flavius Josephus. Translation and Commentary, Volume 9 Life of Josephus* (Leiden, Brill)

Mendelson, Alan (1982) *Secular Education in Philo of Alexandria* (Cincinnati, Hebrew Union College Press)

Milik, J. T. (1976) *The Books of Enoch: Aramaic Fragments of Qumran Cave 4* (Oxford, Clarendon)

Milikowsky, Chaim (1988) 'Which Gehenna: Retribution and Eschatology in the Synoptic Gospels and in Early Jewish Texts', *NTS 34*, pp.238–49

Miller, Patricia Cox (1988) '"All the Words Were Frightful": Salvation by Dreams in the Shepherd of Hermas', *VC 42*, pp.327–38

Miller, Patricia Cox (1994) *Dreams in Late Antiquity: Studies in the Imagination of a Culture* (Princeton NJ, Princeton University Press)

Minear, Paul S. (1962) 'The Cosmology of the Apocalypse', in William Klassen and Graydon F. Snyder (eds), *Current Issues in New Testament Interpretation: Essays in Honor of Otto A. Piper* (London, SCM), pp.23–37

Mitchell, Margaret (1991) *Paul and the Rhetoric of Reconciliation: An Exegetical Investigation of the Language and Composition of 1 Corinthians* (Louisville KY, Westminster John Knox Press)

Mócsy, András (1974) *Pannonia and Upper Moesia: A History of the Middle Danube Provinces of the Roman Empire* (London, Routledge & Kegan Paul)

Mondi, R. (1989) 'ΧΑΟΣ and the Hesiodic Cosmogony', *HSPh 92*, pp.1–41

Moore, Stephen D. (1989) *Literary Criticism and the Gospels: The Theoretical Challenge* (New Haven and London, Yale University Press)

Morgan, Teresa (1998) *Literate Education in the Hellenistic and Roman Worlds* (Cambridge, CUP)

Morray-Jones, Christopher R. A. (1993a) 'Paradise Revisited (2 Cor 12:1-12): The Jewish Mystical Background of Paul's Apostolate. Part 1: The Jewish Sources', *HTR 86.2*, pp.177–217

Morray-Jones, Christopher R. A. (1993b) 'Paradise Revisited (2 Cor 12:1-12): The Jewish Mystical Background of Paul's Apostolate. Part 2. Paul's Heavenly Ascent and its Significance', *HTR 86.3*, pp.265–92

Morray-Jones, Christopher R. A. (2006) 'The Temple Within', in April D. De Conick (ed.), *Paradise Now. Essays on Early Jewish and Christian Mysticism* [SBL Symposium Series 11] (Leiden, Brill), pp.145–78

Morray-Jones, Christopher R. A. (2009) 'The Ascent into Paradise: Paul's Apostolic Calling and its Background', in Christopher Rowland and

Christopher R. A. Morray-Jones, *The Mystery of God: Early Jewish Mysticism and the New Testament* (Leiden, Brill), pp.341–419

Most, Glenn W., ed. and trans. (2006) *Hesiod I. Theogony, Works and Days, Testimonia* [LCL] (Cambridge MA, Harvard)

Moyise, Steve (1995) *The Old Testament in the Book of Revelation* [JSNT Sup 115] (Sheffield, Sheffield Academic Press)

Moyise, Steve (2000) 'Intertextuality and the Study of the Old Testament in the New Testament', in *Ibid.* (ed.), *The Old Testament in the New Testament: Essays in Honour of J. L. North* [JSNT Sup 189] (Sheffield, Sheffield Academic Press), pp.14–41

Müller, Hans-Peter (1960) 'Die Plagen der Apokalypse: Eine formgeschich-tliche Untersuchung', *ZNW 51*, pp.268–78

Murray, A. T., trans., rev. William F. Wyatt (1999) *Homer, Iliad, Volume 1, Books 1–12* [LCL] (Cambridge MA, Harvard)

Mussies, G. (1971) *The Morphology of Koine Greek as used in the Apocalypse of John: A Study in Bilingualism* (Leiden, Brill)

Musurillo, Herbert, trans. (1958) *St Methodius. The Symposium: A Treatise on Chastity* (Westminster MA, The Newman Press) [ACW 27]

Nautin, Pierre (1973) 'Ciel, Pneuma et Lumière chez Théophile d'Antioch. Notes critiques sur Ad Autol 2,13', *VC 27*, pp.165–71

Naveh, J. (1986) 'A Medical Document or a Writing Exercise? The So-Called 4Q Therapeia', *IEJ 36*, pp.52–5

Newsom, Carol (1985) *Songs of the Sabbath Sacrifice: A Critical Edition* (Atlanta GA, Scholars Press)

Newsom, Carol (1990) 'He has Established for Himself Priests: Human and Angelic Priesthood in the Qumran Sabbath Shiroth', in L. H. Schiffmann (ed.), *Archaeology and History in the Dead Sea Scrolls*, [JSP Sup 8] (Sheffield, Sheffield Academic Press), pp.101–20

Nickelsburg, G. W. E. (1981) 'Enoch, Levi and Peter: Recipients of Revelation in Upper Galilee', *JBL 100*, pp.575–600

Nickelsburg, G. W. E. (2001) *I Enoch 1* [Hermeneia] (Minneapolis, Fortress Press)

Nickelsburg, George W. E. (2005) *Jewish Literature Between the Bible and the Mishnah* [2nd edn] (Minneapolis, Fortress Press)

Nickelsburg, G. W. E and VanderKam, James C. (2004) *1 Enoch: A New Translation Based on the Hermeneia Commentary* (Minneapolis, Fortress Press)

Niditch, Susan (1996) *Oral World and Written World. Ancient Israelite Literature* (Louisville KY, WJK Press)

Niehoff, Maren (2001) *Philo on Jewish Identity and Culture* [TSAJ 86] (Tübingen, Mohr Siebeck)

O'Hear, Natasha (2010) *Contrasting Images of the Book of Revelation in Late Medieval and Early Modern Art: A Case Study in Visual Exegesis* (Oxford, OUP)

Oakes, Peter (1998) 'Jason and Penelope Hear Philippians 1:1-11', in Christopher Rowland and Christopher H. T. Fletcher-Louis (eds), *Understanding, Studying and Reading: New Testament Essays in Honour of John Ashton* (Sheffield, Sheffield Academic Press), pp.155–64

Oakes, Peter (2001) *Philippians: From People to Letter* (Cambridge, CUP) [SNTSMS 110]

Oakes, Peter (2009) *Reading Romans in Pompeii: Paul's Letter at Ground Level* (Minneapolis, Fortress Press/London, SPCK)

Ong, Walter J. (1982) *Orality and Literacy: The Technologizing of the Word* (London and New York, Metheun)

Orlov, Andrei A. (2005) *The Enoch-Metatron Tradition* [TSAJ 107] (Tübingen, Mohr Siebeck)

Osborn, Eric (2001) *Irenaeus of Lyons* (Cambridge, CUP)

Osiek, Carolyn (1999) *Shepherd of Hermas* [Hermeneia] (Minneapolis, Fortress Press)

Pack, Roger A., (ed.) (1963) *Artemidori Daldiani Onirocriticon Libri V* (Leipzig, Teubner)

Pàmias, Jordi and Geus, Klaus, (eds) (2007) *Eratosthenes/Sternsagen (Catasterismi)* (Oberhaid, Utopica)

Parsons, Mikeal C. (2003) 'Luke and the *Progymnasmata*: A Preliminary Investigation into the Preliminary Exercises', in Todd Penner and Caroline Vander Stichele (eds), *Contextualizing Acts: Lukan Narrative and Greco-Roman Discourse* [SBL Symposium Series 20] (Atlanta GA, SBL), pp.43–63

Patillon, Michel and Bolognesi, Giancarlo, (eds) (1997) *Aelius Théon: Progymnasmata* (Paris, Les Belles Lettres)

Pattemore, Stephen (2004) *The People of God in the Apocalypse: Discourse, Structure and Exegesis* (Cambridge, CUP)

Patterson, L. G. (1997) *Methodius of Olympus: Divine Sovereignty, Human Freedom, and Life in Christ* (Washington DC, Catholic University of America Press)

Paul, Ian (2000) 'The Book of Revelation: Image, Symbol and Metaphor', in Steve Moyise (ed.), *Studies in the Book of Revelation* (Edinburgh, T&T Clark), pp.131–47

Paulien, Jon (1988) *Decoding Revelation's Trumpets: Literary Allusions and Interpretation of Revelation 8:7-12* (Barrien Springs MI, Andrews University Press)

Paulien, Jon (2000) 'Criteria and the Assessment of Allusions to the Old Testament in the Book of Revelation', in Steve Moyise (ed.), *Studies in the Book of Revelation* (Edinburgh, T&T Clark), pp.113–30

Pearson, Brook W. R. (1997) Review: 'Bruce J. Malina, *On the Genre and Message of Revelation: Star Visions and Sky Journeys* (Peabody MA, Hendrickson, 1995), *JSNT* 65, p.126

Penner, Todd (2003) 'Reconfiguring the Rhetorical Study of Acts: Reflections on the Method in and Learning of a Progymnastic Poetics', *PRSt* 30, pp.425–40

Perrot, Charles (1988) 'The Reading of the Bible in the Ancient Synagogue', in M. J. Mulder (ed.), *Mikra: Text, Translation, Reading and Interpretation of the Hebrew Bible in Ancient Judaism and Early Christianity* (Assen, Van Gorcum/ Philadelphia, Fortress Press), pp.137–59

Perry, Peter S. (2009) *The Rhetorics of Digressions: Revelation 7:1-17 and 10:1-11:13 and Ancient Communication* [WUNT 268] (Tübingen, Mohr Siebeck)

Petersen, David (1985) *Haggai and Zechariah 1–8: A Commentary* [OTL] (London, SCM)

Pétridès, S. (1903) 'Oecumenius de Tricca, ses oeuvres, son culte', *Échos d'orient* 6, pp.307–10.

Pomeroy, Sarah B. (1981) 'Women in Roman Egypt: A Preliminary Study Based on Papyri', in Helen P. Foley (ed.), *Reflections of Women in Antiquity* (Philadelphia, Gordon & Breach), pp.303–22

Pomeroy, Sarah B. (1984) *Women in Hellenistic Egypt: From Alexander to Cleopatra* (New York, Schocken Books)

Pomeroy, Sarah B. (1998) 'Education', in Jane Rowlandson (ed.), *Women and Society in Greek and Roman Egypt: A Sourcebook* (Cambridge, CUP), pp.299–312

Pongratz-Leisten, Beate (2001) 'Mental Map und Weltbild in Mesopotamien', in Bernd Janowski and Beate Ego (eds), *Das biblische Weltbild und seine altorientalischen Kontexte* (Tübingen, Mohr Siebeck), pp.261–79

Porter, Stanley E. (1989) 'The Language of the Apocalypse in Recent Discussion' *NTS* 35, pp.582–603

Porter, Stanley E. and Pitts, Andrew W. (2008) 'Paul's Bible, His Education and His Access to the Scriptures of Israel', *JGrChJ* 5, pp.9–41

Prigent, Pierre (1972) 'Hippolyte, commentateur de l'Apocalypse', *TZ* 28, pp.391–412

Prigent, Pierre, trans. Wendy Pradels (2004) *Commentary on the Apocalypse of St. John* (Tübingen, Mohr Siebeck)

Prigent, Pierre and Stehly, R. (1973) 'Les fragments du De Apocalypsi d'Hippolyte', *TZ* 29, pp.313–33

Rajak, Tessa (1983) *Josephus: The Historian and His Society* (London, Duckworth)

Ramelli, Ilaria L.E. (2007) 'Christian Soteriology and Christian Platonism: Origen, Gregory of Nyssa and the Biblical and Philosophical Basis of Apokatastasis', *VC* 61, pp.313–56

Ramsay, W. M. (1904) *The Letters to the Seven Churches and their Place in the Plan of the Apocalypse* (London, Hodder & Stoughton)

Rapske, Brian (1994) *The Book of Acts and Paul in Roman Custody* (Grand Rapids MI, Eerdmans)

Ratzinger, Joseph (1956) 'Beobachtungen zum Kirchenbegriff des Tyconius im "Liber regularum"', *REAug 2*, pp.173–86

Reardon, B. P., (ed.) (2008) *Collected Ancient Greek Novels* (Berkeley/ London, University of California Press) [2nd edn]

Reeves, John C. (1992) *Jewish Lore in Manichean Cosmogony* (Cincinatti, Hebrew Union College Press)

Resseguie, James L. (2009) *The Revelation of John: A Narrative Commentary* (Grand Rapids MI, Baker Academic)

Reydams-Schils, Gretchen J., (ed.) (2003) *Plato's Timaeus as Cultural Icon* (Notre Dame, University of Notre Dame Press)

Richardson, E. C., (ed.) (1896) *Hieronymus liber De viris inlustribus: Gennadius liber De viris inlustribus*, *TU 14.1*

Rochberg-Halton, Francesca, (ed.) (1993) 'Mesopotamian Cosmology', in Norriss S. Hetherington, *Cosmology: Historical, Literary, Philosophical, Religious and Scientific Perspectives* (New York, Garland), pp.37–52

Rogers, John H. (1998a) 'Origins of the Ancient Constellations: I. The Mesopotamian Traditions', *JBAA 108.1*, pp.9–28

Rogers, John H. (1998b) 'Origins of the Ancient Constellations: II. The Mediterranean Traditions', *JBAA 108.2*, pp.78–89

Römer, Cornelia (2003) 'Ostraka mit christlichen Texten aus der Sammlung Flinders Petrie', *ZPE 145*, pp.183–201

Rousseau, A., trans. (1995) *Irénée de Lyon. Démonstration de la prédication apostolique* (Paris, Les Éditions du Cerf) [SC 406]

Rowland, Christopher (1982) *The Open Heaven: A Study of Apocalypticism in Judaism and Early Christianity* (London, SPCK)

Rowland, Christopher, with Gibbons, Patricia and Dobroruka, Vicente (2006) 'Visionary Experience in Ancient Judaism and Christianity', in April D. DeConick (ed.), *Paradise Now and Not Yet: Essays on Early Jewish and Christian Mysticism* (Atlanta GA, SBL) pp.41–56

Runia, David T. (1986) *Philo of Alexandria and the Timaeus of Plato* (Leiden, Brill)

Runia, David T. (2001) *On the Creation of the Cosmos According to Moses. Introduction, Translation and Commentary* (Atlanta GA, SBL)

Rüpke, Jörg, (ed.) (2007) *A Companion to Roman Religion* (Malden MA, Oxford, Blackwell)

Russell, Donald A. (2001) *Quintilian/The Orator's Education* [LCL] (Cambridge MA, Harvard) (5 vols)

Safrai, S. and Stern M., *et al* (eds) (1974) *The Jewish People in the First Century: Historical Geography, Political History, Social, Cultural and Religious Life and Institutions*, Volume 1 (Assen, van Gorcum)

Sale, William (1966) 'The Popularity of Aratus', *CJ 61*, pp.160–4

Salmond, S. D. F., trans. (1995) 'Hippolytus: Treatise on Christ and Antichrist', in Alexander Roberts and James Donaldson (eds), *The Ante-Nicene Fathers: Volume 5* (Grand Rapids, MI, Eerdmans) [repr.], pp.204–19

Sandnes, Karl Olav (2009) *The Challenge of Homer: School, Pagan Poets and Early Christianity* [Library of New Testament Studies 400] (London and New York, T&T Clark/Continuum)

Savage, John J., trans. (1961) *Saint Ambrose / Hexameron, Paradise, and Cain and Abel* (New York, Fathers of the Church) [FOTC 42]

Schaefer, B. E. (2005) 'The Epoch of the Constellations on the Farnese Atlas and their Origin in Hipparchus's Lost Catalogue', *JHA 36*, pp.167–96

Schams, Christine (1998) *Jewish Scribes in the Second Temple Period* [JSOT Sup 291] (Sheffield, Sheffield Academic Press)

Schmid, Josef (1955) *Studien zur Geschichte des griechischen Apokalypse-Textes, 1. Teil: Der Apokalypse-Kommentar des Andreas von Kaisareia* (Munich, Karl Zink Verlag) [MTS]

Schmidt, Francis (1990) 'Jewish Representations of the Inhabited Earth During the Hellenistic and Roman Periods', in A. Kasher, U. Rappaport and G. Fuks (eds), *Greece and Rome in Eretz Israel: Collected Essays* (Jerusalem, Yad Izhak Ben-Zvi/The Israel Exploration Society), pp.119–134

Schmidt, Thomas C. (2010) *Hippolytus of Rome: Commentary on Daniel* (Create Space) www.chronicon.net (accessed 10/3/2011)

Schüssler-Fiorenza, Elizabeth (1985) *The Book of Revelation: Justice and Judgement* (Philadelphia, Fortress Press)

Schwartz, Seth (1990) *Josephus and Judaean Politics* (Leiden, Brill)

Scott, James M. (1995) *Paul and the Nations* [WUNT 84] (Tübingen, Mohr Siebeck)

Scott, James M. (2001) *Geography in Early Judaism and Christianity: The Book of Jubilees* [SNTS MS 113] (New York/Cambridge, CUP)

Sedlaček I. and Chabot, I.-B. (1906) *Dionysii bar Salibi Commentarii in Evangelia* (Paris, E. Typographica Republica) [CSCO 101]

Segal, Alan F. (1990) *Paul the Convert: The Apostolate and Apostasy of Saul the Pharisee* (New Haven and London, Yale)

Sharples Robert W. and Sheppard, Anne, (eds) (2003) *Ancient Approaches to Plato's Timaeus* (London, Institute of Classical Studies)

Sider, David and Brunschön, Carl Wolfram, eds and trans. (2007) *On Weather Signs/Theophrastus of Eresus* [Philosophia Antiqua 104] (Leiden, Brill)

Sidnell, Philip (2006) *Warhorse: Cavalry in Ancient Warfare* (London and New York, Continuum)

Siegert, Folker (1996) 'Philo of Alexandria', in Magne Sæbø (ed.) *Hebrew Bible Old Testament: The History of Its Interpretation, Volume I/1: Antiquity* (Göttingen, Vandenhoeck & Ruprecht), pp.162–88

Skarsaune, Oskar (1987) *The Proof from Prophecy: A Study in Justin Marty's Proof-Text Tradition: Text Type, Provenance, Theological Profile* [NovT Sup LVI] (Leiden, Brill)

Skarsaune, Oskar (2007) 'Justin and his Bible', in Sara Parvis & Paul Foster (eds), *Justin Martyr and his Worlds* (Minneapolis, Fortress Press), pp.53–76, 179–87

Small, Jocelyn Penny (1997) *Wax Tablets of the Mind: Cognitive Studies of Literacy and Memory in Classical Antiquity* (London, Routledge)

Small, Jocelyn Penny (2007) 'Memory and the Roman Orator', in William Dominik and Jon Hall (eds), *A Companion to Roman Rhetoric* (Malden MA/Oxford, Blackwell), pp.195–206

Smalley, Stephen S. (2005) *The Revelation to John: A Commentary on the Greek Text of the Apocalypse* (London, SPCK)

Smith, Christopher R. (1994) 'Chiliasm and Recapitulation in the Theology of Ireneus', *VC 48*, pp.313–31

Smith, Morton (1981) 'Ascent to the Heavens and the Beginning of Christianity', *Eranos Jahrbuch 50*, pp.403–29

Solmsen, Friedrich (1966) 'Aratus on the Maiden and the Golden Age', *Hermes 94*, pp.124–8

Spitaler, Anton and Schmid, Josef (1934) 'Zur Klärung des Ökumenius-problems', *Or Chr 3*, pp.208–18

Steinhauser, Kenneth B. (1987) *The Apocalypse Commentary of Tyconius: A History of its Reception and Influence* (Frankfurt, Peter Lang)

Steinhauser, Kenneth B. (1993) 'Tyconius: was he Greek?', *SP 27*, pp.394–9

Steinmann, Andrew E. (1992) 'The Tripartite Structure of the Sixth Seal, the Sixth Trumpet and the Sixth Bowl of John's Apocalypse (Rev 6:12-7:17; 9:13-11:14; 16:12-16)', *JETS 35*, pp.69–79

Sterling, Gregory E. (1992) *Historiography and Self-Definition: Josephos, Luke-Acts and Apologetic Historiography* [NovT Sup. 64] (Leiden, Brill)

Sterling, Gregory E. (2004) 'The Place of Philo of Alexandria in the Study of Christian Origins', in Roland Deines and Karl-Wilhelm Niebuhr (eds), *Philo und das Neue Testament. Wechselseitige Wahrnehmungen* (Tübingen, Mohr Siebeck)

Stevenson, Kenneth W. (2001) 'Animal Rites: The Four Living Creatures in Patristic Exegesis and Liturgy', *SP 34*, pp.470–92

Stewart-Sykes, Alistair, ed. and trans. *The Didascalia Apostolorum: An English Version with Introduction and Annotation*, (Turnhout, Brepols)

Stock-Hesketh, Jonathan (2000) 'Circles and Mirrors: Understanding 1 Enoch 21–32', *JSP 21*, pp.27–58

Stone, Michael (1976) 'Lists of Revealed Things in the Apocalyptic Literature', in F. M. Cross, W. E. Lemke and P. D. Miller (eds), *Magnalia Dei: The Mighty Acts of God* (New York, Doubleday), pp.414–52

Stone, Michael E. (1990) *Fourth Ezra: A Commentary on the Fourth Book of Ezra* [Hermeneia] (Minneapolis, Fortress)

Strazicich, John (2007) *Joel's Use of Scripture and the Scripture's Use of Joel: Appropriation and Resignification in Second Temple Judaism and Early Christianity* [Biblical Interpretation Series 82] (Leiden, Brill)

Stuckenbruck, Loren (1997) *The Book of Giants from Qumran: Text, Translation and Commentary* [TSAJ 63] (Tübingen, J C B Mohr)

Suggit, John N. (2006) *Oecumenius: Commentary on the Apocalypse* [FOTC 112] (Washington DC, Catholic University of America Press)

Sutton, E. W. and Rackman, H., ed. and trans. (1942) *Cicero/De oratore, Books I–II* (Cambridge MA and London, Harvard) [LCL]

Swete, Henry Barclay (1906) *The Apocalypse of St John: The Greek Text with Introduction, Notes and Indices* (London, Macmillan)

Swiggers, Pierre and Wouters, Alfons, trans. (1998) *Dionysius Thrax, Τέχνη Γραμματική* (Leuven, Peeters)

Tabor, James D. (1986) *Things Unutterable: Paul's Ascent to Paradise in its Greco-Roman, Judaic and Early Christian Contexts* (Lanham MD, University of America Press)

Tate, Marvin E. (1990) *Psalms 51–100* [WBC] (Dallas TX, Word)

Taub, Liba Chaia (1993) *Ptolemy's Universe: The Natural, Philosophical and Ethical Foundations of Ptolemy's Astronomy* (Chicago, Open Court)

Tavo, Felise (2005) 'The Structure of the Apocalypse. Re-examining a Perennial Problem', *NovT* 47, pp.47–68

Taylor, C. (1901) 'Hermas and Cebes', Part I, *JP* 27, pp.276–319

Taylor, C. (1903) 'Hermas and Cebes', Part II, *JP* 28, pp.24–38 and 94–8

Taylor, Joan E. (2003) *Jewish Women Philosophers of First-Century Alexandria – Philo's 'Therapeutae' Reconsidered* (Oxford, OUP)

Thackeray, H. St John (1926) *Josephus I. The Life. Against Apion* [LCL] (Cambridge MA, Harvard)

Thackeray, H. St John (1929) Lecture V. 'Josephus and Hellenism: His Greek Assistants', *Josephus. The Man and the Historian* (New York, Jewish Institute of Religion Press), pp.100–24

Theissen, Gerd (2001) 'The Social Structure of Pauline Communities: Some Critical Remarks on J. J. Meggitt, *Paul, Poverty and Survival*', *JSNT* 84, pp.65–84

Thom, Johan C. (2005) *Cleanthes' Hymn to Zeus: Text, Translation and Commentary* (Tübingen, Mohr Siebeck)

Thomas, David Andrew (2008) *Revelation 19 in Historical and Mythological Context* (New York, Peter Lang)

Thompson, Leonard L. (1990) *The Book of Revelation: Apocalypse and Empire* (Oxford, OUP)

Thrall, Margaret E. (1994) *A Critical and Exegetical Commentary on The Second Epistle to the Corinthians, Volume 1* [ICC], (Edinburgh, T&T Clark)

Thrall, Margaret E. (2000) *A Critical and Exegetical Commentary on The Second Epistle to the Corinthians, Volume 2* [ICC], (Edinburgh, T&T Clark)

Tilley, Maureen A. (1996) *Donatist Martyr Stories: The Church in Conflict in Roman North Africa* (Liverpool, Liverpool University Press)

Tilley, Maureen A. (1997) *The Bible in Christian North Africa: The Donatist World* (Minneapolis, Fortress Press)

Toher, Mark (2003) 'Nicolaus and Herod in the "Antiquities Judaicae", *HSPh 101*, pp.427–47

Tolmie, D. F. (2005) *Persuading the Galatians: A Text-centred Rhetorical Analysis of a Pauline Letter* (Tübingen, Mohr Siebeck) [WUNT 190]

Too, Yun Lee (2001) 'Introduction: Writing the History of Ancient Education', in *Ibid.* (ed.) *Education in Greek and Roman Antiquity* (Leiden, Brill), pp.1–22

Toomer, G. J. (1984) *Ptolemy's Almagest* (London, Duckworth)

Torjesen, Karen J. (1986) *Hermeneutical Procedures and Theological Method in Origen's Exegesis* (Berlin and New York, Walter De Gruyter)

Tov, Emmanuel (2004) *Scribal Practises and Approaches Reflected in the Texts Found in the Judean Desert* (Leiden, Brill)

Troupi, Maria (2006) *Menander, Euripides, Aristophanes: Intertextual Transformations of Genre and Gender* (unpublished PhD thesis, University of London)

Tsagarakis, O. (2000) *Studies in Odyssey 11* (Stuttgart, Franz Steiner Verlag)

Tsirpanlis, Constantine N. (1990) 'The Antichrist and the End of the World in Irenaeus, Justin, Hippolytus and Tertullian', *PBR 9*, pp.5–17

Tuplin, Christopher J. (1989) 'The False Neros of the First Century AD', in Carl de Roux (ed.), *Studies in Latin Literature and Roman History, Volume 5* (Brussels, Latomus), pp.364–404

Ulfgard, Håkan (1989) *Feast and Future: Revelation 7:9-17 and the Feast of Tabernacles* (Stockholm, Almqvist & Wicksell)

Ulfgard, Håkan (2009) 'The Songs of the Sabbath Sacrifice and the Heavenly Scene of the Book of Revelation', in Anders Klostergaard Petersen *et al* (eds), *Northern Lights on the Dead Sea Scrolls: Proceedings of the Nordic Qumran Network 2003–2006* (Leiden, Brill) [STDJ 80], pp.251–66

vanBeek, Larry (2000) '1 Enoch among Jews and Christians: A Fringe Connection?', in Stanley E. Porter and Brook W. R. Pearson (eds), *Christian-Jewish Relations Through the Centuries* [JSNT Sup 192] (Sheffield, Sheffield Academic Press), pp.93–115

VanderKam, James C. (1984) *Enoch and the Growth of an Apocalyptic Tradition* (Washington, CBA)

VanderKam, James C. (1989) *The Book of Jubilees: A Critical Text* [CSCO 511] (Leuven, Peeters)

VanderKam, James C. (1994) 'Putting Them in Their Place: Geography as an Evaluative Tool', in John C. Reeves and John Kampen (eds), *Pursuing the Text: Studies in Honor of Ben Zion Wacholder on the Occasion of his Seventieth Birthday* [JSOT Sup 184] (Sheffield, Sheffield Academic Press), pp.46–69

VanderKam, James C. (1996) '1 Enoch, Enochic motifs, and Enoch in Early Christian Literature', in James C. VanderKam and William Adler (eds), *The Jewish Apocalyptic Heritage in Early Christianity* [CRINT 3/4] (Minneapolis, Fortress Press), pp.32–101

van der Toorn, Karel, Becking, Bob and van der Horst, Peter W., (eds) (1999) *Dictionary of Deities and Demons in the Bible* (DDD) [2nd edn] (Leiden, Brill)

van Dijk, Gert-Jan (1997) ΑΙΝΟΙ ΛΟΓΟΙ ΜΥΘΟΙ. *Fables in Archaic, Classical and Hellenistic Greek Literature. With a Study of the Theory and Terminology of the Genre* (Leiden, Brill)

van Henten, Jan W. (2000) 'Nero *redivivus* demolished: The Coherence of the Nero Traditions in the Sibylline Oracles', *JSP 21*, pp.3–17

van Kooten, Geurt Hendrick (2003) *Cosmic Christology in Paul and the Pauline School: Colossians and Ephesians in the Context of Greco-Roman Cosmology* [WUNT 171] (Tübingen, Mohr Siebeck)

van Kooten, Geurt Hendrick (2005) 'Wrath Will Drip in the Plains of Macedonia': Expectations of Nero's Return in the Egyptian Sibylline Oracles (Book 5), 2 Thessalonians, and Ancient Historical Writings', in A. Hilhorst and G.H. van Kooten (eds), *The Wisdom of Egypt: Jewish, Early Christian, and Gnostic Essays in Honour of Gerard P. Luttikhuizen* (Ancient Judaism and Early Christianity 59), (Leiden, Brill), pp.177–215

van Kooten, Geurt Hendrick (2007) 'The Year of the Four Emperors and the Revelation of John: The "Pro-Neronian" Emperors Otho and Vitellius and the Images and Colossus of Nero in Rome', *JSNT 30*, pp.205–48

Vanni, Ugo (1991) 'Liturgical Dialogue as a Literary Form in the Book of Revelation', *NTS 37*, pp.348–72

Vardi, Amiel D. (2003) 'Canons of Literary Texts at Rome', in Margalit Finkelberg and Guy G. Stroumsa (eds), *Homer the Bible and Beyond: Literary and Religious Canons in the Ancient World* (Leiden, Brill), pp.131–52

Varneda, Pere Villalba I (1986) *The Historical Method of Flavius Josephus* (Leiden, Brill)

Vasaly, Ann (1993) *Representations: Images of the World in Ciceronian Oratory* (Berkeley, University of California Press)

Vercruysse, Jean-Marc (2004) *Tyconius. Le Livre des Règles* (Paris, Les Éditions du Cerf) [SC 488]

Vercruysse, Jean-Marc (2006) 'La composition rhetorique du Liber Regularum de Tyconius', *SP 43*, pp.511–16

Vercruysse, Jean-Marc (2010) 'Tyconius a-t-il lu Origène?', *SP 46*, pp.155–60

Viré, Ghislaine, (ed.) (1992) *De Astronomia Hygini* (Stuttgart, Teubner)

Wallis, Robert E., trans. (1994) 'Victorinus On the Creation of the World and Commentary on the Apocalypse', in Alexander Roberts and James Donaldson (eds), *The Ante-Nicene Fathers. The Writings of the Fathers down to AD 325, Volume 7* (Grand Rapids MI, Eerdmans), pp.339–60

Webster, T. B. L. (1995) *Monuments Illustrating New Comedy*, 3rd rev. and enlarged edn by J. R. Green and A. Seeberg (London, Institute of Classical Studies), *Volume 1*

Weinrich, William C. (2005) *Ancient Christian Commentary on Scripture: New Testament XII. Revelation* (Downers Grove IL, Intervarsity Press)

Weinrich, William C., trans., and Oden, Thomas C. (ed.) (2011a) *Greek Commentaries on Revelation: Oecumenius and Andrew of Caesarea* [Ancient Christian Texts](Downers Grove IL, Intervarsity Press)

Weinrich, William C., ed. and trans. (2011b) *Latin Commentaries on Revelation: Victorinus of Petovium, Apringus of Beja, Caesarius of Arles, Bede the Venerable* (Downers Grove IL, Intervarsity Press)

Weiser, Artur, trans. Herbert Hartwell (1962) *The Psalms* [OTL] (London, SCM)

Welborn, L. L. (2005) *Paul the Fool of Christ: A Study of I Corinthians 1–4 in the Comic-Philosophic Tradition* (London, T&T Clark/Continuum)

West, M. L., trans. and comm. (1978) *Hesiod/Works and Days* (Oxford, Clarendon)

White, Joel (2008) 'Paul's Cosmology: The Witness of Romans, 1 and 2 Corinthians, and Galatians', in Jonathan T. Pennington and Sean McDonough (eds), *Cosmology and New Testament Theology* [Library of New Testament Studies 355] (London and New York, T&T Clark, Continuum), pp.90–106

White, Robert, trans. (1975) *The Interpretation of Dreams: The Oneirocritica of Artemidorus* (Park Ridge, New Jersey)

Whitmarsh, Tim (2001) *Greek Literature and the Roman Empire: The Politics of Imitation* (Oxford, OUP)

Wiles, David (1991) *The Masks of Menander: Sign and Meaning in Greek and Roman Performance* (Cambridge, CUP)

Wilken, R. L. (1967) 'The Homeric cento in Irenaeus, "Against Heresies 1.9.4"', *VC 21*, pp.25–33

Wilken, Robert Louis (2004) 'Christian Formation in the Early Church', in John van Engen (ed.), *Educating People of Faith: Exploring the History of Jewish and Christian Communities* (Grand Rapids MI, Eerdmans), pp.48–62

Williams, Frank, trans. (1994) *The Panarion of Epiphanius of Salamis, Volume 2, Books II and III. (Sects 47–80, De Fide)* (Leiden, Brill)

Wilmart, André (1958) *De decem uirginibus*, in A. Hammann (ed.), *Patrologia Latina Supplementum, Volume 1* (Paris: Éditions Garnier Frères), pp.172–4

Winston, David (1979) *The Wisdom of Solomon* [AB 43] (New York, Doubleday)

Wiseman, T. P. (2008) *Unwritten Rome* (Exeter, University of Exeter Press)

Wolff, Hans Walter, trans. Kohl, Margaret (1974) *Anthropology of the Old Testament* (London, SCM)

Wolff, Hans Walter, trans. Jansen, Waldemar *et al.* (1977) *Joel and Amos* [Hermeneia] (Minneapolis, Fortress Press)

Woolf, Greg (2000) 'Literacy', in Alan K. Bowman, Peter Garnsey and Dominic Rathbone, (eds), *The Cambridge Ancient History* [2nd edn], *Volume 11. The High Empire, AD 70–192* (Cambridge, CUP), ch 30

Worthington, Ian, (ed.) (2007) *A Companion to Greek Rhetoric* (Oxford, Blackwell)

Wright, J. Edward (2000) *The Early History of Heaven* (New York, OUP)

Wright, M. R. (1995) *Cosmology in Antiquity* (London and New York, Routledge)

Wyatt, N. (2005) 'Sea and Desert: Symbolic Geography in West Semitic Thought', in *Ibid.*, *The Mythic Mind: Essays on Cosmology and Religion in Ugaritic and Old Testament Literature* (London, Equinox), pp.38–54

Yadin, Yigael (1983) *The Temple Scroll* (Jerusalem, Israel Exploration Society)

Yarbro Collins, Adela (1976) *The Combat Myth in the Book of Revelation* [HDR 9] (Chico CA, Scholars Press)

Yarbro Collins, Adela (1984) *Crisis and Catharsis: The Power of the Apocalypse* (Philadelphia, Fortress)

Yarbro Collins, Adela (1996a) 'The Seven Heavens in Jewish and Christian Apocalypses', in *Ibid.*, *Cosmology & Eschatology in Jewish and Christian Apocalypticism* (Leiden, Brill), pp.21–54

Yarbro Collins, Adela (1996b) 'Numerical Symbolism in Jewish and Early Christian Apocalyptic Literature', in *Ibid.*, *Cosmology and Eschatology in Jewish and Christian Apocalypticism* (Leiden, Brill), pp.55–138

Yarbro Collins, Adela (2007) *Mark* [Hermeneia] (Minneapolis, Augsburg Fortress)

Yates, Frances Amelia (1966) *The Art of Memory* (London, Routledge & Kegan Paul)

Yonge, C. D., trans. (1993) *The Works of Philo: Complete and Unabridged* (Peabody MA, Hendrickson)

Young, Frances M. (1989) 'The Rhetorical Schools and their Influence on Patristic Exegesis', in Rowan Williams (ed.), *The Making of Orthodoxy: Essays in Honour of Henry Chadwick* (Cambridge, CUP), pp.182–99

Young, Frances M. (1997) *Biblical Exegesis and the Formation of Christian Culture* (Cambridge, CUP)

Young, Frances M. (2003) 'Alexandrian and Antiochene Exegesis', in Alan J. Hauser and Duane F. Watson, *A History of Biblical Interpretation: Volume 1: The Ancient Period* (Grand Rapids MI, Eerdmans), pp.334–54

Young, Ian M. (1998) 'Israelite Literacy: Interpreting the Evidence. Part 1', *VT 48*, pp.239–53

Ziegler, Joseph, (ed.) (1943) *Septuaginta. Vetus Testamentum Graecum Auctoritate Societis Litterarum Gottingensis, Volume 13. Duodecim Prophetae* (Göttingen, Vandenhoeck & Ruprecht)

Zimmerli, Walther, trans. James D. Martin (1983) *Ezekiel 2: A Commentary on the Book of the Prophet Ezekiel Chapters 25–48* [Hermeneia] (Minneapolis, Fortress Press)

INDEX OF REFERENCES

20.13	211
20.13-21.2	206
20.14	70
20.15	70
21-22	203
21.1	72, 184
21.1-22.20	184
21.8	70, 118
21.20	131n. 38
21.21	61
22.1-2	209
22.9	79n. 16

JEWISH PSEUDEPIGRAPHA

Apocalypse of Abraham

	42, 62
15.2-4	44n. 30
30.14-16	3

Apocalypse of Zephaniah

4.1-7	101, 101n. 89
6.1-17	103n. 97
6.7-9	101, 101n. 89
6.15	103n. 97

II Baruch

4.2-7	47
55.3	103n. 97
63.6	103n. 97

III Baruch

	42, 57, 58, 60, 62, 63
4	56
4-9	57
4.8	57
16.3	3

I Enoch

1-36	7, 38, 42, 42n. 24, 43 43n. 26, 47, 78, 83, 85, 88, 101, 122, 212
1-105	48n. 45
1.1-32.6	43n. 26

6-11	43, 43n. 27
10	110, 111
10.4	111
10.4-8	111
10.6	70
10.11-13	111
10.12	111
12-16	43, 43n. 27
12-36	42n. 23
12.1-3	43
13.4	43
14	38, 39n. 2, 42, 42n. 22, 43, 46, 47, 60, 78, 82n. 27
14-16	105
14.8	44, 46, 54, 60, 63, 66, 66n. 110, 67, 71, 85n. 41
14.8-9	44, 45
14.8-23	59, 105
14.8-25	66
14.8-16.4	47
14.9	44, 45, 46, 67, 106
14.10	45
14.10-14	44, 106
14.11	45, 47, 47n. 42
14.12	46, 67
14.13	45, 67
14.15	46, 66n. 111
14.15-23	105, 106
14.15-25	45
14.17	47, 47n. 42
14.18	46, 67
14.20	46
14.22	46, 118
14.25	46, 66n. 111, 67n. 112
15.2	43
16-17	75
17	86, 89, 119
17-19	39n. 1, 43, 47, 50, 50n. 47, 51, 71, 78
17.1-2	89n. 55

17.1-7	51
17.4	51, 89
17.5	50, 71, 89
17.7	51, 71
17.7-8	87n. 48, 88, 89, 90, 104, 109, 119
17.8	86n. 42, 100
18.1-5	51, 51n. 50
18.2	50
18.2-3	51, 68, 71
18.6	111
18.6-8	51
18.6-16	84, 85
18.10	51
18.12	50, 71
18.13	84
18.14	71
18.15	84
19.1	47
19.3	51
19.3-21.9	43n. 26
20-36	47, 47n. 44
20.1	66
20.1-8	47
20.2	103n. 97, 104
20.8	103n. 97
21-32	59
26.1	48n. 45
34-36	101
34.1-36.4	101n. 87, 101n. 88, 111
37-71	42, 43, 43n. 25, 65, 65n. 106, 110n. 115, 115, 118
56.5-7	18n. 52, 42, 101
72-82	101, 101n. 87, 101n. 88, 111
76	101
76.1	101
76.4	101
76.10-11	101, 104
76.11-12	89n. 55
80.4-6	84

GENERAL INDEX

abyss 51, 60–2, 70–1, 84, 85–90, 91–2,
    100–1, 102–4, 111, 115, 119,
    122–3, 127–9, 133–4, 144, 152,
    167–9, 186, 187–9, 191–2, 204–
    6, 209–11, 213
Adams, E. 40, 52, 85
Alexander, L. 12, 39
Alexander, P. 68, 106, 109, 115, 116
allegory 31, 53–4, 73, 117, 121, 124, 125,
    126, 127–9, 133–6, 138–41, 144,
    145–7, 150–1, 201, 208, 211, 213
alphabet 10–11, 35, 76
angel of the abyss 91–2, 102–4
Apocalypse
    cosmology 60–72
Aratus 6, 17–19, 37, 74, 84, 121-2, 133-
    51, 210-14
Aristotle 12, 16, 21, 36, 41, 80–1, 143,
    198–200, 215
astronomical exegesis 17–19, 111, 130–3,
    134-6, 138, 143, 145–50
Aune, D. E. 2, 3, 5, 55, 60–8, 70–2, 76,
    78–9, 84–5, 95, 102–5, 108, 110–
    11, 115, 117, 124, 126, 130, 155

Babcock, W. S. 174–9, 181–2, 186, 187,
    189–92
Bagnall, R. S. 22, 23
Barclay, J. M. G. 27, 33–6, 73
Bar-Ilan, M. 26
Bartsch, S. 125–6
Bauckham, R. 2, 104
Bautch, K. C. 39, 47, 50–1, 70, 87, 89–90
Beale, G. K. 2, 3, 66, 72, 76, 78, 80, 108,
    130
Beck, R. 132, 138, 145, 146, 154
Berggren, J. L. 18, 19
Black, M. 18, 43, 51, 84, 88, 101
Bøe, S. 96, 97, 99, 115
Boll, F. 130–4, 139
Bonner, S. 10–12
border maps 68–70, 108–12, 115, 117,
    119–20, 206
Borgen, P. 29, 53–4, 127

bowl 2–3, 115, 117–8, 164–5, 184–5,
    201, 203
Brent, A. 145, 155, 166, 215
Bright, P. 175–9, 181, 189
Bruce, F. F. 99, 158

Campbell, G. 2
Carruthers, M. J. 80–1, 83, 215
celestial sphere/globe 17–20, 122, 133–41,
    144, 148, 150
celestial temple 44–7, 56, 59–60, 62–8,
    82, 105–8, 167–9, 183–4, 208–9
Cerrato, J. A. 145, 162, 215
Charles, R. H. 3, 61–4, 66–8, 71–2, 78,
    101–2, 106–7, 111, 115, 117,
    130–1
Charlesworth, J. H. 64, 106–7
Chevalier, J. M. 130–2
Childs, B. S. 96, 117
Chyutin, M. 44, 63, 105
Cicero 10, 18, 24, 30, 36, 53, 81, 83, 123,
    159, 178–81, 198, 199, 212
Clay, J. S. 41, 114, 128
Cole, S. G. 22, 25
Collins, J. J. 57, 104
Colson, F. H. 29–30, 127–8
constellation 7, 17–19, 84–5, 121, 122,
    124, 129–151, 210, 212–13
Corinthians, II, 12:1-10
    cosmology 54–60
cosmic geography 38, 39–40, 48–50, 68,
    71, 75, 83, 85–6, 101, 105, 111,
    150, 186, 188, 204, 209–10
cosmological templates 39–42
Crenshaw, J. L. 26, 94, 206
Cribiore, R. 9–16, 22–6, 76, 122

Daley, B. E. 170
Davila, J. R. 102, 103, 106
Day of the Lord 4, 95
De Groote, M. 193–8, 200, 202, 204–8
De Villiers, P. G. R. 194, 197, 201
Dines, J. M. 96, 99
disc, terrestrial 38, 40, 43, 47, 51, 53, 71,